The God of Egypt

Placing the Biblical Exodus in Egyptian History
Second Edition

By
Pamela Dawn O'Neal

Cover Photography by Brian O'Neal
Cover Art by Auburn Dawn

This edition published in 2020 by
Broken Oak Publishing
PO Box 255
Ridgetop, TN 37152
An imprint of
Lightning Source Industries
1246 Heil Quaker Blvd.
LaVergne, TN 37086

ISBN 978-0-9795020-5-7

Printed in the United States of America

October 2020

Contents

Akhenaten and Family

The God of Egypt
Introduction

For millennia, Akhenaten, the illustrious, controversial pharaoh of Egypt's magnificent Eighteenth Dynasty has remained an enigma. His utter rejection of the conventional polytheistic religion that was fundamental to Egyptian culture and that had secured and supported pharaonic power for centuries seems inexplicable. Certainly there have been those throughout history who have questioned Akhenaten's sanity. Accusations of heresy and megalomania have prevailed, but this book will examine another theory. Fundamental to this hypothesis is the answer to the question, who was the Aten that Akhenaten sought so desperately to worship? This book will suggest that Aten was more than just a randomly selected member of the vast, established Egyptian pantheon; Aten was not the sun, and Atenism did not precipitate Hebrew monotheism. The disk of the Aten was merely a symbolic representation of the one God who has always existed, the God of the Bible, the Great I Am, the God of Moses. In fact, the one God who brought the land of Egypt both to power and to its knees was the intended recipient of Akhenaten's sincere adulation. The radical religious revolution of Akhenaten was one man's heroic attempt to honor the one God that Egypt had forgotten and had offended, the one true God who has always been the God of Egypt.

To support this theory, it must be plausibly established that the Hebrew exodus occurred just prior to the Amarna period. Under such conditions, the ten plagues set the stage for the extreme actions/reactions of Pharaoh Akhenaten. If one deity demonstrated complete domination over the authority of the pharaoh and over every other object of Egyptian worship, it would only make sense to seek the favor of that deity. Akhenaten may well have reasoned that Egypt's very survival was in the bargain.

Of course, placing the exodus anywhere in Egyptian history is difficult and speculative but perhaps not impossible. At least the academic conversation in the last few years has moved beyond the notion that there is absolutely no evidence to support a Hebrew exodus or even to suggest a Hebrew presence in Egyptian history. Nevertheless, due to the interpretative nature of the evidence, various scientific, academic, political, social, and religious agendas, and the focus and purpose of both the Biblical account and ancient Egyptian records, a definitive consensus for the placement of the exodus may never be.

Yet, who most likely served as pharaoh during the time of Joseph? Who were the Hyksos? Who was the daughter of the pharaoh that drew Moses from the Nile? Who was the pharaoh of the exodus? For the purposes of this discussion, names, timelines, and order of ascensions will be considered less important than events. This book will seek harmony between the account of the Old Testament and the secular history of ancient Egypt. A correlation of events, the sequence of events, circumstances, and behavior will help answer questions and weave the framework upon which a case for the God of Egypt will ultimately rest.

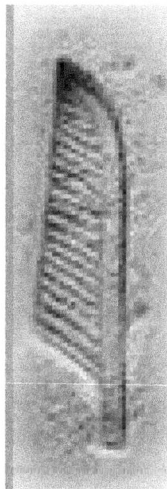

**Mentuhotep II
Wearing the Atef Crown of Upper Egypt**

Chapter 1
Binder of the Two Lands

Near the end of Egypt's Eleventh Dynasty, something remarkable occurred, for the first time since the days of Menes, Egypt, a land that had long been divided, was united under the rule of one pharaoh, Mentuhotep II.[1] Though the turbulent history of the First Intermediate Period and the vicious wounds on the bodies of over sixty soldiers buried in the Tomb of the Warriors that adjoins the mortuary temple of Mentuhotep II suggest a time of conflict, the latter reign of Mentuhotep II is largely considered peaceful.[2] Somehow, Mentuhotep II, over the course of less than a decade, overcame centuries of ancestrally established nomacracies ("great chieftains"), won the veneration of all the various nomes (major cities and their surrounds), and united Egypt. He ushered in the Middle Kingdom as perhaps the most powerful pharaoh to that time, and reigned in relative peace for approximately forty years.[3] Could it be that Mentuhotep II was pharaoh during the time of Joseph?

The last eleven chapters of Genesis discuss Joseph's extraordinary rise to power in Egypt. According to the account in Genesis chapter 41, God endowed an imprisoned slave, Joseph, with the ability to interpret the vivid, unsettling dreams of a pharaoh. In Pharaoh's first dream, seven frail cows consumed seven fine, fat cows, but they remained emaciated. Similarly, his second dream envisioned a stalk of grain with seven mature heads, "plump and good," being swallowed by a stock of seven shriveled heads. With God's help, Joseph successfully interpreted these dreams to mean that there would be seven "fat" years in Egypt when the harvest would be plentiful, but this time of prosperity would be followed by seven "lean" years of a famine so severe that the years of plenty would be utterly forgotten (King James Version, Genesis 41.1-30).

Pharaoh was so impressed by Joseph's insight, he appointed Joseph to be a vizier, an official second in power only to the king himself (Genesis 41.40). His trust in Joseph was not misplaced. Joseph faithfully oversaw the ponderous task of organizing and implementing a plan (based on collecting a fifth of production) to store massive amounts of grain in preparation for the coming famine. Joseph was a humble servant and did not seek in any way to usurp the tributes of the throne. For seven years, plenty of grain was collected and stored in silos in cities throughout Egypt (Genesis 41.33-49).

Then, just as predicted, a terrible famine came. Though famine in the ancient world was not particularly uncommon, this particular famine seems unprecedented. According to the scriptures, this famine was "over the face of the whole earth." In all lands, there was no bread—except in Egypt. Therefore, if this passage is taken literally, people of all the earth came to Joseph in Egypt to buy grain (Genesis 41.50-57). In an ancient Egyptian hymn to Atum, one of the earliest deities of Heliopolis (the biblical On), Atum "fashioned men of different natures and created their life. He made them differ in colour [sic], each from the other."[4] Though the Egyptians of the Eleventh Dynasty were largely isolationists, ancient Egyptians were obviously aware of a vast array of human appearance. Perhaps people of the whole world did come to Egypt to buy grain.

At any rate, it would be safe to say that Egypt probably sold grain to its neighbors and to much of the known world. Egypt was the considered breadbasket of the ancient world principally because Egypt was often well situated during times of regional drought. Unlike its neighbors, who were largely at the mercy of precipitation for production of their crops, Egyptians, of necessity, had mastered irrigation. Evidence of "small-scale irrigation" is even seen in pre-dynastic Egypt.[5] By taking full advantage of the annual Nile inundation, there was usually bread in Egypt; and for hundreds of years, ancient peoples turned to Egypt when they needed to buy grain.[6] Therefore, Egypt stood to prosper during times of famine when grain would have been a crucial commodity.[7] Indeed, reliefs from as early as the Fifth Dynasty "depict Asiatics praising the king with uplifted arms as they arrive in Egypt." There is no indication that these foreigners were captives. They seem to have been allowed into Egypt to engage in trade.[8] Certainly, such rejoicing would have accompanied transactions sustaining the lives of their families during times of drought.

Genesis speaks of Abraham traveling to Egypt under similar circumstance (Genesis 12.10). Abraham was originally from Ur, an urban center in the prestigious Sumerian/Babylonian/Chaldean empires.[9] He also had significant familial ties to Haran, another thriving Mesopotamian metropolis[10] Nevertheless, when famine came, Abraham immediately thought of Egypt.

Still, the universal famine in Joseph's time was deviant. It was devastating even to the Egyptians; even their breadbaskets were empty. In fact, according to the scriptures, only the pharaoh (and those whom he chose to honor) prospered under this famine's unrelenting distress.

> And there was no bread in all the land; for the famine was very sore, so that the land of Egypt and all the land of Canaan fainted by reason of the famine. And Joseph gathered up all the money that was found in the land of Egypt, and in the land of Canaan, for the corn which they bought: and Joseph brought the money into Pharaoh's house. And when money failed in the land of Egypt, and in the land of Canaan, all the Egyptians came unto Joseph, and said, Give us bread: for why should we die in thy presence? For the money faileth. And Joseph said, Give your cattle; and I will give you for your cattle, if money fail. And they brought their cattle unto Joseph: and Joseph gave them bread in exchange for horses, and for the flocks, and for the cattle of the herds, and for the asses: and he fed them with bread for all their cattle for that year. When that year was ended, they came unto him the second year, and said unto him, We will not hide it from my lord, how that our money is spent; my lord also hath our herds of cattle; there is not ought left in the sight of my lord, but our bodies, and our lands: Wherefore shall we die before thine eyes, both we and our land? Buy us and our land for bread, and we and our land will be servants unto Pharaoh: and give us seed, that we may live, and not die, that the land be not desolate. And Joseph bought all the land of Egypt for Pharaoh; for the Egyptians sold every man his field, because the famine prevailed over them: so the land became Pharaoh's. And as for the people, he removed them to cities from one end of the borders of Egypt even to the other end thereof. Only the land of the priests bought he not; for the priests had a portion assigned them of Pharaoh, and did eat their portion, which Pharaoh gave them wherefore they sold not their lands. Then Joseph said unto the people, Behold, I have bought you this day and your land for Pharaoh: lo, here is seed for you, and ye shall sow the land. And it shall come to pass in the increase, that ye shall give the fifth part unto Pharaoh, and four parts shall be your own, for seed of the field, and for your food, and for them of your households, and for food for your little ones. And they said, Thou hast saved our lives: let us find grace in the sight of my lord, and we will be Pharaoh's servants (Genesis 47.13-25).

Joseph's pharaoh, through the forewarning of a prophetic dream and through the shrewd 20% investment of a loyal vizier, emerged from this devastating natural disaster with unimaginable wealth and power. He essentially owned all of the riches, all of the livestock, all of the land, and all of the people in Egypt, not to mention of its neighbors. Certainly, it is safe to say of the pharaoh in the time of Joseph, that—like Mentuhotep II—there had not been such a pharaoh since the days of Menes. Indeed, the empire of Mentuhotep II spread beyond the borders of Egypt. Akhtoy, the Chancellor and Chief Treasurer of Mentuhotep II, speaks of the king's terror and influence spreading throughout Sinai and Canaan. Furthermore, through the reorganization of government and the managing of pharaoh's new holdings, Joseph established an on-going 20% revenue that was regularly collected as tribute. Notably, according to the Wilbour Papyrus, during the Twelfth Dynasty, a tribute of five measures on each "arura" of grain was accessed. Only temples and other pious foundations were tax exempt. Could this "five measure" taxation at the dawning of the Middle Kingdom be evidence of the collection of a "fifth part" of the increase that was implemented by Joseph after the seven years of famine? Furthermore, under Mentuhotep II a new relationship emerged between the pharaoh and his subjects. Far from acting independently as kings in their own right, only nomarchs who were considered "helpful" to the king were recognized. Under a corvée system, Egyptians were conscripted to do physical labor and military service. Those who attempted to circumvent the corvée were dealt with severely. Could such harsh treatment of Egyptian citizens indicate a sudden loss of manpower due to the death of many in a severe famine? Could the corvée also imply that in the days of Mentuhotep II, beyond the traditional role of subjects as servants of the king, people utterly sold themselves to the pharaoh as slaves?[11]

Are there other indications that point to Mentuhotep II as the pharaoh during the time of Joseph? Memorialized in the large limestone sarcophagus of one of Mentuhotep II's wives, Ashait, is the storage of large amounts of grain being gathered into silos under the watchful eye of an overseer. Above this, a herdsman is driving a row of fat cattle. The beautiful queen is pictured sniffing a lotus blossom and being fanned by an attendant while another servant offers her a choice duck. Placidly perched on her throne, the queen is sufficed for all eternity. In the afterlife, it seems Ashait could anticipate a never ending supply of ducks for her table, servants to see to her every need, perpetually healthy herds of cattle, and storehouses of grain, securing her wealth and welfare throughout eternity. Could it be that the scenes engraved into the stone vault of Mentuhotep II's beloved wife tell the story of the conspicuous time in which she lived, a time when the household of Mentuhotep II secured power and prosperity through silos of grain overseen by a trusted vizier? Facsimiles of granaries and similar reliefs were also found among the grave goods of Mentuhotep II's concubines and in the tombs of two of his highest-ranking officials.[12]

The Visions of Neferti, arguably a papyrus of historical fiction believed to have been composed in the Eighteenth Dynasty, is set at the rise of the Middle Kingdom and tells the story of a pharaoh who unites "The Two Lands of Egypt." Neferti attributes that achievement to "Amememhet the Triumphant," a successor of Mentuhotep II. Nevertheless, this piece of literature indicates a jumbled cultural memory of drought, famine, and unification of Egypt at the turn of the Middle Kingdom. "The canals are dry. They can be crossed on foot. One searches for enough water to sail. The canals have turned into dry land. Dry land replaces water." All of these phrases indicate drought. The story also describes hunger, "Everyone says, 'I want.'"[13]

Inscriptions preserved in the tombs of various nomes and officials from the time of Mentuhotep II may present a similar picture of drought and famine at the beginning of the Middle Kingdom. The Suit nomarch of Heracleopolitan writes:

I was rich in grain. When the land was in need, I maintained the city with kah [spirit] and heket [grain measures]; I allowed the citizen to fetch for himself grain; and his wife, the widow and her son. . . . I filled the pastures with cattle, every man had many breeds, the cows brought forth twofold, the fields were full of calves.

Here is what the assistant treasurer of the Gebelen nome says:

I sustained Gebelen during unfruitful years, there being 400 men in distress. But I took not the daughter of a man, I took not his field, ... The nome of Thebes went up stream [to Gebelen for supplies]. Never did Gebelen send up-stream or down-stream to another district [for supplies].

Benihasan of Oryx-nome reports:

There was no overseer of serf-laborers whose people I took for [unpaid] imposts, there was none wretched in my community, there was none hungry in my time. When years of famine came, I plowed all the fields of the Oryx-nome as far as its southern and northern boundary, preserving its people alive, and furnishing its food, so that there was none hungry there in.[14]

Like the optimistic depictions that adorn the coffin of queen Ashait, these three men were carving their desired reputations in eternity. Ancient Egyptians often did not present their lives as they actually were but rather as they desired them to be. Idyllic scenes of vibrant, young, healthy people engaged in carefree sports and leisure, surrounded by lotus blossoms and luscious foods may grace the walls of countless tombs, but modern medical examinations of the mummies that occupied those tombs tell a much different tale. Ancient Egyptians were commonly stricken with parasites, chronic illnesses, and injuries that would have made their lives uncomfortable and unpleasant. It's small wonder that they longed for a picture-perfect afterlife and made every effort (according to their ideology) to secure it. Writings, drawings, and other artistic expressions had more than just aesthetic appeal to Egyptians; they were believed to be powerful/magical means of devising the future. Things that were preserved in these ways were expected to become true even if they did not, in fact, represent the truth of the time in which they were recorded. With this understanding, it may be said that the men of the Eleventh Dynasty who left these glowing epitaphs of themselves were not necessarily describing experiences as they were but as they wished. Each of these men wished to be the hero of his land who was rich in grain and livestock, who preserved hungry people during a distressing time, and who others turned to for supplies but who never had need of charity or supplies from anyone else. Perhaps these three were among those "appointed officers" who were proposed by Joseph in Genesis 41.34-35. Although it is also possible that the similar wording in these three inscriptions may suggest nothing more than formulaic language, as if such was the expected or conventional thing to say during the time in which they lived, nevertheless, each of these nomarchs seems to give himself sole credit as if he had, single-handedly, devised the rationale behind the rations that had been preserved and that had sustained the people living in his district.

Yet, reading between the lines, the reality from these three Eleventh Dynasty nomes seems to be that, actually, there were many hungry people at that time; there was famine, need, and distress. People were deeply in debt; they lost their lands, cattle, herds, and families; and Egyptians were pressed into slavery at the perceived hand of an overseer. The described conditions sound very like the unique circumstances that existed in Egypt during the time of Joseph, and these three nomarchs longed to be like the pharaoh of that time.

Of course, given the time in which they lived, Mentuhotep II is most likely the pharaoh whose status these men coveted and longed to realize in the next life. After all, it stands to reason that not everyone was happy with the rise of Mentuhotep II. Surely several nomarchs longed to be monarchs, and what demigod doesn't dream of godhood? "The nome of Thebes" (despite the spiteful chagrin of the Gebelen nome's assistant) had managed both. Since Mentuhotep II was located in Thebes (the Greek name of the Egyptian city originally known as Wesi), the bitter Gebelen treasurer is likely making reference to him—albeit disrespectful reference, by reducing the all-powerful pharaoh, Mentuhotep II, to his former standing of just the ruler of a "nome."[15]

Curiously, the fact that Mentuhotep II was Theban could be another indicator that he was the pharaoh at the time of Joseph. At the beginning of the Middle Kingdom, Amun was a relatively obscure god throughout Egypt, but he was an important deity in Thebes.[16] Of course, in the New Kingdom Amun was the premier god in Thebes, ousting Mentu as patron, and after he was combined with Ra, (which may have happened as early as the Middle Kingdom) Amun-Ra was considered to be the king of gods in all Egypt.[17] Amun was represented by a ram, though he was not the only god in Egypt to be represented in that way.[18] Regardless of the archaeological record that indicates the widespread consumption of sheep throughout Egypt, through the discovery of countless bones with obvious signs of preparations for cooking, nevertheless, the farming and consuming of sheep (at least by foreigners) could have been viewed as an abomination to Egyptians who were loyal to a pharaoh or a region that considered rams to be especially sacred. Perhaps this helps explain why the Egyptians associated with Joseph refused to eat with the Hebrews (Genesis 43.32).[19] Egyptians coming out of the First Intermediate Period harbored a longstanding cultural prejudice against foreigners. Yet, the Egyptians in Joseph's day seemed to have had a particular aversion to shepherds, as evidenced in Genesis 46.34; perhaps this negative sentiment was held because shepherds "lord over" and eat sheep or perhaps foreign shepherds did not or could not regard sheep with the reverence prescribed by Amun worshippers. However, a difference in cultural opinion, between Egyptians and Hebrews, over the proper use of sheep and cattle is again evident in Exodus 8.26.

Although there is some debate, it is generally accepted as fact that Mentuhotep II united all of the territories of all the nomes in Egypt under the double crown within a relatively short period of time. The only real question is how. Human nature and history dictate that tribal leaders, patriarchs, autocrats, and warlords do not relinquish turf easily; in fact, they usually defend their bearings to the death. Rarely would charisma or diplomacy alone conciliate. Despots must be utterly defeated and have no other choice but to abdicate their lands and holdings, either through battle or through some other extraordinary circumstance. Indeed, evidence from the First Intermediate Period leading up to the reign of Mentuhotep II, strongly indicates a volatile time in Egyptian history. Violent power struggles between the various regions of Egypt had been ongoing. Through the vying for power of Mentuhotep II's predecessors, some suggest that much of the unification of Egypt was settled by the time of his rule and Egypt was largely divided between two strongholds. However, the hubris in tomb inscriptions left by nomes through the reign of Mentuhotep IV seem to challenge the bona fide effectiveness of any civil war that may have occurred and seem to suggest ongoing disputed loyalties. Therefore, perhaps civil war was not a sufficient means to unite Egypt. However, if there had been a severe famine and if Mentuhotep II controlled the only grain supplies, it is feasible that he could have *bought* the unification of Egypt with grain and could have succeeded in a way that war could not.

But what of the sixty soldiers who obviously died in horrific assault and were buried near Mentuhotep II's mortuary temple in Deir el-Bahari? Do they indicate that through the power of Mentu, the Theban god of war (and his namesake), Egypt was united by force? Certainly it seems they were honored for valiant service and sacrifice to the pharaoh, perhaps most honored by the placement of their final burials, but it is highly unlikely that the unification of Egypt, over the course of the First Intermediate Period, could have been accomplished with only sixty casualties. Perhaps they are select representatives of a much larger number of Theban troops. Perhaps they gave their lives in the final battle to defeat Herakleopolis or in a struggle to achieve some strategic piece of Egypt's eventual unification. Perhaps they died in a desperate effort to maintain one critical holding in Egypt. Yet, the condition of these soldiers' bodies is puzzling. The men were in the prime of life, none were embalmed, only two were buried in coffins, the rest were simply wrapped in linen—a burial not even to the standards of a middle class Egyptian. They appear to have been buried at the same time, but may not have died at the same time or at the same place. Six of the bodies had been exposed for some time before they were collected because they obviously served as carrion for scavengers. The reed shafts and ebony tips of the arrows still embedded in some of the bodies make it clear that these soldiers were fighting fellow Egyptians, yet there are no signs of hand-to-hand combat. When Mentuhotep II began his reign, there were two prominent great houses—Herakleopolis (in the faiyum) and Thebes.[20] Despite the fact that Egypt was further subdivided into forty-two nomes, Egypt was still "the Two Lands," Upper and Lower Egypt.[21] Upper Egypt included all land south of Memphis, and Lower Egypt was the land to the north.[22] The faiyum, of Lower Egypt, included the richest, most fertile soil of the   River Valley. It would have been crucial for the pharaoh during the days of Joseph to wield enough control over parts of the faiyum to exact tributes from that area in order to accumulate 20% of the total grain harvested in Egypt during the seven years of plenty. If Joseph's pharaoh was centered in Upper Egypt, in Thebes, that goal could have been problematic. It is possible that parts of the Delta in Lower Egypt would have needed to be taken by force. Rabbi Zlotowitz, in *The Family Chumash Bereishis*, notes that the Hebrew text implies that the toll was to be "exacted from them [landowners] even against their will." Perhaps the sixty soldiers died in that effort.

A monument erected to the founder of the Twelfth Dynasty memorializes grain being stored in silos. Large silos for holding grain have been discovered at the Middle Kingdom site named Hetep-Senusret. These silos could have supplied five thousand people with grain.[23] It could be that, for the pharaoh in the time of Joseph, diplomacy was sufficient to secure a fifth of the grain produced during the seven years of plenty—even from areas of the Two Lands where the pharaoh's supremacy might have been disputed. Convincing the various nomes to donate 20% of an overwhelming surplus could have been perceived as a small price for good relations with the nomarch of Thebes and his "inferior," foreign representative. It was also a small price to appease Egyptian paranoia of the supernatural and to offset the imagined ramifications of a prophetic dream. After all, if the biblical account is true and a fifth of the yield was so plenteous that the storekeepers lost count of the volume, there must have been grain to burn in the faiyum! People are less likely to quibble over things that are plentiful, but such is not the case for precious commodities that are in short supply. After the famine had depleted the excess, the reserves of grain collected by Joseph would have become prime targets in need of secure defense. It is not hard to imagine that there were those who gave their lives to protect the pharaoh's precious storehouses against marauders who were desperate. Perhaps the sixty men buried at Deir el-Bahari died defending what Mentuhotep II immortalized on his queen's coffin; perhaps they gave their lives securing the silos of "the nome of Thebes." In fact, even commoners at the rise of the Middle Kingdom, instead of being accompanied by more standard benign utensils and regalia, were buried with weapons, indicating a time of violence. Violence often accompanies desperation.[24]

The pharaoh presented in scripture from the days of Joseph, at first glance, seems to have been ruling all of Egypt, suggesting that perhaps Egypt was already united when Joseph arrived. Genesis 40.1, for instance, refers to this pharaoh as "the king of Egypt," not a king. However, in chapter 41, verse 35, Joseph suggests that pharaoh store grain "in the cities under Pharaoh's authority," possibly indicating a limited administration. With this interpretation, the pharaoh's comment in Genesis 41.41, "See I have set you over all the land of Egypt," may be considered grandiose language. Yet it may also be that the pharaoh was merely acknowledging that the fate of all Egypt was resting in Joseph's hand. (Actually, the fate of all Egypt was in the hand of the one God who was in the process of making Egypt into the world power.) Nevertheless, it seems clear that the post-famine dominion of the pharaoh in Genesis 47 was vastly greater than it was in chapter 41. There is no doubt that after the famine the pharaoh of Joseph was the undisputed ruler of the Two Lands. If Joseph's pharaoh was not Mentuhotep II, what other pharaoh rose to such absolute, undisputed power during his rule?

Still, was there a significant famine in the time of Mentuhotep II? The fixation on hunger and grain expressed in the writings from the nomes of that time period and the importance that sustenance is given in the etchings on Ashait's funerary vault suggests at least a fear of famine. Prayers were being sung to Min, the god of the Eastern Desert, asking for rain during the reign of Mentuhotep II. Writing from a man named Montuhotep, Son of Hapi, dated to the reign of Mentuhotep II records a "low Nile."[25] Core samples obtained from the ice atop Mount Kilimanjaro indicate a drought around the end of the First Intermediate Period, and there is evidence to indicate a prolonged famine reminiscent of the account in Genesis 41-47.[26] A Theban man from the Eleventh Dynasty wrote about conditions so horrendous, residents of Upper Egypt were eating their own children.[27] Perhaps this helps explain why even common people were carrying weapons.

Heqanakhte is a significant voice from this time period, though some argue to place him later. Nevertheless, he was a farmer and landowner, living near Thebes, but in his old age he became the priest and

Typical Middle Kingdom Farmer

caretaker of the ka and tomb (Theban Tomb 315) of Ipi, Mentuhotep II's vizier. Acting as the ka-priest for such an illustrious dignitary was a great honor, but Heqanakhte was still preoccupied with the grain production on his farmland that he had placed in the charge of his oldest son, Merisu. Letters that Heqanakhte wrote to Merisu were found discarded in a shaft of Ipi's tomb; and they seem to express the old farmer's preoccupation, confusion, frustration, and eventual desperation in a time of famine.

In his, presumed, first letter, dated to "the 5th year," (perhaps referring to the fifth year of plenty), it's easy to detect the old man's pride in his new title, in his fields, and in the generous harvest that had regularly rewarded diligence. In this letter, Heqanakhte inventories an abundance of grain, cattle, and seven thousand loaves of bread. He seems to anticipate another year of surplus and advises Merisu to apply strategies that have proven fruitful in the past:

A message from the ka-priest Heqanakhte to Merisu, Whatever can be inundated on our land, you are the one who ploughs it. A warning to all my people, and to you! Listen, I consider you responsible for it. Put your back into ploughing, do your utmost; look after my seed corn, look after all my property. See, I consider you responsible for it. Take great care with all my property!

When this admonition didn't prove sufficient to produce the desired yield, Heqanakhte assumed that Merisu—not a drought or famine—was the problem. It's understandable that Heqanakhte might not have been aware of a famine or a drought, especially in its beginnings. The climate in Egypt is so dry, even a total lack of rainfall could easily go unnoticed. Yet, inundations sometimes failed, perhaps explaining why Heqanakhte may not have been confident that all his land could be irrigated. Still, if there had been seven years of tremendous plenty and surplus, it's easy to understand how such experience could have skewed Heqanakhte's expectations. Still, Heqanakhte advises Merisu to store grain in as many as thirteen places and to sell a stand of timber. In a second letter, he urges Merisu further (notice the use of singular "god"):

> Take great care! Hoe all my land, sieve with the sieve, hack with your noses into the work. Look,
> if they are diligent, god will be thanked for you; and I will not have to make things hard for you.

In a third correspondence, Heqanakhte expresses his growing frustration with the lack of produce, his mounting dissatisfaction with Merisu, and his disapproval of the quality and quantity of grain he has received. (Note: "GOING WITHOUT" was written with stress strokes in the original manuscript.):

> Now, what do you mean by having Sihathor (a second son) coming to me with old, dried-out, northern barley from Memphis, instead of giving me ten sacks of good, new barley? Fine— you're happy, eating good new barley while I'm GOING WITHOUT! Isn't that so? Your ship has come in for you, when in fact you do nothing but evil. If you had sent me the old barley simply to keep the new barley intact, what could I have said "Well done"? But since you won't assign me a single bushel from the new barley, I won't assign one to you—for the rest of eternity!

Eventually, Heqanakhte seemed to grasp the dire circumstance and understood more of the scope of the disaster. Softened somewhat, he encouraged Merisu:

> Bear this in mind: being half alive is better than being plain dead. Listen, you say hunger only about [real] hunger. Look, they are beginning to eat people here! Listen, there is no body to whom your sorts of rations are given anywhere. So make the most of it until I return.[28]

In this series of letters, Heqanakhte certainly seems to describe an abrupt, drastic change in crop yield. He describes a situation that did not improve but continued to decline. Fear of his family dying, horror for the dreadful actions of desperate people, resolve to make the best of what he has, and resignation to reality characterize the old farmer's conclusion. If Heqanakhte was describing the famine that occurred in the days of Mentuhotep II's vizier, Joseph, sadly, it is unlikely that conditions improved in the next few years. Hopefully, Heqanakhte's recent appointment to ka-priest for Ipi's tomb included him in the portion assigned to priests by Pharaoh and allowed him to keep his cherished land (Genesis 47.22). In fact, "there is nobody to whom your sorts of rations are given anywhere" seems to indicate that Heqanakhte did receive special portions from Pharaoh and that he shared what he got with his sons. Therefore, he urged them to "make the most of" what they were receiving, assured them that they would not die, and reminded them that there is a big difference between being hungry and starving.

Genesis 41.45 says that Joseph was assigned a new name. It's important to note that the highly respected Egyptologist Dr. K. A. Kitchen has analyzed the name that pharaoh gave to Joseph, Zaphenat-Pa'aneah (as it is translated in the Bible). Kitchen concluded that, in the original Egyptian, Zaphenat-Pa'aneah was likely something more akin to Zatenaph-Ipi-ankh(u). Dr. Kitchen also points out that Ipiankhu or Ipi, for short, was a fairly common Middle Kingdom name, but not later. If Mentuhotep II was the pharaoh of Joseph, perhaps he named Joseph "Ipi" after a former vizier who passed away, or perhaps Joseph *was* the Ipi that Heqanakhte served as ka-priest. Naming and renaming can be tied to establishing dominion, going all the way back to Genesis 1.26 and 2.19, 20, where God gave man dominion over earthly creatures and had Adam name them. It could be that assigning a name to Joseph was a mark of Pharaoh establishing authority over the Hebrew or incorporating him into the structure of the king's administration. Perhaps Mentuhotep II was so well pleased with the performance of Joseph early on in the seven years of plenty that he was having a Theban tomb prepared for Joseph before the drought began. Certainly, tombs were often made ready well before the death of the tomb's intended occupant, and it seems reasonable to assume that a caretaker for the site might also have been assigned. Interestingly, more than ample supplies required for the mummification process were found in Ipi's Theban tomb (TT 315) along with a chest that contained canopic jars and a sarcophagus, presumed empty, indicating that Ipi was likely embalmed at this location but, in keeping with the tradition of Lower Egyptian pharaohs, according to the precedence set in the Old Kingdom by pharaoh Djoser, perhaps only Ipi's viscera was interred in his Theban tomb. Mentuhotep II was the first pharaoh from Upper Egypt to have his organs buried, separately from his body, in canopic jars. The fact that the pharaoh, another of his highest officials, Meket-Re, and Ipi were all embalmed in this same fashion indicates that Mentuhotep II ordered the same quality of preservation for these two men as for himself. Indeed, the mere location of Ipi's tomb, in close proximity to Mentuhotep II's temple, nestled among the resting places of Mentuhotep II's highest officials shows the great regard that the pharaoh held for Ipi. Ipi's tomb, like Meket-Re's tomb, provided a separate burial chamber for Ipi's personal servant, a man named Meseh.[29]

Similar dire circumstances to those reported in the letters of Heqanakhte are described in The Admonitions of Ipuwer, also known as The Dialogue of Ipuur and the Lord of All, which has long been suspected of dating to the Middle Kingdom. Though some dispute the time period of Ipuwer and contend that his poem is propaganda and not history, Ipuwer certainly seems to lament a time of great distress and famine:[30]

> O, but the desert is throughout the land; the nomes are ravaged [laid waste], . . . well-married women are saying: "If only we had something to eat!" . . . What can we do about this, when all has fallen into ruin? O, but laughter is ruined, and [no longer] sounds; There is only groaning throughout the land, mixed with laments.[31] "Destroyed are the abundant gifts for the children"; there are no unripe or ripe sycamore figs . . . O, but the officials are hungry, because of affliction . . . the robber has all his belongings taken. O, but every flock, their hearts weep; the cattle are groaning at the state of the land.[32] O, but men eat only plants, and wash them down with water; now they cannot find seeds, plants, or birds, and fodder is taken from the pig's mouth. No one can be benevolent, when they are bent double with hunger. O, but the grain is ruined on every side; . . . they are stripped of clothes, everyone is saying, "There is nothing!" The storehouse is bare, its keeper stretched out on the ground.[33]

Conditions must have been dire for Egyptians to consider taking anything from the mouth of a pig. According to Herodotus, pigs were considered unclean and anything that had come in contact with a pig was unclean.[34] Though the writings of Ipuwer are poetic, vague, and admittedly open to interpretation, the time he describes does sound somewhat like the famine in the days of Joseph. Famine was severe, the property of noblemen was forfeited, livestock was distressed, and people were bankrupt. Furthermore, Ipuwer goes on to say in Stanza IX, "Look, he who had no seed [grain] is the lord of a granary; he who took out loans of grain for himself is someone who lends it out."[35] Certainly, that could have been an observation made in the days of Joseph and in the days of Mentuhotep II.

Is it possible that the biblical account of Joseph's slavery and the eventual immigration of his family to Egypt occurred at the dawn of the Middle Kingdom? Dr. John S. Holladay, Jr. says, "clearly there had been an active Asiatic presence in the region since . . . the Eleventh Dynasty . . . ."[36] Research of Dr. Kitchen supplies further insight to place Joseph in the Middle Kingdom, if not at the time of Mentuhotep II. The slave price paid for Joseph is consistent with slave sales in the Middle Bronze Age.[37] On the imposing stela of Hammurabi, where 282 laws are posted from the first city-state in the First Dynasty of Babylon, it states that a slave should sell for twenty shekels of silver.[38] Joseph was sold by his brothers for a very similar price—twenty pieces of silver (Genesis 37.28). Since recorded sale prices for slaves increase over time, prices paid for slaves become indicative of a timeframe for the transaction. For example, slaves in the Third Dynasty of Ur (about the time of Abraham) brought ten shekels of silver, in the 13th and 14th centuries BC, a slave was sold for thirty shekels, and by the Persian Empire in the 4th and 5th centuries, a slave cost 90-120 shekels of silver.[39] Significantly, in Exodus 21.32, Moses prescribes compensation to be paid to a slave's owner, for a slave killed by a neighbor's ox, to be thirty shekels, indicating that the time of the Exodus falls between 1250 and 1500 BC. Menahem, who lived shortly before the fall of the northern kingdom of Israel and about 200 years before the rise of the Persian Empire, bought back some slaves from Pul the King of Assyria for fifty shekels (II Kings 15.20).[40]

Of course, the mere fact that Joseph was purchased by an Egyptian may help to place him near the rise of the Middle Kingdom. During the chaotic era that immediately followed the Middle Kingdom, the Second Intermediate Period, it seems that Egyptians themselves were enslaved in their own country. Ipuwer said, "O, but there is no one who can leave," which certainly sounds like slavery. According to the testimony of soldiers such as Ahmose son of Ebana and others, by the time of the warrior kings of the Eighteenth Dynasty, slaves in Egypt were obtained and awarded as trophies through the spoils of war. Actually, this was a practice that likely began in the Middle Kingdom. By that time, there would have been little need for a high-ranking military officer like Potiphar to buy a slave (Genesis 37.36). Yet, the fascination with Joseph expressed in Genesis 39.1-12 may also help to place him in the 11th Dynasty. Various tombs of noblemen from that time express interest in the "exotic world of the Asiatics."[41]

Furthermore, in his book *On the Reliability of the Old Testament*, Kitchen observes that the gifts Joseph received from the pharaoh provide clues to his era. The scripture says in Genesis 41.42, "And Pharaoh took off his ring from his hand, and put it upon Joseph's hand, and arrayed him in vestures of fine linen, and put a gold chain about his neck." Such adornments were customary during the Middle Kingdom.[42] An image of Amenemhat III, from the Twelfth Dynasty, depicts the young man wearing a pendant on a chain around his neck. The Septuagint refers to the gift that Joseph received as a "necklace of gold."[43] But perhaps a better translation of the Hebrew word "rabiyd" suggests that Joseph was more likely given a gold chain collar. Intriguingly, a relief of Mentuhotep II at Dendara displays the pharaoh donned in just such a chain-collar necklace. Furthermore, numerous statues of Mentuhotep II show the king wearing distinctive knee-length linen robes that he wrapped tightly around his upper body. The Hebrew word beged, translated as "vestures," may also well be interpreted to mean, "robe."

However, to some, the next verse in Genesis poses a problem for placing the story of Joseph within a Middle Kingdom window. "And he [Pharaoh] made him [Joseph] to ride in the second chariot . . ." (Genesis 41.43). This is the earliest mention of a chariot in the Bible, and "chariot" may be a poor understanding. Obviously, Joseph was given access to some form of transport that usually carried the pharaoh, perhaps even a human-powered palanquin. Of course, from early on, the Nile served as the main "highway" in Egypt, rendering extraneous roads and wheeled vehicles superfluous.[44] Most scholars believe that the Egyptians did not use true chariots, at all, before the time of the Hyksos, several decades past Mentuhotep II, and that this reference to the pharaoh's "second chariot" is, at best, "little more than a wheeled platform" perhaps drawn by horses.[45] Yet, Kitchen leaves the window open a bit by suggesting that chariots were introduced "no later than the Hyksos." Chariots were included among the imports of the Hyksos according to the stela of Kamose.[46] Certainly chariots existed in other cultures well before the days of Mentuhotep II. For instance, the Standard of Ur, that is believed to date to 2500 BC, clearly depicts chariot-like war wagons. It is nearly impossible to believe that, as active as Egypt was in trade with other cultures, Egyptians, even well before Mentuhotep II, were unaware of chariot technology.[47] It is equally unlikely that they did not possess the engineering capability to have chariots.

What about horses? Remains of horses dating to perhaps as far back as 1700 BCE have been found in Egypt at Buhen, Tell el-Daba, and Tell el-Maskhuta.[48] It is curious to note that part of the mortuary temple of Mentuhotep II is called "Bab el-Hosan" or "Gate of the Horsemen."[49] This designation seems to suggest the use of horses in the days of Mentuhotep II; however, it is more likely that the Arabic label refers to a misadventure of Howard Carter, when his horse "discovered" the buried chamber. Nevertheless, Dr. David Rohl builds an argument for chariots in Egypt during the Middle Kingdom based on an evident use of chariot gloves.[50] Rohl poses the rhetorical question: in a climate as hot as Egypt, why wear leather chariot gloves if not to drive a chariot? Furthermore, in Genesis 44, Joseph's brothers left at daybreak with their donkeys. Later, Joseph sent his Egyptian servants to go after his brothers, fully expecting his servants to overtake them (Genesis 44.3-4). Perhaps the Egyptian servants of Joseph had transportation that was faster than donkeys.

K. A. Kitchen also suggests that a pervasive interest in divination and dream interpretation could help place Joseph in the Middle Kingdom. Two small figures, likely from the Middle Kingdom, seem to demonstrate the practice of using a cup to tell the future.[51] Genesis 44.1-5 describes a silver cup that Joseph used for a similar purpose, but Joseph is probably more commonly known for his ability to interpret dreams. Papyrus Chester Beatty III Recto possesses grammar and vocabulary that Dr. Kitchen identifies as "good Middle Egyptian." This document delineates a sort of index for possible images one might encounter in a dream, categorizes each image as "good" or "bad," and assigns a corresponding, vague interpretation.[52] The events that transpire in Genesis 40 and 41 certainly indicate that Joseph was in Egypt during a time when it seems that Egyptians from all walks of life believed in prophetic dreams. A cupbearer, a baker, and a pharaoh all had dreams that they found to be troubling; and from the prison to the palace, all of these Egyptians were anxious to have their dreams interpreted. Of course, a superstitious belief in the power of dreams to predict the future or to connect one to the supernatural could likely be found at any place and any time in human history. Yet, it is the prevalence of such preoccupation that may set the Middle Kingdom apart as the likely time of Joseph.

It is worthy to note that the reverence for dream interpretation displayed by the Egyptians in Genesis 40 and 41 was not universal. Genesis 37 relates two prophetic dreams of Joseph that predict his eventual rise to a place of authority over his brothers and even above his father. Far from receiving the interpretation of these dreams with fear and respect, his brothers rebuked and despised Joseph for having the audacity to even dream such a farcical suggestion (Genesis 37.5-10). Later, in verse 19, his brothers further denigrate a belief in dream interpretation through their sneering observation, "Behold, this dreamer cometh." Of course, the ultimate irreverence toward Joseph's dreams is revealed in the next verse where his own brothers plot to kill Joseph " . . . and we shall see what will become of his dreams" (Genesis 37.20). Such brazen disregard stands in sharp contrast to the fearful credibility dreams were being afforded in Egypt.

Dr. Kitchen also finds a case for placing Joseph within this time period based on the positions that Joseph held while he was in Egypt. Joseph began his slavery as a house servant for the captain of Pharaoh's bodyguard, Potiphar (Genesis 39.1-2). Such domestic servitude was more common to the Old and Middle Kingdoms than to the New Kingdom.[53] Yet, as might be expected after 100 years of civil war and subsequent depletion of able-bodied Egyptian servants, the Middle Kingdom saw a rise in the number of foreign slaves (largely serving in domestic positions) who came to Egypt from the region of Canaan, while there is much less evidence of foreign slaves in any capacity during the Old Kingdom.[54] New Kingdom slaves were predominantly foreign and were often pressed into hard labor, especially involving building.

Perhaps part of an explanation for this astute observation by Dr. Kitchen may be found in the curious verses Genesis 43.32 and 46.34. " . . . the Egyptians, which did eat with him, by themselves: because the Egyptians might not eat bread with the Hebrews; for that is an abomination unto the Egyptians" and " . . . every shepherd is an abomination unto the Egyptians" (which was a sentiment leveraged by Joseph as a strategy to relocate his relatives to Goshen, some of the choicest land in Egypt). Even hundreds of years past the time of Joseph, Juvenal, the first century Roman poet, wrote about Egypt, "Every table abstains from animals that have wool: it is a crime to kill a kid."[55] Whether this abhorrence concerning sheep on the part of Egyptians was religious or merely cultural, it does speak to the fact that Joseph was in Egypt during a time when there was some prejudice against foreigners, particularly against shepherds. People who are prejudiced are usually reticent to tolerate customs that are different from their own. They tend to be separatists as was demonstrated by the Egyptians preferring not to eat or to live in the same place with foreigners. Separatists also tend to be arrogantly self-reliant, as in the statement of the nomarch's assistant who asserted that Gebelen never needed help from anybody. A notion of inherent Egyptian superiority is echoed in the Middle Kingdom narrative, The Tale of Sinuhe, where even a run-away Egyptian is considered a "King [among] the Bedwin [Bedouin]."[56]

Sentiments and behaviors like these seem to favor a placement for Joseph between the end of the Old Kingdom and prior to the graffiti and other evidences that indicate an expanded involvement with foreigners during the Middle Kingdom.[57] In Mentuhotep II's mortuary temple, there is a relief of foreigners offering tributes to the pharaoh, a scene that certainly would have been true of the pharaoh of Joseph.[58] However, accepting gifts and accepting people are not the same thing; overcoming bigotry is often slow business.

Still, there are always those individuals who are willing to defy convention and be more pragmatic. Potiphar promoted Joseph (who had proven himself to be valuable) to overseer in charge of his entire estate, his house, and his land (Genesis 39.4-5). Being appointed to act, as the superintendent of a plantation was a practice found more in the Middle and New Kingdom.[59] When Joseph distinguished himself before Pharaoh, the king was willing to overlook cultural prejudice and appoint Joseph to the highest office that a pharaoh could grant: vizier.

Egypt had a long history of highly trusted, high-ranking officials (though perhaps not such elevated officials who were foreigners). Even on the Narmer Palatte, the king is depicted in a grand procession with his vizier, led by nomarchs who are proudly displaying their respective standards.[60] Uni and the legendary Imhotep are just two examples of trusted officials with extensive powers from the Old Kingdom.[61] Certainly there were others in the Middle Kingdom, such as Ipi, who were high-ranking officials directly under Pharaoh. At this time, there was a "royal commissioner" who looked after the business of the pharaoh; and probably working

The Narmer Palatte

under him, were "overseers of the crown-possessions" who were in charge of the royal herds in each nome.[62] Incidentally, Genesis 47.6 says Pharaoh requested that some of Joseph's brothers be put in charge of his livestock. Sesostris III, of the Twelfth Dynasty, wrote of his trusted vizier:

My majesty sendeth thee my heart being certain of thy doing everything according to the desire of my majesty since thou hast been brought up in the teaching of my majesty thou hast been in the training of my majesty and the sole teaching of my palace.[63]

From the Twelfth Dynasty, Schetepibre, a high-ranking official in the administration of Amenemhat III expressed his loyalty to the crown and warns those who are untrustworthy: "Fight for his name; purify yourselves by his oath, and ye shall be free from trouble. The beloved of the king shall be blessed, but there is no tomb for one hostile to his majesty and his body shall be thrown into the waters." [64] In fact, the absolute loyalty of pharaoh's advisors was deemed so important, young men were raised and trained in the king's house in order to ensure devotion. [65] Unfortunately, a successor of Mentuhotep II, Amenemhat I, was too trusting of his adviser. This is especially odd to consider since it is possible that before becoming pharaoh, Amenemhat I, the son of commoners, may have been a vizier himself. Mentuhotep II created the duel positions of Governor of Upper Egypt and Governor of Lower Egypt.[66] Perhaps Joseph served as vizier in northern Egypt, and Amenemhat I is the Amenemhat who claimed to be "overseer of the south and witness to two desert miracles." Could this curious title adopted by Amenemhat be a reference to surviving the worst famine on record and living to see the unification of Egypt, both of which could have seemed to be impossible "miracles" never to happen again? Most have speculated that the "two miracles" of Amenemhat I were finding a well in the wake of a freak storm and witnessing the chance birth of a gazelle atop a slab of stone being quarried to use for a sarcophagus lid. However, wet-weather wells and gazelles being born are common occurrences, not really rising to the criteria of miracles. Certainly, in the New Kingdom the job of being pharaoh's right hand was considered too big for one vizier, but whether this was the case in the Middle Kingdom is still a matter of debate. Mentuhotep II was also known to have had a vizier named Khety. Yet, Mentuhotep II additionally created a new (though not unprecedented) office of "royal sealbearer," who, unlike other bureaucrats in his administration, had "wide supervisory duties." In light of Joseph being given the right to wear pharaoh's ring, the king's seal, along with its accompanying authority, perhaps Joseph was the royal sealbearer while

Amenemhat and Khety served as upper and lower governors in the administration of the newly united Egypt. Perhaps Amenemhat went on to serve as vizier through the administration of Mentuhotep IV.[67] Nevertheless, this same Amenemhat eventually became pharaoh (an occurrence that Shaw speculates to be one of Amenemhat's two miracles), and in The Instruction of King Amenemhat I, he bears a bitter caution to his son:

> Harden thyself against all subordinates . . . he who ate my food made insurrection; he to whom I gave my hand aroused fear therein.[68]

Significantly, Amenemhat I relocated the royal residence from Thebes to Itj-Tway, an obscure site just south of Memphis.[69] Memphis was the traditional capital of Egypt, especially during the Old Kingdom. However, Mentuhotep II had established the capital of his government in Thebes, presumably because it was his hometown.[70] Furthermore, if Mentuhotep II was the pharaoh of Joseph, he would have had the luxury of operating out of the southern part of Egypt because he had a proven and faithful "right-hand-man" to watch over his interests in the north. Joseph would have been especially eager to be in northern Egypt after his family moved there because that was the location of Goshen. In fact, Joseph could easily have maintained the bureaucratic capitol in Memphis while living in Goshen with his family, which seems to have been the case with rulers during Egypt's Second Intermediate Period. Indeed, Ipi was granted land by Mentuhotep II just outside of Memphis and elsewhere in the Delta.[71]

Nevertheless, since Itj-Tway means "binder of the two lands," it seems fairly obvious that Amenemhat I envisioned this new location as the center of a new government for a united Egypt.[72] Was Amenemhat I moving away from something or closer to something? Was Amenemhat I moving north merely to distance himself from his ancestral province of Thebes and to establish more of a presence in the north? Was he attempting to facilitate the consolidation of Upper and Lower Egypt? Probably yes, but if Mentuhotep II was the pharaoh during the famine in the days of Joseph, there could have been more behind Amenemhat I's reasoning.

If the biblical record is to be believed, the pharaoh of Joseph benefited tremendously from the supernatural insight, wise counsel, and faithful service of his vizier. Pharaoh's observation proved true: "Can we find such a one as this is, a man in whom the Spirit of God is? . . . there is none so discreet and wise as thou art"(Genesis 41.38-39). Successors of this pharaoh would have been unbelievably foolish not to take notice of the successful relationship between the crown and this divining vizier. In fact, verse 8, in the opening chapter of Exodus, seems to indicate that pharaohs recognized the renown of Joseph for some time.

The Bible records that Joseph lived a long and vital life of 110 years (Genesis 50.22-26). Hence, it may be more than coincidental that to wish one a life span of 110 years, "as is due to a holy man," became an Egyptian blessing.[73] Since he was thirty when he accepted the office, according to the scripture, it's possible that Joseph served the government in Egypt, in some capacity, for eighty years (Genesis 41.46). Whether the numbers are accepted as literal or not, it cannot be argued that eighty years would constitute a long time. It perhaps indicates that Joseph was available to serve subsequent pharaohs. However, it is also possible/probable that at some point Joseph requested and was granted release from office in order to enjoy a life near his family in Goshen. After all, such rewards for faithful service were sometimes granted in Egypt.[74] Joseph had never sought eminence, and after years of separation, it is likely that he only longed to be near his elderly, beloved father who lived for seventeen years after coming to Egypt (Genesis 47.28). Joseph no doubt had earned some respect—and probably a little fear, especially since he had proven an ability to communicate with God! To a superstitious people, such power would have carried fearful weight. It is hard to imagine that any reasonable request made by Joseph would have been denied.

Notwithstanding, the events surrounding the death of Jacob in Genesis 50 seem to imply that while Joseph was still an important man in Egypt, there had been a change in his relationship with the pharaoh. In verse 2, Joseph possessed the authority to command Egyptians, to have his father mummified, and to commission a seventy-day national period of mourning, which adhered to Egyptian tradition.[75] However, his request of the pharaoh in verses 4 and 5 seems curiously apprehensive. Of course, regardless of his rank, Joseph was only a glorified servant of the king; it may be, therefore, that Joseph was merely recognizing the absolute authority of the monarch and was expressing the appropriate, expected protocol.

The Papyrus Bulag 18, a document from the 13th Dynasty, outlines Middle Kingdom divisions of the palace. The kap was the innermost circle, residence of the royal family, their personal servants, and nursery attendants. The interior overseer of the kap was the only officer that could move freely between the various levels of the palace. The wahy was the audience area where banquets and other official business of the pharaoh were conducted. The khenty was the outer court. The vizier ran this. Nevertheless, Joseph, second only to pharaoh, making a request of Pharaoh's "household" that they speak to Pharaoh on his behalf, at the time of his father's death, sounds disassociated as if this was a new administration of a different pharaoh. The Twelfth Dynasty legend of Sinuhe seems to confirm the tremulous change of climate that could accompany the coronation of a new pharaoh. Furthermore, if Mentuhotep II was the pharaoh who appointed Joseph, the lineage of his successor is suspect. Mentuhotep III was likely the son of Mentuhotep II by his wife, Queen Tem, but Mentuhotep IV may have been a usurper.[76] The Eleventh Dynasty fell nineteen years after the death of Mentuhotep II. Therefore, the amiable association of Mentuhotep III and Mentuhotep IV with officials who had served a former pharaoh is also suspect. However, the fact that Joseph's request was so generously granted implies an abiding appreciation and respect (Genesis 50.7-11).

Other allowances could be made to explain Joseph's cautious protocol. Every pharaoh was an individual with his own personality and temperament. Mentuhotep II, who came to the throne around age twenty and died around seventy, was a pharaoh who reassessed himself at times during his life because he changed his Horus more than once. For instance, early in his career, Mentuhotep II's Horus name was Netjeryhedjet, which means "the divine one of the white crown," indicating a presumptuous despot, albeit with limited jurisdiction. Yet, his final Horus name, Sematawy, "the one who unites the two lands," could be seen as more relative.[77]

Genesis 39 and 40 provide perhaps some insight into the disposition of the pharaoh who first elevated Joseph. Early on, he seems to have been a man who was demanding, exacting, dictatorial, and given to fits of rage. Though he may have considered himself to be merciful and visionary, he demonstrated the capacity to be callously, arbitrarily cruel. When Potiphar impounded Joseph, the young Hebrew found himself in the company of a prison full of people who had found themselves on the wrong side of Pharaoh's favor (Genesis 39.20-22). These were probably the lucky ones. While Joseph was there, Pharaoh lost his temper with two more servants, his cupbearer and his baker, and he threw them into prison as well (Genesis 40.1-2). The scripture indicates that these men had "offended" Pharaoh; but he seems to have been easily offended because, based on the dreams and hopes of both of these men, their greatest desire was to be reinstated as faithful servants of the king (Genesis 40.6-17). Now, it may be that this is an unfair character analysis; perhaps the pharaoh had reasonable grounds to hang the baker. Perhaps a preponderance of new evidence vindicated the cupbearer. Yet, seemingly on a whim, three days later, Pharaoh dispatched both of these men from the dungeon. To one, he granted absolution of his offense and returned him to his former duties. The other prisoner, however, seemingly to entertain the pharaoh on his birthday, was executed (Genesis 40.20-22). Such rash behavior does not seem to paint the picture of a particularly charming, evenhanded, levelheaded potentate who would have lords standing in line to relinquish their lands, status, families, and fate into his hands. According to scripture, people didn't give themselves over to Joseph's pharaoh because of his charisma but because of the dire circumstance. There is no one who suggests that Mentuhotep II managed to unite Egypt through congeniality.

However, people and circumstances can change. The pharaoh, who may have elevated Joseph rather capriciously, appears to have developed great confidence in Joseph and fondness for him over time. In a passage that's similar to Genesis 50.4, in Genesis 45.16-23, when a rumor of Joseph's good fortune reached Pharaoh's ear, the king overflowed with genuine gracious kindness. He was thoughtful and deeply sympathetic. If this is the same pharaoh who promoted the Hebrew prisoner, Joseph's trustworthiness had tamed the tyrant. Yet, if this is the demeanor of a new pharaoh, it may indicate endemic pharaonic complacency.

Amenemhat I began his administration as an assertive presence, but, over time, he trusted an advisor who proved to be untrustworthy. There is debate over the exact order of kings in the Middle Kingdom.[78] If, however, this was the time period of Joseph, and if Joseph was still living—even if Joseph was not his acting vizier—it makes sense that Amenemhat I would seek to move the center of government closer to Joseph's discerning consult. It is hard to imagine Joseph being willing to leave Goshen. In fact, Amenemhat I built a palace and a temple in Goshen.[79] Still, Amenemhat I learned a caustic lesson about trust. For decades it had been safe for Pharaoh to trust the service of the Hebrew, Joseph. Yet, even among his kinsmen, in that generation, the level of Joseph's integrity was rare. Sadly, even if Amenemhat I had trusted Joseph's brethren to fill the office of vizier, "insurrection" and "fear" would not have been foreign to the treachery demonstrated by conspirators who were capable of betraying their own brother, selling him into slavery, and lying to their father.

Ruins of Mentuhotep II's Mortuary Temple

Of course, it is also possible that Amenemhat I's motives for moving to Goshen were more menacing. In The Prophecy of Neferty, a fictional account of Amenemhat, written much later, Amenemhat I is credited with saying, "Asiatics will fall to his sword, Libyans will fall to his flame, Rebels to his wrath, traitors to his might, As the serpent on his brow subdues the rebels for him. One will build the Walls-of-the-Ruler, To bar Asiatics from entering Egypt . . ." Perhaps, beyond his animosity and distrust of the Asiatics living east of Egypt, Amenemhat was also suspicious and fearful of the growing population of Asiatic immigrants occupying Goshen. He didn't expel the foreigners living in the delta, but he may have moved closer to them to stay more keenly aware of their activities. Certainly, there was a growing contempt for Asiatics in Egypt, especially those from Canaan and Syria.[80]

Do other circumstances support the idea that Mentuhotep II was the pharaoh during the days of Joseph? Besides emerging from seven years of famine with unrivaled power, the pharaoh of Joseph accumulated tremendous wealth. Is there evidence of increased wealth in the days of Mentuhotep II? By the days of Amenemhat I there is evidence of a definite rise in the standard of living, even for the Egyptian middle class. An unexpected increase in means would certainly have helped to fund the "renaissance" in Egypt, as Shaw characterizes the Middle Kingdom. There was a sudden influx of silver, a precious metal that could not be mined in Egypt.[81] Semi-precious stones, both native to Egypt and not, were plentiful in royal jewelry of that time.[82] In fact, the jewelry of the Twelfth Dynasty "is considered to be some of the most exquisite ever made—either in Egypt or elsewhere."[83] Magnificent gold work and "especially lavish embellishments" with semi-precious stones like cornelian, amethyst, lapis lazuli, turquoise, and jasper would certainly signify jewelry of a pharaoh with opulent wealth. The bustle of Middle Kingdom building projects also indicates ample resources. Mentuhotep II's mortuary temple, The House of Millions of Years, was vast and innovative, two adjectives not associated with the comparatively meager memorials of his Theban predecessors nor with a lack of funds.[84] Relocating the capital, building new palaces and temples all demonstrate little concern over wealth on the part of Amenemhat I. Furthermore, early pharaohs of the Middle Kingdom built "a vast catch basin which provided water enough to carve twenty-seven thousand acres out of the desert and convert it to farmland," an elaborate, expensive project that would have certainly served as insurance against future famines.[85] The resulting lake occupied ninety square miles of the Faiyum and was seventeen feet deep.[86] Amenemhat I also built fortresses to secure the borders of northern and southern Egypt.[87] Beyond the borders, pharaohs at the dawn of the Middle Kingdom expanded the interests of Egypt in every direction.[88] The wealth and manpower that would have been required to launch successful campaigns into Nubia, Punt, Libya, Kush, and the Sinai do not seem to be consistent with the undertaking of a tentatively united kingdom on the heels of generations of civil war.[89]

But what of the God of Egypt? What was understood about him at this time? Ancient inscriptions and even imagery on the Narmer Palette seem to suggest that "divinity" was likely associated with Egyptian royalty before pharaonic history.[90] In the final analysis, Mentuhotep II, however, may not have considered himself to be a god; though on a stela where he seemed to congratulate himself for all the land he had acquired, it appears that someone chiseled over the original likeness of Mentuhotep II in order to replace his image with a god, and some observers contend that Mentuhotep II intended to be worshipped. A relief in a shrine found in Deir el Ballas, shows Mentuhotep II worshipping some unidentified diety.[91] Mentuhotep II's comparative modesty seems to have characterized the iconography of several Middle Kingdom pharaohs.[92] In contrast to the "god-kings of the Pyramid Period," Mentuhotep II's mortuary temple, though it underwent many revisions over the course of his reign, stands in a scale more human than divine.[93] Perhaps Mentuhotep II intended his mortuary temple to be a house of worship for millions of years, but not, necessarily, a place to worship the pharaoh or Egyptian gods. Years later, in the Eighteenth Dynasty, Thutmose III built a shrine to Hathor inside Mentuhotep II's temple, but the design that Mentuhotep II approved for his mortuary included doorways and aisles too narrow to ever accommodate festival processions of the golden barque of the god Amun.[94] Though the scriptures portray a pharaoh who appears sovereign, aside from the instance where Joseph invoked Pharaoh's office as part of an oath, there is no real indication that Joseph's pharaoh held any claims to divinity (Genesis 42.15-16). Could it be that Mentuhotep II, like the pharaoh in the days of Joseph, experienced an encounter with a true God and was therefore reticent to stand in comparison? If so, the chiseled correction on the congratulatory stela of Mentuhotep II is ironic; the pharaoh in the days of Joseph did not procure the power and riches at the rise of the Middle Kingdom and ultimately unite the land of Egypt, God, the God of Joseph did.

It is important to note that in the Eighteenth Dynasty, there was a recalled impression that a god had given pharaoh to be "lord of all the foreign lands." Therefore, imperialism and military campaigns "in order to extend the frontiers of Egypt" were believed to be divinely intended.[94] It may well be that from an Egyptian perspective the warrior pharaohs of the New Kingdom were merely staking claim to lands and labor that was rightfully Egypt's. After all, perhaps at the dawn of the Middle Kingdom, the same lands had been given to the king of Egypt in exchange for grain. Indeed, there is evidence that from the days of Mentuhotep II, regular patrols were made of regions surrounding Egypt, as if an eye was being kept on Egyptian holdings. In fact, even the slightest objection of foreigners to Egyptian rule was considered illegal, "outlawry, rebellion."[95] However, though the gift seems to have been strongly remembered, the giver was not. Credit for pharaoh's divine right to rule was extended over time to Amun, the patron god of Thebes. It is probably safe to say that Amun was not the God of Joseph, nor was Amun the God who deserved this recognition.

So, who was the God of Joseph? Though some may argue that Joseph worshiped Egyptian gods, students of the Bible accept that the only God recognized by Joseph was the God of the Bible, the one true and living God who made the world and everything in it (Genesis 39.9; 41.16; 38-39; Hebrews 11.22; Jeremiah 10.10). Therefore, it is significant to note that Pharaoh arranged a marriage between Joseph and Asenath the daughter of Potipherah, priest of On (Genesis 41.45). Surely Pharaoh could have arranged a marriage between Joseph and any eligible woman in Egypt. He could have enjoined the daughter of any nobleman, any general, any official, including a daughter of pharaoh himself, although there seems to be no indication that Mentuhotep II had any surviving daughters.[96] Buried in his funerary complex at Deir el-Bahari was a five-year-old girl, Mayet, who might have been the daughter of Mentuhotep II. Another of his wives, Henhenet, died in childbirth and was buried with the undeliverable baby still inside her.[97] Though Rabbinic tradition suggests that Asenath was actually adopted by Potipherah and was selected by Pharaoh as a wife for Joseph because she may have been the illegitimate daughter of Dinah, Joseph's sister; perhaps it is more reasonable to advocate that pharaoh's selection of Asenath, the daughter of a priest, was not based on nationality but on spirituality. Out of all the gods worshiped throughout Egypt, did Pharaoh associate the ideology of On with that of Joseph and, therefore, consider Asenath to be a compatible soul mate for his honored vizier? Perhaps no other priests in Egypt had daughters. Perhaps Asenath was the most beautiful. Perhaps some unknown factor swayed Pharaoh.

It is largely accepted that On is the place Egyptians would have known as Iwnw or "Pillar Town," according to the renowned Archaeologist Dr. Donald Redford.[98] On is also synonymous with Heliopolis, a city that in Greek means "house of the sun."[99] On is the most ancient religious center in Egypt and has exhibited the sun as a symbol in many different ways.[100] Manifestations of the sun included Khepri depicted as a scarab beetle; Ra seen as a bird, a ram, and a man; Amun-Ra considered to be a man wearing two tall plumes; Horus and Re-Harakhte, the falcon gods, at times also represented the sun; as did the Eye of Ra and Horus. Aten was symbolized by a disk; and Atum was seen as an old man.[101] In the central story of On, its creation myth, "Before anything existed or creation had taken place, there was darkness and endless, lifeless water" when "the All," the one God, who created everything (including Himself) brought "a mound of fertile silt . . . from this watery chaos."[102] Genesis 1 says:

> In the beginning God created the heaven and the earth. And the earth was without form, and void; and darkness was upon the face of the deep. And the Spirit of God moved upon the face of the waters . . . . And God said, Let the waters under the heaven be gathered together unto one place, and let the dry land appear. (Genesis 1.1-9)

While the creation mythology of On is only one of several creation myths attributed to a plethora of gods across Egypt, fading echoes resonating back to the Genesis account can be detected in nearly every creation myth. Another celebrated myth in this regard is the Ptah creation myth, mainly promoted in Memphis but recopied

**Mentuhotep II
Wearing the Double Crown
of a United Egypt**

and preserved in stone by Shabacu during the era of great Nubian pharaohs.[103] While, to some, the Ptah creation myth most closely resembles the biblical story; it is, nevertheless, hard to believe that similarities between the On creation myth and Genesis are coincidental. It seems that there must be an underlying truth, some reality, in the congruency of these ancient accounts. Is it possible that Pharaoh married Joseph to the daughter of the priest of On because she shared a similar belief in "the All," the one God? In fact, the concept of a universal god was integral to On.[104]

In the book of Hebrews, the writer introduces a fascinating concept: an eternal priesthood "after the order of Melchizedek" (Hebrews 7.17). Melchizedek was a mysterious character indeed, "first being by interpretation King of righteousness, and after that also King of Salem, which is, King of peace; Without father, without mother, without descent, having neither beginning of days, nor end of life; but made like unto the Son of God; abideth a priest continually" (Hebrews 7.2-3). Melchizedek was a high priest of the God of the Bible, the God of Abraham who was the patriarch of Joseph (Genesis 14.18-29). If there was an ancient order of such priests, could it be that the ancient priests of On originated from this same order? Could this be the reason that Pharaoh connected Joseph with Asenath?

Could it be that the original god of On was understood to be the same God who needed no further introduction to Pharaoh when Joseph interpreted his dreams? Could it be that this same God was known and worshipped in other ancient places by other ancient priests such as Jethro the father-in-law of Moses? (Exodus 3.1)[105] Joseph simply told Pharaoh, "God shall give Pharaoh an answer" (Genesis 41.16). There is no indication that the God of Joseph was a "foreign" god that needed identification or explanation. Pharaoh seemed to know God, the God of Joseph (or at least to know about him), the Lord of All, the one God, the God who had spoken to him in troubling dreams, the God who during this pharaoh's reign was actually the Binder of the Two Lands, the "Ancient of Days" who had always been the universal God, and the one true God of Egypt (Daniel 7.9-22).

Citations

1. Saleh & Sourouzian 67; Hoerth, *Archaeology* 130; Silverberg 3; Shaw 130-131, 149; Winlock, *Excavations* 3; Winlock, *Rise* 31
2. Woldering 105, Shaw 151, Clayton 74
3. Wilson 127, Shaw 152-153, Wiseman 84, Hoerth, *Peoples* 267; Winlock, *Rise* 22; Breasted, *History* 131
4. Aldred 243; Hamlin 30, Aling, *Egypt* 4, 49
5. Hoerth, *Archaeology* 129
6. Beegle 36
7. Vos76
8. Redford, *Joseph* 196
9. Vos6
10. Vos25
11. Redford, *Joseph* 237, Shaw 173-174, Aling, *Egypt* 15; Winlock, *Rise* 35, 44
12. Saleh & Sourouzian 68, and Image 69b, Shaw 154; Winlock, *Excavations* 24, 44; Winlock, *Rise* 42-43
13. Matthews 235-240; Parkinson, *Sinuhe* 134-139
14. Breasted, *History* 160-161; Shaw 128-130; T. Stewart 131
15. Oakes and Gahlin 10; Silverberg 14, Shaw 152, 174, Hoffmeier 109
16. Newby 124; Hawass 12
17. Hoerth, *Archaeology* 138; Aldred 135
18. Assmann 61; Redford lecture "City of the Ram and Fish"
19. Silverberg 4, Lewy, *Origin* 1, 5, Gray 177
20. Rohl 16, Shaw 151, Clayton 74; Winlock, *Rise* 29
21. Silverman 27; Winlock, *Excavations* 124-127
22. Hoerth, *Archaeology* 127; Silberberg 3
23. Zlotowitz 235, Holness 27, Clayton 74
24. Shaw 151, 177
25. Kees 47; Shaw 130; Winlock, *Rise* 32-33
26. Rohl 16, Zagorski Web
27. Rohl 77; Shaw 129; Winlock, *Excavations* 60-62
28. Ray 23-35, Shaw 162, Clayton 75
29. Kitchen, *Reliability* 346; Rohl 350; Winlock, *Excavations* 55; Winlock, *Rise* 47; Allen, *Officials* 4, 16, 23-24; *Egypt Engineering an Empire*; Curtis
30. Parkinson, *Sinuhe* 166, Van Seters 104, Aling, *Egypt* 20; Kitchen, *Reliability* 387
31. Stanza III; Parkinson, *Sinuhe* 173-174
32. Stanza V; Parkinson, *Sinuhe* 175-176
33. Stanza VI; Parkinson, *Sinuhe* 177
34. Champollion 87
35. Parkinson, *Sinuhe* 181
36. Oren 198, Hoffmeier 98
37. Kitchen, *Reliability* 48; "The Patriarchal Age: Myth or History?"
38. Kitchen, *Reliability* 50
39. Vos 9; Kitchen, *Reliability* 52, Van Seters 12
40. Kitchen, *Reliability* 52; A. Myers 816
41. Stanza I; Parkinson, *Sinuhe* 171, Breasted, *History* 226, Shaw 161, 182, Hoffmeier 114; Kitchen, *Reliability* 346
42. Kitchen, *Reliability* 349, Monet plate 40
43. Vos50
44. Hoerth, *Archaeology* 127; R. Smith 65-66
45. Hoerth, *Archaeology* 151
46. Kitchen, *Reliability* 349, Shaw 195
47. Vos 13, Shaw 161, 178, Aling, *Egypt* 45
48. Oren, 355, Aling, *Egypt* 45
49. Oakes and Gahlin 188
50. Rohl 285-286, Shaw 154
51. Kitchen, *Reliability* 351
52. Kitchen, *Reliability* 352
53. Kitchen, *Reliability* 349, Aling, *Egypt* 31, 34
54. Kitchen, *Reliability* 247, 371; Shaw 182, Aling, *Egypt* 31
55. Silverberg 1
56. Breasted *Records I* 235; Parkinson, *Sinuhe* 31-34
57. West 17, Shaw 165, Van Seters 33
58. Breasted, *History* 153
59. Kitchen, *Reliability* 349
60. *The Great Pharaohs of Ancient Egypt*
61. Monet 59, 67
62. Breasted, *History* 162
63. Breasted, *History* 166
64. Breasted, *History* 167
65. Breasted, *History* 166
66. Tyldesley, *Pharaohs* 70, Shaw 152, Hoerth, *Peoples* 267
67. Tyldesley, *Pharaohs* 70; O'Connor and Cline 201, Shaw 152, 156, 174, Hoerth, *Peoples* 263, Aling, *Egypt* 48; Winlock, *Excavations* 4, 9; Winlock, *Rise* 34, 44, 55; Allen, *Officials* 15; Gardiner 93
68. Breasted, *History* 179, Shaw 156, 158
69. Silverman 28; Winlock, *Rise* 54
70. Tyldesley, *Pharaohs* 66
71. Tyldesley, *Pharaohs* 66, 86; Winlock *Excavations* 58; Winlock, *Rise* 51
72. Mertz 128
73. Leca 31; Parkinson, *Sinuhe* 112-113; Kitchen, *Reliability* 351
74. Bryan 276
75. Aldred 181
76. Breasted, *History* 180; Parkinson, *Sinuhe* 27-28, Tyldesley, *Pharaohs* 70, Shaw 150, 155-156, 176; Winlock, *Rise* 48, 53
77. Shaw 151-152, Hoerth, *Peoples* 266, Clayton 73; Winlock, *Rise* 30-31
78. Dodson and Dyan 85-87, Shaw 160
79. Rohl 266, 270
80. Parkinson, *Sinuhe* 206-207, Shaw 158-159, 163
81. Casson 24, Shaw 150, 159
82. Casson 23
83. Oakes and Gahlin 58, Shaw 165; Winlock, *Rise* 150
84. Woldering 130, Hoerth, *Peoples* 268; Winlock, *Excavations* 30-31
85. Casson 21, Van Seters 92
86. Vos47
87. Silverman 28-29, Shaw 159, Van Seters 17
88. Breasted, *History* 180
89. Breasted, *History* 180; Hoerth, *Archaeology* 139, Shaw 156, 159

90. Oakes and Gahlin 343, Aling, *Egypt* 19
91. Breasted, *History* 181; Winlock, *Rise* 37
92. Rohl 16, Shaw 152
93. Woldering 115; Winlock, *Rise* 38
94. Redford, *Akhenaten* 16-17; Winlock, *Excavations* 53, 80; Winlock, *Rise* 41, 88-90
95. Redford, *Akhenaten* 17. Shaw 152, Wiseman 86, Hoerth, *Peoples* 267
96. Dodson and Dyan 85
97. Tyldesley, *Pharaohs* 69, Shaw 154
98. Allen web, "Heliopolis"; Redford email; Winlock, *Excavations* 43
99. A. Myers 781
100. Oakes and Gahlin 156
101. Silverman 119
102. Oaks 301
103. Shanks and Meinhardt 57
104. Assmann 152
105. Greenberg 40

War Chariots

Chapter 2
The Shepherd of All

There is little disagreement that the unprecedented unification that was realized under Mentuhotep II, at the dawn of the Middle Kingdom, was all but gone by the end of the Thirteenth Dynasty. Perhaps the dismantling of the double crown began when prominent families and nomarchs began to vie again for positions of power.[1] The permutation of offices, titles, and shared powers between the nomes and the pharaoh seems to have reconfigured with every Middle Kingdom change of administration, and sometimes, more frequently than that.[2] However, the absolute power of Mentuhotep II was never realized again by the "Great House" because, after regaining a foothold at the beginning of the Twelfth Dynasty, powerful families and ambitious officials voraciously retained position and influence until the days of Rome.[3] Aristocrats, bureaucrats, governors, and officers are partly to blame for the discord and chaos that defined the end of the Middle Kingdom and remained through the Second Intermediate Period. The enigmatic "revolving door" that ushered in a dizzying succession of pharaohs in the second half of the Thirteenth Dynasty may indicate an aristocratic design of shared and circulated authority, but it is also evidence of a weak central government and instability. After all, on the watch of these later Middle Kingdom rulers, Nubia successfully broke away and established self-rule under a line of Nubian kings.[4] Some pharaohs during this time of upheaval didn't even hold the crown long enough to last through the official days of mourning for the former monarch.[5]

The copious figure of Sebekemsaf, a member of the Thirteenth Dynasty's ruling class, perhaps lends deeper insight into the dysfunction that contributed to the fall of Memphis. Perhaps a slothful decadence and bloated self-importance had numbed the sensibilities of the upper crust. Furthermore, the "rigid formalism" displayed in Sebekemsaf's statue "is characteristic of spiritual decline."[6] The Words of Khakheperreseneb, a lament from possibly the end of the Twelfth Dynasty, is wrung with anguish over the lack of honesty and the love of wrongdoing that prevailed throughout the land. Perhaps the ruling class well before the end of the Thirteenth Dynasty was out of control, unfocused, unprepared, and too out of shape to fend off the coming degradation. But not even they were mostly to blame for the disgraceful bedlam of the Second Intermediate Period—that dubious distinction belongs to the mysterious Hyksos.[7]

For decades, experts have debated the identity and the modus operandi of the Hyksos. Who were the Hyksos? Perhaps it shouldn't be surprising that modern observers have difficulty identifying the Hyksos; it seems that ancient Egyptians were unsure about them too. Were they Syrians, Phoenicians, Sea People, Amorites, Amalekites, the Amu, the Mentiu, Minoans, Chaldeans, Hurrians, Indo-Aryans, Bedouins, Asiatics, Canaanites, or some other group? Were they invaders or immigrants? Did they conquer Lower Egypt quickly through military conquest or slowly through societal encroachment? All of these theories have been proposed.

What seems to be certain is that the Hyksos were considered foreigners. "Hyksos" is the Greek form of an Egyptian word, "Heqau-Khasut," which simply means "foreign rulers" or "rulers of foreign lands."[8] Therefore, "hyksos" was more of a description, than a proper noun. In an "episode [that] clearly stands out as a unique phenomenon, previously unparalleled, a time when foreign lords imposed their rule in Egypt . . ."from their capital city, Hwt-wa'ret, which translates to us through Greek as "Avaris," the Hyksos ruled Egypt's entire northern region after the fall of the Thirteenth Dynasty.[9] Eventually, Ahmose, the Theban pharaoh who reclaimed Lower Egypt and ushered in the Eighteenth Dynasty as the New Kingdom, defeated the Hyksos.

Certainly, The Visions of Neferti describes Asiatic ascendancy and chaos associated with the Middle Kingdom.[10] Ipuwer also seems to lament a time of foreign dominance in Egypt. "Everywhere the foreigners have become people [Egyptians]."[11] "every nobody is a well-born man, those who were people [Egyptians] are now aliens, . . ."[12] "things are done that have never happened before, and the king [has been deposed] by wretches." Such statements indicate that Ipuwer was describing foreigners displacing Egyptians and Egyptian government. Since Ipuwer says foreigners had never conquered Egypt before, it can be assumed that the "nobodies," the foreign rulers he deplored were the Hyksos.[13]

Ipuwer calls these foreigners "tribes of the desert," "marsh-dwellers," and "Asiatics" which suggests a nomadic, Bedouin, or Semitic people; but also people who lived in the Delta.[14] The fact that Ipuwer does not identify this race of foreigners more specifically may imply uncertainty, but it could be an intentional offense on Ipuwer's part to purposely not bring notoriety to the aggressors by refusing to mention their name. Still, perhaps the foreigners were a conglomeration of many different peoples, or perhaps they were a race of people that was simply unidentifiable to Ipuwer. It does seem that, at times in their history, Egyptians had difficulty distinguishing the Amu of Syria from the Mentiu of the deserts of Sinai and Palestine. In their depictions, the Amu and the Mentiu look very much alike, "the same profile, the same pointed beard, the same long hair, . . . the same garb."[15] Perhaps other nationalities were ambiguous to Egyptians as well. The Hyksos, along with other inhabitants of Canaan, may well have been indeterminate to the Egyptians and could have been generically considered "Asiatic." Consistent with the sentiments expressed in Genesis 43.32 and 46.34, all "Asiatic Bedu [Bedouins]" were despised; therefore, it seems that little distinction of Asiatics mattered from an ancient Egyptian perspective.[16] An Egyptian text, The Teaching for King Merikare, expressing sentiments from the Eleventh Dynasty, vividly expresses the low opinion of Semitic tribes, "He has been fighting since the Time of Horus! He cannot prevail; he cannot be prevailed over. He does not announce the day of battle, like a thief whom a gang has rejected. . . . Lo, the vile Asiatic! . . . Don't give them a thought!"[17]

Ipuwer is also vague about *how* these foreigners came to power. Statements such as: "barbarians of outside have come into Egypt," "the land has [been] despoiled of kingship, by a few (lawless) people" and "cows are given to the plunderers," could suggest a violent, overwhelming invasion.[18] In fact, it has long been suggested and debated that the Hyksos possessed weaponry and technology that was superior to the Egyptian army, leading to the idea that the Hyksos were advanced, organized, cunning, sophisticated, and/or militaristic, i.e., Syrians, Phoenicians, Minoans, Amorites, etc. Of course, the writings of Kamose and Ahmose may have contributed to this inflated impression of the Hyksos. Kamose says:

Sekenenre

Behold! I am come, a successful man! What remains is in my possession, and my venture prospers! As mighty Amun endures, . . . the Asiatic has perished! Does your heart fail, O you vile Asiatic, you who used to say: "I am lord without equal from Hermopolis to *Pi-hathor* upon the *Rekhly* water. Avaris on the Two Rivers, I laid waste without inhabitants; . . . What a happy home-trip for the Ruler [Kamose] with his army ahead of him! They had no casualties, nor did anyone blame his fellow, nor did their hearts weep![19]

In like manner, Ahmose, on his triumphal stela, boasts in vicious abusive language and cheers his glorious defeat of the Hyksos. [20] It was both propaganda and hopeful, prophetic language that led Kamose and Ahmose to paint the Hyksos as a favored opponent who had invaded Egypt as an evil, unprovoked aggressor, but whom the superior Theban pharaohs had utterly thwarted and caused to flee in fear. Yet the skull of Ahmose and Kamose's predecessor, Sekenenre Taa-ken, stands in ghastly evidence to Hyksos brutality and superiority. Kamose's own subsequent demise is highly suspicious testimony to his flair for exaggeration—certainly to his overstated victory.

Still, the "vanguardist" Hyksos invasion theory does not seem consistent with Ipuwer's depiction of Egypt being taken over by allegedly lowly foreigners who lived in tents.[21] In fact, Ipuwer's observation, "the marsh-dweller is carrying a shield" would tend to indicate that the shield-carrying "invaders" were people who had been *living* in the Delta.[22] "And look, they have fallen into rebellion"; a statement like this would lead one to believe that people who were once contained and in the good graces of the government had staged an uprising.[23] Ipuwer paints a picture of foreigners, once serving in low estate among the Egyptians, becoming wealthy and powerful:

O, but the plunderer robs everywhere; the servant is taking as he finds, . . . O, but beggars have become lords of wealth someone who could not earn sandals for himself is a lord of riches, . . . O, but gold . . . and all our jewels are strung on the necks of servant girls.[24]

Ipuwer also describes the foreigners/Hyksos as:

Foreigners . . . skilled in the [crafts] of the Marshland [the Delta], . . . he who could not make a sarcophagus is a lord of a tomb. Look, . . . someone who could not make a coffin is a lord of a treasury. And look at these changes of mankind! He who could not build himself a room is a lord of walls. Look, the colonial tenants . . . now what they make is tents, like foreigners. [25]

Who were these alien "barbarians" from outside who came into Egypt, these desert dwellers who lived in tents, skilled in agriculture—especially tending flocks and herds ("crafts of the Delta"), who came to Egypt, begging with their hands out, asking only to be considered as servants, despised by Egyptians, yet allowed to establish a colony, lavished with great wealth, and honored in burial with sarcophagi and tombs?

Genesis 14.6; 16.7; and 21.14, 20, and 21 describe the region where Abraham and his family sojourned as a desert wilderness, the Hebrew word *midbar*. Genesis 30.43; 31.17; and 32.7, 15 make it clear that Abraham, Isaac, and Jacob owned and used camels just like the Bedouin caravan of traders described in Genesis 37.25. (Incidentally, Genesis 12.16 indicates that some of Abraham's camels came from Egypt, though camels are not indigenous to Egypt and there is no record of camels as permanent residents in Egypt before the Persian Period. Yet, perhaps the camels that pharaoh gave to Abraham had been recently acquired in trade for grain during the same drought that brought Abraham to Egypt in the first place.) Abraham, Isaac, and Jacob lived in tents (unlike Asiatic Canaanites who were city dwellers) (Genesis 12.8; 18.1; 24.67; 25.27; 26.17, 25; 31.25; and 35.21). The Hebrew patriarchs were quite skilled in farming according to Genesis 26.12, but the family of Jacob was especially shrewd in tending livestock (Genesis 30.29-43). Indeed, it was their standing as shepherds that caused the Hebrews to be considered an "abomination" to Egyptians (Genesis 46.34). The Hebrews came as aliens, as foreigners to Egypt; furthermore, they identified themselves as having been shepherds for generations, "And Pharaoh said unto his [Joseph's] brethren, What is your occupation? And they said unto Pharaoh, Thy servants are shepherds, both we, and also our fathers" (Genesis 47.3). They settled in Goshen, in "the Marshland," the Delta, the best land of Egypt, and practiced their "works" and crafts so well that they were put in charge of Pharaoh's own herds (Genesis 47.6). In fact, while Asiatics were captured from Canaan and pressed into service as slaves on various building projects throughout the Middle Kingdom, there is evidence of some Asiatics who were listed among specialized Egyptian workers—not slaves. "There are donkey drivers (who presumably knew the road), soldiers, and even chieftains from Retjenu [Canaan]."[26]

The family of Jacob arrived in Egypt destitute. Joseph came as a slave (Genesis 37.36). Joseph's brothers came bowing their faces to the ground, begging permission to buy grain, and recognizing themselves as no more than servants (Genesis 42.5, 6, and 10). Yet, unlike any other foreigners affected by the great famine in the time of Joseph, the ancient Hebrews didn't remain destitute. Joseph gave them back all the silver they paid for grain, and riches of Egypt were lavished upon them (Genesis 42.25):

Pharaoh said unto Joseph, Say unto thy brethren, This do ye; lade your beasts, and go, get you unto the land of Canaan; and take your father and your households, and come unto me: and I will give you the good of the land of Egypt, and ye shall eat the fat of the land. (Genesis 45.17-18)

Furthermore, Genesis 50 says both Jacob and Joseph were mummified; Joseph's coffin is mentioned specifically in verse 26, and he was originally buried in Egypt, presumably in a tomb. Could the Hyksos have been Hebrews? If the Hyksos were the ancient Hebrews, why would Ipuwer have such difficulty identifying them?

Although approximately seventy Hebrews came to Egypt as a nation "of promise," they were not yet a recognizable nation (Genesis 36.31; 46.3-27). They were in reality just the family of one man, Jacob, also known as Israel (Genesis 32.28). Though they were "the children of Israel," there is nothing in scripture to indicate that they identified themselves as "Israelites" at this time (Genesis 45.21). Furthermore, Joseph didn't necessarily identify himself as a Hebrew either, but as being from "the land of the Hebrews," a notable difference (Genesis 40.14). It's true that, according to the biblical text, Potiphar's wife and Pharaoh's cupbearer both identified Joseph as a "Hebrew"; each of them were personally acquainted with Joseph, and obviously classified him as a "Hebrew"—an "alien" (Genesis 39.14, 17; 41.12). It is likely that "Hebrew" was not considered a proper noun but is better understood as a common word, meaning "foreigner"—a term that in ancient times was often a term of derision. [27] Therefore, it is highly understandable and consistent that Ipuwer, as an outside observer, would have viewed the "Hebrews" as aliens, nondescript, detestable foreigners. For three generations, the Hebrews had been "sojourners." They didn't really belong *anywhere*—"they were but a few men in number; yea, very few, and strangers . . . when they went from one nation to another, from one kingdom to another . . ." (Psalms 105.12-13). Although they probably had adopted and adapted "identifiers" from many different cultures, they were only in the very beginning stages of distinguishing themselves as a people. Still, they were no longer associated with Ur; they did not belong in Haran; they were strangers in Canaan; and they certainly were not Egyptian (Genesis 17.8). The ancient Hebrews were "foreigners" everywhere they went! Ipuwer's classification was accurate. In fact, "Hebrew" was not embraced as an ethnic identity or as the proper name for the language of Israel until the intertestamental period.

For decades, archeologists, Egyptologists, and historians have said that there is no evidence of a Hebrew presence in ancient Egypt. When it is understood that the Hebrews came to Egypt as a family—not a nation—it's a small wonder that the record of them is lacking. What symbols would identify them? Judah had a signet (a seal), a bracelet (a twined cord), and a staff to give Tamar, but what would Judah's seal have looked like? (Genesis 38.18) The only mention of any markings left by the Hebrew patriarchs were incidental stones that Jacob erected (Genesis 28.18; 31.45; 35.14). Joshua, some five hundred years past Jacob, wrote on the stone altar he erected, but there is no mention in scripture of any monument made by Jacob being modified or autographed in any way other than being anointed with liquids (Joshua 8.32). The only land the Hebrews are recorded to have owned was a burial cave in a field in Hebron that Abraham bought from Ephron the Hittite and a similar field near Shechem that Jacob bought (Genesis 23.16-19; Genesis 33.19; Joshua 24.32). There is nothing in scripture to indicate that the Hebrews in the days of Jacob had a distinctive architecture (other than tents), pottery, dress, tools, weapons, writing, or even language, except for the fact that an interpreter was used between Joseph and his brothers when they first came to Egypt (Genesis 42.23; Psalms 81.5).

The only customs that seem to have set the Hebrews apart were circumcision and monotheism, but even these were not exclusive to or necessarily identifiable to Hebrews. Hebrew circumcision predated the Law of Moses, but circumcision, for instance, had also been practiced in Egypt since the Sixth Dynasty at least (Genesis 17.10; John 7.22).[28] Others, besides Hebrews—and pre-dating Hebrews—were monotheistic as well; although, based on the vast archeological record of multiple deities in nearly every culture on earth, monotheism was decidedly unpopular. Nevertheless, rarity should not be mistaken for non-existence. Enoch "walked with God"; evidently, Enoch's faithful monotheism identified him as atypical in his generation since, sadly, the notion of multiple gods—as even a possibility—seems to reach all the way back to the Garden of Eden, according to the Bible (Genesis 5.21-24). Eve was obviously swayed by, or was at least open to, the serpent's wicked proposal that even a human being could be like "gods" (Genesis 3.5). Noah, too, was a monotheist; and this extraordinary ideology selected him for preservation during the universal flood (Genesis 6.8, 22). Two other examples are: Melchizedek, the king of Salem and "priest of the most high God" to whom Abraham paid due homage; and Job, who worshiped the God of the Bible but who was probably not a Hebrew since he was from the land of Uz (Genesis 14.18; Job 1.1; John 8.39). Furthermore, Job seems to pre-date Exodus because God spoke to Job directly, indicating that he lived in the Patriarchal Age, the days before Moses and the prophets, and Job didn't worship God as prescribed by the Law of Moses; instead, Job appears to have offered sacrifices for himself and for others seemingly at his own home and without the mediation of a priest (Job 1.5; 38.1; 42.8; Leviticus 6).[29] Some biblical scholars regard the book of Job as the oldest book of the Bible, although Genesis records events that, obviously, predate Job. Since Sabeans and Chaldeans pillaged Job's livestock, it is possible that this tested monotheist was a contemporary of Abraham (Job 1.13-22; Genesis 11.28). However, since the names of Job's friends indicate associations with certain tribes of people living in and near Canaan, Job was more likely a contemporary with the generations just following Joseph. Issachar, Joseph's brother, had a son named Job; perhaps one was named after the other, or perhaps the parallel is merely coincidental; but the Job from Uz did not move to Egypt, neither is a great famine mentioned as part of the many trials that he suffered (Genesis 46.13).

Hyksos Dagger

Ruins and artifacts excavated from the Hyksos' capital, Avaris, also seem ambiguous in identifying the Hyksos. Hyksos pottery is a confusing conglomeration of Syrian and Canaanite forms, yet with Egyptian influences and, sometimes, made with Egyptian raw materials.[30] Houses in Avaris are similar to Syrio-Palestinian, Syrian, and Mesopotamian structures.[31] Yet, the finest examples of Minoan frescos ever found were discovered in Avaris.[32] The Hyksos left no inscriptions in a native language or any mythological or religious texts.[33] Articles of Baal worship, suggesting ties to several regions in Canaan, and even to Babylon, Syria, and Phoenicia, have been found in Avaris.[34] It also seems that the Hyksos adopted worship of the Egyptian god Seth, but assigned him Baal's Canaanite consort, Anat.[35] Most ancient idols were designated consorts because the male deity was believed to be balanced by a female counterpart, but that female partner wasn't usually from a different culture.[36]

In fact, the scriptures may connect the ancient Hebrews to Seth worship. In Numbers 24.17, when Balaam the son of Beor was being prohibited by God from cursing the Hebrews, he said, " . . . there shall come a Star out of Jacob, . . . and shall . . . destroy all the children of Sheth." "Sheth" is a variation of "Seth," who was one of the sons of Adam, but "Sheth" is obviously also very similar to the name of the Egyptian god "Seth" (I Chronicles 1.1). Since Noah was descended from the Seth who was Adam's son, all "post-flood" mankind are the children of Seth (Genesis 5.6-30). Therefore, Balaam was either prophesying the destruction of all mankind or only the destruction of Seth worshipers, i.e. anyone who would rather worship an entity like Seth and/or the stars in the sky than trust God and his "star" (Matthew 2.2-10; Revelation 22.16).

As Balaam and the king of Moab, Balak, stood atop Mount Peor, they could see the Hebrews camped on the edge of Canaan, tribe by tribe (Numbers 23.28-24.2). Forty years prior, as punishment for their grumbling against God and for their lack of faith and lack of faithfulness, God had sentenced every Hebrew of that generation (who was older than a teenager when he/she left Egypt) to die in the wilderness (Numbers 9.1; 14.28-35). Therefore, many Seth worshipers who may have been among them when they left Egypt were likely dead by the time Balaam and Balak looked down on the Hebrews.

Yet, just as God had eliminated the Seth worshipers from among the Hebrews, he was poised to destroy all remaining worshipers of Seth in Canaan (Numbers 26.64-65). It's generally believed that the Hyksos worshiped Seth because he was most like Baal, a familiar god of Asiatics. However, as a fertility god, Baal was also analogous to Osiris.[37] Nevertheless, by tying Baal to Egyptian deities, it was easier for Baal worshipers in Canaan who were allied with the Hyksos to become Seth worshipers as well, much as Seth was married to Anat.

It is likely that Balaam and Balak would not recognize these Hebrews as being former rulers in Egypt;

after all, the escaping Egyptian slaves, even though they were a menacing mob, would not have looked much like the formerly aristocratic Hyksos (Numbers 22.5). Also, Balak and Balaam were likely not alive during the time of the Hyksos reign. But God remembered the Hyksos and their endorsement of Seth worship, and through the reluctant pronouncement and prophesy of Balaam, God made it clear that he would not abide false gods.

Manetho (an Egyptian high priest and historian from the Ptolemy period, in the third century BC) also seems to have associated the Hyksos with the Hebrews because he says that they (the Hyksos) went on to build Jerusalem. Interestingly, Manetho and others further describe the Hyksos as "brothers of the princes of Retjenu"—an apt categorization of Joseph's family.[38] Certainly the Hebrews went on to conquer the land that included Jerusalem in the days of Joshua (Joshua 11.16-23). They defeated the king of Jerusalem just as they defeated the king of Jericho (Joshua 12.9-10). There is little question that Jericho was conquered by the Hebrews in the occupation of Canaan; therefore, there can be little question that Jerusalem was conquered too, by Joshua before the days of David.[39] That famous city eventually became the Hebrews' governmental and religious capital (Joshua 10.22-28; II Samuel 5.7; Nehemiah 11.1). Josephus (a Jewish historian employed by the Roman government) subscribed to Manetho's assessment of the Hyksos association with Jerusalem.[40] However, Manetho and/or Josephus likely intended no ill will toward the Hebrews by identifying them with the Hyksos. Though these two men were not perfect or without agenda, fundamentally, they were simply endeavoring to be historians. If the Hyksos were the Hebrews, why did they incorporate so many different cultures, exhibit so many different religions, and worship so many different gods? From the day that the Hebrews came into Egypt, they were a mixed race.[41] Rebecca, Isaac's wife, urged their son Jacob to return to her family in Haran to arrange himself a marriage. However, Jacob and his Syrian father-in-law Laban had cause to distrust each other. Perhaps it was for this reason that the scriptures never say anything about Jacob encouraging his own sons to return to Haran to look for wives, though its not unlikely that Leah, Rachel, or the two concubines, Bilhah and Zilpah, may have urged their sons, following Rebecca's example (Genesis 30.3, 9). Nevertheless, Jacob's sons (of necessity) were married to women of nationalities other than Hebrew. Therefore, the group of individuals who came to Egypt as Joseph's family probably represented, by marriage, an array of cultures, influences, and religions. In fact, though Hebrews are rightly associated with monotheism, very rarely in their ancient history were they exclusively monotheistic.[42] The Hebrew patriarch, Abraham, originated from a polytheistic family (Joshua 24.2). Members of Jacob's household and his father-in-law possessed and, presumably, worshiped idols (Genesis 31.30, 34; 35.2-4). Hebrews worshiped Egyptian gods (Joshua 24.14). The ancient Hebrews cast and worshiped a golden calf (Exodus 32.4-8). Before they even possessed the land of Canaan, some Hebrews had already engaged in worshiping Canaanite gods and were considering further worship of Canaanite gods (Numbers 25.1-3; Joshua 24.15). Often, Hebrews were led into the worship of foreign gods through marrying foreign women. For this reason, as part of the commandments given to Moses, God warned the Israelites not to marry indigenous women from the promised land (Exodus 34.15-16).

Of course, the Law of Moses did not exist in the time of Joseph; therefore, aside from the example set by Abraham, Isaac, and Jacob, who went to family in Haran to arrange marriage, it seems that Joseph and his brothers were relatively free to marry whomever they chose (Genesis 24.2-4; 28.2). Joseph was married to an Egyptian woman (Genesis 41.45). Judah, for one, had a Canaanite wife, Shua (Bathshua); Simeon was also married to a Canaanite woman (Genesis 38.2; 46.10; I Chronicles 2.3). The nationalities of Jacob's other daughters-in-law are unknown in the scriptures. It is probable that the seventy to seventy-five male immigrants who entered Egypt as the "Hebrews" had wives representing many different cultures (Genesis 46.26; Acts 7.14). Therefore, while the Hyksos may have been predominantly composed of Hebrews, they undoubtedly embraced and included others from many different places.[43] In fact, the Hebrews and the Hyksos were always a mixture of races from the day they entered Egypt until the day they left (Exodus 12.38; Numbers 12.38). Consequently, it is not surprising that they agglomerated many different styles of crafts—including polytheism.

How is it that the Hyksos/Hebrews settled in Avaris? Joseph's family came to Egypt in the second year of the famine (Genesis 45.6). Joseph promised to provide for them and keep them from being impoverished

(Genesis 45.11). Pharaoh promised them the "best" in Egypt, including land and possessions (Genesis 45.17-20). The Hebrews may have immigrated to Egypt in tents, but tents certainly were not the best accommodations in Egypt. Despite the fact that the Hebrews assured Pharaoh that they were merely "sojourners" in Egypt, it is highly likely that Joseph and Pharaoh built houses—built a city—especially for Jacob and his offspring in Goshen (Genesis 47.4). A town would have defined an area for the Hebrews to inhabit, and it would have secured their safety and seclusion; and as Ipuwer observed, the tent dwellers possessed walls.

Dr. Manfred Bietak heads a team of Austrian archeologists who have worked for decades excavating Avaris. His meticulous work and intriguing findings reveal that the first residents of this small town located along the Pelusiac Branch of the Nile Delta (in the region commonly associated with Goshen), lived in Egyptian-style huts "approximately 25 m^2, which is a very modest amount of space for one family."[44] Yet, indications of a semi-nomadic presence in the town are evidenced by Bedouin-style cooking pots. The ancient Hebrews came to Egypt as an extended family of nomadic people. They likely traveled very lightly and had few possessions that were not biodegradable.[45] In fact, Genesis 46.6-7 stresses that they only brought their livestock and progeny with them into Egypt. Still, it is not hard to imagine that, from an archaeological perspective, these particular Hebrew "Bedouins" from the early Middle Kingdom would appear highly Egyptianized. Joseph was so Egyptianized that his own family didn't recognize him (Genesis 42.8). Furthermore, Pharaoh and Joseph started "Egyptainizing" Jacob's family even before they left Canaan:

> Now thou art commanded, this do ye; take you wagons out of the land of Egypt for your little ones, and for your wives, and bring your father, and come. Also regard not your stuff; for the good of all the land of Egypt is yours. And the children of Israel did so: and Joseph gave them wagons, according to the commandment of Pharaoh, and gave them provision for the way. To all of them he gave each man changes of raiment; but to Benjamin he gave three hundred pieces of silver, and five changes of raiment. And to his father he sent after this manner; ten asses laden with the good things of Egypt, and ten she asses laden with corn and bread and meat for his father by the way. (Genesis 45.19-23)

It is unlikely that the pharaoh of Egypt sent Jacob's family Asiatic-style clothing and goods. It is also unlikely that Jacob would have refused the generous gifts sent by Pharaoh and by Joseph. It was unwise to disobey the command of a pharaoh, "not to concern themselves with their 'stuff,'" therefore it's perhaps more of a mystery as to why they bothered bringing their crude cooking pots; nevertheless, they did (Genesis 47.1). However, these foreigners arrived in Egypt with Egyptian clothes, Egyptian wagons, Egyptian food, and the finest Egyptian wares. It stands to reason that Egyptian houses were built for them too. It also stands to reason that not many foreign artifacts from that original group would be easy to classify. In fact, only 20% of the pottery found in Avaris from this time period is not Egyptian.[46] It's also highly likely that Joseph would have lived with his family in Avaris and would have been buried there, even if he possessed tombs elsewhere.

Dr. David Rohl has reached a similar conclusion. He too believes that Avaris was the home of the Hebrews and of Joseph. In the earliest layer of Avaris, is the foundation of a Syrian-style villa, complete with gardens that represent the footprint of the residence of Jacob, according to Dr. Rohl.[47] The villa dates back to the early Middle Kingdom (the time of Mentuhotep II), and Asiatic artifacts have been found on the site. In particular, there is "extremely fine" Levantine Painted pottery ware that has its origins in Syria according to Dr. Bietak.[48] This assumption fits very nicely in a connection with Jacob, who spent at least fourteen years in the Padan-Aram region of Syria and married two women from there. It is very feasible that broken pottery from the sophisticated potters' wheels in Haran would be found in the remains of a place where Jacob may have lived.[49]

At some point, in the Twelfth Dynasty, there was a "hiatus" of habitation in Avaris; the village lay essentially unoccupied and "was resettled by Canaanites."[50] What could account for this occurrence? Upon the death of the Hebrew patriarch, Jacob, there was a mass funeral procession from Egypt to Hebron in Canaan. According to Genesis 50.7-8, the company included all of the Hebrews and their servants, the royal servants of Pharaoh, and all the "elders of the land of Egypt." Only the Hebrews' small children, flocks and herds, and presumably their caretakers, stayed behind. Such an event could certainly account for a temporary vacancy in Avaris. The undertaking of such a pilgrimage, no doubt, took some time. It is also likely that, impressed by the imperial entourage that accompanied the Hebrews and becoming cognizant of the good life that the former nomads were living in Egypt, several opportunistic Canaanite in-laws, would-be friends, and suddenly-cozy-cousins would have been eager to emigrate to Egypt on the return trip (Genesis 36.12).

Subsequent to this interim in occupancy, Dr. Bietak's findings also indicate that, later in the Twelfth Dynasty, the Syrian-style villa was razed, and a grand Egyptian-style palace, complete with a garden tomb as part of its complex, was constructed on the same location.[51] What could account for this? After the death of Jacob, there was no need for Jacob's villa. Rohl is convinced that the Egyptian-style palace was built to be the later-life dwelling of Joseph.[52] Perhaps it was built during his absence and was presented to the celebrated vizier as a pharaonic present intended to cheer Joseph upon his return from the sad task of burying his father. In fact, as suggested in the first chapter of this book, if the pharaoh at the time of Jacob's death was a different pharaoh than the one who welcomed the Hebrews into Egypt, building this palace may have been a goodwill gesture on the part of the new king, intended to build a rapport or even to curry favor with Joseph.

Dr. Rohl's analysis of Dr. Bietak's findings on the site of this mysterious palace, especially his explanation of evidence in the on-site tomb that suggests a systematic evacuation of its contents and its occupant, is compelling. Of course, the Bible says that Moses gathered "the bones" of Joseph and took them with him in the Exodus, an apt description of Joseph's remains in Avaris if his viscera were buried elsewhere: say, in Ipi's tomb at Deir el Bahri (Exodus 13.19). As Dr. Rohl proposes, Moses' respectful emptying of Joseph's tomb would probably not have resembled the usual desecrating, ransacking operations of ancient tomb robbers.[53] He also speculates that a shattered statue is the likely head and shoulders of a monument dedicated to Joseph, though any likeness to Joseph is completely lost because the figure's face is long removed, and no identifying inscriptions remain.[54] Nevertheless, it is interesting to note that in his refurbished version of this cult statue that Dr. Rohl attributes to Joseph, the figure is positioned and is wearing a robe that is, at the very least, reminiscent of the pose and the Sed-Festival robe of Mentuhotep II in his most famous statue.

Other clues that tie the Hyksos to Canaan and to the Hebrews include: various bronze daggers and spears, copper belts, pottery that suggests an Asiatic origin, and the remains of sheep consistent with the type of sheep commonly found in the Levant of the Jordan Valley and Asia Minor.[55] Donkeys and sheep, animals long associated with Hebrews, were buried with some residents of Avaris (Genesis 22.3, 42.26, 44.13).[56] Jewelry found in Avaris is indicative of Canaan. Burial customs of the inhabitants of Avaris were (by the Thirteenth Dynasty) very Canaanite, not Egyptian. Of course, these burials were not really Hebrew either, since the Bible records Hebrews burying their dead in caves, but a possible explanation for this dissimilarity will follow shortly. 80% of the weapons found in 50% of the graves in this Goshen city were Syrio-Palestinian, but perhaps the most arousing and controversial discoveries are the nine clay seals that Dr. Bietak unearthed in Avaris, which appear to bear the name "Yakob," or Jacob. In the History Channel documentary, *Exodus Decoded*, Bietak says, "It's very strange that we found nine seals with the name Yakob here. It's a Biblical name, by the way. The original was probably mounted on a ring worn on the finger, and this gives us a new puzzle." [57]

Jacob's Seal

Many are quick to correlate these seals with the signet ring given to Joseph by Pharaoh (Genesis 41.42). Of course, this is a problematic conclusion. It is highly doubtful that Pharaoh's ring had Jacob's name on it, and even if subsequent signet rings were made especially for Joseph by pharaoh, they would probably not have displayed Joseph's Hebrew name or his father's name since Pharaoh, himself, had given Joseph an Egyptian name, recorded in Genesis as "Zaphenath-pa'neah" (Genesis 41.45). It is, therefore, unlikely that these seals are any direct evidence of Joseph. However, in light of the signet of Judah in Genesis 38, it is possible that the seals are evidence of the Hebrew patriarch Jacob. If his son, Judah, had a signet, it's likely that Jacob did too. At least it heightens the possibility against alternative theories that suggest that these nine seals are merely generic impressions of a common Asiatic name that could have represented any number of individuals. Even a rudimentary examination of the seal, makes it clear that this Jacob was *no* commoner. The name "Yakob," written in Egyptian hieroglyphs, is contained inside a cartouche or "shenu." This oval-shaped name ring, drawn to resemble a tied rope, was reserved for royal names. So, we can deduce that this Jacob was considered to be a king in his own right, the leader of his people. At the very top of the seal is the symbol for Aten, a deity with very interesting ties to the God of Abraham, Isaac, and Jacob, the God of the Bible. Obviously, the Jacob who owned this seal identified himself with Aten. The decorative swirls on either side of the cartouche appear to symbolize water, perhaps indicating that this Jacob lived between two rivers, just as Kamose identified Avaris to be. And the ankh symbol at the bottom of the seal says that this Jacob was blessed.[58]

Mounting evidence has steered several experts to conclude that Hebrews inhabited Avaris. Yet, were the Hebrews the Hyksos? Some say that the Hyksos were an invading force that attacked and occupied Avaris after the Hebrews left Egypt in the Exodus.[59] Others say that the Hyksos were foreigners ruling Egypt when the Hebrews arrived or that the Hyksos came to Egypt during the Hebrew sojourn.[60] There are those who say that it was a Hyksos pharaoh who enslaved the Hebrews.[61] Still others believe that the Hebrews were allied with the Hyksos and that "the exodus" was Ahmose's expulsion of the whole lot of them.

The response to these arguments probably rests in the strata of Avaris itself. Apparently, Avaris was originally a relatively small Egyptianized-Asiatic settlement consisting of a few huts and the Syrian-style villa that was, perhaps, the house of Jacob. In little over a decade, the villa was dismantled and a grand Egyptian-style palace, perhaps the residence of Joseph, was built atop the villa's foundation. The palace was eventually vacated as well, but the city of Avaris continued to expand; large houses were built (complete with servants' quarters). Though there is evidence to suggest that the residents of this booming Avaris were highly "Egyptianized," they retained some Asiatic customs, especially burial practices, yet the demographics of graves in Avaris are puzzling. Female remains outnumber males, and there are disproportionately large numbers of infant remains, children under eighteen months of age.[62] More puzzling still is the evidence of a terrible disaster that struck the city around the end of the Thirteenth Dynasty. Mass graves with bodies strewn haphazardly, with no evidence of funerary rituals or grave goods, suggest a time of great tragedy. Following this calamity, Avaris was all but deserted.[63] However, within a relatively short time, the city was rebuilt, remodeled, and repopulated by mostly military troops with seemingly strong Asiatic chauvinism. This refashioned Avaris was also the site of Canaanite and Egyptian-style temples. Eventually, through the Fifteenth Dynasty, Avaris expanded again to incorporate a "fortified" palace and was, obviously, a center of trade between the Hyksos and the entire Mediterranean region, although goods exported by the Hyksos remain a mystery.[64] The research of Dr. John S. Holladay, Jr. strengthens the observation of vigorous trade even more. He writes, "new cross-cultural insights brilliantly illumine the situation in the Eastern Nile Delta, particularly with respect to the function of Avaris, probably the most important external trading node in the proto-Phoenician Canaanite trading diaspora."[65]

Do the early layers of Avaris suggest a correlation to the first fourteen chapters of Exodus, or is there another explanation? A major obstacle prohibiting a Hebrew exodus at any time near or during the Second Intermediate Period is the Egyptian army. *Major* military operations conducted in Syrio-Palestine from the days of Ahmose certainly through Thutmose III (really until Akhenaten) simply are not consistent with the early history of the Israelites in Canaan.[66] Conflicts between the settling Hebrew tribes and the various inhabitants of Canaan (i.e., Amorites, Ammonites, Midianites, Philistines, etc.) would have seemed like mere skirmishes compared to the well-documented force of the formidable Egyptian army conquering and holding land after land, city after city, throughout the Levant all the way to the Euphrates, yet there is no mention of pharaonic conquest or any significant, successful Egyptian military involvement (with the Hebrews or with any of their neighbors) throughout the entire books of Exodus, Leviticus, Numbers, Deuteronomy, Joshua, Judges, Ruth, I Samuel, and II Samuel which cover nearly five centuries of Hebrew history!

A lesser reason that makes the Exodus unlikely before the New Kingdom is the use of the title "pharaoh" in the books of Moses. Although the Hebrew Bible is sometimes credited with coining the term, the Egyptian word "Per-O," meaning "Great House," is believed to be the basis of the title "pharaoh."[67] Thutmose III may have been the first king of Egypt referred to as the "Great House," the "Per-O." It was likely a reference to the Amun-Ra temple complex at Karnak that Thutmose III expanded into what was the largest building in the world for millennia.[68] Therefore, it is perhaps more likely that employing the term "pharaoh" may indicate that Hebrews at the time of the exodus were more familiar with Egypt in the days of Thutmose III and after.

Of course, there are those who contend that the Old Testament scriptures, even the books of Moses, did not exist in written form until the time of the Babylonian captivity. No earlier copies of the books are known to be extant and, therefore, are theorized in some academic circles never to have existed at all. It is then argued that, until the 6th century BC, the Old Testament was largely a collection of oral traditions, which may or may not have been embellished over time, though Galatians 3.15 upholds the integrity of the Law.

However, something tangible was preserved on stone tablets and placed inside the Ark of the Covenant according to the Biblical account (Exodus 24.12; I Kings 8.9). Historical writing was also prescribed (Exodus 17.14). Deuteronomy 28.58 certainly seems to indicate that the Law of Moses was written and was not only oral. Written copies of *all* the laws and statutes were encouraged (Deuteronomy 17.18). Prophets were told to write in a book intended to be read (Isaiah 34.16; Jeremiah 30.2). Written "scrolls/books," were found in the temple renovation in the days of Josiah, prior to the Babylonian captivity. How long had they existed? How long had they been lost? Far from an oral tradition, carefully preserved, the scriptures record that not even the high priest seemed to have been knowledgeable of what was *written* in those lost books (II Kings 22.8).

Hyksos Scarab
Top and Belly

Perhaps a re-examination of the layers of evidence at Avaris may suggest a different hypothesis for the placement of the exodus. It does seem likely that the early Syrian-style villa of stratum H=d/2, from the early Middle Kingdom, that housed mostly Egyptianized Canaanites was built for Jacob and his sons, although the scriptures do insinuate that Jacob liked living in a tent (Genesis 25.27).[69] Furthermore, Jacob's stated intention was to be a visitor in Egypt (Genesis 47.4). Therefore, it is not certain that the old man would have opted to move into a villa even if one was built for him. Regardless, it makes sense that the Egyptian-style palace that was erected later would have served quite nicely as a dwelling and business place for Joseph during the last decades of his life, following the death of his father. Furthermore, Dr. Rohl's analysis of the tunnel carefully dug to remove the contents of the tomb on that location seems irrefutable.

On the other hand, assuming that a disproportionate number of women and infants buried in Avaris offers evidence of a pharaonic edict to eradicate Hebrew male children is questionable (Exodus 1.15-22). Josephus provides the explanation that, for some time after the death of Jacob, Hebrews continued to bury their "fathers" in Hebron.[70] Steven seems to confirm Josephus on this point (Acts 7.15-16). Dr. Bietak finds it "unthinkable" that such expeditions would have been allowed to proceed across the borders of Egypt without special permission. Obviously, such permission was granted to residents of Avaris; and the scriptures bear out, in the last chapters of Genesis, that the ancient Hebrews were treated as special when they first arrived in Egypt and when they returned to Canaan to bury Jacob.[71] Significantly, in the Wadi Gaza and the Jezreel Valley, the discovery of several scarab amulets from Egypt, some inscribed with the names of Hyksos kings, suggest an ongoing tie between the Hyksos and the Hebron region of Canaan.[72] This same area of Canaan corresponds to the territory of Judah where Abraham likely lived and where the burial cave of the Hebrew ancestors would have been located. Perhaps the disproportionate number of females and children buried in Avaris confirms that the Hebrews in Avaris only buried adult male bodies in Hebron; perhaps only some Hebrew males—those who were particularly loyal to Hebrew tradition and patriarchy—opted to be buried in Hebron. Perhaps the bodies buried in Avaris represent only part of the Hebrew population, foreign allies of the Hebrews, servants of the Hebrews, and/or lesser wives. Shocking evidence that supports the possible human sacrifice of Egyptian slave girls buried with their masters indicates a disturbing prejudice in Avaris against both Egyptians and women.[73]

On the other hand, the disproportionate number of males to females may reflect the ancient Hebrew practice of polygamy. Abraham had multiple wives, as did Jacob. Polygamous families tend to have disproportionately large numbers of children; therefore, correspondingly large numbers of infant deaths should not be surprising. Polygamy, however, was not common in Egypt. Only Egyptian royal families were polygamous; most Egyptian men simply could not afford more than one wife and considered the practice objectionable.[74] Yet, affording multiple wives was probably not an issue for post-famine Hebrews; they were, likely, quite wealthy! Polygamy is a practice that arguably promotes the degradation of women, historically reducing females to little more than property and possibly indicating why the female dead in Avaris were not extended the select courtesy of burial with the illustrious Hebrew ancestors in Hebron.

What about the mass of the uncelebrated dead in Avaris; do they verify the tenth plague, as some say? Bietak is certain they represent some sudden catastrophe.[75] Manetho says, in the Aegyptiaca, fragment 42, his record of the fall of the Thirteenth Dynasty, "a blast of God smote us."[76] Did a literal "blast" precede the invasion of Memphis? What could explain Manetho's ominous illustration and sequence of events?

Carbon dating of an olive branch from Santorini places the eruption of Thera between 1630-1600 BC. This is, at least, a step in the right direction (from the previously assigned date of 1500 BC) to place the eruption of Thera at the time of the Avaris mass graves. Solidified mud and ash associated with Thera, and an accompanying tsunami, devastated coastal settlements in the Egyptian Delta. Ash and pumice from the super eruption encased structures in the vicinity of the Egyptian fortress of Tharo. "Scientists suggest that trade winds may have carried a blizzard of ash to Egypt from Santorini, over 700 miles away."[77] Certainly the earthquakes, ash clouds, and poisonous gases associated with a massive volcanic explosion would constitute a catastrophe. Terrified by the darkness, disaster, and death, the residents of Avaris would have evacuated the city in a panic. And, depending on the prevailing winds, Avaris could have been devastated by the eruption of Thera while an area perhaps as near as Memphis was not. Yet, the massive explosion of Thera was probably heard in Memphis. It is, therefore, understandable how such an event could be described as "a blast," and to a superstitious people, as "a blast from God." Several have speculated that parts of the writings of Ipuwer may be describing a volcanic event. Pumice, which has been positively linked to Thera, has been found in Avaris.[78] Though initial examination of this pumice does not seem to support a placement at the end of the Thirteenth Dynasty, Dr. Bietak explains that the pumice could have washed to the shores of north Avaris via the sea.[79] However, agricultural activity that has been part of the Egyptian Delta since antiquity is also somewhat problematic to an undisturbed reading of the various strata in Avaris.[80] Of course, Thera is far from the only volcano in the volatile region of the Mediterranean; volcanoes also occupy Sinai. So, Ipuwer may well be describing volcanic activity from any number of places in ill-omened phrases like "Behold, the fire has begun to rise—"[81]

If Avaris was deemed uninhabitable by its residents during a calamity at the end of the Thirteenth Dynasty—regardless of the nature of the disaster, i.e., volcano, earthquake, plague, pestilence, etc.—where would her refugees have gone? The choices for these displaced Asiatic immigrants would have been limited. Could they have returned to their ancestral country? After living in Egypt for decades, the land that their ancestors had left behind was probably occupied by opportunistic squatters who would not want the successors back. Besides, if these residents of Avaris were ancient Hebrews, they didn't have land (other than a couple of burial plots) to return to, and by now, there were many more Hebrews than just seventy. Could they expect the Egyptians to share shelter with them? There is nothing to indicate that Egyptian sympathies toward shepherds and/or Asiatics had changed. In fact, the writings of Senusret I indicate that sentiments toward Asiatics had not changed in the Middle Kingdom. Even though there is evidence to indicate that the early residents of Avaris were "Egyptianized" Asiatics, it does not mean they were not still "loathsome" foreigners to Egyptians. After all, Joseph was so highly "Egyptianized" that his own brothers didn't recognize him, yet not even Joseph, second only to the pharaoh, fully accepted as an Egyptian. The wording of Genesis 43.32 sounds as if even the Egyptians who served Joseph and ate in his house (with him) still preferred to eat by themselves.

Could Hebrews, acting as Hyksos, have been capable of employing force? Manetho describes the

Hyksos as an "obscure race" that came from "regions of the East."[82] At the end of the Thirteenth Dynasty, Memphis was the capital of Egypt, Avaris was east of Memphis, but any group of Asiatics (Hebrews included) would have been considered by the Egyptians as having originated or "come from" the East. As discussed earlier, it is not surprising that the Hebrews would have been considered "obscure," hidden and/or hard to identify—even by this time. They were still a nation without a nation; and if they had largely sequestered themselves inside the walls of Avaris, what occasion would Egyptians have to become well acquainted with Jacob's descendants? Manetho goes on to report:

> [the] invaders . . . marched in confidence of victory against our land. By main force they easily seized it without striking a blow; and having overpowered the rulers of the land, they then burned our cities ruthlessly, razed to the ground the temples of the gods, and treated all the natives with cruel hostility, massacring some and leading into slavery the wives and children . . .

According to Dr. Rohl, Manetho calls the Hyksos "shepherd kings."[83] As already established, there is a strong correlation between Hebrews and shepherds. Since, in the biblical account, shepherds were held by Egyptians in such low esteem, it seems that "shepherd kings" would have been a title of contempt, in keeping with Egyptian sentiments toward Asiatics and toward the Hyksos expressed over time. Associating the Hyksos with shepherds is perhaps echoed in Ipuwer's reference to "the shepherd" in Stanza XII of his lament.[84]

Yet would Hebrews have been capable of aggression like Manetho reports? Genesis 14 tells how Abraham, the first Hebrew, with only 318 men, defeated the armies of several kings just to save the life of one of his relatives (Genesis 14.14-15). Assuming that ancient Hebrews were aware of the promises made to their patriarchs, in Genesis 15 and 28, they could have been very confident indeed, as Manetho asserts that the aggressors "marched in confidence of victory." Any "Egyptianized" people would presumably have been motivated to stay in Egypt. At any rate, having been displaced from their city, the former residents of Avaris were, no doubt, anticipating the application of force to acquire new housing, no matter where they went. Would it make more sense to apply that force quickly and nearby or after having been weakened by time and long travel? The ancient Hebrews, especially, would probably not have been eager to leave Egypt; they had lived a privileged life there! Josephus says, "they lived happily in Egypt."[85] And why not? They had been given the best that Egypt had to offer. They had flourished in a famine when everyone else had suffered great loss. Some may have felt destined and entitled to greatness in Egypt, but were they capable of such "fierce-facedness," "wrongdoing," and "plunder" as Ipuwer characterizes? (Genesis 46.3) [86]

Granted, both Manetho and Ipuwer were speaking from an Egyptian perspective about perceived assailants who conquered their land; anger and despair no doubt shaded their opinions. It should also be noted that Ipuwer implicates only "a few people" in the overthrow of the government, which of course suggests that *not* all ancient Hebrews were violent or treacherous, but then, it only takes a few ringleaders.[87] Nevertheless, Joseph's brothers had certainly demonstrated treachery when they sold him into slavery and lied to their father (Genesis 37). Joseph's brothers were obviously disagreeable by nature because Joseph urged them not to quarrel with each other—this, even after overflowing kindness had been demonstrated toward them (Genesis 45.24). They also fully expected revenge for their treachery and did not really believe that Joseph's goodness toward them was genuine (Genesis 50.15). This perhaps lends further insight into the underlying character of these particular men. Even Joseph, who loved them, acknowledged that they, his own family, were capable of intentional evil (Genesis 50.20). In fact, in this family, rancor had been generational. Jacob was conniving and cruel to his brother, Esau, and deceitful to his own father, Isaac (Genesis 25 and 27). Laban, Jacob's father-in-law (who was also his uncle), had demonstrated betrayal (Genesis 24.29, 29). Jacob mistreated Laban in return (Genesis 30). If the Hebrew forefathers were capable of such ruthless behavior against their own relatives, how much more likely is it that ancient Hebrews might mistreat strangers? In fact, if ancient Hebrews, acting as the Hyksos, had massacred unprepared, unsuspecting people, had plundered their possessions, and had shown no mercy, even to women and children, it would not have been the first time.

In Genesis 34, there is recorded the disturbing a story of the violation of Dinah, Jacob's daughter, and the subsequent vicious retaliation of her brothers. According to scripture, Shechem, a prince in Canaan, committed an immoral act; he molested Dinah, but he also, according to scripture, loved her deeply and begged his father to arrange for him a marriage with the girl. Rabbi Zlotowitz seems to indicate that Genesis

Asiatics in Egypt

34.1 suggests that it may have been Dinah who first violated the accepted codes of restraint.[88] Regardless, Jacob's sons were indignant and insisted that "such a thing" could not be tolerated—although Jacob's sons were not above similar behavior. After all, Genesis 35.22 and 38.13-26 describe the repulsive indiscretions of Reuben with his own father's concubine and of Judah with his daughter-in-law. (Such things should not have been tolerated either; Genesis 49.4 and I Chronicles 5.2 show that Reuben was punished). Shechem and his father, Chamor, went to Jacob seemingly to do the "honorable" thing: to seek reconciliation, to offer restitution, and to plead for the hand of Dinah in marriage. Dinah's brothers, however, were uninterested in forgiveness. Instead, they conspired to feign a hope of good will with Chamor's people. They imposed Hebrew religious practice (circumcision) on the Hivvites but only used it to gain a cruel military advantage. Then, with their victims sufficiently subdued, two of the brothers, Simeon and Levi, mercilessly attacked the incapacitated city of Chamor ("confidently" according to Genesis 34.25). They killed not only Shechem and Chamor, but also *every* male. They enslaved the women and children and helped themselves to whatever they wanted. It is important to note that nowhere in this story does the scripture indicate that God instructed the Hebrews to enact such vengeance or that he aided them in any way. Genesis 34.30 makes it clear that Jacob did not at all approve of what transpired; even on his deathbed, Jacob continued to denounce his sons' violent actions against the Hivvites and the dishonor that they brought on their father through these acts of treachery (Genesis 49.5-6). Nevertheless, apparently without divine aid, through their own ruthless skill, an entire city was destroyed by the hand of only two Hebrews.

Is it possible, therefore, that a few ancient Hebrews might have been able to overpower "the rulers of the land" in Memphis? Exodus 1.7 seems to indicate that they could, " . . . the children of Israel were fruitful, and increased abundantly, and multiplied, and waxed exceeding mighty; and the land was filled with them." Stratas F-G in the excavation of Avaris confirm exponential population growth.[89] Ancient Hebrews—far from being slaves—in the early wake of Joseph, were rich, successful, skilled, feared, unified, strong, and numerous. They had every advantage. The Hyksos, though a minority group in Egypt, were armed with advanced armor, bows, and chariots—expensive technology from Asia and Canaan that could have been easily procured by a wealthy sub-group through trade.[90] The Hebrews had understandable reason to be confident of victory; and if some catastrophe had placed them in a desperate situation, they had motive for aggression.

"Egyptian texts such as the Brooklyn Papyrus attest to the presence of a sizable Asiatic population in the eastern Delta during the Twelfth and Thirteenth Dynasties."[91] If the Hyksos already inhabited the Delta before the fall of Memphis, they would not have been weakened by engaging Egyptian troops stationed in the fortress on the northeastern border between Egypt and Canaan. Also, there would have been no occasion to warn Memphis of a military conquest of the Asian outpost and of the approach of hostile forces. Dr. Bietak says,

"Archaeological evidence gives the impression of the gradual growth in power of an Asian-dominated province of the northeastern Delta."[92] It is more likely, therefore, that the conquering of Lower Egypt was accomplished—not by an invading army from an outside country, but by immigrants who had been welcomed into Egypt by a pharaoh's open arms, by foreigners who had been enjoying the finest land and accommodations in Egypt for decades, by alien colonists who had multiplied to strength in numbers and who finally rebelled against their gracious hosts and supplanted the natives.

There is strong evidence to support the notion that Hebrews inhabited Avaris at the dawn of the Middle Kingdom. They arguably had ample resources, numbers, and finances to launch an offensive. As a testament to the wealth and commercial connections of those in Avaris, artifacts and writings yield extensive evidence of imports of goods from regions as far away as Crete, Palestine, and Syria.[93] According to the findings of Dr. Bietak, trade with Syria and Lebanon seems to have "figured importantly" from early in Avaris.[94] Could there have been imports of advanced weapons?

In fact, there were. On a stela recording spoils acquired in the vicinity of Avaris, Kamose reports the confiscation of 300 Hyksos ships, filled with—among other precious goods—bronze weapons, and "axes without number."[95] Curiously, the goods listed in the manifests of these vessels were not Canaanite in origin, which suggests the knowledge and procurement of advanced weapons from distant ports of call.[96] Of course, Hebrews were not really Canaanite in origin either. Their ancestral roots were beyond Canaan. Abraham and Sarah came from Ur; Abraham sought a wife for Isaac from their relatives in Haran, and Jacob married into and lived with family in Syria. Therefore, they were well acquainted with more advanced civilizations that existed outside of Canaan. Canaan was a good place for the Hyksos to seek extra manpower, logistics, and strategic locations, but Canaan was not a good source of advanced technology.

However, it is likely that most of the sons of Jacob considered Canaan as "home" since the family had "settled" in Hebron (Genesis 35.27). They had relatives that comprised several nations, inhabiting the Levant region. Of course, their maternal relatives lived mostly to the north in Padan-Aram. The Edomites, the family of Jacob's twin brother, Esau, were located just south of Hebron. The Amalekites were also likely descendants of Esau, "specifically of his son Eliphaz;" although it's possible that they merely merged with the existing Amalekites mentioned in Genesis 14.7 since they occupied the same region of Kadesh.[97] The Moabites and Ammorites, descendants of Lot, Abraham's nephew, occupied areas around the Dead Sea. The Midianites, children of Abraham through his wife Keturah, lived as Bedouins in the area. It is therefore likely that many of Jacob's sons were married to women who came from these various tribes located in the region of Canaan. Although there is no real indication that Hebrews placed much stock in these distant familial ties, it is not hard to imagine that the early Hebrews may have felt more accepted and more kinship with peoples in and around Canaan than they did with the Egyptians. The distribution of Egyptian scarabs from the Hyksos period found in Palestine has led Dr. Dapha Ben-Tor to conclude that there was a special connection between Avaris and Canaan. It is a connection that "supports kin relations between the two populations."[98] Of course, people are often eager to claim kinship with a rich family; wealth and power have long been facilitators for "friendships." The Hebrews also had a history of accord with the early Philistines, the people who inhabited the Plain of Philistia (Genesis 21.32; 26.26-31). Perhaps that is why the Hyksos were able to establish a second capitol in that region. Perhaps the location of Sharuhen, the Hyksos' second capitol, also indicates that these coastal residents of Canaan and seafarers were especially allied with the Hyksos.[99]

The ancient Hebrews and the Hyksos share a similar obscure background, a connection to the same places, and a comparable history of cruelty and treacherous behavior. However, the Hebrews are uniquely set apart from all other ancient people by the special treatment that they received during the severe famine in the days of Joseph which resulted in affording the Hebrews a place of supreme wealth and privilege, an advantage not shared by any other race of people at that time. Given this analysis, the Hyksos were likely Hebrews.

"O, but" as if it is to be read as one story, Ipuwer seems to run together a famine, an influx of a group of tent-dwelling nomads, the deposing of nomes, the redistribution of wealth to people who did not earn it, the terrifying effects of a volcano, the chaos of anarchy, Egyptians being treated like foreigners by aliens who were acting like Egyptians, infanticide, the overthrow of the rightful government, and the worship of a new God. If Ipuwer is lamenting the time from the famine of Joseph, in the days of Mentuhotep II, to the rise of the Hebrews/Hyksos in Egypt, it is somewhat puzzling to ponder the currently accepted time frame suggested for these events. If Ipuwer is not simply using time as a literary device, i.e., mingling the distant past with the present to enhance the sense of bedlam that is being experienced by the speaker, then either Ipuwer was a prophet, was extremely long-lived, or perhaps too much time has been allotted for this chaotic period in conventional chronology. His admonition reads like an eyewitness account from beginning to end.[100]

As a note: Due to the many references to death, destruction, plunder, and especially in passages such as "O, but the river is blood" and "O, but gold and lapis lazuli, silver and turquoise, carnelian and amethyst, diorite and all our jewels are strung on the necks of servant girls," there are those who interpret the writings of Ipuwer to be a lament over the ten plagues, the plundering of Egypt, and other events during the time of the Hebrew exodus. However, such statements could also have described the distress, carnage, and redistribution of wealth at the rise of the Hyksos. For instance, in just a few lines before Ipuwer says, "the river is blood," he explains the occurrence: "many dead are buried in the river; the flood is a grave, for the embalming-place has become the flood."[101] The river had turned to blood because it was filled with massacred bodies; this was not the case when Moses turned the water to blood in the first plague.

On the other hand, "foreigners have become people [Egyptians]," "he who could not make a sarcophagus for himself is a lord of a tomb," "Look, he who had no seed is a lord of a granary," and "he who could not build himself a room is a lord of walls" seem more consistent with people looking to stay, to live, and to be buried in Egypt rather people who were exiting. In fact, if Ipuwer were describing Hebrew slaves at the time of the exodus, he would hardly say that they couldn't build; building was what they were pressed to do. Furthermore, the Hebrews at the time of the plagues already possessed walls and houses with lintels and doorposts (Exodus 12.22). And though the Hebrews plundered the Egyptians in Exodus 12.35-36, they hardly could have taken granaries and tombs. It is, therefore, more likely that Ipuwer is describing the arrival and rise of the Hebrews/Hyksos, not the exodus. In fact, the chaos described by Ipuwer may constitute "the storm" described by Ahmose on his Tempest Stela; and the "dearth" of wealthy grave goods during the latter 17th Dynasty could better reflect Theban domination and taxation by the Hyksos rather than plundering in the exodus.[102]

Hyksos Kings

The investigation of Dr. Bietak, in stratas E-D, suggests that after the catastrophe at the end of the Thirteenth Dynasty, Avaris was redesigned and used by the Hyksos as a military outpost; a large citadel formed the western edge of the city along the banks of the Nile.[103] Manetho corroborates this finding:

> [Auris/Avaris] he [the Hyksos king, Salitis] rebuilt and fortified with massive walls, planting there a garrison of as many as two hundred and forty thousand heavily-armed men to guard his frontier. Here he would come . . . , partly to serve out rations and pay his troops, partly to train them carefully in maneuvers and so strike terror into foreign tribes.[104]

Dr. Bietak also reports that inhabitants of the new Avaris were less Egyptianized than its former residents. The idea that a military might tend to distinguish itself from the general population is understandable. An "us-versus-them" mentality must be maintained in order to perceive an enemy. If Egyptians were the perceived enemy of the Hyksos, who then was the "us"? Based on Dr. Bietak's work, they were Asiatic people who had come from Canaan and who had strong cultural ties to the residents of Avaris from before the catastrophe at the end of the Thirteenth Dynasty.[105] If then the previous residents of Avaris were largely Hebrews, so was the Hyksos army of Salitis.

It is most likely that the Hyksos were, predominantly, composed of Hebrews who came to Egypt as a fledgling nation; a mixture of races, cultures, and religions (by marriage); devastated by famine; in low estate; living in tents; and skilled in animal husbandry. They were granted privilege in Egypt due to the overwhelming celebrity of Joseph, who (with the support of Mentuhotep II) built homes for Jacob's family, in Avaris, Goshen. The early Hebrews prospered greatly in Avaris. Joseph lived out the end of his long life there in a palace and was buried in a garden tomb. Therefore, for at least eighty years, and perhaps longer, the Hebrews prospered and co-existed peacefully in Egypt. They increased greatly in numbers, and Avaris grew accordingly. Even though they were highly Egyptianized, they retained certain customs such as their burial practices and, probably, polygamy. They also probably continued to marry foreign women (from Canaan, Syria, Minoa, Cyprus, and other places) and, accordingly, made cultural accommodations for their wives' various customs and beliefs.[106] For the most part, the Hebrews were a peaceful people, content to keep to themselves, as the Egyptians also preferred. However, some catastrophe, near the end of the Thirteenth Dynasty, forced the Hebrews to leave Avaris; yet, having become accustomed to the best in Egypt, they marched on Memphis.

Historically, the ancient Hebrews had demonstrated themselves capable of ruthless cruelty and amazing military success. Further encouraged by legends and prophecies that foretold victory and greatness in Egypt, they embraced their heritage, regrouped, and through sheer confidence, great numbers, and affluence that would have provided access to the best equipment that wealth and trade could afford, they routed the existing government and set their own ruler on the throne. They took whatever accommodations they desired and mercilessly slaughtered those who stood in their way. Thus they filled the land of Lower Egypt, essentially dividing Egypt in half between Cusae and Siut, and may have extended their conquest throughout the Two Lands and beyond (Exodus 1.7). [107]

The Hyksos/Hebrews oppressed and ruled the north while the Great House in Thebes maintained a tentative control over Upper Egypt—tentative because the Hyksos in the north excised taxes from the south.[108] Beyond that, the true reaches of the Hyksos/Hebrew kingdom are still unknown. It may be that they expanded their conquests to include parts of Nubia and Canaan and perhaps even Phoenicia and Syria.[109] There were certainly diplomatic and economic ties between the Hyksos and a wide-range of other cultures. "Textual and especially archaeological data furnish evidence of the substantial trade contacts with Canaan and beyond, up to Syria and around the Mediterranean."[110] Evidences of the Hyksos have even been unearthed in places as far away as Knossos and Bagdad.[111] Avaris was turned into a military housing and training facility also, eventually, serving as the spiritual center and capital city, housing the Hyksos king, and the "shepherd kings" maintained their overbearing, despised authority in Egypt until the dawn of the New Kingdom.

The Hebrews/Hyksos—drunk with power and hedonism—fell into debauchery. As is often the case with those who come into great wealth and power suddenly, without truly earning their fortune, the shepherd kings were not good stewards. They were irreverent, destructive, gluttonous, and pitiless to Egyptians in their wake. Adding further insult, they advanced the worship of Seth, the nemesis of Osiris, the antagonist of On, the evil god of chaos.[112] In fact, Seth is analogous to Satan, although the ancient Egyptian concept of a devil is quite different from the biblical. Egyptians believed that a healthy balance between good and evil maintained order in the universe. The Bible teaches that the universe was not created for evil and that God's strength is absolute; God and Satan do not balance each other; they are by no means equal. Though some disagree, nevertheless, Montet suggests that Seth was the Egyptian god most reminiscent of Canaanite religion.[113] The Hyksos rulers even insisted that Seth was the *only* god and tried to impose this twisted monotheism on Egyptians.[114] This behavior combined traditional Hebrew monotheism with a propensity to paganism that characterized many ancient Hebrews. And if the Hyksos were the Hebrews, their deplorable behavior represents one of the lowest points in Hebrew history. From an Egyptian perspective, the Egyptians had sheltered these uncouth, tent-dwelling shepherds, shared the fat of their land with the aliens, allowed them to flourish, and then the ungrateful "wretches" repaid their generous hospitality with sedition. Egyptian bewilderment and indignation resonates in the words of Ipuwer and Manetho. "Yet what the Egyptians resented most of all were the acts of vandalism committed by the Hyksos, who destroyed shrines and killed sacred animals"[11]

In fact, behavior strikingly similar to that attributed to the Hyksos is recounted in the Song of Moses:

Jacob is the lot of his inheritance.
He found him in a desert land,
and in the waste howling wilderness;
he led him about, he instructed him,
he kept him as the apple of his eye.
As an eagle stirreth up her nest,
fluttereth over her young,
spreadeth abroad her wings,
taketh them, beareth them on her wings:
So the Lord alone did lead him,
and there was no strange god with him.
He made him ride on the high places
of the earth, that he might eat
the increase of the fields;
and he made him to suck honey
out of the rock,
and oil out of the flinty rock;
Butter of kine, and milk of sheep,
with fat of lambs, and rams
of the breed of Bashan, and goats,
with the fat of kidneys of wheat;
and thou didst drink
the pure blood of the grape.
But Jeshurun waxed fat, and kicked:
thou art waxen fat,

thou art grown thick,
thou art covered with fatness;
then he forsook God which made him,
and lightly esteemed
the Rock of his salvation.
They provoked him to jealousy
with strange gods, with abominations
provoked they him to anger.
They sacrificed unto devils, not to God;
to gods whom they knew not,
to new gods that came newly up,
whom your fathers feared not.
Of the Rock that begat thee
thou art unmindful, and hast forgotten
God that formed thee.
And when the Lord saw it,
he abhorred them,
because of the provoking of his sons,
and of his daughters.
And he said, I will hide my face from
them, I will see what their end shall be:
for they are a very froward generation,
children in whom is no faith.
(Deuteronomy 32.9-20)

The Hebrews, at the time of Jacob, were starving in the desert wilderness of Canaan; but God had his "eagle" eye on them. He pushed them out of the nest and carried them safely to Egypt; and at that time, they were largely faithful to him as their only God (Genesis 35.2-4). In a hard time, a devastating famine—i.e., "the rock," he gave them the best of Egypt: the best land, the best foods—honey, oil, cheese, milk, fat lambs, even the best imported foods, and the best wine. (Notice that lines 13-20, as represented above, is probably not describing the Hebrews' post-exodus forty years of wandering in the desert, when, according to their own testimony, they had little to eat or drink. That's why God sent them manna, but even though it seems, according to Exodus 16 and Numbers 11.5-8, that manna could vary in taste, it hardly was the variety of foods described in this part of Moses' song.) But "Jeshurun," which means "the upright one," grew spoiled and rebelled. Ancient Hebrews probably *were* spoiled by all the best in Egypt; they forsook God and worshiped strange gods, i.e., probably Baal, other foreign gods, and Egyptian gods, particularly Seth (a devil, the Egyptian god of chaos), and sacrificed to demons, i.e., Apophis, the serpent demon.[116] Even "new gods that came newly up" may be evidenced in examples like the Minoan frescos found in Avaris. God was disgusted by their idolatry and by their mistreatment of other people, in this case, Egyptians (who were also "his sons and daughters"). As mentioned in the first chapter, later pharaohs credited Amun with Egypt's sovereignty over "all the foreign lands."[117] If the Hebrews/Hyksos had remained faithful to the God of their forefathers, perhaps pharaohs would have retained the knowledge of Joseph and of his God. Egyptian and Hebrew history could have been so different, but Hebrews acting as the Hyksos turned their back on God. Therefore, God turned his back on the Hebrews. He allowed them to be conquered, enslaved, and he didn't look after how they were treated. They had behaved wickedly; they were an evil generation, ungrateful and unfaithful. Of course, Moses' song is not only a recounting of the past; it is also a prophetic song intended as a warning. When this song was written, the Hebrews were standing on the edge of the land God had promised them; Moses was warning them not to repeat this pattern of God's goodness, Hebrew's rebellion, and God's punishment.

Paul echoes the notion that the Hebrews became exceedingly powerful while they were in Egypt. "The God of this people of Israel chose our fathers, and exalteth the people when they dwelt as strangers in the land of Egypt, and with an high arm brought he them out of it" (Acts 13.17). In Egyptian iconography and throughout most of the ancient world, an uplifted arm was a depiction of military strength and the subduing of one's enemies. It is usually assumed that God's "high arm," here in verse 17, was raised against Egypt when he brought the plagues and orchestrated the exodus. However, could it also be that God raised his arm in the form of Ahmose as he brought the Hebrews/Hyksos out of the exalted station of greatness he had allowed them to enjoy? In their "greatness," had they forgotten God and had made themselves his enemy?

As if the death and destruction, subjugation and taxation were not enough, the Hyksos king, Apophis, taunted the Egyptian ruler in Thebes. An antagonizing letter was (recounted years later as having been) sent from Avaris haughtily declaring," One [messenger] has come [to thee] concerning the pool of the hippopotami which is in the city [Thebes], for they permit me no sleep, day and night the noise of them is in my ear."[118]

Hyksos Woman & Baby

Soon after (as the tale continues), all ties were severed between Upper and Lower Egypt. The pharaoh of Thebes refused to worship Seth, refused to pay taxes to the Hyksos, refused to do anything the Hyksos king required, and cut all lines of communications with Memphis and Avaris.[119] Dr. David O'Connor suggests that perhaps even as early as the Thirteenth Dynasty, "[Theban] leaders and elite were largely restricted to Southern Egypt, and their contact with Middle Egypt and the Delta [was] perhaps relatively slight."[120] Therefore, it is highly likely that—growing up essentially estranged from Lower Egypt, the Hebrews/Hyksos, the history of their humble beginnings, the vizier and pharaoh who acted as their benefactors, and their propitious rise to power: ". . . there arose up a new king over Egypt, which knew not Joseph" (Exodus 1.8). Ahmose was only a boy when Sekenenre and Kamose died. Sequestered in Thebes, he didn't know Joseph or the Hebrews; he only knew the detestable foreigners in Lower Egypt that ferociously slaughtered his father.[121]

It took three pharaohs (perhaps more, since more than one pharaoh was named Sekenenre) leading armies against the Hyksos, perhaps as long as thirty years, but finally, in a chronicle sounding very like that of "Ameny" from *The Visions of Neferti*, "the Asiatics [fell] to his slaughtering," and Ahmose emerged victorious.[122] He claims to have chased the Hyksos out of Egypt, and obviously some did escape in retreat to Palestine. Certainly, the tomb of one of Ahmose's most loyal fighting men—Ahmose, son of Ebana—yields detailed description of the pharaoh's tenacious pursuit and eventual defeat of the Hyksos.[123] Ahmose claimed victory in the expulsion of the Hyksos from borders not even near Egypt; but based on the biblical account, it is more likely that Ahmose is the pharaoh who enslaved the Hebrews (Exodus 1.9-11).

There is no doubt that Ahmose utterly defeated the Hyksos and reunited Upper and Lower Egypt; the only question is why he would view eviction of the enemy as a greater victory than enslavement of the vanquished? Perhaps it was better for Ahmose's public image at the time; it proved him a strong, vigorous pharaoh who had the stamina to chase Egypt's enemies to the ends of the earth if necessary. Perhaps it is how he wanted to be remembered—that he had humiliated the Hyksos; they had fled from him like scared rabbits. Perhaps he thought things would be better for him in eternity if he had done no more than expel the Hyksos; after all, mercy is an admirable quality that can make one's heart light. Perhaps there were those in Egypt who would sleep easier if they thought that the Hyksos threat was completely gone, far away from Egypt and that no Hyksos still existed within the country's borders. After all, the scripture seems to indicate that even after they had been subdued and enslaved, a residual fear of the Hebrews—the aliens—remained.[124]

> And he [Pharaoh] said . . . , Behold, the people of the children of Israel are more and mightier
> than we: Come on, let us deal wisely with them; lest they multiply, and it come to pass, that,
> when there falleth out any war, they join also unto our enemies, and fight against us, and so get
> them up out of the land (Exodus 1.9-10).

Another important observation is found in a letter from Ahuserre Apophis (a Hyksos king) sent to the king of Kush (Upper Nubia) encouraging him to attack Thebes from the south and further implying that the Hyksos would join in the battle, attacking Thebes from the north. Together they would then destroy the rulers of Thebes and would split the spoils of war between them. Since such an attack never occurred, the veracity of Ahuserre Apophis in his gracious offer to share lands and goods with Kush is left to speculation. However, the notion that Thebes had long felt "hemmed in" between the Hyksos and their potential allies is well documented.[125] This passage in Exodus indicates that a large number of Hebrews having been enslaved, could—if given the opportunity—ally themselves with enemies of Egypt from any direction, and would flee the country. In other words, the pharaoh in Exodus is implicating Hebrews with Hyksos-like behavior. They were potentially capable of amassing an attack, had ties to potential allies in multiple directions, and had proven a propensity to retreat rather than be subjugated. In fact, a corresponding ominous fear shades the history surrounding the Second Intermediate Period. Fragments of a sarcophagus from the Thirteenth Dynasty depict men from the Delta as figures bearing the crests of Lapwings, synonymous with "enemies."[126] These images suggest mistrust of a potentially hostile presence residing in the Delta prior to the fall of Memphis. Furthermore, in the tombs of Thutmose III and Amenhotep II, Apophis (pictured in the *Amduat* as a serpent demon) is not banished, but rather, is subdued daily.[127] If it is possible that Apophis in the renderings of mythological, continuous battles in the underworld might also represent the Hyksos Apophis and his people, then the tombs of these two Eighteenth Dynasty pharaohs indicate that the Hyksos were not all banished beyond the borders of Egypt as Ahmose recorded. The people of Apophis were, in fact, pursued, conquered, enslaved, and were being humiliated and subdued on an ongoing basis; a menacing threat was pressed into serving Ra. Even though it is likely that the Hyksos king in the days of Ahmose was Khamudi, Apophis was an infamous name that had been associated with several Hyksos kings.[128] It's then reasonable to suggest that, for some time, the name "Apophis" may have been synonymous with "Hyksos" to Egyptians.

Did Ahmose exile or enslave the Hyksos? Probably both. Ahmose, son of Ebana speaks of pressing after the retreating Hyksos to Sharuhen, the Hyksos' stronghold in the Plain of Philistia. Ahmose and his army besieged Sharuhen for three years until it fell. Then the tenacious pharaoh continued to pursue fleeing Hyksos to perhaps as far as Syria.[129] Ahmose, son of Ebana speaks of obtaining Hyksos slaves in multiple places. "One [Ahmose] gave to me the gold of bravery besides giving me the captives for slaves." Pharaoh obviously granted slaves to Ahmose, son of Ebana as the spoils of war.[130] Ahmose also awarded slaves to one of his naval officers who writes, "I took captive there one man and three women, total four heads. His Majesty gave them to me for slaves."[131] But these are not the only evidences that Ahmose enslaved the Hyksos/Hebrews.[132]

In the twenty-second year of Ahmose, he re-opened the quarry at Maasara, a site that had been idle since the Hyksos had obtained power; and he decorated its entrance with a stela. The carved images reveal three overseers, armed with weapons, imposing the forced labor of Asiatic foreigners depicted with pointy beards. Not even the animals being used in Ahmose's depiction of slave labor are indigenous to Egypt. They are the hunched-back oxen usually associated with Asiatics.[133] However, not all of the slaves in this relief are of the

41

same nationality. The third slave can be identified as Libyan by the characteristic side-lock on his head. Therefore, it is possible that extreme prejudice was applied to all foreigners within the borders of Egypt during the time of Ahmose. All foreigners were seen as Hyksos, or at least as enemies and were either killed, expelled, or enslaved. Nevertheless, since these slaves indicate Asiatics and neighbors of Egypt in alliance with Asiatics during the time of Ahmose, these quarry slaves are likely Hyksos. To add insult to injury, Ahmose commissioned the stones from this quarry to build temples in Memphis, Thebes, Luxor, and probably Karnak to the very gods that the Hyksos had tried to eliminate in their monotheistic promotion of Seth.[134] It seems to indicate that Ahmose employed a "divide and conquer" mentality in dealing with these Hyksos slaves. He divided them into smaller groups (perhaps to prevent them from organizing a large-scale revolt) and pressed them into service at numerous building sites all over Egypt. Exodus 1.11 paints a similar picture of the Hebrew enslavement, "Therefore they [the Egyptian administration] did set over them [Hebrew slaves] taskmasters to afflict them with their burdens. And they built for Pharaoh treasure cities, Pithom and Raamses."

Apparently, Manetho mentions something similar. "Lepers" from Avaris were enslaved by a pharaoh and forced to work in the quarries.[135] A sage named Amenophis predicted divine retribution for mistreatment of the lepers.[136] These lepers, according to the Egyptian priest, eventually organized under a leader who called himself "Moses." In the centuries that transpired between the days of the Hyksos and Manetho, it isn't hard to imagine that the foreigners, the outsiders, that were the Hyksos, could become confused with lepers, outcasts. Perhaps the calamity responsible for the mass deaths in Avaris was a swift plague with properties reminiscent of leprosy. Shaw argues that the mass graves in Avaris were the result of pestilence. Nevertheless, residents of Avaris were not all expelled, as Manetho affirms. Furthermore, Manetho's connection between Avaris and Moses further suggests a correlation between the Hyksos and the Hebrews.

Yet, it also seems that Ahmose's "shrewd" dealings with the Hyksos were not completely popular. He was opposed by several nomes, and he deposed them just like he did the Hyksos. He confiscated their lands, titles, and possessions and made them permanent properties of the crown. It's possible that from that time on, heredity was no longer a prerequisite for the office of nomarch as Ahmose tightened his grip on the power of the central government.[137] Those nomes that remained loyal to the king collected taxes for the pharaoh, lent their power to his standing army, and left biographies glorifying their military victories at his side.[138]

Yet what, exactly, was the nomarchs' point of dissension with Ahmose? Were the contentious nobles upset that foreigners no longer ruled Egypt? Did they not like Egypt reunited under a centralized government? Were they opposed to relinquishing the double crown to the ruling family of Thebes? Or did they object to Ahmose's answer to the Hyksos problem? Could it be there were Egyptians who were uncomfortable with *any* Hyksos or Hyksos sympathizers living anywhere on earth—and certainly not living within the borders of Egypt, not even as slaves. "He turned their heart to hate his people, to deal subtly with his servants" (Psalms 105.25).

The pursuit and enslavement of the Hebrews/Hyksos and their collaborators likely continued under Amenhotep I and was obviously compounded under the rule of Thutmose I. Ahmose son of Ebana writes: [His Majesty] went to Retjenu [Canaan] to vent his wrath throughout foreign lands. His Majesty arrived at Naharin [the region just northeast of Canaan also known as Huran/Syria]. . . . Then his Majesty made a great heap of corpses among them. Countless were the living captures of his Majesty from his victories.[139]

Even continuing on into the early reign of Thutmose II, the population of slaves captured in Canaan increased in Egypt according to Ahmose-Pennekheb who indicated that "many prisoners were taken" and that Egypt's control of the entire region of Palestine was reinforced.[110]

It is worthwhile to take note of Josephus' account of the events that transpired during this time period: Egyptians grew delicate and lazy, as to painstaking; and gave themselves up to other pleasures, and in particular to the love of gain. They also became very ill affected towards the Hebrews, as touched with envy at their prosperity; for when they saw how the nation of the Israelites flourished, and were become eminent already in plenty of wealth, which they had acquired by their virtue and natural love of labour [sic], they thought their increase was to their own detriment; and having, in length of time, forgotten the benefits they had received from Joseph, particularly the crown being now in another family, they became abusive to the Israelites, . . . [141]

Josephus seems to describe fairly well the conditions in Egypt during the second half of the Thirteenth Dynasty: "delicate and lazy." He too is of the understanding that the Hebrews, like the Hyksos, became prosperous, numerous, and "eminent." However, he absolves the Hebrews of any wrongdoing and suggests they were simply enslaved because of their affinity for honest, hard work, leading to success that made Egyptians jealous. Yet, it is difficult to follow the logic that if the Hebrews had a "natural love of labour," why did they have to "accustom themselves to hard labour?" Human nature dictates that people tend to treat others the way that they have been treated. Past abuse leads to mistreatment and distrust. The pharaoh, who did not know Joseph, feared and distrusted the Hebrews, as Exodus 1.9-10 seems to indicate. Cruelty is never justified, but it is likely that the Egyptians had reason to fear the ancient Hebrews.

Asserted Hebrew innocence in the face of unprovoked aggression, as recorded by Josephus, is reminiscent of the sentiment expressed in a correspondence written by Apophis. After Kamose learned of Apophis' letter to the King of Kush, conspiring an alliance between the Hyksos and Kush to overthrow Thebes, the pharaoh took aggressive steps to address the Hyksos threat. In response, Apophis writes:

Kamose-the-Brave, given life, is attacking me on my soil, although I have not attacked him in the manner of all he has done against you. He is choosing these two lands to bring affliction upon them, my land and yours, and he has ravaged them.[142]

Though Ipuwer seemed uncertain of exactly what to name the foreigners who brutally conquered Egypt, he does seem to remember Joseph and to associate the Hyksos with him. In Stanza XII, Ipuwer writes, "Surely, Utterance, Perception, and Truth are with you—but it is chaos that you have put throughout the land, and the noise of tumult."[143] Pharaoh considered Joseph to be discerning, dependable, and wise; he gave Joseph unparalleled authority, yet Joseph was also responsible (in the eyes of Ipuwer) for bringing the Hebrews/Hyksos to Egypt. Therefore, if Stanza XII refers to Joseph, then Joseph was ultimately responsible (in the eyes of Ipuwer) for the chaos that was unleashed on Egypt during the Second Intermediate Period.[144]

However, in words reminiscent of Psalms 80.1, "Give ear, O Shepherd of Israel, thou that leadest Joseph like a flock;" Ipuwer also, perhaps, cites the God of Joseph in Stanza XI. Ipuwer cries:

He is the shepherd of all; there is no evil in his heart. Yet although he has made the day to care for them, his herd is small, and fire is in their hearts! If only he had realized their character in the first generation! Then he would have struck down opposition, and stretched out his arm against them, and destroyed the flock of them and their heirs.[145]

The God of the Bible's true followers have always been few. In his time, it seems Enoch was the only man on earth who walked with God (Genesis 5.22). Enoch's great grandson, Noah, was also, apparently, the only righteous man on earth (Genesis 6.5-8). Job was in the minority (Job 1.8). Abraham was unique (Hebrews 11.8-12; James 2.23). Jesus also describes God's true followers as "few" (Matthew 7.13-14). Even if Joseph's God (the Shepherd of All) is rightly associated with the Hebrews (who were shepherds by trade), sadly, as a majority, many ancient Hebrews throughout their history were often unfaithful to God. God, however, is faithful, and he keeps his promises—although there came a time when God considered taking Ipuwer's advice:

The Lord said unto Moses, I have seen this . . . is a stiff-necked people: Now therefore let me alone, that my wrath may wax hot against them, and that I may consume them" (Exodus 32.9-10)

The God of the Bible *never* allowed ancient Hebrew idolatry to go unpunished. The sad Hyksos chapter in Hebrew history was no exception (Daniel 9.5-12; Ezekiel 20.4-8). For their disgraceful ingratitude for the hospitality that had been lavished upon them and especially for their abhorrent thanklessness to God demonstrated by embracing the evil god Seth and encouraging others in idolatry with them, God allowed the Hyksos/Hebrews to be overthrown and enslaved in Egypt. He did not forget his promise to make them a great nation, but a Hyksos definition of greatness was not the same as God's.

As a question, if the Hebrews were in Egypt 430 years, to the day, as Exodus 12.41 states, but for approximately half of that time they lived in luxury and eminence, why did God tell Abraham that they would be enslaved and afflicted for 400 years of their time in Egypt? (Genesis 15.13; Acts 7.6) This was, in the first place, prophetic language and may not have been meant to be taken completely literally, but may have been a representative number of years. However, there is more than one kind of slavery (John 8.34). When the Hebrews first arrived in Egypt, no doubt they were overwhelmed with gratitude to God and praised him for all he had done for Joseph and for their family. If the prophecy given to Abraham was literal, then perhaps the Hebrews' period of faithfulness lasted about thirty years, but after the death of their patriarch, Jacob, and as they began to forget the circumstances that brought them to Egypt, many may also have began to turn away from God, perhaps not even Joseph was able to persuade them to remain faithful. God does not recognize partial loyalty. Jesus said, "No man can serve two masters: for either he will hate the one, and love the other; or else he will hold to the one, and despise the other. Ye cannot serve God and mammon" (Matthew 6.24). Therefore, as soon as any Hebrews allowed their heads to be turned by the riches that they were enjoying in Egypt and began to serve themselves, they became slaves of the cruelest master, and from God's perspective they were afflicted, whether they recognized it or not. Of course, any Hebrews who persisted in loyalty to God and did not approve apostasy were likely despised and afflicted by their own countrymen.

It's possible that Galatians 3.17-19 may also be referencing the appalling behavior of the Hyksos/Hebrews. The 430 years mentioned in verse 17 is clearly recalling the Hebrew sojourn in Egypt, and verse 19 makes it clear that the Law of Moses was bound on the Hebrews because of their "transgressions." Because they had proven themselves to be rebellious and irreverent, God gave them laws to guide and teach them. People who honor God obey him, and those who humbly serve their fellow man are great in God's eyes (Matthew 5.19; 20.26). "He is righteous in all his ways, and holy in all his works" (Psalms 145.17). Though some would disagree that ancient Egyptians possessed the concept of a universal God, Ipuwer maintains, "He is the shepherd of all," Moses echoes "the Lord [is] the God of the spirits of all flesh, . . .be not as sheep which have no shepherd" (Numbers 27.16-17).[146] Though he often has not been acknowledged or worshiped as God, he has always loved all people on earth (Genesis 12.3; 18.17-18; Isaiah 45.22; John 3.16). He *is* the God of Egypt, and he is the Shepherd of All.

Citations

1. Silverman 28; Shaw 175; Winlock, *Rise* 150
2. Aldred 127; Shaw 176
3. Monet 73
4. Tyldesley, *Egypt* 60; Hoerth, *Archaeology* 141, Shaw 148, 171, 173
5. Monet 38
6. Woldering 129
7. Parkinson, *Sinuhe* 146-148; Hoerth, *Peoples* 269
8. Oren 113; Woldering 106
9. Oren *ixx, xxiii*
10. Matthews 235-240; Parkinson, *Sinuhe* 135-136; Kitchen, *Reliability* 387
11. Stanza I; Parkinson, *Sinuhe* 170, Van Seters 5
12. Stanza IV; Parkinson, *Sinuhe* 174
13. Stanza VII; Parkinson, *Sinuhe* 178; Winlock, *Rise* 151
14. Aldred 117; Van Seters 108,118, 119; Winlock, *Rise* 97
15. Monet 108
16. Redford, *Joseph* 235; Kitchen, *Reliability* 466-467
17. Silverman 42; Parkinson, *Sinuhe* 212, 223
18. Stanzas III, IV, VII, & VIII; Parkinson, *Sinuhe* 173,175,178, 180, Aling, *Egypt* 21
19. Oren 14-15
20. Monet 216
21. Stanza X; Parkinson, *Sinuhe* 182
22. Parkinson, *Sinuhe* 170; Van Seters 118
23. Stanza VII; Parkinson, *Sinuhe* 178; Van Seters 120
24. Stanzas I, II, & III; Parkinson, *Sinuhe* 171,173
25. Stanzas IV, VII, VIII, & X; Parkinson, *Sinuhe* 175, 179, 180, 182
26. Redford, *Joseph* 197; Shaw 169; T. Stewart 159
27. Assmann 41; Gray 177, 186, 188, 193; Lewy, *Origins* 3-7
28. Oakes & Gahlin 459
29. Peloubet 320, 489
30. Redmount 184-186; Van Seters 26, 67
31. Rohl 353; Oren 98
32. Reeves 224; Shaw 219
33. Oren *xxi*
34. Monet 114
35. Monet 115; Van Seters 177
36. Shanks & Meinhardt 35
37. Silverberg 198
38. Aldred 9; Velikovsky 87; Newby 140, Van Seters 123-125, 164
39. Davis 32
40. Velikovsky 89; Josephus 610-611
41. Silverberg 21
42. Shanks & Meinhardt 27-56
43. Oren 98

44. Oren 97
45. Oren 97, 99; Hoerth, *Peoples* 299, Kitchen, *Reliability* 246
46. Oren 98
47. Rohl 355
48. Oren 98
49. Oren 98
50. Bietak 7
51. Oren 98
52. Rohl 356
53. Rohl 363
54. Rohl 365-368
55. Rohl 272
56. Rohl 272
57. Remount 184, Rohl 271, *Exodus Decoded*
58. Silverman 235; Collier 3; Bunson 51; Oren 14-15
59. Rohl 271
60. Vos 52-53
61. Hoerth, *Archaeology* 149
62. Rohl 270-271
63. Rohl 279
64. Rohl 270, Shaw 195
65. Oren 203
66. Oren *xxiv*; Galford 34; Breasted, *History* 227, 259-260, 264; Silverman 50; Aling, *Egypt* 86
67. Newby 46
68. D. Stewart 62
69. Oren *xxiii*
70. Josephus 55; Kitchen, *Reliability* 184
71. Oren 103
72. Oren *xxii, xxiii*; Van Seters 61-62
73. Rohl 288
74. Vos 69
75. Rohl 279
76. Rohl 280
77. *The Final Torments*; Morrison
78. *The Final Torments*
79. Oren 125
80. Oren 125
81. Stanza VII; Parkinson, *Sinuhe* 178
82. Rohl 280; Shaw 167; Winlock, *Rise* 96
83. Rohl 17; Engelbach 37; Van Seters 120; Winlock, *Rise* 97
84. Parkinson, *Sinuhe* 185
85. Josephus 55
86. Parkinson, *Sinuhe* 170, 171
87. Stanza VII; Parkinson, *Sinuhe* 178
88. Zlotowitz 190
89. Oren *xxiii*
90. Casson 24; Hoerth, *Archaeology* 141; Aldred 130, 131; Greenberg 17; Van Seters 60
91. Oren *xxii*
92. Oren 111; Van Seters 18
93. Silverman 31; Redmount 185
94. Oren *xxii*
95. Oren *xxiii*, Shaw 195; Van Seters 55-59
96. Oren *xxiii*; Winlock, *Rise* 158-163
97. A. Myers 45
98. Ben-Tor 189
99. Breasted, *History* 227
100. Allen, *Theban* 17
101. Stanzas II & III; Parkinson, *Sinuhe* 172, 173; Winlock, *Rise* 169
102. Stanzas I, VII, & IX: Parkinson, *Sinuhe* 170, 179, 181; Shaw 220-221
103. Oren *xxiii*, 115
104. Rohl 280; Winlock, *Rise* 97
105. Rohl 280; Van Seters 192
106. Oren 99, 104
107. Monet 114
108. Rohl 280; Van Seters 71, 167
109. Oren *xxii-xxiv*; Breasted, *History* 227
110. Oren *xxii, xxiv*
111. Breasted, *History* 218; Oren *xxii*
112. Oakes & Gahlin 294, 310, & 314; Winlock, *Rise* 100, 102
113. Monet 114-117; Aling, *Egypt* 54
114. Monet 158
115. Monet 115
116. Oakes & Gahlin 277, 309
117. Redford, *Akhenaten* 17
118. Breasted, *History* 223; ten-Berge & van de Gooterge 232
119. Monet 115, Shaw 205; Winlock, *Rise* 102
120. Oren 57
121. Silverman 31; Hoerth, *Archaeology* 157, Hoffmeier 122; Hoerth, *Peoples* 286
122. Breasted, *History* 224; Parkinson, *Sinuhe* 138-139; Shaw 210
123. Breasted, *History* 226-227
124. Oren *xxii;* Shaw 161; Lewy, *Origins* 5
125. Monet 119; Winlock, Rise 100
126. Monet 24
127. Hornung 27
128. Oren 114
129. Breasted, *History* 227; May 63
130. Breasted, *History* 227
131. Breasted, *History* 226; Redford, *Joseph* 198
132. Hoerth, *Archaeology* 158
133. Saleh & Sourouzian figure 119; Breasted, *History* 227
134. Breasted, *History* 252, Shaw 220
135. Assmann 33
136. Assmann 31, Shaw 190
137. Oren 61; Greenberg 49
138. Breasted, *History* 229, 234; Aldred 127
139. Tyldesley, *Hatshepsut* 70-71; Greenberg 45
140. Tyldesley, *Hatshepsut* 82
141. Josephus 55
142. Ryholt 181
143. Parkinson, *Sinuhe* 186
144. Parkinson, *Sinuhe* 186
145. Parkinson, *Sinuhe* 185
146. Silverberg 89

Nephthys, Osiris, Isis, and Horus

Chapter 3
One Who Answers Prayers

And Pharaoh charged all his people, saying, "Every son that is born ye shall cast into the river, and every daughter ye shall save alive." And there went a man of the house of Levi, and took to wife a daughter of Levi. And the woman conceived, and bare a son: and when she saw him that he was a goodly child, she hid him three months. And when she could not longer hide him, she took for him an ark of bulrushes, and daubed it with slime and with pitch, and put the child therein; and she laid it in the flags by the river's brink. And his sister stood afar off, to wit what would be done to him. And the daughter of Pharaoh came down to wash herself at the river; and her maidens walked along by the river's side; and when she saw the ark among the flags, she sent her maid to fetch it. And when she had opened it, she saw the child: and, behold, the babe wept. And she had compassion on him, and said, This is one of the Hebrews' children. Then said his sister to Pharaoh's daughter, Shall I go and call to thee a nurse of the Hebrew women, that she may nurse the child for thee? And Pharaoh's daughter said to her, Go. And the maid went and called the child's mother. And Pharaoh's daughter said unto her, Take this child away, and nurse it for me, and I will give thee thy wages. And the woman took the child, and nursed it. And the child grew, and she brought him unto Pharaoh's daughter, and he became her son. And she called his name Moses: and she said, Because I drew him out of the water. (Exodus 1.22-2.10)

This is a remarkable story but not completely unprecedented. In fact, it heralds the distant echoes of the mythologies of two great ancient cultures. The Legend of Sargon, a Mesopotamian myth from the days during the rise of Ur, bears a striking resemblance to the story of Moses. Sargon, the illegitimate—therefore marginalized and probably endangered—son of a high priestess, was hidden in a pitch-sealed, reed basket and set adrift in "the River," the Euphrates. The baby lived and was drawn out of the water by Akkl, who was "a drawer of water" by trade. Akkl raised the boy as his own son and trained him in gardening, presumably through the art of irrigation. According to the saga, the Mesopotamian goddess, Ishtar, smiled on Sargon and helped him to achieve greatness.[1] Sargon, whose name means, "the king is legitimate," became king of Akkad; and in his writings, he boasted that his kingdom spanned from "the Lower Sea [the Persian Gulf] and its islands to the Upper Sea [the Mediterranean Sea] and its islands."[2]

Jochabed, Moses' mother, must have been a woman who liked to hear stories and who placed some faith in what she heard (Exodus 6.20; Hebrews 11.23). Since the ancestral roots of the Hebrews reached all the way back to Ur, it is very plausible that Sumerian mythology was part of ancient Hebrew oral tradition. Likely, Jochabed had been told the story of Sargon from childhood and implemented the tenuous strategy obtained from Sargon's mother in a similar, desperate hope that her baby would also be rescued. Interestingly, in the Exodus account there is no indication that Jochabed was appealing to the God of the Bible. In fact, only the meaning of her name, *Yôkebed*, "the Lord is majesty" indicates knowledge of the one God.[3] According to the book of Hebrews, however, it seems that both Jochabed and her husband, Amram, were, in fact, demonstrating faith in the God of the Bible when they audaciously defied the pharaoh and floated their infant son in the Nile (Hebrews 11.22-23). It may also be that the faith of Amram is echoed in the name of Moses' second son, Eliezer: "For the God of my father, said he, was mine help, and delivered me from the sword of Pharaoh" (Exodus 18.4).

Of course, the story of baby Moses also reverberates with Egyptian mythology in the legend of Isis and Osiris. Osiris, killed by his evil brother, Seth, was placed in a coffin and committed by Isis to the Nile in hopes that she would restore life to her brother/husband some day.[4] Furthermore, in fear of Seth's retaliation against her son, Horus, Isis hid the child among the bulrushes of the marshy Nile Delta and placed him under "the watchful eye of the protective cobra-form goddess Wadjet."[5] It is not hard to imagine that both Moses' mother and his adopted mother were influenced by these myths that each contributed to the saving of Moses' life.

Young Hatshepsut

No doubt, the daughter of the pharaoh, who remains unnamed in scripture, was reminded of the dilemma and sympathy of Isis when she found, hidden among the bulrushes on the banks of the Nile, a basket—that might as well have been a casket—for a baby who was as good as dead. The introductory passage of the second chapter of Exodus allows us to identify several characteristics of this Egyptian princess. She was compassionate: she saved the life of the helpless infant (Exodus 2.6). She was accepting: well aware that "This is one of the Hebrews' children," she was willing to rise above prejudice and bigotry (Exodus 2.6). She was brave: it was a very brave thing indeed to transgress Egyptian law. The agonized expression on the face of the mummy who is commonly identified as "the screaming man" serves as a testimony to the fact that not even members of the royal family were above execution for rebellion.[6] She was equitable: the Egyptian princess was certainly well within her rights to simply order the Hebrew slave woman to nurse the child without any compensation whatsoever. Yet, she was a person who highly valued the role of a wet-nurse and paid wages for the Hebrew woman's service (Exodus 2.9). She was innovative: adoption occurred in Egypt, but adoption—especially the adoption of a foreign child—into the royal family by a mere princess was unprecedented (Exodus 2.10).[7] In fact, rulers of ancient Egypt were so reluctant to share the royal family with outsiders, they routinely married siblings. She was ambitious: she saw and seized an opportunity to have a son (something she apparently desired) because she named the baby "Moses," a name that isn't an exact match for the Hebrew *Môsheh* or the verb *mashah* (meaning "drawing out [of the water]"). Yet, it may well be that Hebrews living in Egypt for nearly three centuries developed an Egyptianized dialect now lost to us. After all, "Moses" is a name more easily akin to Egyptian *Mose*, *Moses*, and *Messes* are all forms of "*ms*" which doesn't precisely mean "drew out" either, but does means "child of" or "born of." If this is the case, pharaoh's daughter essentially, called the child "son" (Exodus 2.10).[8] She was decisive and bold: she obviously had great confidence in her relationship with her father, in her own reasoning, and in her ability to defy convention. She was powerful—powerful enough to successfully superimpose her will. These characteristics are very much in keeping with a woman who is arguably *the* greatest, most famous daughter of a pharaoh. Could "the daughter of Pharaoh" who adopted Moses be Hatshepsut?

Hatshepsut was the beloved daughter of Thutmose I who was appointed to be king by Amenhotep I. It's intriguing that Josephus, in his account of the story of Moses, calls pharaoh's daughter "Thermuthis," which is not hard to imagine as a modification over time of "Thutmoses," perhaps indicating a distant recollection in Hebrew history that connects the daughter of the pharaoh in the story of Moses to the family of "Thutmoses I."[9]

The identity of Thutmose I's father remains uncertain, but his mother's name was Seniseb. Most believe that Seniseb was not royal because the most illustrious title she is known to have attained was "king's mother."[10] Amenhotep I and his queen, Ahmose-Meryetamun (rightful successors to Ahmose), failed to produce a heir; therefore, Amenhotep I chose his most trusted general (Thutmose I) to be his beneficiary. Some evidence suggests that Amenhotep I may have fortified the credentials of Thutmose I by sharing the end of his reign as co-regent with his appointee.[11] It's likely that the legitimacy of Thutmose I as pharaoh was further strengthened by his marriage to the king's sister, Queen Ahmose, who is a confirmed member of the Ahmose royal family since recent (exclusively maternal) mitochondrial DNA analysis has confirmed a familial relationship between Hatshepsut and Ahmose-Nefertari.[12] In fact, Hatshepsut's mother (Queen Ahmose) was probably the daughter of Ahmose and Ahmose-Nefertari, an impressive pedigree indeed.[13] Thutmose I was, no doubt, a proven and fiercely loyal servant of Amenhotep I and of the Ahmose line of pharaohs. Amenhotep I led only one documented military campaign in his career; he was just not the warrior that his Hyksos-fighting predecessors had been.[14] Somehow, it seems respectful and tactful that if Amenhotep I could not produce an heir to carry on his family's warrior legacy, he could at least appoint someone who shared their battle-ready spirit. Certainly, in that respect, Thutmose I was an excellent choice to serve as a "son" to Amenhotep I.

Yet, what would have motivated Thutmose I's young daughter, Hatshepsut, to want a son? The clear intention of the early pharaohs of the Eighteenth Dynasty seems to have been to preserve the throne of Egypt within the royal bloodline of the latter kings of the Seventeenth Dynasty, Sekenenre Taa-ken and Queen Ahhotep and Sekenenre Tao I and Queen Tetisheri.[15] "The monarch's right was always bound up with his divine nature, transmitted by royal blood."[16] Not only do brother-sister marriages attest to that objective, but Ahmose and Ahmose-Nefertari's remarkable tribute to their grandmother, Tetisheri, demonstrates an ardent familial reverence. It is a reverence that is further implemented in Ahmose's stele of homage to his mother, Queen Ahhotep.[17] Yet, perhaps the greatest honor, advocating his family's divine right to rule, was bestowed on Ahhotep and Ahmose-Nefertari, when Ahmose pronounced each of these women to be the "god's wife."[18] This sacred title was passed on to Ahmose-Meryetamun; but when she failed to produce a suitable heir, the weighty charge of god's wife fell to Hatshepsut.[19] Hatshepsut, then, needed a son (or at least a proxy) through which she could rule until the throne could be securely preserved by a male child, legitimately born into the Ahmose bloodline. This was a charge that, in time, was passed on to Hatshepsut's daughter, Neferure—the next in line god's wife—to (hopefully) produce a male heir to keep the throne of Egypt within the bloodline of Ahmose. In Egyptian culture, a male pharaoh meant *maat* (order), stability, the opposite of chaos; he also provided the reproductive organ associated "with fertility of herds and crops."[20] Hatshepsut and Neferure were the only living links to the bloodline of the preferred royal family, but they were not male.

There had been, of sad necessity, a long-standing tradition in Hatshepsut's family of queen mothers ruling Egypt until a crowned prince reached autonomy. Ahhotep, Hatshepsut's great-grandmother, served as co-regent with her young son, Ahmose, after the death of her husband, Sekenenre Taa-ken, and the subsequent death of Kamose.[21] Hatshepsut's grandmother, Ahmose-Nefertari, also ruled Egypt while her son, Amenhotep I, was still a child.[22] Beyond that, Ahmose-Nefertari held the traditionally male title, Second Prophet of Amun.[23] Hatshepsut's mother, Queen Ahmose, is depicted standing behind a young Thutmose II since he was called "a hawk in the nest" at the time of his father's death, but Thutmose II's biological mother (likely not royal) may have been deceased.[24] Thutmose II was apparently too young to accompany his army into Kush during the first year of his reign; however, he was old enough to be married to Hatshepsut at the time of his ascension, though Hatshepsut, most believe, was also too young to rule.[25]

In contrast, when Hatshepsut found herself a young widow, Thutmose III (Thutmose II's only son; the son of a concubine) was perhaps an infant or he could have been as old as ten, but he seems to have been too young to be married to Neferure, the only child of Hatshepsut and Thutmose II.[26] This situation would have posed an authoritative problem for Hatshepsut. Thutmose III was neither Hatshepsut's son nor her son-in-law, and the crown prince's mother, Mutnofret, was alive and well. There was, therefore, no precedent for Hatshepsut to act as co-regent (though she clearly did). Neither Thutmose III nor Mutnofret carried the Ahmose bloodline; for that reason, Hatshepsut could not relinquish the throne to them and guarantee the lineage of Ahmose.[27] "This aspect of Hatshepsut's reign takes us back to . . . the uninterrupted sequence of legitimate kings ruling in a single line of succession descended from the gods. Hatshepsut's reign was simply made to conform to the ideal image."[28] She had no choice but to find a way to hold on to the throne until a male heir from the rightful bloodline of Ahmose could hopefully be produced. Technically, with the possible exception of the last ruler of the Twelfth Dynasty, who may have been a woman, Hatshepsut went against Egyptian law and certainly against tradition by becoming pharaoh.[29] Sir Alan Gardiner observes that it is unimaginable to suspect that a woman could have ruled Egypt "without masculine support."[30] A *"moses,"* a son (even an adopted son), therefore, could have provided the gender validation that Hatshepsut needed, especially if her father, Thutmose I had added his own "masculine support" by approving the adoption of a son for Hatshepsut.

It is feasible that Thutmose I could have approved Hatshepsut's adoption of a son for several reasons. He wanted the throne of Egypt to remain in the Ahmose-Amenhotep I bloodline; his only living male heir,

Thutmose II did not satisfy that aspiration. He believed that Hatshepsut was more suitable to rule Egypt than was her half brother, not only because of her pedigree, but also because of her constitution and her character. Hatshepsut possessed an impressive array of leadership qualities.[31] She was probably healthier, stronger, smarter, and generally better suited to the position of pharaoh than Thutmose II, making her the more shrewd choice for a successor to the throne. Had Hatshepsut been male, Thutmose I's choice of successor would have been easy. It's even possible that Hatshepsut's father approved the adoption of Moses because he too was moved with compassion. After all, it's one thing to issue a pitiless edict of infanticide sight unseen; it is quite another to look into the innocent eyes of a helpless infant and act with callused cruelty.

Stephen seems to indicate that the same pharaoh who enslaved the Hebrews ordered the death of Hebrew baby boys (Acts 7.18-19). According to the theory in this book, that would mean it was Ahmose who first "dealt subtilly" with the Hebrew population explosion in this cruel manner. However, the pharaoh who called for the slaughter of Hebrew baby boys on the birthing stool seems to have gotten squeamish about enforcing his own egregious order if, in fact, it was the same pharaoh (Exodus 1.16). After all, the pharaoh who was enforcing the heinous law knew that Shiphrah ("Beauty") and Puah ("Splendor") were directly disobeying the state's command and called them to give an account, yet he was willing to accept their seemingly flimsy excuse of not being fast enough to attend the labor of "vigorous" Hebrew women (Exodus 1.15-19).[32] It's a wonder that the two midwives were not executed on the spot! Of course, scripture attributes this "wonder" to God (Exodus 1.20). In defense of the midwives testimony, however, the sheer number of births per day required to produce the exponential growth of the Hebrew population described in scripture would have made the job of midwife impossible for only two women to attend. Nevertheless, the reluctance of the pharaoh that Shiphrah and Puah stood before perhaps suggests a lack of battle hardness and a lack of experience in having children, characteristics both more consistent with Amenhotep I than with his father Ahmose. Perhaps then it was Ahmose who issued the initial decree that ordered the midwives to commit neonaticide against newborn Hebrew males; yet it was Amenhotep I who, arguably acting in cowardice, was left to enforce his father's law.

A significant amount of time must have passed between the initial order to kill the Hebrew male infants on the birthing stool and the subsequent heartless command to cast the babies into the Nile (Exodus 1.22). Verse 20 indicates that enough time passed for the Hebrews to grow strong, increasing in numbers; and verse 21 suggests that enough time had transpired for God to bless the midwives with families of their own (Exodus 1.15-21). Under this hypothesis, enough time could have transpired for Ahmose to have ordered the decree in verse 15, for Amenhotep I to have been left to enforce it, but it easily could have been Thutmose I who compounded the law by commanding that Hebrew baby boys be cast to a watery grave (Exodus 1.22).[33] As indicated by the nouns and pronouns used throughout this passage in Exodus, the pharaoh at that time, is consistently male. This fact is reinforced in Hebrews 11. The hideous order to cast Hebrew infant boys into the Nile could not have been in effect for more than three years prior to the birth of Moses because Aaron was living, and he was three years older than Moses (Exodus 7.7). Thutmose I ruled some twelve years past the death of Amenhotep I, and he spent much of that time away from Egypt on military campaigns. As a seasoned military tactician, Thutmose I was no doubt accustomed to using death as an insensible means to subdue an enemy. Acts 7.19 describes the callused calculations of the pharaoh, who ordered the Hebrew baby boys to be cast into the Nile, as shrewd and subtle. As the delegate of Amenhotep I and of the Ahmose family bloodline, Thutmose I would simply have been implementing a calculated strategy to successfully accomplish the original objective of his superior. As a father who had lost all of his sons (except for one sickly boy), Thutmose I was probably hurt and angered by observing the Asiatic Hebrews/Hyksos with multitudes of strong, healthy sons. Yet, surveying the precipice of his own mortality, perhaps even Thutmose I was given to second thoughts; conceivably, his daughter could have moved him to compassion. Thutmose I seems to have loved Hatshepsut very much and probably wanted to grant her heart's desires, her hearts "devices."[34] If she had wanted to spare a baby and adopt him as her son, perhaps Thutmose I would have been inclined to acquiesce to Hatshepsut's request and could not bear to appear cruel and heartless in her eyes. Furthermore, if a providential hand had provided such an unexpected avenue for "the god's wife" to rule Egypt through an adopted male child, perhaps Thutmose I was afraid to defy the will of a god.

It is also possible that Thutmose I would have agreed to an adoption because he may have had reason to suspect that his own death was eminent. A CT scan of the mummy that is currently identified as Thutmose I was conducted as part of the passionate work overseen by Dr. Zahi Hawass. The images revealed a clear cause of death—an arrowhead imbedded in the body.[35] Although there is reason to doubt the identity of this particular mummy, Dr. Hawass declared that this arrowhead "will re-write history."[36] Perhaps Thutmose I knew that his life was in jeopardy, and he was concerned about his successor. Thutmose II appears to have been weak; medical examinations suggest that he had a diseased heart and died young, at about 30.[37]

For whatever reason, the pharaoh of Exodus 1.22-2.10 must have agreed to let his daughter adopt Moses. If he hadn't, it likely wouldn't have gone well for Moses, Moses' family, and/or for the princess! Since the Bible only identifies Moses' benefactor as Pharaoh's daughter, it is likely that the young woman was not yet married. Hatshepsut was probably married when she was around twelve years old.[38] Therefore, it is possible that she adopted Moses when she was about eleven, an age when many young girls are enamored by babies.

Hatshepsut seems to have been especially close to her father. Her name, meaning "foremost of the noble ladies" must have been "given or at least approved by her father."[39] She was devoted to him and demonstrated so by erecting two magnificent obelisks to the memory of Thutmose I. One of them reads, "How like her this is, how worthy of her father."[40] Yet, perhaps most telling of Hatshepsut's devotion to her father is the fact that she arranged for Thutmose I to share her tomb, the first and deepest tomb in the Valley of the Kings.[41] Two stone sarcophagi were found in the burial chamber of Hatshepsut. On one of them is carved this tender tribute, "She [Hatshepsut] made it [this sarcophagus] as her monument to her father whom she loved, the good god, lord of the Two Lands, Aakheperkare, son of Re, Tuthmosis [Thutmose] the justified."[42] In comparison, Hatshepsut's mother is rarely mentioned; but it was Hatshepsut's full intention to spend eternity with her beloved father.[43] Some have speculated that Hatshepsut may even have ruled for a time with her father as co-regent.[44]

Hatshepsut always insisted that Thutmose I intended for her to be king. Of course, no witnesses exist to corroborate her testimony, and most believe her depiction of Thutmose I's Address to the Court, from the walls of her temple at Deir el-Bahari, is pure fantasy.[45] However, depictions of Hatshepsut sharing equal status with Thutmose II on monuments at Karnak suggest that she and her half-brother/husband may have functioned as co-regents, perhaps at the assertion of their father.[46] A curious sandstone statue may also stand as evidence of Hatshepsut's claims to her father's endorsement. The figure depicts a miniature (adult) pharaoh Hatshepsut, sitting on the lap of her nurse, Inet, with her feet atop the nine bows which represent a pharaoh's military supremacy.[47] Obviously, from the inscription on the back of the statue, Hatshepsut, as an adult, commissioned this statue, suggesting that she had been destined for kingship from her nurse's knee. However, could it be that Thutmose I, Hatshepsut's warrior father who probably most identified with the pharaonic iconography of the nine bows, always had envisioned Hatshepsut serving as pharaoh and that Inet could endorse Hatshepsut's claims? Could it be that Thutmose I did approve of his daughter adopting a son to that end? In ancient Egyptian culture, if a male heir was not available to carry on the family profession, a son would be adopted.[48] In this case, a son (Thutmose II) was available, but he was unable to carry on the Ahmose family bloodline—or he had not yet proven himself able of producing an acceptable male heir. It may be that Thutmose I felt that he had failed his founder, Amenhotep I, in the regard of preserving the Ahmose family and agreed to allow Hatshepsut to adopt a son. In fact, another commemoration, perhaps, proves that Thutmose I did just that.

Senenmut & Neferure

51

The Cenotaph at Gebel es Silsila contains the earliest known mention of a very mysterious component in the life of Hatshepsut, Senenmut. The epitaph to Senenmut reads, "steward of the god's wife and steward of the king's daughter." Since there is no mention of Neferure anywhere on the monument and the mantle associated with it only refers to Hatshepsut in her role as king's daughter, this commemorative archway can be dated to Thutmose I.[49] The inscription not only suggests Thutmose I's knowledge of Senenmut but also his approval.

The relationship between Hatshepsut and Senenmut has long been fuel for speculation. "He was not Vizier, he was not Chief Priest, yet he may have had more real power than Hapuseneb who held both these offices . . . . Senenmut's position was anomalous."[50] Certainly, phrases where Senenmut is referred to as "beloved" of Hatshepsut, "the real favorite of the king [Hatshepsut]," and "one who entered in [love], and came forth in favor, making glad the heart of the king every day, the companion, and master of the palace, Senenmut" put together with scandalous graffiti from the cliffs above Deir el-Bahari have led many to suspect a disreputable love affair.[51] Hatshepsut's attachment to Senenmut was clearly unusual. In the National Geographic documentary, *Secrets of Egypt's Lost Queen,* Dr. Kara Cooney says that the female pharaoh and Senenmut's relationship is so unusual, it is unprecedented: "It's just weird!" Yet, what if Senenmut was not Hatshepsut's lover? What if Senenmut was Hatshepsut's son—her adopted son? What if Senenmut was Moses? Most, in fact, six of the ten statues known to exist of Senenmut depict him with Neferure. In most of these, the subjects' bodies are largely obscured; the faces are the emphasis—and they seem to be given equal emphasis. These statues of Senenmut and Neferure represent an unusual collection. Though block statues had been part of traditional Egyptian art since the Middle Kingdom, most Egyptian art, depicted bodies as strong and whole.[52] Such representations were perhaps not as much vanity as they were security. It was believed that art would have the ability to house the soul of the individual depicted. So, Egyptians depicted themselves as whole, young, and strong—an image befitting the *ka*. After all, who would want to occupy a body that only had one leg or one arm? Yet, what did the person who commissioned these statues of Senenmut and Neferure want?

Sometimes over-analysis is counterproductive. It could be that poses, like those arrangements displayed of Senenmut and Neferure, exist right under our noses; they adorn nearly every desk, in every office, in every modern workplace because every doting parent loves to see the faces of their children set together as a consolidated group. To almost any mother, the faces of her children are the most important faces on earth—especially if that mother is alone. Hatshepsut was a single mother in an extremely high-stress occupation. As such, the faces of Senenmut and Neferure were pleasing to her; they reminded her of joy and brought her back to the center of her heart. It is especially fascinating that Neferure is consistently, in the statues with Senenmut, depicted as very young. Though parents intellectually know that their children must mature, most wish that they could keep them little for longer; there is often especially a desire to keep the baby as "the baby." Hatshepsut and Thutmose II may have had an older daughter, Neferubity, who died very young—so young that some have even questioned her existence altogether.[53] Perhaps Neferubity was stillborn, but it is unknown how much time separated the birth of the two sisters. If Hatshepsut was eleven when she adopted Senenmut/Moses and was twelve when she married Thutmose II, then allowing for a pregnancy with Neferubity, it is unlikely that Neferure was born before Hatshepsut was fifteen; and, due to the death of Thutmose II, Neferure could not have been born after Hatshepsut's late twenties. Therefore, Senenmut was probably between four and sixteen years older than Neferure, most likely five to ten years older. In fact, when viewing the statues of Senenmut and Neferure from this new perspective, the childlike characteristics in Senenmut's face become striking. Yet, there is a consistently clear message of which child is oldest.

The fact that Senenmut's age is somewhat ambiguous in his earliest statues is not surprising. As mentioned above, Hatshepsut, in perhaps her earliest statue, is depicted as an adult. Statues (and other forms of Egyptian art) during this time period tended to be more about symbolism than realism.[54] Therefore, the image that a statue projected about Senenmut was more important than having the figure look like Senenmut. The red quartzite block statue of Senenmut, now in the British Museum, is believed to be the earliest image of him.[55] It is thus considered because Senenmut is seen by himself (without Neferure) and because Hatshepsut is still holding the title of god's wife; after she became king, she passed that distinction on to Neferure. Details of Senenmut's body are obscure; yet, in this block statue, he is wearing a striped *nemes* head cloth (often associated with royalty) and a false beard (like a pharaoh). Therefore, his image is certainly presumptuous for a mere official but not for a son.

Nevertheless, when interpreting carefully what is inscribed about him on this statue, a different image of Senenmut emerges. At the top of the statue, Senenmut is desired to be "one who followed the king (Thutmose III) in his footsteps from the days of his youth, who acted as his confidant, his attendee, significantly involved with happenings in the palace, . . . having become well acquainted with the character of the king." In other words, the monument advances the notion (and the hope) that Thutmose III and Senenmut would grow up together as best friends, especially close to each other because (inserting the rest of the inscription omitted above in the ellipsis) Senenmut enhanced Horus and had received the highest approval.

There are several candidates who could be identified as the "Horus" that Senenmut "adorns." The phrase could mean that Senenmut somehow reflected the glory of Horus, the god, by reminding others of Horus in some way; that he enhanced Horus, the young pharaoh Thutmose III, by helping him be a better man; that he adorned the memory of Horus, Thutmose I, by fulfilling his wishes for his daughter; or that he augmented Horus, Hatshepsut, by acting as her male representative.[56] Perhaps in the inscription, Senenmut is approved and his position is strengthened by all of the above. Nevertheless, someone of authority "purified," sanctioned, Senenmut and desired him to be viewed as Thutmose III's lifelong friend. The foot of the statue is more explicit as to the identity of Senenmut's adorning patron.

> My mistress [Hatshepsut] repeated favors for me . . . she made me great, she enriched me; I was promoted to the front of the officials, she having realized my excellence in her opinion; she appointed me chief spokesman for her estate, the palace, . . . and a judge in the whole land![57]

If Senenmut was Moses, Hatshepsut indeed did him countless favors—not the least of which was allowing him to live! She certainly made him great, and his life was enriched exponentially! She promoted him to the front of her officials; after all, she had not adopted any of them or called them "son." Exodus 2.2 says that Moses' mother thought he was a "goodly" child; if Senenmut was Moses, Hatshepsut seems to have shared a similar opinion of his "excellence"—as did God: "Moses was . . . exceeding fair" (Acts 7.20). As to being the "spokesman for her estate, . . . judge in the whole land," these accolades and titles, though most highly exalted, were likely purely honorary; and if Senenmut was a child, such pronouncements were certainly contrived. However, "Titles in ancient Egypt were not necessarily indicative of actual employment, but rather served to place a man in the social hierarchy."[58]

Further reinforcing the idea that Senenmut/Moses was adopted by Hatshepsut very near the death of Thutmose I is the statement on the statue dedicated to Senenmut that is now housed in Berlin, "I was in this land under Hatshepsut's command from the moment of the death of her predecessor, I being in life under the mistress of the two lands."[59] Certainly, Moses was "in life"; he was in the land of the living, by the good graces of pharaoh's daughter, the mistress of the two lands.

However, "spokesman" in this case, *r-hry* is analogous to being the "mouthpiece and mediator."[60] It is an ironic thought that if Senenmut was Moses, he was destined to serve in exactly this same capacity, as the spokesman and mediator for God. Yet, Moses argued with God, trying to get out of having to act as a spokesman. Being "chief spokesman" was just another way, in Egyptian culture, of being considered to be a king; Moses wasn't interested in being either the king of the Egyptians or king of the Hebrews.[61] Nevertheless, if Moses' argument, "I am slow of speech, and of a slow tongue," is taken literally, it is possible that Moses may have suffered from some sort of physical speech impediment (Exodus 4.10-12). In actuality, Hatshepsut's "son," if he indeed suffered from such a disability, may never have been required to talk *for* her; his mere presence and existence was enough to give her the right to speak, and his figure alone could have served as a mediator between Hatshepsut and the throne. In fact, Senenmut is called "The Prince and Count; the only mouth which speaks with silence."[62]

From his many monuments, Senenmut is identified with some eighty different titles.[63] "Senenmut has more titles than anyone in Egypt."[64] Ancient Egyptians were obsessed with titles, but no one person could have possibly attended to such a great number of endeavors.[65] Though he is considered to be Hatshepsut's chief architect and is especially credited with several illustrious building projects, including Hatshepsut's mortuary temple, also known as Djeser-Djeseru, Holiest of Holies, "precisely what role Senenmut played in the construction at these sites . . . is problematic; other officials of Hatshepsut's reign are far more precise concerning their roles in various architectural activities."[66] In fact, Senenmut is credited with building *all* of Hatshepsut's monuments. Interestingly, Hatshepsut's mortuary temple was likely inspired by and built beside the mortuary temple of Mentuhotep II, perhaps as a nod to her reverence for the Middle Kingdom, the prosperity and governmental style of that time, and/or perhaps to Mentuhotep II himself.[67] However, it is also perhaps a nod to Mentuhotep II's fortunate connection to and rise to power through a Hebrew second-in-command. If Senenmut was Moses, Hatshepsut may well have identified with Mentuhotep II's great fondness and appreciation for Joseph.

However, perhaps not all of Senenmut's titles were merely honorary; it is possible that Senenmut did have some battle experience.[68] An inscription in (TT 71) Theban Tomb 71, a tomb prepared for Senenmut, reads, "I seized . . . the land of Nubia."[69] Josephus records similar information about Moses, appointed by pharaoh to lead the Egyptian army as their general:

> [Moses] came upon the Ethiopians before they expected him; and, joining battle with them, he
> beat them, and deprived them of the hopes they had of success against the Egyptians, and went
> on in overthrowing their cities, and indeed made a great slaughter of these Ethiopians.[70]

Often times when the throne changed hands, the resolve of the new monarch was challenged by attempted coups in outlying territories, hoping to throw off the bonds of Egyptian hegemony. Upon the death of Thutmose II, it is very likely that such a revolt occurred in Nubia. Evidence exists to suggest that Hatshepsut addressed the enemy by leading the army herself and being personally engaged in combat. In a badly damaged block from the eastern colonnade of Hatshepsut's mortuary temple, her Nubian campaign is said to have been conducted in a way "as was done by her victorious father, the King of Upper and Lower Egypt." It is possible that Hatshepsut took Senenmut with her to fight the Nubians; he would have been in his late teens or early twenties at that time. Princes of such age often accompanied pharaohs in battle. Ti, who was a treasurer of the king, wrote:

> I followed the good god, the king of Upper and Lower Egypt, Maatkare [Hatshepsut], may she
> live! I saw him overthrowing the Nubian nomads, their chiefs being brought to him as prisoners.
> I saw him destroying the land of Nubia while I was in the following of His Majesty.[72]

The prolific Egypt historian Joyce Tyldesley believes that the pronoun "him" in the above passage refers to Hatshepsut. However, Ti clearly identifies Maatkare (Hatshepsut) as "she." Could it perhaps be that Senenmut/Moses is the "him" who, acting as Hatshepsut's proxy, was "overthrowing Nubians" and "destroying the land"? Certainly, the phrase "their chiefs being brought to him as prisoners" sounds like one who could, rightfully, take credit in saying, "I seized . . . the land of Nubia." It is also possible that Hatshepsut merely sent Senenmut/Moses to do battle in Nubia as her representative. Josephus says that Moses fought in "Ethiopia," yet he qualifies that by describing it as the country "who are next neighbours [sic] to the Egyptians," more likely Nubia (or the biblical Kush), the modern-day Sudan—not Ethiopia, at least not as it is known today.[73]

Of course, Josephus' sensational account of Moses' Ethiopian campaign also includes an implausible encounter with flying serpents that Moses overcame by devising "a wonderful strategem," involving pet ibises transported by the Egyptian army in basket arks reminiscent of the vessel that once preserved Moses' life. According to the first century historian, these amazingly congenial birds possessed a convenient snake-killing spirit that would have made even Kipling's Rikki-tikki-tavi proud. Josephus' tale is further embellished with romantic intrigue as an exotic Ethiopian princess falls in love with the dashing Moses and betrays her own people on the condition that Moses marry her. Some may consider Numbers 12.1 as evidence to corroborate this fantastic portion of the Josephus account. However, it is probably more likely that Aaron and Miriam's objection to the "Ethiopian woman" Moses married was intended as an affront to Zipporah. Zipporah, the daughter of a Midianite priest, is the only wife Moses is known to have married, unless Hobab, the father-in-law of Moses is evidence of a subsequent marriage (Exodus 2.16, 21; Judges 4.11).

It is appropriate to note, however, that during the time just before the exodus, the scriptures say, "Moreover the man Moses was very great in the land of Egypt, in the sight of Pharaoh's servants, and in the sight of the people" (Exodus 11.3). The Egyptians believed that if something was written, it had the potential to become true. Perhaps in this case, it did, and another title given to Senenmut was warranted: God did indeed make Moses/Senenmut "the greatest of the great in the whole land."

However, many of the monuments of Senenmut and Neferure identify Senenmut with another title—the young princess' tutor. Under the theory that Senenmut was probably less than ten years older than Neferure, it is unlikely that he actually served in the capacity as tutor to the princess. It is more likely that he was responsible for looking after her in the way that, as her big brother, he was "in charge." There was a royal school in the palace where boys, especially, were educated. Among the subjects taught were reading, writing, arithmetic, and music. Princes began their lessons at five or six years old.[74] However:

> The extent to which Neferure was actually educated by any of her tutors is hard for us to assess .
> . . . If Neferure was truly being raised to inherit the throne, we might suspect that she was given
> the education appropriate to a crown prince. In general, however, royal women were less likely
> than their brothers to be literate.[75]

In fact, in his tomb at El-Kab, an official named Ahmose-Pennekheb claims that he educated Neferure when she was a child, and at some point, Neferure's care was given over to an administrator named Senimen.[76]

If Senenmut was Hatshepsut's adopted son, then based on the estimated age of Hatshepsut at the time of her death, Senenmut's actual age in the British Museum red block statue may have been between 15-20 years old. If that is the case, why is so little known about him before this? "Both male and female royal children tended to be relatively obscure in infancy and childhood." It's possible that for the first few years of his life, Moses lived with his biological family. Three years old was the Egyptian expected age of weaning, and the way that the scripture reads, Jochabed may have kept Moses with her until the baby was weaned.[77]

> And Pharaoh's daughter said unto her, Take this child away, and nurse it for me, and I will give thee thy wages. And the woman took the child, and nursed it. And the child grew, and she brought him unto Pharaoh's daughter, and he became her son. (Exodus 2.9-10)

If Moses was essentially sequestered for three years, perhaps Thutmose I died before ever even becoming aware of Hatshepsut's adopted son. Perhaps the whole scheme *was* completely that of the pharaoh's daughter.

However, other evidence suggests that Jochabed and even her other children were heavily involved with the royal family and were in Moses' life for much longer than three years. Nevertheless, the arrangement is still odd; royal nurses were not usually slaves. "Throughout the Dynastic Age the position of royal wet-nurse was an honorable post of some influence and importance, often given as a reward to the mothers and wives of the élite courtiers."[78] Bonds with the royal nurse were often very strong, lasting a lifetime.[79] The nurse's children served as playmates to the royal offspring.[80] Hatshepsut, herself, loved and highly valued Inet, the wet-nurse who had tended her, so much so, Hatshepsut provided a

Hatnofer's Chair from Tomb 71

private tomb for Inet in the Valley of the Kings.[81] It does seem, from the scriptures, that Moses was well acquainted with his brother, Aaron, and his sister, Miriam. Exodus 4.14 certainly makes it sound as if Moses and Aaron knew each other, and Miriam is highlighted very early in the exodus (Exodus 15.20).

Of course, above a wet-nurse, motherhood was highly valued in Egyptian society, but being the mother of a son was especially relished because it brought recognition that translated into power. If Senenmut was Hatshepsut's son, her male counterpart, her figurehead, her ticket to legitimacy as an acting regent; he was an external extension of herself, her *ka* (her royal-divine spirit); he served as her alter ego.[82] It is curious that in the depiction of Hatshepsut's birth on the walls of Deir el-Bahari, Amun says to Khnum (the creator):

> Go, to make her together with her ka, from these limbs which are in me; go, to fashion her better
> than all gods; [shape for me,] this my daughter, whom I have begotten. I have given to her all life
> and satisfaction, all stability, all joy of heart from me, ...[83]

Khnum, in the relief, proceeds to form Hatshepsut on a potter's wheel as two *male* children.[84] One is Hatshepsut (certainly a child who was loved as much as any son ever was), and the other is her *ka*, her divinely-given right to rule, her male persona, perhaps Senenmut/Moses. In fact, Hatshepsut referred to having multiple *kas*.[85] "Hatshepsut must have seen in Senenmut a kindred soul."[86]

Thutmose III with Hatshepsut, Appearing as a Male Figure

Senenmut was indispensable to Hatshepsut. Tyldesley says, "Senenmut is generally credited with being the political force behind Hatshepsut's assumption and exercise of kingship."[87] Yet, he was perhaps more a force of presence than of person. Some Egyptians thought that *maat* was in jeopardy if the pharaoh was not male.[88] If Hatshepsut had been born a male, she would not have needed Senenmut at all. However, just because Hatshepsut believed that her bloodline, her prowess, and the unusual circumstances made her the best choice to lead Egypt as pharaoh, does not mean that she wished to be a man or even that she pretended to be a man. In fact, when Hatshepsut depicts Amun saying to her, "Welcome my sweet daughter," Thutmose I saying to her, "Come, glorious one," and saying of herself, "to look upon her was more beautiful than anything," it sounds like she was very happy as herself; she enjoyed being a woman.[89] Putting on a false beard was like putting on a crown; it was simply part of the attire of a pharaoh "held at the point of the chin by a strap on each side, which passed round the jaw and in front of the ear and was attached to the crown itself."[90] Therefore, when Hatshepsut wore the false beard, she was not saying, "I'm a man"; she only signifying, "I'm a pharaoh." Senenmut/Moses may very well have been the male completion of Hatshepsut's pharaonic image; he was the extension of Hatshepsut's *ka*, providing her a powerful male form. Could it be that when Hatshepsut appears in relief, statuary, and portraiture as a form without breasts, with broad shoulders, and in full male attire, it's actually Senenmut/Moses appearing as her stand-in?[91] After all, one of Senenmut's inscriptions says, " . . . he causes her to appear, he bears her beauty, for the life, prosperity, and health of the King of Upper and Lower Egypt, Makere [Hatshepsut], living forever."[92] With a son as her male representative, Hatshepsut was glad to be a mother.

Moses said, "Honour thy father and thy mother" (Exodus 20.12). In year seven of Hatshepsut's pharaonic reign, tragedy befell Senenmut. His mother, Hatnofer, died. She was mummified and buried in an anthropoid coffin.[93] Her head and shoulders were covered in a beautiful, golden funeral mask.[94] Many expensive grave goods accompanied her body, including canopic jars, a serpentine heart scarab set in gold, scarab rings, two silver pitchers and a silver bowl (silver was more valued than gold), three funerary rolls of papyrus and leather, boxes and baskets containing linen sheets, cosmetic implements, a razor wrapped in linen, a beautiful blue bowl dated to the early reign of Thutmose II, a necklace of faience lentoid beads, bread, and fruit. Hatnofer was laid to rest in a burial chamber beneath Tomb 71, high in the cliffs above Deir el-Bahari; and several others were interred with her.[95]

Senenmut's father, a man named Ramose, was evidently exhumed from an earlier meager burial and relocated to Tomb 71. Ramose, whose badly decomposed body had originally been buried in mud, was re-wrapped in sheets of linen that were marked with Neferure's name.[96] Also, a scarab inscribed with "god's wife Neferure" was tied to the finger of the body of an elderly woman, Sitdjehuty, likely Senenmut's grandmother, stricken with tuberculosis of the spine.[97] Obviously, Neferure was also close to these dead. Besides these, there were five other human bodies in Tomb 71. According to funerary papyri found inside Hatnofer's mummy wrappings, Senenmut had three brothers: Amenemhat, Minhotep, and Pairy, and two sisters: Ahhotep and Nofrethor.[98] One of the remaining five mummies in Hatnofer's tomb was an unidentified boy, no older than twenty. He was wrapped in a reed mat, and, like Ramose, he had also been exhumed from an earlier burial and reburied in Tomb 71. There were two other young men—one named Amenhotep and another named Hormae, the latter buried with a lute, attributable to the Hyksos. Two anonymous young women, in anthropoid coffins, were also buried in Tomb 71.[99] Since two wooden figures inscribed with the name Ahhotep "beloved sister, the justified" were located nearby, it is assumed that Ahhotep, Senenmut's sister, was among the deceased; but nothing is known about the body of Nofrethor.[100] In Senenmut's second tomb, 353, located beneath Hatshepsut's mortuary temple, his brother, Amenemhat, is "entrusted with the execution of his funerary rites" and Senenmut's sister is depicted there as well.[101] The dead accounted for in Tomb 71 seem to indicate that Senenmut, perhaps, had a surviving brother and sister. In fact, two unfinished shafts off of Tomb 71 may have been intended as eventual burial chambers for his two remaining siblings.[102] After Hatnofer's burial chamber was sealed, work began to finish out the rest of Tomb 71 as a place for Senenmut himself to be interred.

It has been assumed that the anonymous burials in Tomb 71 were all members of Senenmut's family and/or his extended family, including, perhaps, spouses of his siblings. The suggestion that Senenmut came from a family that was bourgeois but somewhat well off seems to be largely based on the fact that several of the people in Tomb 71 were placed inside wooden coffins. During the Eighteenth Dynasty, only the wealthiest Egyptians could afford such coffins.[103] Also, the fact that Senenmut was well educated is seen as indicative of an origin with means. It is estimated that only about 5% of the Egyptian population was literate.[104] However, if Senenmut was adopted as an infant into the royal family, he would have been given access to the best education in Egypt (Moses received such); under those circumstances, Senenmut's literacy would have no bearing on his family's biological affluence or lack thereof (Acts 7.22). Furthermore, most of the dead in Tomb 71 were not originally buried in wooden coffins; they were reburied in them. Several of the bodies in Tomb 71 were badly decomposed and had originally been buried in mud and rocks. It has been suggested that some of the occupants of Tomb 71 were servants. It seems more likely that all of them were servants, or worse, slaves. Many slaves worked as minstrels, like Hormae. Certainly the extremely poor conditions of Ramose's original burial suggests that his family was incapable of providing better for their patriarch, though they clearly loved him—even Neferure cared for him.[105]

Yet, Hatnofer seems central to Tomb 71 as if she was, for some reason, the most prized and honored. The riches afforded Hatnofer seem to have been lavished on her—not by her own family—but by the royal family of Hatshepsut. What service could this woman have provided that was considered so valuable? How is it that Neferure was so well acquainted with these lowly people?

A beautiful, ornately carved and ebony inlaid chair buried with Hatnofer may hold the explanation. Adorned with the Egyptian god, Bes, the protector of the nursery and god of childbirth, this chair would have been especially well suited to the assignment of a wet-nurse.[106] In some cases, a nurse was considered a counterpart to a tutor, i.e., "father-tutor" or "father-nurse."[107] Based on the obvious involvement of Neferure in the burials in Tomb 71 and her attachment to the people interred there, it seems more likely that much of Neferure's care and training, though perhaps not her formal education, may more be ascribed to Senenmut's mother than to Senenmut himself.

Perhaps another analysis of Tomb 71 points to Senenmut's similarity to Moses. Not only does it seem possible that Senenmut's mother was employed by the royal family as a wet-nurse, but Hatnofer's chair was dismantled to save space and was placed inside of a large tambourine composed of red-stained leather stretched over a wooden frame. It is presumed that this instrument was used for rituals.[108] Like Hormae's lute and Hatnofer's tambourine are evidence of musicians in Senenmut's family, Moses' family was also musically talented. Both he and his sister Miriam wrote and sang songs, and Miriam played the tambourine (Exodus 15.1-21; Deuteronomy 32.1-43). In fact, the tambourine (the Hebrew word "toph") seems to have been a popular musical instrument in Hebrew celebration since "all the women" joined Miriam in playing their "timbrels" (Exodus 15.20).[109] Based on it's prevalence in Egyptian art, sistrums were perhaps more common in Egyptian rituals. However, sistrums are rarely mentioned in scripture.[110] Could the presence of a Hyksos lute and a tambourine in the burial chamber of Hatnofer suggest that Senenmut's family was Hebrew as was Moses?

Yet, if Senenmut was Moses, why is there such a discrepancy in the names? Egyptians rarely referred to their rulers by the names they were given at birth.[111] Therefore, if Senenmut was originally named "Son," or "Moses," it was likely not common knowledge. "Senenmut," fascinatingly, means "Mother's brother"; if Hatshepsut adopted him when she was just a child, Senenmut, approximately only a decade younger, may well have felt more like a brother to Hatshepsut, more of a "senenmut" than a "moses." In fact, it was common for Egyptians to have multiple names and nicknames and secret names. For instance, Senenmut's mother, Hatnofer, was also known as Tjutju.[112] Hatnofer was identified in her coffin with the title "House Mistress," not a very prestigious epithet; but it was a designation that might well have described Jochabed too.[113] Sometimes pharaohs assigned new names to people, as was the case with Joseph and centuries later with Jehoiakim (Genesis 41.45; II Kings 23.34). It is perhaps worth mentioning that Hatshepsut and Hatnofer share a common first syllable. If Hatshepsut bestowed the name Hatnofer on this woman, perhaps she was partly identifying her to herself. Yet, the appellation assigned to Ramose is perhaps more compelling. Accompanying his body was the comment "the worthy." The name of Moses' father, Amram, means "the exalted," a notable synonym.[114] Furthermore, "ra" and "ram" is contained in both names. However, it is perhaps more important to note that, as Robert Silverberg points out, "the father of Moses without doubt prefixed to his son's name that of an Egyptian god like Amun or Ptah, and this divine name was gradually lost in current usage, till the boy was called 'Mose.'"[115] Senenmut's father, Ramose, had just such a name, offering yet another possible connection between Senenmut and Moses—especially if, perhaps, the name Ramose had been assigned to the father of Moses by the daughter of the pharaoh sometime after Moses was adopted. Of course, if Hatshepsut was the person who named Moses, both her father, her husband, and her stepson shared the name "Mose" with the prefix "Thot."

Other apparent dissimilarities between Senenmut and Moses are worthy of examination. Senenmut had five siblings, of which only two may have survived their parents; in the scripture, only two siblings of Moses are listed (Numbers 26.59). For that reason, it is usually assumed that Aaron and Miriam were Moses' only siblings and that Miriam, therefore, was the sister of Moses who watched over him in the bulrushes. However, the name of that sister is never provided in scripture. Could it be that Moses' watchful older sister was actually Ahhotep, the beloved and justified?

I Chronicles 6.3 may support the premise that Miriam was younger than Moses because she is listed after Moses. Since Aaron is listed first, and he was definitely older than Moses, it is possible that this verse lists the siblings according to birth order (Exodus 7.7). Of course, Miriam is also listed last in Micah 6.4; but in this instance, Moses, not Aaron, is listed first. Therefore, Micah was obviously not organizing the three by birth order. Yet, Aaron was likely not the firstborn since, on the night of the tenth plague, he may well have left the safety of the blood-covered house (Exodus 12.31). Nevertheless, just because other siblings of Moses are not listed in scripture does not necessarily mean that they never existed. The Bible doesn't even provide an exhaustive list of the siblings of Jesus, but more siblings than are named definitely existed (Matthew 13.56; Mark 6.3). For that matter, no one is exactly sure how many siblings Hatshepsut had either.

Another discrepancy between Senenmut and Moses may be found in the age of their predecessor.

According to Exodus 6.20, Amram lived to be 137 years old. Yet, an examination of Ramose's mummy, conducted by Dr. Douglas Derry, presumably in the first half of the twentieth century, estimated Ramose to have been about sixty when he died.[116]Regardless of this disparity, it is certainly true that either age would have been considered advanced for that time.

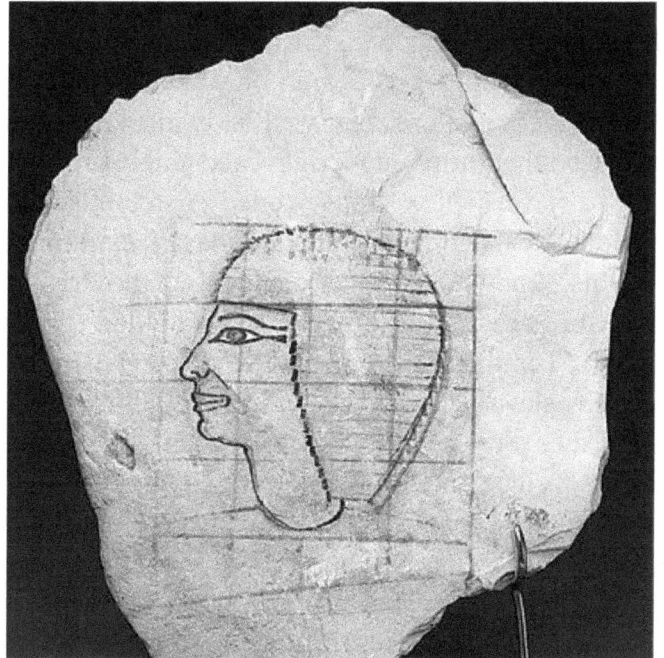

Senenmut Sketched on Ostrica

Beyond Senenmut's family members, two very unusual committals were also found in Tomb 71. A small mare, just a little over twelve hands high, was mummified and placed inside a coffin. Accompanying the filly is the earliest example of an Egyptian saddle. Pottery bowls with food in them were also provided.[117] Furthermore, a mummified monkey was laid to rest with a container of raisins nearby.[118] These animals provide insight to Senenmut as a child. A man might revere a gallant steed, serving him well in battle, but it is much more likely that a boy (an indulged boy, based on the presence of the saddle) would grieve to this extent over the loss of a foal. And even though Egyptians were known to mummify all kinds of animals, a monkey carefully buried with its favorite food seems more consistent with the sentiments expressed by a child for a pet.[119]

Why have most experts assumed that Senenmut was an adult when he entered the life of Hatshepsut? Perhaps it is because drawings of Senenmut often depict him with wrinkles around his mouth and chin.[120] In fact, to some, wrinkles are considered Senenmut's most defining feature.[121] However, wrinkles are not always representative of age. Furthermore, if Senenmut had been an adult or even an old man in Hatshepsut's court, as some have suggested, it is unlikely that Neferure would have known his mother and father, and certainly not his grandmother as is evident from the findings in Hatnofer's tomb. Perhaps Senenmut's wrinkles do not imply age. It is probable that Senenmut was pudgy. More than one of his statues shows Senenmut having "a smooth, soft body with rolls of flesh around his middle, evidence of a sedentary life of ease and affluence."[122] If that is the case, the life of Senenmut was very different from that of his family buried in Tomb 71. Hatshepsut, herself, was so heavy at the time of her death that her viscera could not be removed through the side incision commonly used in the mummification process. Instead, her organs were removed through her pelvic floor.[123] Hatshepsut may have developed excessive eating habits from her nurse, Inet, who based on the appearance of her coffin, was "an unusually large woman."[124] If Senenmut shared Hatshepsut's diet, he was likely overweight too. In fact, the wrinkles under his chin have been described as manifestations of a double chin.[125] It was probably not common for ancient Egyptians to be overweight; therefore, artists had little practice or formulas depicting double chins and chubby cheeks.

Yet, some have proposed a more sinister interpretation, suggesting that such drawings of Senenmut were unkind caricatures, subtlety-depicting Senenmut as "other," "different," and/or "foreign."[126] Certainly, the rolls of fat depicted on Eti, the queen of Punt, were intended to be interpreted as a shocking deformity by the artists who decorated the walls of Hatshepsut's mortuary temple, evoking a burlesque sympathy for "The ass which bears his wife [Eti]."[127] Perhaps some of the same "artists" were responsible for the derogatory graffiti in the cliffs above Deir el-Bahari that maligned the character of Senenmut and Hatshepsut. Undeniably, there was a disturbing undercurrent of disdain for Senenmut and Hatshepsut. Some definitely did not like the looks of the royal picture of which Senenmut was a part.

In fact, could it be that unflattering representations of Senenmut are rooted in an even deeper prejudice? "Humour [sic] would have been the only weapon that the workmen could use to attack their superiors."[128] If

Senenmut was Moses, his Hebrew/Hyksos heritage would, no doubt, have been disdained. Indeed, the next most defining characteristic used to represent Senenmut was a "prominent hooked nose, present on both the ostraca and wall sketch[es], . . . [and] on some statues that portray Senenmut in which the face has survived intact."[129] An exaggerated nose may well be evidence of an inartistic Hebrew stereotype. However, "some scholars have proposed that these [renderings] accurately represent Senenmut's nose."[130]

Nevertheless, thinly veiled contempt for the Hebrew adopted son of the daughter of the pharaoh may well have existed, and it may not have been limited to prejudiced Egyptians. Among his many titles, Senenmut was also known as "Superintendent of the Royal Slaves."[131] Ironically, it may have been Hebrew slaves who were the "artists" responsible for the unkind caricatures and the disrespectful graffiti in the cliffs above Deir el-Bahari. Temple building was a Hyksos slave duty prescribed under Ahmose.[132] According to scripture, some Hebrew slaves resented the elevated station of Moses and castigated his authority when they contended, "Who made thee a prince and a judge over us?" (Exodus 2.14) Though Moses went on to be the leader and judge of all Israel, "prince" and "judge" were also two of the titles ascribed to Senenmut (Exodus 18.13). At times in his life, Senenmut may have been unaware of the scope of prejudice against him. Nevertheless, through the painful process of burying the members of his family, he was no doubt aware of the disparity that existed between life in the royal family and life as a slave. Of course, Moses also was aware of a level of aversion to him as well (Exodus 2.14). At times, he must have wondered where, if anywhere, he really belonged.

Kings of the Eighteenth Dynasty lived primarily in Luxor, but multiple palaces existed all along the Nile, especially between Memphis and Thebes.[133] Pharaohs often moved from palace to palace. A document from the Nineteenth Dynasty describes the preparations that were in order to welcome a pharaoh.

> Get on with having everything ready for pharaoh's [arrival] . . . have made ready 100 ring stands
> for bouquets of flowers . . . 1000 loaves of fine flour . . . cakes, 100 baskets . . . dried meat, 100
> baskets . . . milk, 60 measures . . . grapes, 50 sacks . . .

One can only imagine how many times in one trip the above scene was enacted. It could take as long as three weeks to travel by boat from Memphis to Thebes. Yet, there was a much greater distance in lifestyle between Thebes and Armant, the small village where Senenmut was likely born along the western bank of the Nile, just south of Luxor.[134] It is significant to note that on the monument that ties Senenmut to Armant, he is called "overseer of prophets," suggesting that there were prophets in Senenmut's home town, among his people, or in his family.[135] Prophets were definitely in Moses' family (Exodus 7.1; 15.20; Numbers 12.2).

Is it possible that Moses could have been born in Armant, a town in Upper Egypt? Didn't the Hebrews live in Lower Egypt, in Goshen? The family of Joseph settled in Goshen; and over time, Goshen was, no doubt, considered to be the homeland of Hebrews in Egypt, i.e., their dwelling place (Exodus 8.22). The Hyksos maintained a capital at Avaris, in Lower Egypt; but after the Egyptians enslaved the Hebrews/Hyksos, they continued to multiply and were pressed into "all manner of service" (Exodus 1.14). It stands to reason that as the Hebrews were forced into various projects and tasks and were assigned to different masters, they would have been compelled to live throughout the land of Egypt (Exodus 1.7). In fact, one Eighteenth Dynasty official from Upper Egypt reported having forty-five Asiatic slaves; of course they may or may not all have been Hebrew Asiatics.[136] The scriptures never specify what town was the birthplace of Moses. However, the Nile flows from Armant to nearby Luxor, the home of royalty during this part of the Eighteenth Dynasty.

In Tomb 71, the remains of a grand stone sarcophagus were found, smashed into thousands of pieces. It's obvious that this crypt was intended as the final resting-place for the body of Senenmut. The quartzite coffin is decorated with Isis and her sister Nephthys at each end of the vault and the four sons of Horus and two Anubis figures on the sides.[137] A connection between Isis, Horus, and the princess who found Moses has already been discussed, but it is compelling to note that the protective funerary goddess Nephthys, whose name means "Lady of the House" is certainly similar to "House Mistress" the title associated with Hatnofer.[138] Is it possible that Hatshepsut and "her sister" Hatnofer/Jochabed acted as the Isis and Nephthys who preserved and protected Senenmut/Moses? The answer, of course, must remain conjecture; however, in another ironic correlation, the goddess Nephthys wears a basket on her head.[139] Unlike Nut, the sky goddess, whose image adorned the inside lids of sarcophagi fairly consistently across time, only words of comfort from Isis and Nephthys had commonly accompanied the dead since the Old Kingdom. Therefore, representations of these deities were an unusual addition to find on a sarcophagus though they had been common components of burials in Egypt for hundreds of years.[140]

By piecing the rubble together, enough can be told about the sarcophagus of Senenmut to recognize it as a near duplicate to Hatshepsut's own sarcophagus.[141] Obviously, these sarcophagi were commissioned and designed by the same person, but who? Only a pharaoh could have obtained the quartzite from which the sarcophagi were made. Only a pharaoh could order stone to be quarried, and all quarried stone was the possession of pharaoh. Only a pharaoh could have secured the transport of the heavy stone slabs on barges from Gebel Ahmar to Thebes.[142] Only a pharaoh could have engaged the stonecutters and sculptors. It seems likely that an image of Nephthys at the head of the sarcophagus and of Isis at the foot were preferences ordered by the pharaoh Hatshepsut since her own sarcophagus was decorated in this same fashion, as were the sarcophagi she had made for Thutmose I and for Senenmut; but images of the two sisters carved into the stone of sarcophagi by Hatshepsut started a trend that persisted in the Valley of the Kings at least through Thutmose IV.[143] Yet, perhaps Hatshepsut only provided the materials. Perhaps she only approved Senenmut's conceptions. Christine Meyer, who has examined Senenmut's statues extensively from an Art History perspective, concluded that Hatshepsut and Senenmut's monuments have striking stylistic similarities, indicating a singular mind.[144] Perhaps an examination of style is in order.

Egyptian artists did not sign their work. In fact, there isn't even a word in ancient Egyptian for "artist."[145] It was the client—or in those days, more properly, the patron—who received the credit. "That he [Senenmut] should have tried to sign his work, or rather that he should have tried to get, with the gods if not with his contemporaries, some of the credit accruing from his work is an anecdote well worth adding to our knowledge."[146] Even more brazen, Senenmut is credited with asking Hatshepsut's permission to have his image cast in every kind of precious stone and placed in every temple of Upper and Lower Egypt.[147] More likely, however, the many monuments and accomplishments attributed to Senenmut were subject to the initiation and consignment of Hatshepsut; only she possessed the power to implement them, and upon closer examination, a new image of Senenmut is revealed.

Supposedly, Senenmut said of himself, "I was the greatest of the great in the whole land; . . . I was a foreman of foremen, superior of the great, [overseer] of all [works] of the house of silver, conductor of every handicraft."[148] Either Senenmut was a manifold genius and an egomaniac; or, perhaps, the real Senenmut had very little in common with the super image that was created for him. In fact, almost none of the titles he was given were reasonably "earned." Similarly, almost none of the monuments ascribed to Senenmut were doubtlessly his conceptions.

It has been concluded that Tomb 71, in the cliffs above Deir el-Bahari, and Tomb 353, beneath *Djeser-Djeseru*, were under construction at the same time.[149] Even though both of these tombs were being made to honor (and were presumably being overseen by) the same man, Senenmut, they are very different projects. Hatshepsut's mortuary temple is considered to be one of the most beautiful buildings of all time.

> The building has many effective aspects. Horizontal and vertical accents on the temple are counterpoised and have further relationship to the horizontal lines of the . . . gigantic cliffs into which we are imperceptibly led. Designing this structure to fit into its natural environment is a conscious triumph of architectural planning. Finally, the simple geometry of verticals, horizontal, open squares, and rectangles is beautifully balanced by the chase simplicity of individual columns.[150]

The attention to line, shape, space, and composition is just not the same in the jumble of coffins and artifacts crammed into the burial chamber beneath Tomb 71. Depth of feeling is present in both Tomb 71 and Tomb 353. Both tombs tell a passionate story, but they simply do not represent the same emphasis, subject, style, or talent. Even a casual observer can see that the same mind was not chiefly responsible for both the burial chamber of Tomb 71 and Tomb 353. Perhaps Senenmut (and Neferure) did oversee the burials in the chamber beneath Tomb 71, though Hatshepsut, no doubt, was involved in the project—especially in the layout and design for the tomb itself. However, Hatshepsut's discriminating taste is clearly evident in every aspect of her mortuary temple, including in the associated Tomb 353.

In fact, the almost sixty niches, clandestinely tucked behind doors inside Hatshepsut's mortuary temple that depict Senenmut worshiping Amun and adoring Hatshepsut, are probably not representative of Senenmut's sentiments. Although Senenmut likely cared very deeply for Hatshepsut and was undoubtedly grateful to her, it was probably not his idea to have "his name established on every wall . . . in the temples." The ending of this statement is probably more closely related to the truth: "Thus spoke the king [Hatshepsut]." The discrete images of Senenmut in Djeser-Djeseru could not have been made without Hatshepsut's knowledge and approval. Only royals were permitted access to such religious spaces.[151] Senenmut was probably uncomfortable with public exposure, aware that under such scrutiny he was not really approved by many. It must have been intimidating to be cast in the limelight of Hatshepsut. She was a "phenom": poetic, creative, aesthetic, passionate, and visionary. Hatshepsut was a woman with an agenda. Comparing himself to her, it's a small wonder that "the spokesman who spoke in silence" doubted his own eloquence (Exodus 4.12). Senenmut was probably quiet, obedient, sensitive, and amiable with a conciliatory nature that easily endeared him to those who were close to him. In fact, it was probably his inherently meek nature that made the placement of his images in unobtrusive niches somehow representative. Ironically, Senenmut's genuine humility and faithful acquiescence would have made him an almost irresistible object of admiration. "Before honour is humility" (Proverbs 18.12).

It is very doubtful that Senenmut was an egotist; it would be uncharacteristic of selfish ambition to tenderly descend and seek to honor the powerless paupers in Tomb 71. Comparing the disposition of Moses and Senenmut, a picture of a similar personality emerges. As the scripture says, "Now the man Moses was very meek, above all the men which were upon the face of the earth" (Numbers 12.3). Hebrews 3.2 says, "Moses was faithful in all his house." Likewise, it was said of Senenmut, "It came to pass in every respect, as was commanded by doing according to the desire of his majesty [Senenmut was a] true servant, without his like."[152] If Senenmut was Hatshepsut's adopted son, he was raised to be a faithful servant. Certainly, the same could have been said of Moses, being raised in pharaoh's household (Acts 7.21). Furthermore, it should be noted that Senenmut/Moses would also have been conditioned to graciously bow to the will of a woman.

With that understanding, it is perhaps easier to comprehend the meaning of a very strange passage in Exodus. As Moses was on his way back to Egypt to confront Pharaoh:

. . . the Lord met him, and sought to kill him. Then Zipporah took a sharp stone, and cut off the foreskin of her son, and cast it at his feet, and said, Surely a bloody husband art thou to me. So he let him go: then she said, A bloody husband thou art, because of the circumcision. (Exodus 4.24-26)

Circumcision was a practice of Egyptians and Hebrews, but it was apparently not a custom of the Midianites. Therefore, it seems that Zipporah, Moses' wife, was opposed to circumcising her sons. Moses probably knew the will of God in this matter or else God would likely not have been so angry with him, and Zipporah wouldn't have immediately known what to do in order to save Moses' life. Yet, it seems that Moses hadn't pressed the issue of circumcising their sons with Zipporah. Instead, as he had been habituated, he went along with the woman's wishes and let Zipporah have her way. God, however, did not.

What were Hatshepsut's wishes? What was her agenda? Yes, it was her agenda to rule Egypt in the continuance of her royal Ahmose bloodline, but it was more than just that. Senenmut, it seems, was part of her agenda too. She truly adored him; he was her heart's delight, and she strongly desired to validate those feelings in the eyes of others. She wanted others to see Senenmut as one who deserved to be highly favored, in part, because he was a reflection of herself. In his many monuments and titles, she wanted Senenmut to be respected and admired because Hatshepsut wanted to be respected and admired. Senenmut was important to her; therefore she designed for him to be important to Egypt because Hatshepsut wanted to be remembered as important.

Hatshepsut was ambitious and competitive. She was out to do great things. She meant for her children to do great things too. It wasn't enough for Neferure to just be her daughter; she was "god's wife." Yet, Hatshepsut had even greater designs for Neferure. At Deir el-Bahari, there is strong evidence that Hatshepsut intended for Neferure to follow in her political footsteps as well. Neferure, in wall reliefs, is deified and seen as being groomed to carry on the throne in the bloodline of Ahmose.[153] Indeed, Neferure was the only person who could.

It wasn't enough for Senenmut/Moses just to be Hatshepsut's son either; he was deemed "the greatest of the great." On the obelisk erected in memory of Thutmose I, Hatshepsut said, "Now, my heart turns this way and that as I think what people will say, those who see my monuments in years to come, and who shall speak of what I have done."[154] Perhaps Hatshepsut was concerned about how history would remember her decision to claim the throne. Perhaps she wondered if her building projects would be admired and appreciated. But, could this statement be a reference to some other controversial act that her father had permitted her to do? Was she wondering if people in the future would validate her decision to adopt Senenmut/Moses? Unfortunately, human nature usually resists being told what one's opinion ought to be. Many people living in the days of Hatshepsut did not agree that Senenmut deserved to have the favor and the life that he was living. However, Egypt was at peace and was prosperous; for these exhibitions of *maat* (i.e., order), Hatshepsut was praised.[155] It is noteworthy that buried beneath the obelisk that Hatshepsut erected, there were found two statues holding hands: Hatshepsut and Neferhotep I, a pharaoh from the Thirteenth Dynasty who was credited with restoring *maat*.[156]

With an eye to the future, Hatshepsut's agenda also involved writing her own daring narrative and projecting it to be/to become true. Hatshepsut was a romanticist. She loved fantasy; she, like Jochabed, no doubt had "heard stories of the gods from her nurse or her mother."[157] Yet, "For Hatshepsut mythology and politics were intermeshed."[158] She believed that she could manufacture reality. "The scenes [in her temple at Deir el-Bahari] by themselves are by no means timid or apologetic; they are miraculous and joyful . . . Nor should [they] be regarded solely as a propaganda exercise . . . ."[159] In her birth scene, Hatshepsut drew heavily from mythology, including from the collection of Middle Kingdom stories found on the Westcar Papyrus.[160] And, her tale of the divine conception of the pharaoh was an idea as old as the Fifth Dynasty.[161] Therefore, if Amun, appearing in the form of Thutmose I, impregnated Hatshepsut's mother; if the god Khnum, assisted by the frog-headed goddess, Heket, fashioned Hatshepsut's living body and soul; if multiple goddesses attended her birth as midwives; if she was suckled by Hathor, then Hatshepsut had simply fit the accepted story line. The story gave her a divine right to rule.[162] Clearly, the birth story was intended to validate Hatshepsut as a legitimate pharaoh.

However, James Breasted observes that part of the final scene in Hatshepsut's birth story is "impossible to explain." The child, Hatshepsut and her *ka*, stand before a kneeling, unfamiliar Nile-god, "and in the

lower row of the same scene appears before another unknown divinity." The lioness goddess, Pakhet, makes a record of the event, and Hatshepsut "is launched upon" her career.[163] "Osiris as well as the Nile were revered as gods of fertility; hence it follows that Osiris *is* the Nile and vice versa," and while a connection between Osiris and baby Moses has already been suggested, Osiris is not depicted.[164] Could it be that this mysterious scene at the end of her birth story recalls the day Hatshepsut found something significant at the edge of the Nile. Could it be that Hatshepsut and Moses together are shown thanking the true God of the Nile for delivering a baby boy safely to her and thanking the "unknown" God of Amram and Jochabed, because through this gift of a male figure, a son to be her surrogate image, Hatshepsut had obtained the authority to rule Egypt? If Hatshepsut was the pharaoh's daughter who drew Moses from the Nile, it could have been at that very moment, as she granted life to a helpless infant, that she first realized, as she also wrote on a Karnak obelisk, "as my father Amon favors me, as my nostrils are filled with satisfying life," she had breathed life to Moses.[165]

In a similar perplexing scene, from Senenmut's shrine in the cliffs at Gebel Silsila, Hatshepsut is "embraced by the crocodile-headed god Sobek and by Nekhbet, the vulture goddess of Upper Egypt." Tyldesley says other experts describe the relationship envisioned here as "peculiar" and "unusual."[166] Again, crocodiles are reminiscent of the Nile and vultures are associated with the dead, but crocodiles are also representative of the god Sobek and therefore with pharaonic might, and vultures are also associated with Mut and Nekhbet, goddesses of motherhood and tutelage. The baby in the basket was spared from the crocodile and from the vulture; and, through the gift of Senenmut/Moses, Hatshepsut was simultaneously granted might to be a pharaoh and ability to be a mother. Because of an unexpected blessing granted to Hatshepsut, Egypt had been blessed with pharaonic strength and with prosperity.[167] Hatshepsut was especially grateful.

As Hatshepsut filled the walls of Djeser-Djeseru, recording her dreams coming true, she continued to draw, heavily, from Egyptian mythology and literature. For example, her Punt relief is very reminiscent of The Tale of the Shipwrecked Sailor, another Middle Kingdom story.[168] In fact, the manifest of goods recorded from Hatshepsut's Punt expedition reads like a copy of the exotic cargo brought to Egypt in the sailor's tale.[169] It is as though, in her travels to Punt, Hatshepsut was setting about the business of bringing fantasy to life.[170] Incidentally, included in that story, friends of the sailor are retrieved from the water and are miraculously brought back to life; Moses was saved from a similar fate.[171] If Hatshepsut could make this story true, why couldn't the rest of the walls of her temple be made true as well?

Due to her obvious love of literature and legend, Hatshepsut likely shared favorite stories with Senenmut. On the magnificent astronomical ceiling (the first of its kind) in Senenmut's Tomb 353 is the bull-headed constellation Meskhe-tiu, the constellation of Orion (in ancient legend, this constellation was also Nimrod, the mighty hunter), and the significant star in Egyptian culture, the star of renewal, Sothis, among other heavenly bodies (Genesis 10.9).[172] One can imagine the daughter of the pharaoh holding her adopted son in her lap on a warm September evening, pointing at the stars and telling her favorite stories to him. It was perhaps a cherished memory that Hatshepsut wished to preserve for eternity. In Hatshepsut and Senenmut are " . . . intertwined stories of a remarkable woman and an able man, the echoes of which have not been hushed up entirely in spite of every effort on the part of their antagonist and the lapse of thirty-four centuries."[173]

In fact, on that same ceiling, Hatshepsut and Senenmut's names are forever linked. He was her son; she gave him life. As one of his inscriptions says, "I was in life under the Mistress of the Two Lands."[174] Every child is "in life" because of the care of their mother. The bond between mother and child is eternal. Yet, why is Neferure not honored in this way? Under the theory proposed in this book, Senenmut/Moses played a unique role and provided a unique bond with Hatshepsut that Neferure could not. He was the male child, the tiny fragment of the eternal divine that breathed life into Hatshepsut's political career.

It is an ironic thought to consider the place that folklore played in the life of the legendary Moses. The beginning of his life is too like the legend of Sargon, and his rescue from the Nile is too like the story of Isis and Osiris to be coincidental. Perhaps it isn't out of place that the middle of his life should echo another favorite Egyptian folk tale, The Story of Sinuhe. Ironically, this Middle Kingdom story recounts the adventures of a legendary favorite of the Egyptian court, assigned to the care of a princess named Nefru.[175] Upon the death of the king he served, Sinuhe fled Egypt in fear for his life from the successor to the throne. The former Egyptian nobleman, was taken in by a sheik, married the sheik's oldest daughter, rose to favor in the foreign Palestinian kingdom of the Retjenu, and returned to Egypt in his old age.[176] Sinuhe's story is certainly not unlike the story of Moses who fled Egypt at 40 years old, in fear for his life, was taken in by a man of "eminence," married Zipporah the daughter of Reuel/Jethro the Priest of Midian, rose to favor in a foreign land, and returned to Egypt at eighty years old (Exodus 2.11-4.20).[177] Interestingly, in Senenmut's Tomb 71, plans were found that calculated the layout of that tomb to correspond to The Story of Sinuhe.[178]

However, perhaps the resemblance of The Tale of Sinuhe to the life of Moses is also more than coincidence. Since the earliest version of the story, the Theban Papyrus Berlin 3022, is dated to the Twelfth Dynasty and is set at the death of Amenemhat I, it's possible that The Tale of Sinuhe was somewhat inspired by the story of Joseph.[179] The tale is a comment on the difference between life in Egypt and life in Palestine, with the main character, ultimately, preferring Egypt. At the end, Sinuhe returns to the royal court and is "reborn as a true Egyptian."[180] Is it possible that Sinuhe was originally not a true Egyptian but was a foreigner who rose to unprecedented status as a nobleman? Is it possible that Hatshepsut was so intrigued by this story that she purposely called Moses, her foreign baby, "Senenmut" because it sounded somewhat like Sinuhe? Is it even possible that Neferure's name was intended to somewhat echo Nefru? If so, it is yet another example of the weighty influence that literature played in Hatshepsut's view of life.

Hatshepsut truly did believe that she was pre-destined to rule Egypt.[181] She was not fabricating truth on the walls of Djeser-Djeseru; she was defending truth, as she understood it. To her way of thinking, she had been created and given life by a deity. By the process of elimination, she was the only member of the royal bloodline who was available to rule Egypt. Therefore, it must have been divine will for her to become pharaoh. If she was the daughter of the pharaoh in Exodus chapter 2, divine will had also provided a son for her. Under this rationale, Thutmose I agreed; he too felt that Hatshepsut was the best available choice to rule Egypt, and by sanctioning her adoption of Moses, he believed that he had secured the throne within the bloodline of Ahmose, in the hands of a strong leader. Djeser-Djeseru eloquently depicts Hatshepsut's version of the truth.

However, even offering a viable scenario under which she could rightfully serve as pharaoh was not all of Hatshepsut's agenda. At her *Speos Artemidos*, Hatshepsut wrote:

> I have done these things by the device of my heart. I have never slumbered as one forgetful, but
> have made strong what was decayed. I have raised up what was dismembered, even from the first
> time when the Asiatics [the Hyksos] were in Avaris of the North Land, with roving hordes in the
> midst of them overthrowing what had been made; they ruled without Re . . . I have banished the
> abominations of the gods, and the earth has removed their footprints.[182]

This is a curious statement. Booth believes it to be pure propaganda since "the restoring of monuments was undertaken by the Theban Seventeenth Dynasty."[183] Indeed, Ahmose had set about restoring the temples and buildings that had been destroyed by the Hyksos. So, what exactly was Hatshepsut claiming to have restored? What had decayed that she had made strong? In the Speos Artemidos, Hatshepsut depicts herself as Pakhet, the lioness-headed deity. Pakhet is also known as "the snatcher."[184] Could this scene be an allusion to Hatshepsut snatching Moses from the Nile and restoring him? Ray notes, "the reference to 'dismemberment' here recalls the death of Osiris, and by implication the miraculous re-animation which reversed this."[185] Like Osiris, Moses was floating "dead" in the Nile until life was given back to him by a princess acting as his Isis.

Yet, perhaps the message on the walls of the Speos Artemidos was intended to be greater still. Hatshepsut was a diligent student of history, especially of the Middle Kingdom. She loved the literature of that time. She fashioned her governmental style after the pharaohs of that period, further consolidating herself with the Middle Kingdom by depicting herself holding hands with Neferhotep I.[186] In keeping with the theory of this book, when the Hebrews first came to Egypt at the rise of the Middle Kingdom, they were not (as Hatshepsut wrote on her obelisk) "roving in hordes" or "overthrowing what had been made"; the Hebrews were not the "vile Hyksos" at that time. They were merely the family of Joseph, the vizier who had done *tremendous* good for Egypt. The memory of the good that had preserved Egypt through a terrible drought and the history of how Egypt came to be united had decayed. Her ancestor, Ahmose, had restored the body of Egypt that had been "dismembered," divided in the days of the Hyksos. Now, Hatshepsut desired to "raise up" that body and return Egypt to the strength of prosperity and good relations with her fellow man.

If Hatshepsut was the daughter of the pharaoh from Exodus 2, Hatshepsut's heart led her to spare the life of a Hebrew child. Either through her association with Jochabed/Hatnofer or through her own extensive study of the Middle Kingdom, Hatshepsut may well have learned about the story of Joseph. It was Hatshepsut's desire to remove the footprints of the Hyksos, their chaos, and their abominable worship.[187] Yet perhaps, through her son, Moses/Senenmut, it was Hatshepsut's agenda to restore a reputation of Hebrew goodness in Egyptian eyes. The Hyksos had been defeated. Hatshepsut now proposed moving beyond a cessation of hostilities and taking the final, greatest step: defeating hatred, the mutual enemy. "Hatshepsut preferred acts of peace to acts of war."[188] Could it be that she was laying the groundwork for what she hoped would be an eventual peace with the Hebrews? In one of the inscriptions on the statue of Senenmut, now in Berlin, it says Senenmut, "entered upon the wonderful plans of the Mistress of the Two Lands."[189] Beyond her plans to rule, could it have been part of Hatshepsut's "wonderful plans" to restore Egyptian appreciation for a Hebrew right hand man like Joseph had been, and to help Egypt (and the former Hyksos) rise above cruelty?

Hatshepsut is well remembered for the glorious obelisks she erected to honor Thutmose I. Topped with electrum, they were intended to beam in the first golden rays of the breaking dawn. Obelisks, in Egyptian iconography, were representations of the first light of creation. In Hatshepsut's obelisks at Karnak, she was announcing the creation of a new day in Egypt, "to return to the perfection of the world at its origins."[190] She and her father together had ushered its dawning. Was this new day a day of ethnic tolerance toward Hebrews, a day of seeing beyond the Hyksos, a day of new possibilities? In her birth scene in Djeser-Djeseru, Hatshepsut envisioned herself as one who would "reign benevolently over the whole earth."[191] Could it be that Hatshepsut's vision included a day of looking beyond prejudice and seeing truth? She was the first monarch since Ahmose to even mention the detested Hyksos.[192] Yet, the truth is that not all foreigners, not all Hyksos, were bad. The truth is that the world was full of foreigners who were potential friends of Egypt, not only enemies. Hatshepsut sought to forge new alliances for Egypt.[193] Not all goods had to be exploited through conquest, tribute, subjugation, misery, and death. Plentiful, wonderful goods could be obtained peacefully through mutually beneficial trade. In fact, her expedition to Punt was only the culmination of several successful trade expeditions, including trips to Phoenicia, Sinai, and unknown lands. John Ray observes that in Hatshepsut's temple at Deir el-Bahari, Senenmut appears almost as the "master of ceremonies."[194] Senenmut was central to Hatshepsut's idealistic conceptions. If Senenmut was Moses, he was a foreigner, he was a Hyksos/Hebrew, but Senenmut/Moses was good. Hatshepsut's love for him was illuminating.

It has *never* been true that *all* Hebrews believed and behaved like the Hyksos. Not *all* Hyksos worshiped Seth; certainly there were always those Hebrews who maintained a belief in the God of Abraham and Joseph. For example, Shiphrah and Puah, the Hebrew midwives, believed in God, and they were blessed by him for their "fear" and for their bravery (Exodus 1.15-21). Amram and Jochabed demonstrated their faith in God as well (Hebrews 11.23). It's hard to imagine the agony of Jochabed. It's hard to imagine being in such an impossible position. Had she failed to obey the order of Pharaoh, her whole family could have been executed; yet placing Moses on the Nile's edge in a tiny reed vessel was almost certainly killing her precious baby boy. However, God blessed her tiny glimmer of faith in his providence, and through Jochabed's desperate hope, God (not Hatshepsut) brought about the rescue of countless people (Matthew 17.20).

If Amram and Jochabed believed in God, and if Moses was Senenmut, why is he depicted worshiping Egyptian gods in Djeser-Djeseru? Based on the evidence in Tomb 71, it is obvious that Senenmut had some exposure to his family. However, the depth of faith that Moses' parents possessed, professed, and/or the scope of their knowledge about God is unknown (Romans 10.17). It is also unknown how much opportunity Moses' parents would have had to teach him about God, although in the naming of Eliezer, Moses seems to have tied his father to whatever rudimentary familiarity with God he held before God spoke to him (Exodus 4.20). However, it's possible that some of Moses' faith could be attributed to his father-in-law since Reuel/Jethro is called "the priest of Midian," he "rejoiced for all the goodness which the Lord had done to Israel," he blessed God and offered sacrifices to him (Exodus 18.1-12). The scripture records Reuel counseling Moses (Exodus 18.17-24). Could it be that Reuel was a priest of Midian in the order of Melchizedek? He seemed to hold some priestly authority that may have superseded Aaron (Exodus 18.12). Reuel obviously had some knowledge of the God of the Bible which should not be too surprising since the name, Reuel, indicates that he may have been a descendent of Esau, Jacob's twin brother. Jethro may not have been a name, but a title. The fact that Reuel was a Midianite, also ties him, distantly, to Abraham; Midian and Edom, the land of Esau, were close neighbors (Genesis 36.10, 17; Genesis 25.1-2). However, it's possible that Reuel, if he was also known by an alternative name, Hobab, may be even more specifically identified as a Kenite, a ascetic, nomadic people associated with the Rechabites (I Chronicles 2.55). Nevertheless, regardless of the influence of Reuel, Moses' early knowledge of God was still obviously lacking because, when he encountered the burning bush in the wilderness of Midian, near Horeb; he did not seem to know much at all about God (Exodus 3.1).[195] He clearly understood that he was in the presence of deity, and he was afraid; he seemed to be somewhat familiar with the names of his forefathers: Abraham, Isaac, and Jacob, and had some recollection that they worshiped a God. However, he could not identify that God and had to ask for his name:

> He said, I am the God of thy father, the God of Abraham, the God of Isaac, and the God of Jacob. And Moses hid his face; for he was afraid to look upon God. And the Lord said, I have surely seen the affliction of my people which are in Egypt, and have heard their cry by reason of their taskmasters; for I know their sorrows; . . . Now therefore, behold, the cry of the children of Israel is come unto me: and I have also seen the oppression wherewith the Egyptians oppress them. Come now therefore, and I will send thee unto Pharaoh, that thou mayest bring forth my people the children of Israel out of Egypt. . . . And Moses said unto God, Behold, when I come unto the children of Israel, and shall say unto them, The God of your fathers hath sent me unto you; and they shall say to me, What is his name? What shall I say unto them? And God said unto Moses, I AM THAT I AM: and he said, Thus shalt thou say unto the children of Israel, I AM hath sent me unto you. (Exodus 3.6-14)

From this passage, it also seems clear that Moses did not expect his fellow Hebrews to have a common knowledge of this God either, although they also may have retained some memory of their forefathers, their history, and an associated God. However, based on the behavior of these ancient Hebrews little more than three months after escaping Egypt, their faith tended to be more easily pagan (Exodus 19.1).

> And when the people saw that Moses delayed to come down out of the mount, the people gathered themselves together unto Aaron, and said unto him, Up, make us gods, which shall go before us; for as for this Moses, the man that brought us up out of the land of Egypt, we wot not what is become of him. And Aaron said unto them, Break off the golden earrings, which are in the ears of your wives, of your sons, and of your daughters, and bring them unto me. And all the people brake off the golden earrings which were in their ears, and brought them unto Aaron. And he received them at their hand, and fashioned it with a graving tool, after he had made it a molten calf: and they said, These be thy gods, O Israel, which brought thee up out of the land of Egypt. And when Aaron saw it, he built an altar before it; and Aaron made proclamation, and said, Tomorrow is a feast to the Lord. And they rose up early on the morrow, and offered burnt offerings, and brought peace offerings; and the people sat down to eat and to drink, and rose up to play. And the Lord said unto Moses, Go, get thee down; for thy people, which thou broughtest out of the land of Egypt, have corrupted themselves. (Exodus 32.1-7)

In the statement, "These be thy gods," it is obvious that the Hebrews, at this point in their history, were superstitious about the power and existence of multiple gods. In fact, their belief system seems to be consistent with most polytheists of the ancient world. Though ancient cultures were most loyal to the gods that were perceived to be associated with their own nation, region, or town, they feared gods of other places too. At least, they believed that deities existed beyond their given pantheon and that those deities had supernatural powers. Going into battle, however, ancient people hoped their own gods would win the day, would make their army victorious and would prove to be more powerful than the gods of their opponents (II Chronicles 32.13-14).

The worship that is described in the episode of the golden calf is very like the idolatrous worship practices in ancient Egypt, where common people were not involved in the day to day services that took place within the temples.[196] However, on feast days, people from all walks of life engaged in mass worship. Based on the description of the Hebrew worship of the golden calf, "the people sat down to eat and to drink, and rose up to play," it would seem that they were probably emulating Egyptian religious feasts associated with multiple hedonistic overindulgences.[197] Certainly more than enjoying quail, manna, and water is implied (Exodus 16.13-15; 15.24-25, 27). In fact, it is possible that they were enacting a specific annual festival that was taking place back in Egypt at that same time. It took the Hebrews three months to reach Sinai, and Moses had been on the mountain for forty days (Exodus 19.1; 24.18). Depending on when the Passover had occurred that year (Passover can fall anywhere from late March to early May on a western calendar), it's possible that this event with the golden calf coincided with the Festival of Osiris. During that festival, which usually accompanied the receding of the Nile inundation, Osiris was represented by a golden ox.[198] Osiris was associated with agriculture, fertility, and rebirth; he was "The Lord of the Land." The fall of the Nile began the planting season in Egypt. Since the Hebrews complained about missing foods that were grown back in Egypt and longed to return to Egypt, it's feasible that they were appealing to "the lord" Osiris to provide for them and take them back to Egypt and the crops that he grew there. They could also have been invoking Ra; he too was depicted as a young bull. Perhaps these Hebrews were appealing to both Ra and Osiris and many other Egyptian gods; after all, Aaron credited "these gods" with bringing them out of Egypt (Exodus 16.3; 11.5; Exodus 32.4).[199]

Nevertheless, it would seem that in spite of all their complaining about hunger and thirst (without the aid of Osiris or Ra), the escaping Hebrews had food enough to make a feast and probably had the means of making beer (Exodus 15.24; 16.3; 17.3). They left Egypt with "flocks and herds and much cattle" (Exodus 12.38). They were warned before Moses ascended Mt. Sinai not to let their animals break through the barrier around the consecrated mountain, so they still had flocks and herds there with them (Exodus 19.13; 34.3). It is likely that some of these animals were sacrificed to make a feast in honor of the golden calf (Exodus 32.5-6).

Bread and beer were key components in the Egyptian diet. In fact, Egyptians were sometimes called "eaters of bread."[200] Beer was a staple and was regularly used in religious festivals; it was believed to "pacify and humor" of the gods.[201] Inscriptions from an early Eighteenth Dynasty tomb lend insight into the endemic abuse of alcohol in Egyptian religious feasts; "drinking into intoxication and celebrating a festive day" were believed to be means of communicating with the gods.[202] Egyptians usually made beer by fermenting barley bread; beer was the main beverage in their diet.[203] Even children drank beer; in fact, it was considered a mother's responsibility to provide beer and bread for her children.[204]

It is also important to note that Aaron acted as a priest between the people and the golden calf. This event occurred before the people had heard the particulars of the religion prescribed in the law that Moses was in the process of receiving on Mount Sinai (Exodus 28.1-3; Deuteronomy 13.9-12). Therefore, as far as we know, Aaron had not yet been identified as a priest—much less, as the high priest of God, although there were those who were considered to be "priests" among the Hebrews before Moses ascended the mountain (3.3; Exodus 19.22). Since there was no Law of Moses at that point, it is likely that these Hebrews, identified as "priests," were priests of Egyptian gods. Compellingly similar to the way that Moses' brother, Aaron, was seen as a "priest" by the people at Sinai; in Tomb 353, Senenmut's brother, Amenemhat, is depicted with Hatshepsut acting as a priest in Senenmut's funerary rites.[205]

There seems to be no real consensus on the significance of the golden calf. It is clear, however, that the Hebrews and Aaron knew that making such an image was contrary to the will of the true God who had brought them out of Egypt. God had spoken directly to the people and told them the Ten Commandments, the second of which clearly says, "Thou shalt not make unto thee any graven image, or any likeness of any thing that is in heaven above, or that is in the earth beneath, or that is in the water under the earth." Certainly the golden calf was a graven image in the likeness of something on earth. They also knew that it was against the will of God to worship a graven image because the third commandment says, "Thou shalt not bow down thyself to them (graven images), nor serve them: for I the Lord thy God am a jealous God . . . ." It is hard to believe that the Hebrews had forgotten what God told them because hearing God speak made such an impression they had trembled with fear and begged Moses, "Speak thou with us, and we will hear: but let not God speak with us [again], lest we die" (Exodus 20.1-19). It seems clear that in worshiping the golden calf, the Hebrews were seeking the leadership of some other gods and that they were willing to credit those gods with having delivered them from slavery in Egypt. The book of Acts seems to imply that there may have been a connection between the worship of the golden calf and celestial bodies, reminiscent of Egyptian festivals and of the bull-headed constellation on the celestial ceiling of Senenmut's Tomb 353:[206]

> And they made a calf in those days, and offered sacrifice unto the idol, and rejoiced in the works
> of their own hands. Then God turned, and gave them up to worship the host of heaven; as it is
> written in the book of the prophets, O ye house of Israel, have ye offered to me slain beasts and
> sacrifices by the space of forty years in the wilderness? (Acts 7.41-42)

In the early 1990s a small "golden" calf was discovered in the ruins of Askelon, an ancient city of the Philistines in southern Palestine, less than thirty miles northwest of Sharuhen.[207] The thin, elongated figure was housed inside a pottery shrine that was shaped like an egg.[208] Eggs have long been an almost universal symbol of fertility, and since Baal was a fertility god that originated in Mesopotamia, it is not hard to imagine a connection between the golden calf and Baal.[209] In Canaanite culture, Baal was equivalent to the fertility god Osiris.[210] The calf figurine in Askelon was dated, by broken pottery around it, to the Middle Bronze Age, a time that coincides with the early Hebrew settlement in Avaris.[211] The Hyksos are known to have associated Baal and Seth and Anat; they were also known to have had a close association with the region of Canaan where the calf figurine was discovered.[212]

Similarly, Archaeologist Amihai Mazar found a bronze bull in 1981 in the ruins of a "high-place," a worship site in the tribal territory of Manasseh. It is very like another bronze bull found at Hazor by Yigael Yigael. "The principal epithet of El, the chief male deity of the Canaanite pantheon in pre-Israelite times, was 'Bull.' . . . Thus the Manasseh shrine or sanctuary . . . was probably associated not with Yahweh but with . . . the old Canaanite deity El."[213]

Therefore, it is perhaps possible to further connect the image of a golden calf with the Canaanite pantheon and with Baal worship. Interestingly, Hazor is about the same distance from the ancient city of Dan as Bethel is from the region of Manasseh. When the kingdom of Israel divided after the death of Solomon, Jeroboam, who was king of the northern tribes, fashioned two golden calves and established both Dan and Bethel as high places for the worship of those idols. Furthermore, Jeroboam said something very reminiscent of Aaron: "behold thy gods, O Israel, which brought thee up out of the land of Egypt" (I Kings 12.25-28). Notice that both Aaron and Jeroboam referred to a golden calf as plural deities. Furthermore, Jeroboam had just returned to Israel from exile in Egypt, which again causes one to wonder if there is not a significant connection between the worship of a golden calf and Egyptian worship, perhaps even Seth worship (I Kings 12.2). Adding further indication that at the time of Jeroboam the golden calves may have been more associated with Egypt than with Canaan is the introduction of Jezebel several years past Jeroboam: "And it came to pass, as if it had been a light thing for him to walk in the sins of Jeroboam the son of Nebat, that he took to wife Jezebel the daughter of Ethbaal king of the Zidonians, and went and served Baal, and worshipped him" (I Kings 16.31). This verse certainly seems to make a distinction between the worship of Jeroboam's golden calves and the worship of Baal, at least as it was introduced by Jezebel, a Phoenician. So does II Kings 10.28-29. Nevertheless, a definite association between the image of a calf and Baal is secured in Hosea 13. In a prophecy against the northern tribes, verses 1 and 2 make a strong connection between Baal and calf worship.

> When Ephraim spake trembling, he exalted himself in Israel; but when he offended in Baal, he
> died. And now they sin more and more, and have made them molten images of their silver, and
> idols according to their own understanding, all of it the work of the craftsmen: they say of them,
> Let the men that sacrifice kiss the calves. (Hosea 13.1-2)

In Egyptian mythology, Seth was sometimes represented as a donkey. Seth in Greco-Egyptian texts was closely associated with the god Iao—so named to sound like the Egyptian word for donkey.[214] However, since the thin, elongated image that represented the Hyksos' Seth was a nondescript animal, perhaps Aaron's golden calf could still be perceived as a throwback to Seth worship.[2155] After all, "calf" is a nondescript word. It has long been assumed that the golden calf was bovine; certainly the calf found at Askelon is a bovine, bull calf. Of course, the *Aphis* bulls of Egypt were bovine, and a golden statue of an *Aphis* bull found in the *Serapaeum* is now displayed at the Louvre.[216] Bovines were central to Minoan worship, and Baal was at times represented by a bull.[217] However, "calf" could refer to the young of many different species. From the Hebrew word "*êgel*," the only further insight is that Aaron's graven image was a male calf. To associate Aaron's calf with Seth makes sense in other ways as well. Seth was the god of the desert.[218] The Hebrews were appealing to a god while they were in the desert wilderness of Sinai (Exodus 19.2). The desert was credited, in Egypt, as the source for gold. Aaron's calf was made of gold. Seth was also the god of chaos, which Egyptians believed had to be appeased before order could be restored. The displaced Hebrews' world was turned upside down; they were seeking direction, order, and purpose. Stephen says that the Hebrews "in their hearts turned back again into Egypt" (Acts 7.39). It makes sense that, from a Hyksos perspective, the Hebrews would have turned back to Seth, Baal, and Anat ("These be thy gods, O Israel") that they credited with their power and success of the past (Exodus 32.4). However, this assumption must remain a speculation; and since Amun-Ra was the premier deity of the New Kingdom, Ra and Osiris remain as likely gods to which Aaron could have been referring.

Also left to speculation is the answer to the question, what happened to Senenmut? Senenmut seems to have just disappeared from Egyptian history. No one knows where Senenmut is buried. Two great tombs for Senenmut have been discovered; and while it seems fairly certain that it was his intention to be buried in the stone sarcophagus found in Tomb 71, there is no indication that he was ever buried in either Tomb 71 or in Tomb 353.[219] Some have speculated that a third tomb of Senenmut exists but remains uncovered. Yet, in another comparison, no one knows where Moses is buried either (Deuteronomy 34.6).

Nevertheless, there are those who believe that Senenmut's "arrogance" finally caused him to fall out of favor with the crown. Yet, there are others those who believe that Senenmut simply died. Regardless, there is no mention of Senenmut after Year 20 of Hatshepsut's reign. If Senenmut was Moses, however, a new scenario develops. In Year 20, Senenmut/Moses would have been around 40 years old. When Moses was approaching 40, major changes occurred in his life (Acts 7.23-29). In fact, it is likely that, due to the condition of Hatshepsut—for months, major changes were in the works for Senenmut/Moses, probably beginning around the time of Year 20 of Hatshepsut's reign.

According to recent medical examinations of the mummy of Hatshepsut, it has been determined that she suffered from several pernicious degenerative and painful ailments. She had cancer; a malignant abdominal tumor was causing her pelvis to deteriorate. In fact, Hatshepsut had serious bone disease in both hips. She probably was diabetic; she had osteoporosis and arthritis, and she suffered with severe dental problems.

In fact, the most likely cause of Hatshepsut's death was an abscessed molar. The diseased tooth broke; half remained in her jaw and half she swallowed. This part of the broken molar was recovered from a canopic jar labeled as containing her preserved viscera and was used to positively identify Hatshepsut's mummy. The abscessed tooth likely broke during what must have been an agonizing attempted extraction. The resulting sepsis was fatal. However, little evidence exists to confirm that such invasive dental procedures were applied or even existed in those days. [220] Though Herodotus explicitly identified medial specialists, including those doctors who dealt with teeth, it is difficult to determine if the practice of dentistry in ancient Egypt extended beyond magic spells and application of medicines. [221] If an extraction was attempted, one wonders why the broken half of Hatshepsut's molar would have been left in the socket?

At any rate, the last several months and perhaps the last couple of years of Hatshepsut's life would have been extremely uncomfortable; she was likely bedridden. The abscessed tooth would have caused her face to be so swollen, she would have been unable to open and close her mouth or to eat. .[222]

Hatshepsut died in Year 22, it's not hard to imagine that, since Neferure had likely been dead for years, her faithful Senenmut saw to her constant care. Since Hatshepsut was not well enough to commission new statues or to build new projects in Senenmut's name, and since Senenmut had probably never cared about such recognition in the first place, it isn't hard to understand why there is no mention of

Thutmose III

Senenmut after about Year 20. Under this scenario, Senenmut did not die; he did not fall out of favor with the queen, but after Year 20, he faded into relative obscurity, donning the humble role of devoted caregiver to the dying queen.[223] Furthermore, after Neferure and Hatshepsut died, there was no longer any hope for continuing the Ahmose bloodline and there certainly would have been little use or support for an adopted prince who was a foreigner. The scriptures say:

> . . . when Moses was grown, . . . he spied an Egyptian smiting an Hebrew, one of his brethren. And . . . he slew the Egyptian, and hid him in the sand. . . the second day, behold, two men of the Hebrews strove together: and he said . . . to him that did the wrong, Wherefore smitest thou thy fellow? And he said, Who made thee a prince and a judge over us? Intendest thou to kill me, as thou killedst the Egyptian? And Moses feared, and said, Surely this thing is known. Now when Pharaoh heard this thing, he sought to slay Moses. But Moses fled from the face of Pharaoh, and dwelt in the land of Midian: and he sat down by a well. (Exodus 2.11-15)

"All of the evidence points to Hatshepsut as the most likely candidate for Moses' stepmother; " and after her death, Moses/Senenmut could have been perceived by Thutmose III as a threat to his crown.[224] However, becoming pharaoh obviously was not an aspiration of Moses (Hebrews 11.24-25). Seeking a place to belong, it makes sense that Moses would have looked into the life of a Hebrew. Then, overcome with grief and anger, Moses murdered an Egyptian, only to find that he was not welcomed by the Hebrews either. Therefore, Moses fled to the land of Midian, and a male pharaoh sought to kill him. Both Moses and Senenmut disappeared.

Based upon the many glowing approvals Hatshepsut left concerning Senenmut, it seems that it would have been nearly impossible for anyone to harm him while Hatshepsut was living; but after she (and Neferure) died, who would have been left to defend Senenmut? Likewise, Moses, from infancy, was sheltered by the daughter of the pharaoh and probably would have been protected by her for as long as she lived. However, if Moses was Senenmut, then, following the death of Hatshepsut, Moses killing an Egyptian official in a crime of passion was just the opportunity Thutmose III had long awaited! "He sought to slay Moses" (Exodus 2.15). Moses fled. Isn't it likely that the incensed pharaoh would pursue him? He held a personal grudge against Moses. Moses—as the adopted son of pharaoh's daughter—held, perhaps, some perceived claim to the throne. Moses was now a murderous fugitive who had insulted the exceedingly generous hospitality of Egyptian royalty (Hebrews 11.24-25).[225]

If an enraged pharaoh were to have launched a pursuit to find Moses, a runaway Hebrew, where is he most likely to have looked? Upon the death of Sinuhe's pharaoh, the court's darling fled to Palestine (the land of the Asiatics), perhaps out of fear of being charged with murder.[226] Sinuhe said, "My heart was distraught . . . my arms spread out in dismay, my senses were disturbed and I trembled all over. I removed myself by leaps and bounds to seek a hiding place for myself."[227] Palestine seems to have been a popular hiding place for Hebrews.[228] Moses' ancestors came from Palestine. The Hyksos fled to Palestine; their allies had been stationed in Sharuhen, a city in Palestine. Moses was a Hebrew and, therefore, a "vile Asiatic." It was most logical for Thutmose III to assume that Moses/Senenmut would have sought refuge in Palestine, the land of the Asiatics. In fact, it is probable that Moses was reminded very much of Sinuhe after he killed the Egyptian taskmaster and (like his mother and his adopted mother) was possibly tempted to reenact folklore. Why Moses fled to Midian is anybody's guess.

Thutmose III, however, didn't go to Midian. Less than a hundred days after the death of Hatshepsut (perhaps less than 90 days, barely allowing time for decency in observing the prescribed days of mourning for a former monarch), the infuriated pharaoh led his army on a targeted military campaign into Palestine supposedly "to defeat a coalition of Syrio-Palestinian city states who were threatening Egyptian hegemony in the region."[229] However, according to Thutmose III's own stated purpose, the new pharaoh was looking for some*one*—his nemesis, "that wretched foe."[230] Thutmose III's meant "to overthrow that vile enemy [the prince of Kadesh] and to extend the boundaries of Egypt in accordance with the command of his father Amen-Re."[231]

Perhaps there really was a prince of Kadesh, who had rallied a weak coalition of Palestinians who actually believed (at least for a few hours) that they could successfully challenge the authority of Thutmose III's new administration and take a stand against Egyptian domination; but perhaps Thutmose III also strongly suspected an alternate identity for this "prince of Kadesh." Perhaps he was actually in pursuit of someone of Hyksos heritage. Perhaps Thutmose III was hunting for the fugitive, Senenmut/Moses. For his entire life, Thutmose III had witnessed and had stood in the overwhelming shadow of the charming Senenmut, perhaps part of him believed that Senenmut *was* capable of nearly super-human accomplishments. It wasn't outside the realm of possibility to assume that Senenmut/Moses, a charismatic, highly educated, Egyptianized Asiatic with vast internal knowledge of the workings of Egyptian government and its military, and with an alleged claim to the throne of Hatshepsut, might have been able to amass an army of former Hyksos allies and other enemies of Egypt in order to pose a credible threat to Thutmose III and to the integrity of Egypt. As further defense of Thutmose III's aggression, it is written on the walls of Amun's temple at Karnak,

> Regnal Year 22 . . . on the first campaign of force, [in order to drive off] in bravery, [in force, in strength, and in righteousness, those who were violating] Egypt's borders. For though it had been [many] years [since the Hyksos were] pillaging, every man [working] at their direction [in the towns of the Delta], yet in the time of others there had come to be troops . . . in the town of Sharuhen, and from Yaradja to the ends of the earth had started to defy His incarnation.[232]

Though Thutmose III clearly associated this alleged uprising with revivification of the Hyksos, he didn't find the object of his animosity (the prince of Kadesh) in Sharuhen, the former Hyksos capital in Canaan. So, he pressed on, finally engaging some pathetic Asiatic forces in battle at Megiddo, in "the first coherent account of a decisive battle" recorded in Egypt.[233] Yet, Thutmose III's stated agenda seems to have been more personal. He was looking for someone in particular; someone who he thought had "entered into Megiddo." Thutmose III was hoping to find "that wretched foe," "the chief of Kadesh," the individual of whom he said, "*he* is there at this moment."[234] Perhaps he not only wanted to find that wretched foe and destroy him once and for all,

Thutmose III wanted to make sure that his final, glorious victory over Senenmut/Moses was well documented. As it stands in history, a victory was recorded, but perhaps not the victory Thutmose III had hoped.

Kadesh was a Syrian city on the Orantes River.[235] It was over a hundred miles from Sharuhen, yet Thutmose III was under the impression that an incredibly charismatic leader from Kadesh had managed to rally together an army from all the Asiatic lands that were subject to Egypt.[236] Which Kadesh? There was another Kadesh. The home of the Amalekites and Edomites was also called Kadesh; that Kadesh was a barren wilderness area in the Negev that bordered Sharuhen on the southeast (Numbers 20.14-22).[237] Perhaps Thutmose III initially believed that the darling favorite of Hatshepsut, Senenmut/Moses was reduced to being the "prince" of a wasteland; he was now "the chief of Kadesh," referring to the Negev neighborhood of Sharuhen. It may have been intelligence obtained in Sharuhen, that convinced the pharaoh that his "wretched foe" was not in the Negev at all and, therefore, caused Thutmose III to press northward. Nevertheless, on the twenty-first day of the ninth month of Year 22, Thutmose III's army descended on the battlefield at Megiddo. The enemy's "army" that was "amassed" there fled in fear to the nearby town of Megiddo. The famous "battle" didn't even last a day. Thutmose III surrounded the town of Megiddo and waited until the residents had no choice but to surrender. The stubborn siege took the better part of a year, finally ending in December.[238]

The Asiatic "army" that Thutmose III encountered at Megiddo certainly does not sound like a well-organized coalition truly prepared for a fight. Generally, people who have been planning an insurrection against a powerful foe have accumulated weapons, troops, and battle plans. The only strategy of that dreaded foe from Kadesh seems to have been retreat. It is also significant to note that though a tent that supposedly belonged to the "wretched foe," "a beautiful [suit] of bronze armor belonging to that foe," and various other belongings "of that foe" were confiscated, the prince of Kadesh was not reported as having been captured or killed.[239] In fact, over the next twenty years, the "Napoleon of Egypt," Thutmose III embarked on nearly annual campaigns in pursuit of his obsession—that foe from Kadesh.[240] Finally, after seventeen long campaigns, Thutmose III achieved at least one of his long-term objectives; he captured Kadesh on the Orantes.[241] It happened in Year 42. However, there is no mention of Thutmose III finding, capturing, or killing the prince of Kadesh on the Orantes, who was most likely a man named Durusha.[242] In fact, if Durusha was the "real" prince of Kadesh, he obviously was not the person Thutmose III was hunting because, upon capture, Thutmose III let Durusha go![243]

One can only imagine Thutmose III's rage and disappointment when he realized he had been chasing the wrong man for twenty years! The frustrated pharaoh returned to Egypt in that same year, Year 42, and began a new campaign—erasing the memory of his nemesis, Senenmut, along with Hatshepsut and Neferure who had supported Senenmut.[244] He had hoped to humiliate and to kill Senenmut/Moses, but he settled for killing his memory instead. It was a daunting task since Hatshepsut had sought to memorialize Senenmut "in every kind of precious stone" and to record his memory on every wall "in every temple of Upper and Lower Egypt."[245]

Clearly, part of Thutmose III's intention was to rewrite history. On the north portico of Djeser-Djeseru, Thutmose III re-carved the inscription of Thutmose I's endorsement to suggest that he, not Hatshepsut, was chosen to rule as pharaoh by his late grandfather—even though it is highly unlikely that Thutmose I was even alive when Thutmose III was born.[246] Throughout Egypt, images of Hatshepsut as king were "destroyed, defaced, or replaced with images of her father or husband."[247] Yet, in some instances, images of Senenmut were destroyed, while adjacent images of Hatshepsut were left untouched.[248] This leads one to wonder if Senenmut, not Hatshepsut, was the main target of Thutmose III's intended *damnatio memoriae*. Furthermore, perhaps recalling the ending of Sinuhe's tale, if indeed Senenmut/Moses was still out there somewhere, and were to return to Egypt as an old man someday, Thutmose III wanted to make sure that Senenmut/Moses saw what he had done to the legacy of Hatshepsut's golden boy. He did not want to leave any existing platform for Senenmut to re-establish himself and/or lay hold to any claim to the throne. Thutmose III wanted no confusion to undermine the secure succession of his son. If Thutmose III held any superstitious notion about The Story of Sinuhe coming true, it certainly seems that he hoped to make Senenmut's story end differently. Pharaoh had no intentions of laying out "the welcome mat" for Moses/Senenmut like the pharaoh of Sinuhe had done.[249]

Most of the damage to Hatshepsut's monuments occurred in Thebes; and in Karnak, Thutmose III completely dismantled Hatshepsut's Red Chapel and walled in her beautiful obelisks.[250] Destruction of images and monuments was not limited to the efforts of Thutmose III. At several times in Egyptian history, various monuments were attacked; and it is possible that "waves" of attackers including some during the Amarna period and even from the Christian era could be responsible for damage done to the memory of Hatshepsut's reign.[251]

Several unsavory motives have been ascribed to the behavior Thutmose III exhibited toward the memory of the last pharaoh from the Ahmose bloodline, from jealousy to outright hatred of his stepmother. Recent theories, however, tend to be more pragmatic, suggesting that the real purpose behind Thutmose III's aggression was simply to secure an undisputed line of ascension for his son, Amenhotep II. In order to firmly establish the Thutmose pharaonic succession, the Ahmose line had to be sufficiently smudged.[252] Yet, who posed a threat to the ascension of Thutmose III's son? No one—unless Senenmut/Moses—was still alive.

Perhaps Thutmose III was jealous—not, necessarily, of Hatshepsut but of the special attention Hatshepsut gave to Senenmut. Thutmose III seems to have had an elevated disdain of favoritism. In the inscription to his vizier, Rekhmire, Thutmose III went out of his way to condemn the practice. "It is an abomination of the god to show partiality. This is the teaching: thou shalt . . . regard him who is known to thee like him who is unknown to thee, and him who is near to—like him who is far."[253] Though this is an instruction intended to make Rekhmire a better judge, it is nevertheless an insight into the thinking of Thutmose III. Perhaps his sensitivity to partiality is a result of firsthand experience. If Senenmut/Moses was the adopted son of Hatshepsut, it must have been difficult for Thutmose III to always stand in distant recognition to her favorite. Even in her Punt reliefs, for example, Senenmut is the central figure while Thutmose III is barely even recognized.[254] "There is no doubt that from the age of about twelve to thirty-two he [Thutmose III] was kept in the background and deeply resented the fact."[255] Likely, 10-15 years older than Thutmose III, Senenmut was already glorified in military victory before the young co-regent had barely ventured beyond the nursery. If Senenmut was Moses, there was almost certainly an added level of contempt for an adopted Hebrew/Hyksos slave being favored by Hatshepsut above Thutmose III, the actual son of Thutmose II. One can only imagine how it must have felt to be dwarfed by countless monuments extolling the excellences of Senenmut, "the greatest of the great in the whole land."[256] Favoritism is a terrible injustice to children in any family, and as demonstrated by the life of Joseph, parental favoritism can breed murderous hatred of the favorite in the heart of his/her siblings (Genesis 37). Perhaps Thutmose III loathed Senenmut and was eager for any excuse to eliminate him, his monuments, and his memory.

However, monuments of Senenmut even reached beyond the borders of the Two Lands. It is a remarkable happenstance that a stela dedicated to Neferure and Senenmut was erected by Hatshepsut in an iconic place readily associated with Moses—Mount Sinai. The monument from Serabit el-Khadim shows Neferure, adorned in the vulture headdress of a queen as she presents an offering to Hathor. Senenmut is seen as her fan-bearing attendant.[257] Though no one knows for certain which summit in the complex of peaks associated with the mountain range of Sinai is the one where the Law was given to Moses, Serabit el-Khadim is a possibility.[258] Under the theory that Senenmut *was* Moses, one can only imagine the strange mixture of strong emotions that he may have experienced when confronted with this memorial from his distant past.

It is remarkable to consider the tremendous prosperity that was realized in Egypt during the reigns of the two pharaohs memorialized at Deir el-Bahari: Mentuhotep II and Hatshepsut. Perhaps it is not coincidental that God had promised Abraham in Genesis 12.3, "I will bless them that bless thee." Good to his word; God remembered Abraham through his descendants, especially through those who, by their faithful behavior, honored the memory of their illustrious progenitor. Abraham was blessed when his legacy was upheld by the faith that his great grandson, Joseph, placed in God; and Joseph was blessed as a result. Abraham was blessed when a pharaoh recognized Joseph's integrity and Moses' value. In other words, when Joseph and Moses were elevated, it was as if Abraham, himself, was made great the land of Egypt. Any pharaoh who blessed Abraham (even indirectly) was blessed—always.

Abraham was blessed by Amram and Jochabed through their demonstration of faith in Abraham's God. Someone heard the prayers of a Hebrew mother and allowed her baby to survive after she, consciously obeying the edict of the pharaoh, cast her son into the Nile; but, conscientiously obeying the orders of her heart, cast him adrift inside a sealed basket. Someone heard the cries of a Hebrew infant and allowed him to be cradled, comforted, and fed. Someone heard the request of a princess and granted her the ability to adopt a son.

However, God also said in Genesis 12.3, "I will curse him that curseth thee." Those shameful descendants of Abraham who dishonored his faithful legacy by worshiping idols and returning evil for good, cursed Abraham. They were penalized severely, but other blasphemous, idolatrous oppressors and "cursers" were about to be punished. God is the one who answers prayers and also doles vengeance (Romans 12.19). The God of Egypt was poised to demonstrate his terrible, sovereign authority over the land of the pharaohs.

Djeser-Djeseru

Citations

1. Hattstein 18, 22; Beegle 53; Kitchen, *Reliability*
2. A. Myers 913-914; Cloud
3. 296A. Myers 585; Hoffmeier 137
4. Silverberg 11
5. Oakes & Gahlin 308, Greenberg 34
6. "Mystery of the Screaming Man"
7. Booth 52
8. Collier and Manley 71, 163, 154; A. Myers 731; Beegle 54; Greenberg 36-37
9. Josephus 56; Shaw 226-227
10. Tyldesley, *Hatshepsut* 62
11. Tyldesley, *Hatshepsut* 62-63
12. Breasted, *History* 255; Janot & Hawass 106; David 131
13. Roehrig 7; Shaw 231
14. Janot & Hawass 100
15. Breasted, *History* 266
16. Bille-De Mot 26
17. Tyldesley, *Hatshepsut* 57
18. Booth 65
19. Tyldesley, *Hatshepsut* 60
20. D. Stewart 52; Bulter 251
21. Aldred 134, Shaw 212, 223; Winlock, *Excavations* 144
22. Booth 67
23. Dodson & Dyan 21
24. Winlock, *Woman Pharaoh* 145, Tyldesley, *Hatshepsut* 70; *Pharaohs* 77
25. Roberts 25
26. Tyldesley, *Hatshepsut* 96, Booth 71, Newby 54
27. Winlock, *Woman Pharaoh* 145, Tyldesley, *Hatshepsut* 97, Breasted, *Records II* 142, Roehrig 7
28. Kemp 264
29. Casson 45, Shaw 170
30. Gardiner 184
31. Tyldesley, *Hatshepsut* 1
32. Beegle 50
33. Petrovich 9
34. Roberts 33
35. *Secrets of Egypt's Lost Queen*
36. *Secrets of Egypt's Lost Queen*, Janot & Hawass 103
37. Tyldesley, *Hatshepsut* 90; Russell 25; National Geographic 88; Harris & Weeks 133
38. Roberts 25, Booth 70
39. Ray 44
40. Ray 55
41. *Secrets of Egypt's Lost Queen*
42. Tyldesley, *Hatshepsut* 125
43. Ray 56
44. Roberts 28
45. Breasted, *Records II* 97
46. O'Connor & Cline 29
47. Tyldesley, *Hatshepsut* 80; Winlock, *Excavations* 211
48. Booth 53
49. Dorman 114
50. Newby 56
51. Breasted, *Records II* 152, 147
52. Cottrell 49, Woldering 248, Bolshakov web
53. Booth 70, Roehrig 102, Roberts 26
54. D. Myers 25
55. Roehrig 121, Dorman 116
56. Dorman 126, Breasted, *Records II* 132, Winlock, *Woman Pharaoh* 151
57. Dorman 116
58. Tyldesley, *Hatshepsut* 185
59. Winlock, *Woman Pharaoh* 145, Dorman 123
60. Dorman 117
61. Ray 72
62. Winlock, *Woman Pharaoh* 138
63. Roberts 33
64. Brier: *Great Pharaohs of Ancient Egypt*
65. Ray 58
66. Roberts 33, Dorman 175-176
67. Tyldesley, *Hatshepsut* 194
68. Galford 51
69. Dorman 169, Tyldesley, *Hatshepsut* 143
70. Josephus 57-58
71. Tyldesley, *Hatshepsut* 141-142
72. Tyldesley, *Hatshepsut* 143
73. Josephus 57; Tyldesley, *Hatshepsut* 141-142; Van Seters 122
74. Galford 28
75. Tyldesley, *Hatshepsut* 88
76. Tyldesley, *Hatshepsut* 88
77. Tyldesley, *Hatshepsut* 55
78. Tyldesley, *Hatshepsut* 48; Beegle 67
79. Tyldesley, *Hatshepsut* 80; Greenberg 34
80. Roehrig 112
81. Galford 22; R. Smith 122
82. Tyldesley, *Hatshepsut* 214
83. Tyldesley, *Hatshepsut* 48, Ray 43, Bolshakov web
84. Breasted, *Records II* 81
85. Tyldesley, *Hatshepsut* 131
86. Breasted, *Records II* 85
87. Winlock, *Woman Pharaoh* 145
88. Tyldesley, *Hatshepsut* 193
89. Roberts 32
90. Galford 49; Breasted, *Records II* 96, 91
91. D. Stewart 51
92. Roberts 27
93. Breasted, *Records II* 150
94. Dorman 170
95. Roehrig 92
96. Dorman 170; Roehrig 92, 94; Winlock, *Excavations* 140
97. Cottrell 51
98. Tyldesley, *Hatshepsut* 166, 196; Winlock, *Excavations* 218
99. Dorman 165-166
100. Booth 91
101. Cottrell 51, Dorman 169
102. Dorman 166, 95
103. Tyldesley, *Hatshepsut* 202
104. Tyldesley, *Hatshepsut* 200
105. Galford 51, Tyldesley, *Hatshepsut* 180
106. Galford 28; Dorman 168; Cottrell 51-52; Tyldesley, *Hatshepsut* 182
107. Dorman 34; Oakes & Gahlin 131, Roehrig 95
108. Roehrig 112, Galford 28
109. Roehrig 95
110. Roehrig 95
111. Vos 70
112. Thompson, *Handbook* 256
113. Ray 40
114. Reeves 185
115. Reeves 185, Ray 43, Greenberg 36
116. Cottrell 51
117. Silverman 206, Freud 5
118. Dorman 169
119. Cottrell 52
120. Tyldesley, *Hatshepsut* 196, Reeves 184
121. Cottrell 52; Ikram 79
122. Roehrig 120
123. Winlock, *Woman Pharaoh* 139
124. Cottrell 54, Roehrig 118
125. Tyldesley, *Hatshepsut* 214

126. Tyldesley, *Hatshepsut* 80
127. Roehrig 120
128. Roehrig 121; Saleh & Sourouzian image 130a
129. Tyldesley, *Hatshepsut* 130, Breasted, *Records II* 108
130. Winlock, *Woman Pharaoh* 191
131. Roehrig 120; Winlock, *Excavations* 139
132. Roehrig 120
133. Winlock, *Woman Pharaoh* 146
134. Breasted, *Hist.* 232; *Rec. II* 146, Tyldesley, *Hatshepsut.*185
135. Tyldesley, *Hatshepsut* 34, 36
136. Dorman 118, Ray 58, Aldred 70
137. Dorman 118-119
138. Aldred 118, Shaw 164
139. Booth 92
140. Watterson 122
141. Oakes & Gahlin 276
142. Hayes 75
143. Booth 92
144. Tyldesley, *Hatshepsut* 200-201
145. Reeves and Wilkinson 36; Hayes 74-75
146. Dorman 111
147. *Great Pharaohs of Ancient Egypt*
148. Winlock, *Woman Pharaoh* 104-105
149. Dorman 125
150. Breasted, *Records II* 147
151. Dorman 108
152. B. Myers 21
153. Tyldesley, *Hatshepsut* 194-195; Winlock, *Excavations* 105
154. Breasted, *Records II* 147
155. *Secrets of Egypt's Lost Queen*
156. National Geographic 88
157. Roberts 30
158. Rohl 16
159. Galford 16
160. Ray 56
161. Tyldesley, *Hatshepsut* 103
162. Tyldesley, *Hatshepsut* 102
163. Silverberg 9
164. Breasted, *Records II* 78-85
165. Breasted, *Records II* 86, Oakes & Gahlin 276
166. Lange & Mirmer, 377
167. Breasted, *Records II* 133
168. Tyldesley, *Hatshepsut* 184
169. Oakes & Gahlin 276-277
170. Parkinson, *Sinuhe* 92-97
171. Parkinson, *Sinuhe* 96-97
172. Ray 51
173. Ray 52; Parkinson, *Sinuhe* 96
174. Winlock, *Woman Pharaoh* 139; Winlock, *Excavations* 139
175. Winlock, *Woman Pharaoh* 143
176. Breasted, *Records II* 153
177. Parkinson, *Sinuhe* 27
178. Beegle 57; Parkinson web; Parkinson, *Sinuhe* 31-35
179. Breasted, *History* 180, 188, 203; A. Myers 577
180. Tyldesley, *Hatshepsut* 194
181. Parkinson, *Sinuhe* 21
182. Parkinson web; Parkinson, *Sinuhe* 42
183. Ray 49
184. Roberts 33
185. Booth 73
186. Ray 48
187. Ray 49
188. Ray 45, *Secrets of Egypt's Lost Queen*
189. Ray 48-49; Kemp 68
190. Casson 42
191. Breasted, *Records II* 152
192. Ray 49
193. Monet 33
194. Tyldesley, *Hatshepsut* 157
195. Roberts 30
196. Tyldesley, *Hatshepsut* 144; Roberts 33; Ray 57
197. Peloubet 316, 343
198. Unger 729, 922; May 67; Tyldesley, *Hatshep.* 103; Assmann 70
199. Bunson 91
200. Bunson 90
201. Breasted, *Records II* 264
202. David 57
203. Oakes & Gahlin 478
204. Oakes & Gahlin 479
205. Silverman 61
206. Oakes & Gahlin 478
207. Dorman 166
208. Redford, *Oxford* 521
209. ROM 11; Dothan & Dothan 45
210. Brinkley
211. 211.Vos 116
212. Silverberg 198
213. ROM 11, Rohl 273; Berling 36
214. Oren 104, Ben-Tor 189
215. Shanks & Meinhardt 29
216. Assmann 37
217. Oakes & Gahlin 294
218. Assmann 72; Oakes & Gahlin 93, 103
219. Reeves 224; Hatstein 29
220. Oakes & Gahlin 294
221. Tyldesley, *Hatshepsut* 201, Dorman 179
222. Davis 68
223. David 61
224. *Secrets of Egypt's Lost Queen*
225. Booth 81; Dorman 67, 97, 136; Winlock, *Woman Pharaoh* 157; Cottrell 55
226. Petrovich 27
227. Josephus 57
228. Parkinson, *Sinuhe* 28
229. Beegle 57-58; Parkinson, *Sinuhe* 28
230. Breasted *Records I* 234-235; Tyldesley, *Hatshepsut* 72
231. Roehrig 261, Hawass 38
232. Breasted, *Records II* 180
233. Tyldesley, *Hatshepsut* 214
234. Roehrig 261
235. D. Stewart 51
236. Breasted, *Records II* 180
237. Tyldesley, *Hatshepsut* 214
238. Breasted, *Records II* 180
239. Eerdman 45; May 59, 69
240. D. Stewart 60; Hoffmeier 109
241. Breasted, *Records II* 185-188
242. Newby 57, 81; Roehrig 262
243. Newby 77; Breasted, *Records II* 169, 214-215
244. Newby 84
245. Tyldesley, *Pharaohs* 115
246. Janot & Hawass 108; Booth 82; Tyldesley, *Pharaohs* 115
247. Dorman 125
248. Tyldesley 95
249. Booth 82; *Secrets of Egypt's Lost Queen*
250. Dorman 136; Winlock, *Excavations* 152
251. Parkinson, *Sinuhe* 35-37, Hoffmeier 111
252. Tyldesley 115
253. Tyldesley 202
254. *Secrets of Egypt's Lost Queen*
255. 255.Breasted,*RecordsII* 267-269
256. Ray 57, Breasted, *Records II* 104
257. Newby 54 258. Breasted, *Records II* 147
258. Cameron & Kuhrt 76 260. y de la Torre

The Sarcophagus of Amenhotep II

Chapter 4
The Father of Terror

Resisting the Proud

Absolute silence, a silence that may be felt, is all around;
a feeling of awe steals over one as it is realized that here,
lying in his lonely coffin,
far away from the haunts of man, beast or bird,
is the shrouded, silent form of the monarch
whose word alone was sufficient to make the world tremble.[1]

In the fourth month of Peret, in the tenth year of Siamun, fifth ruler in Thebes during Egypt's Twenty-first Dynasty, when the priests of Amun-Ra achieved the rank and power of pharaohs, and the Two Lands were, once again, divided; the priests/pharaohs authorized the opening of the tombs in the Valley of the Kings, the rewrapping of several mummies, and the relocating of the bodies of the great rulers who were buried there—all but one.[2] Amenhotep II was the only pharaoh who was rewrapped, "recoffined" ("in his lonely coffin" as Mary Broderick observed), and then replaced within his own sarcophagus, within his own tomb.[3] Why? What was it that caused the priests of the Twenty-first Dynasty to treat Amenhotep II differently from every other pharaoh? Furthermore, within Amenhotep II's tomb, (Kings' Valley 35) KV 35, was placed a cache of royal mummies. Why were these kings and queens not laid to rest with the others in (Deir el-Bahari) DB 320?[4] Was it a matter of convenience? Was it an afterthought? Was there no rhyme or reason to the actions of the priests?

It has long been suggested that the priests were acting in compassion for the dead pharaohs, protecting their bodies from robbers and vandals, securing their peaceful existence in the afterlife. It has been suggested that the priests were hurried in their task, quickly gathering the monarchs and stashing their bodies hastily, under the cover of darkness in order to keep their final internment a secret. It has been suggested that the motivation behind these actions were more lucrative than loving. However, the fact remains that not all pharaohs were treated equally, and the question remains: why?

Amenhotep II certainly did not consider himself to be equal to other pharaohs. Nearly every writer who comments on Amenhotep II alludes to his super ego. "He boasted of his boasting."[5] Though an inflated ego would be an understandable consequence for any human being who held as much power in his/her hand as the ankh (the power of life and death) and who was deified as the center of the universe; still, Amenhotep II stands apart. Even before he was pharaoh—perhaps even before he was the crown prince—Amenhotep II considered himself to be exceptional.[6] On a stela at Giza, he boasts,

... His Majesty rose up ... a fully-grown young man. At eighteen, he was completely mature.
He had learned to master every craft of Montu (the warrior god of Thebes). On the battlefield he
had no equal. He learned to ride and train horses. There was none like him in this great army. ...
not a single man who could draw his bow, nor could he be approached in running.[7]

The quote goes on to say:

... no one who could draw his bow, not among his own army, [or] among the rulers of foreign
countries ... because his strength is so much greater than [that of] any king who ever lived.[8]

Incidentally, Amenhotep II was buried with his bow. It is said that he inspected 300 bows until he found one with craftsmanship worthy of his excellence.[9] Ironically, his bow was of Hyksos design, a composite of wood, horn, and sinew, and was inscribed with the self-gratifying appellations: "Smiter of the Troglodytes, overthrower of Kush, Hacking up their cities ... the Great Wall of Egypt, protector of his soldiers."[10]

Though Amenhotep II is certainly not the only eighteen-year-old male to think himself fully developed and fully taught; obviously he wasn't without need of coaching since his archery instructor, Miny, Mayor of Thinis, is recorded as reminding him, "Span your bows to your ears."[11] Nevertheless, athletic ability and military skills were an excellent way of demonstrating one's prowess to be pharaoh. When word of his young, "energetic" son's bragging reached his father's ears, Thutmose III, sent orders to Amenhotep II's trainers:

> Let him be given the very best horses of the stable of My Majesty which is within the Wall (Memphis) . . . to take charge of them, to make them obedient, to train them, to look after them.[12]

Continuing to boast of his own accomplishments, Amenhotep II says, "He trained horses which had no equal. They never tired when he held the reins; even after a long gallop, they were never lathered with sweat."[13] He amazed other Egyptians by his ability to drive a chariot with the reins tied around his waist while he shot arrows with complete accuracy.[14] Of his personal archery prowess, Amenhotep II states:

> He entered his northern garden and found set up there four targets of Asiatic copper, each of one palm in thickness, and with 20 cubits space between one stand and the next. His majesty then appeared in his chariot like Month (Montu) in his strength; he took his bow and grasped four arrows at once. He drove north, shooting at it like Month in his panoply. His arrows came out at its back. He then shot another stand. This . . . had never been done before; . . . had never been heard in tales—an arrow was shot at a copper target, passed through it and fell to the ground—[15]

After successfully achieving this fantastic feat, part of a stela from Medamud says that Amenhotep II offered a prize to anyone who could duplicate his singular performance—and noted that no one could.[16] Of his rowing skills, Amenhotep II says of himself:

> He rows in the stern of his falcon-ship with a crew of 200 men; they set off and cover half a mile with rowing, when they become weak and their limbs tremble and they cannot breathe the air. Then is his majesty strong under his oar of 20 cubits in length . . . set off . . . after . . . three miles rowing, without ceasing from activity, while people gazed at him in admiration.[17]

Of his ascension to the throne, Egyptian history says:

> King Tuthmosis III went up to heaven; he was united with the sundisk; the body of the god joined him who had made him. When the next morning dawned, the sun disk shown forth, the sky became bright, King Amenhotep II was installed on the throne of his father.[18]

Interestingly, for hundreds of years, Egyptians had believed that the dead, at least dead pharaohs, "merged with the Aten."[19]

Amenhotep II was not the oldest son of Thutmose III. The heir apparent was a boy named Amenemhat B. It is he who is listed as the heir of Thutmose III on the southern wall of Thutmose III's festival hall at Karnak, an inscription that dates to Year 24 of Thutmose III's reign—just two years into Thutmose III's reign without Hatshepsut.[20] In fact, since Thutmose III reigned for perhaps fifty-four years and Amenhotep II became king at eighteen, it is possible that Amenemhat B was considerably older than Amenhotep II. Yet, such an intensely competitive spirit as was demonstrated by Amenhotep II is sometimes spurred by sibling rivalry where children are closer together in age, vying for parental approval and distinction in a similar stage of development.[21] Thutmose III had six wives (maybe seven) and four sons, Amenemhat B, Siamun B, Menkheperre A, and Amenhotep II, two of which (Amenemhat B and Menkheperre A) were likely older than Amenhotep II; and it is even possible that Amenhotep II was the youngest of Thutmose III's sons.[22] Though if Amenhotep II was the same age as a second born son by one of Thutmose III's other wives (for example Amenemhat B's mother was probably Sitiah while Amenhotep II's mother was Meryt-Re), or if Amenhotep II's older brother(s) were deficient in some way, he might have been more motivated to stand out as exceptional.[23] After all, the throne of Egypt was the potential prize. Of course, it is perhaps more likely that Amenhotep II's older brothers died in battle, pursuing the Prince of Kadesh with their father; there is no evidence to suggest that any of Thutmose III's sons were lacking in health or vigor.[24] Amenemhat B, for instance, was charged with being "overseer of the cattle," a physically demanding position.[25] Nevertheless, Amenemhat B died before becoming pharaoh, and there was a family history of poor health and heart disease. Thutmose II, the grandfather of Thutmose III's sons, died young of such a condition.

However, not all of Amenhotep II's bragging was unfounded.[26] The fact that his claims are unusual, even for a pharaoh, indicates that there could be some truth in them.[27] At five and a half to six feet tall, Amenhotep II was taller than most pharaohs; Thutmose III, for example, was barely five foot—although that measurement of Thutmose III is questionable because it may not have included his feet, which were missing from his remains.[28] Perhaps, before Amenhotep II was even eighteen, he served as a general in his father's army and as a commander of the Egyptian navy.[29] He was also appointed to be the governor of Memphis.[30] Amenhotep II was muscular, athletic, and probably had better than average hand-eye coordination.[31] He was an avid hunter. In fact, though he died at around 45 years old, he appears to have been in relatively good health.[32] The many monuments he made to himself unwaveringly advance the idea that Amenhotep II was vigorous and strong throughout his career.[33]

It seems that Amenhotep II was a young man who had everything poised in his favor. Upon the death of Thutmose III, Amenhotep II was full ruler of the greatest empire on earth. The borders of Egypt reached beyond the Fourth Cataract (a large outcropping of rock and associated Nile white water rapids) in the south, encompassed Canaan to the east, and stretched from Lebanon beyond the Euphrates all the way to Syria in the North.[34] From "Egypt's greatest military genius," Thutmose III, Amenhotep II inherited the strongest army, perhaps, ever in Egypt.[35] Certainly, the soldiers who fought under Thutmose III had more experience than any other Egyptian army to that point. For nearly twenty years, in seventeen successful campaigns, they proclaimed the military supremacy of Egypt throughout the Levant and Nubia.[36] By his father,

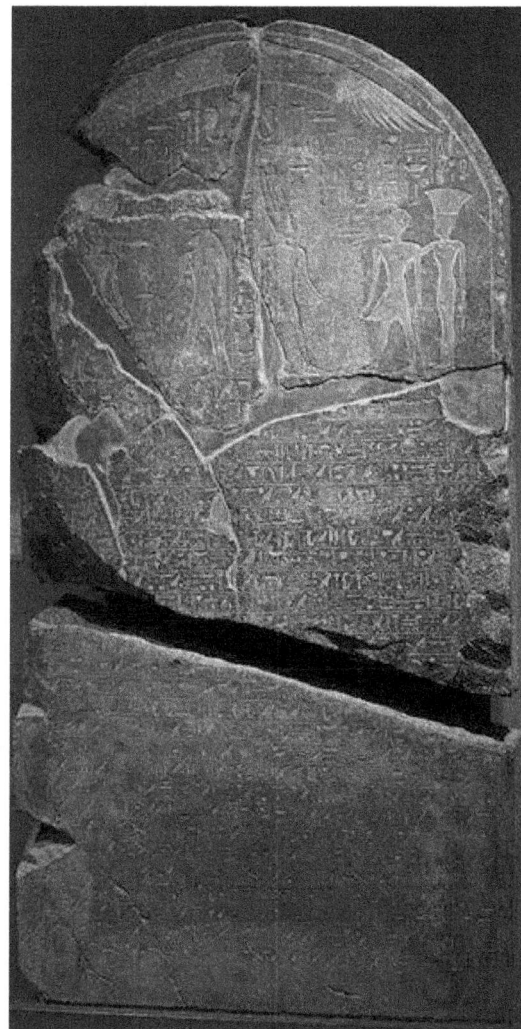

Elephantine Stelae of Amenhotep II

the young pharaoh was well prepared for battle, "to fight—and fight hard."[37] Amenhotep II accompanied Thutmose III on military campaigns in Asia, although the number of times is uncertain. Nevertheless, young Amenhotep II "was the ideal division commander under his father's generalship, leading his troops into rich Syrian cities where they plundered, glutted themselves, anointed themselves with oil daily, and got drunk 'as if at a festival in Egypt.'"[38] Perhaps they enjoyed themselves too much because the young king developed an aberrant taste for brutality that turned him into a "ruthless monarch."[39]

Shortly after the death of his father, the first challenge to Amenhotep II's pharaonic authority materialized as a reported uprising in Takhsy, a city near Kadesh on the Orontes.[40] Without hesitation, Amenhotep II launched his army on a victorious but gruesome campaign. Breaking with the traditions of his fathers, who often captured "the sons of petty Asian kings," brought them back to Egypt for training and indoctrination in Egyptian culture, held them as hostages for guaranteed persistent payment of tributes and as insurance against revolt, and then returned them to their homelands to serve as loyal, Egyptianized vassals; Amenhotep II took "royal ruthlessness to new extremes."[41] He captured seven Syrian princes, personally clubbed them to death, and conveyed their bodies back to Egypt, hanging them upside down on the prow of his

81

flagship. Upon returning to Thebes, he further mutilated the princes' bodies, decapitating them, cutting off their hands, and hanging six of the princes head down on the walls of the Temple of Amun. The seventh he hung in a similar fashion at "Napta near the Fourth Cararact" as a grizzly warning to Nubia.[42] On the Amada and Elephantine stelae that commemorate this deplorable display, Amenhotep II glorifies his "excessive cruelty."[43]

> His Majesty caused this stela to be made, established in this temple in the place of the station of the lord— Life! Prosperity! Health! Engraved with the great name of the Lord of the Two Lands, the son Re, Amenophis, the God who rules in Heliopolis, in the house of his fathers, the gods, after his Majesty had returned from Upper Retjenu, having overthrown all his enemies and broadened the borders of Egypt on the first campaign of victory. It was with his father Amen's joy that his Majesty returned, after he had smitten with his own mace the seven chiefs who were in the district of Takhsy, they being placed upside- down at the bow of the falcon-bark of his Majesty, whose name is called "Akheperure causes the Two Lands to be established." Thereupon six of these enemies were hanged upon the wall of Thebes, the hands likewise. The other enemy was sent to Nubia and hanged on the wall of Napata, in order to cause the victories of his Majesty to be seen forever and ever . . . the limits of the entire land and what Re shines upon. He makes his boundary as he desires without opposition to his hand, just as his father, Amen-Re, Lord of the Thrones of the Two Lands, commanded the son of Re, of his body, whom he loves, Amenophis, the God who rules in Heliopolis, given life, stability, dominion, health and his joy entirely like Re forever, to do for him.[44]

The account of this campaign is corroborated in the writings of Amenemheb and Minmose, two officials who served under Thutmose III and Amenhotep II; and though the young pharaoh also returned from Takhsy with 1,650 pounds of gold, 50 tons of copper, and 550 captured Syrian noblemen with their wives, horses, and chariots, the campaign was actually of "little military significance" and could even be considered to have been "just a raid of a localized area to reinforce an Egyptian presence in the region."[45] But then, *inu*, the Egyptian word often translated as "tribute," is perhaps better understood as "plunder".[46] There was nothing especially brilliant about Amenhotep II's Takhsy campaign; in fact, not even its most shocking and defining feature was completely novel. Thutmose III had once returned from a battle in Nubia with his boat displaying the body of a Nubian chieftain hanging upside down, an arrow still imbedded in his chest.[47] Obviously, this grim exhibition of power had made an impression on the young Amenhotep II who, professing his ominous desire to be considered "greater than any king who has existed," was not to be outdone.

In the final analysis, Amenhotep II's appalling brutality paints a disturbing portrait. Certainly, his excessive violence was intended as a statement, but it was not a statement that was consistent with traditional Egyptian eminence. Yet, the Takhsy butchery is only the opening chapter of The Annals of Amenhotep II, which have been described as "more propaganda designed to inflate the national and international perception of Amenhotep II than they were to catalogue events in his military campaigns."[48] The proposed message was clear—Amenhotep II was terror! However, the intended recipients of that message were not only foreign enemies, but were also Egyptians. More Egyptians witnessed the rotting bodies of the six princes hanging from the Theban temple walls.[49] If there were any subjects, anywhere, who dared to question or challenge the rightful ascension of Amenhotep II, the new pharaoh was uninterested in debate.

Nevertheless, there is debate concerning the number of subsequent military excursions conducted by Amenhotep II. Ancient Egyptian records offer conflicting information.[50] However, most agree that within four years of his Takhsy campaign, Amenhotep II was again prompted to address a challenge to Egyptian dominance in Syrio-Palestine.[51] However, the nature of what prompted this action is speculative. Was there an uprising against Egyptian hegemony? Was there a challenge to the authority of Amenhotep II? Was there a threatened expansion of Mitanni forces, an alliance between the Hurrians and the city-states of Kadesh and Tunip, on the northeastern border of the Egyptian empire?[52] Was there restlessness in the standing army that had become accustomed to regularly flexing its military muscles? Or could it be that Amenhotep II simply desired to emulate his father's frequent forays into Syrio-Palestine? After all, "It seems that both literally and figuratively, the new king may have picked up where his father had left off in terms of dealing with Western Asia."[53]

Whatever his reasons for launching his troops on a second tour, Amenhotep II, acting as the general, unlike Thutmose III, did not seem to possess a purposeful military strategy.[54] He traced the border of Egyptian holdings beyond the Orantes but never pushed into Mitanni or any other unconquered territory, causing some to wonder if he achieved his objective—or if, indeed, he ever even had one.[55] For the most part, he merely rambled through territory that he already owned.[56]

Despite the rhetoric in all of the campaign texts, and especially the references to Amenophis' heroic and athletic exploits, none of the expeditions proved as ambitious or successful enough to rival those of his father, Tuthmosis III, or of his grandfather, Tuthmosis I.[57]

It would seem, from what he wrote concerning his second Asian campaign, that this foray was yet another exercise in propaganda, intended to enlarge Amenhotep II's own bombastic legacy:

Now when the Prince of Naharin, the Prince of Hatti, and the Prince of Shanhar heard of the great victories that I had made, each one tried to outdo his competitor in offering gifts .... They thought on account of their grandfathers to beg his majesty for the breath of life to be given to them: 'We will carry our taxes to your palace, son of Re, Amenhotep (II), divine ruler of Heliopolis, ruler of rulers, a panther who rages in every foreign land and in this land forever.[58]

Since he never even ventured into any "foreign land," obviously, the desired mission of this second campaign was not expansion of Egypt but expansion of a perception of the greatness of Amenhotep II among other kings.

Amenhotep II's propaganda consistently advances the notion of a heroic young pharaoh, fearlessly leading his troops into battle, often pushing his way ahead of the army, to single-handedly destroy the enemy.[59] Perhaps he did, but there is evidence to suggest that even on this campaign where they never so much as ventured into disputed territory, Amenhotep II was lagging at the back of his army.[60] Of course, Amenhotep II would have posterity believe that he was shrewdly positioned in the right place at the right time when his men were attacked from the rear. On the other hand, perhaps Amenhotep II was merely emulating the strategic positioning of his father. In his most famous battle, at Megiddo, Thutmose III's troops urged the pharaoh to "hearken unto us this once; [guard] for us the rear."[61] Perhaps, by the days of Amenhotep II, it was not so much tactical but had simply become conventional for the king to send the army ahead of him.[62]

Nevertheless, the actual account of this "heroic" encounter describes Amenhotep II, having:

. . . crossed over the ford of the Orontes, . . . descried a few Asiatics coming on horses . . . at a gallop. Behold, his majesty was equipped with his weapons of battle, . . . They retreated when his majesty looked at one of them. Then his majesty himself [speared a retreating Asiatic in the back] . . . carried away this Asiatic, his horses, his chariot, and all his weapons of battle. His majesty returned with joy of heart [to] his father, Amon; he (his majesty) gave to him a feast.[63]

For all of his titles and all of his boasting about his unmatched skills, Amenhotep II does not emerge from this encounter appearing to be a great warrior. Instead, his behavior never seems to rise above a hunter on safari.

If Amenhotep II thought that his second campaign would "stabilize and reaffirm" an Egyptian hold over Syria/Palestine, "he was apparently mistaken"; only two years later, he conducted a third campaign into Canaan.[64] However, causing one to again doubt the competence of the young general, his Memphis stela records that this mission was launched in the early part of November.[65] Perhaps he was responding to some urgent intelligence, but for obvious reasons, in the ancient world, November was not the season "when kings go forth to battle" (II Samuel 11.1).[66] Yet, perhaps that is exactly the reason Amenhotep II chose to go to war in winter—after all, "This was a thing that had never been done before; it had never been heard of in tales."[67] Perhaps the challenge itself was the allure.

As with Amenhotep II's other tours, this campaign did not rise to the level of a major military event; rather, the Egyptian army seems used as little more than a raiding party, merely achieving "the acquisition of slaves and booty."[68] In the sequence of unsavory events, the first two Canaanite villages threatened by

Amenhotep II immediately surrendered. The second two towns he utterly destroyed. Just why he was so enraged by these two towns is unknown. Amenhotep II then reported experiencing a reassuring dream from Amun, urging him to proceed with the god's favor and protection. Therefore, he attacked two more towns, captured a large number of prisoners, ordered the digging of two ditches, and set them aflame. It's possible that these fires were simply used to contain the prisoners, but a more compelling argument suggests that Amenhotep II used the flames to have the helpless Canaanite captives burned alive, perhaps as a sacrifice to Amun. Indeed, his own writing on the Amada and Elephantine stelae seems to glorify such behavior. He wrote:

> . . . in the year of terror, without any who can save . . . he makes prisoners [sacrificial victims] out of his enemies . . . There is no limit to what he has done . . . like an action of devouring flame. There is none who can escape the slaughter, like the enemies of Bastet upon the road which Amun has made.[69]

However, since such gruesome human sacrifice was a known Canaanite—but not Egyptian—religious ritual (called *herem*), it is perhaps more likely that Amenhotep II burned these prisoners out of pure cruelty and not as tribute to Amun. "Such brutal treatment of his enemies should not surprise us in Amenophis II's case."[70]

There are those who believe that the "ruthlessness" of Amenhotep II eventually resulted in peaceful subjection throughout the region that made further military aggression unnecessary for the rest of his reign.[71] Amenhotep II ends the stelae that commemorate this campaign by describing the kings of his greatest rivals, Mitanni (who were also known as Hurrians and were allied with Kadesh and Tunip), the Hittites, and Babylon, as fawning over the king of Egypt and begging for "the breath of life" from him. However, such an event is unsubstantiated and is highly suspect.[72]

Furthermore, there is evidence on a fourth pylon at Karnak that points to—not a lasting peace—but to yet another raid on Palestine. Beneath a carving of the king in his chariot are bound prisoners, and the subscript announces that Amenhotep II has "loaded his span with captives" from those who were disloyal to him and has presented spoils to "fill his house" from "the vile foreign land of Retenu [Retjenu]."[73] Two Taanack letters and a fragment of a tablet found in Galilee provide additional evidence to hint at further military actions in the north, and the south wall of the shrine at Ibrim records a military campaign of Amenhotep II into Nubia. Even Punt was a possible target.[74] Some suggest as many as nine military campaigns for Amenhotep II.[75] "It is precisely here that one would like to know whether the remaining seventeen years of his reign were indeed peaceful, or if we merely lack records of additional campaigns."[76]

It does seem to be true that "In Asia the Egyptians recognized no mission but to exploit it," and after the defeat of the Hyksos, Egypt did not encounter a power equal to themselves until they reached Syria.[77] There was no real opposition to Egypt in Canaan. Consistent with the description provided especially in the book of Joshua, the Canaanites lacked political alliance. "Each of the small states was jealous of its own rights and power, and each was equally defensive regarding its independence."[78] When threatened, each city closed its gates and closed ranks.[79] Such myopic strategy was no match for the Egyptian army.

However, it's curious to observe Egyptian military actions in Asia and to deduce, perhaps, another mission: avoid the giants. Though most in the academic world scoff at the very notion, according to the scripture, ancient Canaan was inhabited by "Nephilim," families of giants: the Rephaim, the Anakim, and the Emim (Genesis 6.4, 14.5; Deuteronomy 2.11). Still, a new examination may lend perspective and help whittle the giants, somewhat, down to size. At the time of the Hebrew conquest of Canaan, the Rephaim, represented by Og, the king of Bashan, inhabited the Transjordan (Joshua 12.4).[80] Yet, very few Rephaim remained in those days; in fact, Og was one of the last (Deuteronomy 3.11; Joshua 13.12). However, the Anakim, the descendants of Arba, had three tribes, the Sheshai, the Ahiman, and the Talmai; therefore, they must have been more established (Numbers 13.32-33; Joshua 14.15).[81] The Anakim occupied the hill country of Hebron which was also known as Kirjatharba, the city of Arba, and living in the hill country seems to have distinguished the giants from other Canaanites who occupied the lowlands (Numbers 13.22; Joshua 11.21-23, 15.13).[82]

Though there seems to be no mention of Asiatic giants in Egyptian literature (with the possible exception of "Iy-'anaq" [Anak] in the Execration Texts of Sesostris III and Amenemhet III) and no real evidence of giants in the archaeological record of Canaan, Egyptian troop movements during the Eighteenth Dynasty do circumvent the hill country where the scripture reports that giants lived. Of course, the Egyptian military had a strong naval branch, and chariots largely defined their land forces.[83] Hill country is no battlefield for either a navy or chariots. Chariots maneuver best on flat land, and the passes through the hill country of Palestine were narrow.[84] Certainly, these factors could also account for the Egyptians' obviated routes.

The army of Ahmose pushed through Palestine (presumably by chariot) pursuing Hyksos, not giants.[85] Thutmose I advanced to the Euphrates and may have passed through Nephilim territory, but his records are not very detailed. Furthermore, Thutmose I's focus was arguably more concerned with the dimensions of Egypt than with the dimensions of any potential opponents; after all, he was adequately equipped to hunt elephants.[86] Thutmose III made several passes along the coastal region of Palestine, from the Negeb, into the Plain of Philistia, the Plain of Sharon, through Lower and Upper Galilee, and into the Plain of Phoenicia, in his quest to overpower the "Prince of Kadesh."[87] It stands to reason that he would have mainly utilized the Via Maris (the Sea Road), which passed through Megiddo. Yet, neither the Via Maris nor the Transjordan King's Highway (the two major trade routes through the region) traversed the hill country of Palestine.

The Philistines occupied the coastal region of southern Canaan. Though he was not a Philistine, Goliath, in the days of David, was from Gath and fought with the Philistines. Other giants were said to have lived in Gaza and Ashdod, also cities in Philistine territory (I Samuel 17.4). In Thutmose III's detailed records, why didn't he ever report coming into contact with giants when he went through those places? After all, Thutmose III went through Gaza.[88] In the conquest of Canaan, any giant residents, as reported in the Bible, would have been displaced by the Hebrews and forced to move from their ancestral homes. Some seem to have taken refuge in Philistine territory (Joshua 14.12-15). Under the theory upheld in this book, there is no indication that giants would have been living among the Philistines, along the coast of the Mediterranean, in the days before the latter reign of Amenhotep III. Therefore, probably, Thutmose III never met giants in battle.

When the Hebrews sent spies into Canaan to survey the land, ten out of twelve spies said: "We be not able to go up against the people; for they are stronger than we" (Numbers 13.31-33). In fact, it may have been from the Egyptians (especially from Amenhotep II) that the Hebrews formed such a pessimistic opinion. Egyptian history did not regularly record defeat or humiliation. Yet, perhaps Egyptians were defeated or at least intimidated by the Anakim. If giants had successfully rebuffed the Egyptian army or if a pharaoh had been defeated, by giants or otherwise, it would not have been officially recorded. However, that does not mean that it would not have been known.[89] The loss of lives and equipment and the pharaoh's shame of defeat would no doubt have become common knowledge. Der Manuelian, in his in-depth study on the life of Amenhotep II, proposes that on his third campaign where he spent time rampaging through Canaan, it's possible that Amenhotep II engaged forces in the vicinity of Galilee that caused him to fall back.[90] If the expert army of Amenhotep II had been forced to withdraw by inhabitants—some inflatedly rumored to be giants—in the hill country region of Galilee, that might explain the Hebrews' lack of confidence in their ability to defeat the Nephilim (Joshua 17.15).[91] The humiliation of defeat might also explain Amenhotep II's shocking violence toward the Canaanite captives that he may have incinerated near the end of this same campaign. Perhaps the pharaoh's ghastly behavior was little more than a display of rage and an act of damage control to repair his fearsome image. Amenhotep II always expected to win and considered himself to be a perpetual champion; his extremely competitive personality would have prevented him from being able to concede defeat easily.[92]

Of course, the report given by the ten Hebrew spies was not only faithless; it was also exaggerated (Deuteronomy 1.28-30). According to scripture, certain individuals of the Nephilim reached a height of over nine feet; yet, that is not to suggest that such height was average—even for the Nephilim (I Samuel 17.4). Nine feet, of course, would be considered astronomically tall by today's standard; and when one considers that the average height of an ancient Egyptian or Hebrew was a little over five feet, the description of "giant" becomes more understandable.[93] Yet, though the giants of Canaan may have looked imposing and fierce, in reality, they were probably not as formidable as they appeared. In Genesis 14, the Rephaim and the Emim were defeated by an alliance of four kings: Amraphel king of Shinar, Arioch king of Ellasar, Chedorlaomer king of Ellam, and Tidal king of nations (Genesis 14.1, 5). Yet, when the raiding kings kidnapped Lot, Abraham (then known as Abram) with a band of 318 men overtook and defeated the giants' conquerors. Therefore, if called for, Abraham and his men could likely have easily defeated the giants as well. It's even possible that Abraham freed the Nephilim from their captors—that is, if any of Abraham's allies: Aner, Eshcol, and/or Mamre had requested the giants as part of "their portion." The king of Sodom was certainly interested in possessing the captives of the conflict, but Abraham never lost sight of his prime directive. He only sought to free Lot, his nephew, and Lot's household; Abraham had no desire or intention to prosper from the spoils of war (Genesis 14.21-24).

The Athletic Amenhotep II

Abraham, Isaac, and Jacob all lived in the vicinity of Hebron, the area reported to have had the highest concentration of Anakim, yet there is never any mention of conflict between the ancestral Hebrews and giants. On the contrary, Mamre the Amorite who served as friend and long-time landlord of Abraham, may have been an Anakim due to the association of Amorites and Anakim; however Mamre is never identified as such in scripture (Genesis 14.13). Nonetheless, his name implies great size; "Mamre" means "strength or fatness."[94] Anakim literally translated means, "long necked"; the height of these tall people must have been reminiscent of giraffes.[95] Perhaps, the giants, by nature, were not particularly aggressive; and they may not have been especially skilled in battle either. Arguably the most famous giant, Goliath, provides an example. Goliath was very frightening to Saul's army. This, alone, indicates that Goliath's gigantism was anomalous even among the Anakim; the Israelites didn't encounter nine-foot individuals every day. Goliath was unusually big, well armed, and defiant, but other than identifying him as "a champion" there is no record given of any successes of Goliath on the battlefield. In fact, he is notably remembered for being defeated in a single blow delivered by a mere boy (I Samuel 17.4-11, 45-50). Similarly, other giants of the same family were each defeated by, presumably, average-sized opponents, one on one, in hand-to-hand combat (II Samuel 21.18-22; I Chronicles 20.4-8). Benaiah, one of David's mighty men, is even recorded as defeating a giant who is further identified as an Egyptian, perhaps a mercenary (II Samuel 23.20-23).

The Hebrew spies didn't receive their reticence of the Anakim from their Hebrew ancestors. Neither did their fear of giants stem from the days of the Hyksos. Trails of scarabs found in the vicinity of Hebron from the days of the Hyksos indicate that travelers regularly traversed Anakim territory seemingly without incident. So, some post-Hyksos persons must have successfully rumored a notion (echoed by the ten spies) that the Anakim were invincible. Perhaps the most likely candidates are individuals associated with the army of Amenhotep II.

Of course, it's also possible that the ten spies gave such a negative report because they didn't really want to do battle in the Promised Land. The Hebrews had been not long out of Egypt when the spies were sent into Canaan because it was in response to their faithless report that God sentenced the Hebrews to wander for forty years and to die in the wilderness (Numbers 10.11- 13; 14.28-38). Numerous times, the Hebrews had expressed their desire to return to Egypt. Following the plagues, the Hebrews of the exodus were well aware of the weakened state of the country that had been their home for as long as they had lived; they were also eye-witnesses to the fact that the Egyptian army was gone, perhaps they desired to return to Egypt—not as slaves—but as a conquering army. Delivering an overstated report of impossible odds in Canaan made the prospect of returning to Egypt all the more attractive (Numbers 14.1-4). Furthermore, if the Hebrews had returned to Egypt and re-established their Hyksos dominion, they could have possessed both Egypt and Canaan. Canaan was still part of Egyptian territory at that time.

Nevertheless, even if he was defeated by the Anakim, a person as competitive as Amenhotep II would have been unlikely to "take himself out of the game."[96] He enjoyed the contest of battle too much to be content with peace. In fact, even as late as Year 23 of his reign, there's proof that when Amenhotep II wasn't at war, he longed for the glory of the battlefield. After having a little too much to drink, Amenhotep II sent a letter to his "ol' army buddy," Usersatet, who was serving as his viceroy in Nubia. The pharaoh reminded Usersatet of the satisfaction of fighting in Takhsy and referred to their Syrian enemies as "old women," adding "The people of Takhsy are completely worthless."[97] This is not the language of a diplomat. In his Sphinx stela, he also waxes sentimental over the challenges he enjoyed while training on the Giza plateau.[98] For instance, he had great confidence in his horsemanship and in his archery skills and recalls how he dared anyone to do better. In a way, Amenhotep II's appalling cruelty was perhaps just another dare.[99] He had the best army in the world; he knew it, and secure within the borders of his empire, he dared (tried to provoke) his neighbors to test him, to give him reason to do battle. Merciless hostility is not indicative of a man who is truly interested in good relations with his neighbors. For that matter, neither does a man who keeps a pet lion intend to appear particularly approachable.[100] When his stela says, "the Two Lands remained peaceful," Amenhotep II probably means that the throne passed smoothly from his father to himself, not that he made peace with his enemies.[101] Amenhotep II was an oppressor; he was uninterested in peace. Amenhotep II was once asked by the king of Mitanni to give one of his daughters in marriage to make an alliance between their two nations. Amenhotep II "haughtily refused," saying that no Egyptian princess had ever "suffered the indignity of being married off to a foreign ruler."[102] Though some speculate that Amenhotep II may have forged treaties with his neighbors, his profile is more a pharaoh who did not seek peace and who was not willing to concede or to negotiate with anyone.[103] He was belligerent to a fault. In fact, there are those who contend that the pride, rash behavior, and thoughtless actions of Amenhotep II nearly lost the empire.[104]

Drastic changes occurred in the short eight to ten years of the next administration.[105] Thutmose IV does not appear that he was at all confident of Egypt's standing in the world; on the contrary, his policies seemed more consistent with damage control. He quickly sought an alliance with Egypt's greatest enemy, Mitanni, through marrying a daughter of their king, Artatama I.[106] "For the first time in her history Egypt was taking part in a dialogue on equal terms with someone whom she had conquered on Syrian battlefields."[107] In fact, Thutmose IV may not have perceived his state as equal; the seemingly desperate pharaoh of Egypt appears to have been essentially reduced to begging the king of Mitanni for a treaty between their countries because Thutmose IV wrote to Artatama I seven times requesting a princess before his petition was finally granted and a marriage was arranged.[108] Though there is some debate as to whether "seven" requests is a literal reckoning—in other words, is it merely a poetic attitude, or is it possible that writing seven times was some sort of symbolic penance for the lives of the seven Takhsy princes brutally slaughtered by Thutmose IV's father? At any rate, the excessive correspondence causes one to wonder why the pharaoh is effectively suggested to be the weaker negotiator if there is not at least some truth to the desperation of his situation. The fact that the Mitanni princess kept her foreign name also makes Thutmose IV seem ineffectual. This was not at all the first time that foreign women had become part of the royal harem. However, usually the pharaoh simply took whatever women he wanted, whether through the spoils of war or just from the sheer power of his position (Genesis 12.15).[109] In fact, Thutmose III probably had three Syrio-Palestinian women in his harem: Manuwai, Manhata, and Maruta.[110] Perhaps one such woman, Mutemwia, was even the mother of Amenhotep III.[111] Therefore, why did Thutmose IV feel obliged to ask for a foreign wife; why was he seeking a treaty in the first place; why did Thutmose IV appear to feel so vulnerable?

Thutmose IV does not seem to have been at all confident in the ability of his army. Military actions during his tenure were kept to a bear minimum.[112] In fact, Thutmose IV could not even secure the borders of Egypt itself! A stela at Konosso records that Nubians actually invaded Egyptian soil, coming up into Egypt's "Eastern desert," having "descended from the vicinity of Wawat [Lower Nubia]."[113] Where was the great

Egyptian army of his predecessors, Thutmose III and Amenhotep II? Unlike his father and grandfather, Thutmose IV did not seem to have full confidence in his army. He describes himself as traveling separately from them in the deployment to address this Nubian assault. He writes:

> . . . he commanded that [his army be col]lected immediately. He sent it off in valiance and strength. Proceeding after this by His Majesty . . . in his [golden] ship . . . . spans of horses and troops were accompanying him. His army was with him, the champions in two rows, with the elite troops at his sides, and . . . boats being equipped with his retainers . . . Without waiting for his army to come to him, [he made] a great [carnage] with his powerful scimitar. His terror entered into every belly . . . .[114]

Though this account is likely overstated, and it is highly doubtful that Thutmose IV—single-handedly—put down this incursion. Nevertheless, far from lagging at the rear, why didn't Thutmose IV wait for his army or boast about the strength and ability of his forces?

Egypt had maintained a standing army since the days of Ahmose I; why did Thutmose IV have to scramble an army together or need an army to "be collected immediately"?[115] In the tomb of Tjanuny, the commander of the army under Thutmose IV, elaborate scenes decorate the walls showing squads of new recruits lining up to serve under his command.[116] In another tomb, Nebamum, the Chief of Medjay, is credited with being brought out of retirement to train new recruits: "as a pension from the king. At the time of his promotion he was referred to in the text as . . . 'the old man of the army." Thutmose IV charged Nebamum with the job of drill sergeant.[117] Ptahemhet, whose brother (Nebseney) had been a charioteer in the army of Amenhotep II, is another retired military man who was pressed back into service under Thutmose IV.[118] Userhat, a scribe under Thutmose IV, records a similar scene on the walls of his tomb, (Theban Tomb) TT 56. Userhat's tomb shows raw recruits sitting slump-shouldered, talking to each other, getting their hair cut, and, generally, looking dejected.[119] Yet, a more disturbing picture is presented in the tomb of Horemheb, also a commander under Thutmose IV, where young Egyptian men with their hands tied behind their backs are being conscripted into military service. Why was there such a desperate need for new recruits? Where was the active military? Where was the mighty army that was built and battle-hardened by Thutmose III?

Thutmose IV had "far fewer foreign campaigns," and his army's activities were little more than "police actions." Scholars are at a loss to explain the drastic decline in military campaigns under Thutmose IV.[120] However, if Egypt had suffered the sudden loss of its army, an acute reversal in foreign policy would be explainable; in fact, it would be expected. What happened to the seemingly invincible army that Thutmose III cultivated and that Amenhotep II flaunted? Could it be that they died? Could it be that they drowned? Could it be that Thutmose IV's predecessor, Amenhotep II, was the pharaoh of the exodus?

Of course, this isn't the first time that such a suggestion has been proposed. From the late 19th Century, when the curiously salt-encrusted mummy of Merenptah was discovered, was theorized to have died from drowning in salt water, and was somehow mistakenly associated with Amenhotep II (perhaps because Merenptah was one of the cache of pharaohs interred in Amenhotep II's tomb), the name of Amenhotep II has been suggested to be possibly connected with the exodus. And though many disagree, over the years, several, including Alfred Hoerth, John Davis, Douglas Petrovich, John Rea, Bryant Wood, Rodger Young, and others have come to a similar conclusion, at least placing the exodus within the Eighteenth Dynasty.[121] Vos says, "Amenhotep II is often thought to be the pharaoh of the Exodus."[122] Even Unger's Bible Dictionary lists Amenhotep II as the likely pharaoh of the exodus. As the events in ancient Egypt are presented in this book, there is no other candidate who could be the pharaoh who died in the Red Sea.

According to scripture, the life of Moses divides, roughly, into three periods: forty years in Egypt, forty years in Midian, and forty years wandering in the wilderness (Acts 7.23; Exodus 7.7; Deuteronomy 2.1-7). Therefore, if Hatshepsut was the daughter of the pharaoh who rescued Moses from the Nile, there must be less than one hundred years between the days of Hatshepsut and the exodus. If Hatshepsut adopted Moses when she was around eleven years old, that would easily account for the first forty years of Moses' life because

Hatshepsut's mummy depicts a woman who was 50-52 years old when she died.[123] The problem begins with the forty years Moses spent in Midian (Acts 7.30).

Immediately after the death of Hatshepsut, Thutmose III began nearly twenty years of campaigns into Syrio-Palestine, searching for his nemesis, "the prince of Kadesh," who he probably believed was actually Moses/Senenmut.[124] Moses fled Egypt to escape a pharaoh who was seeking to kill him, and he remained in Midian until after the death of that pharaoh (Exodus 2.15, 23). Although the official statement of ascension seems to suggest that Amenhotep II was installed as pharaoh upon the death of his father, most experts accept the assertion found on Amenhotep II's Sphinx stela that he shared a co-regency with Thutmose III for about two years, and most also agree that Amenhotep II reigned for twenty-six years, though there is some uncertainty surrounding the end of Amenhotep II's reign.[125] Twenty years, plus two years, plus twenty-six years, is forty-eight years; and for a literal interpretation of scripture, that's too long for Moses to be in Midian. However, in Acts 7.23, Stephen says, concerning the age of Moses when he fled Egypt, "as a time of forty years was being filled for him [Moses]." According to the (KJV) King James translation, this phrase is interpreted: "when he [Moses] was full forty years old"; however, perhaps a better understanding of the meaning is, "when he [Moses] was approaching the age of forty," as it appears in the New American Standard translation (NASB).[126] If Hatshepsut actually died when she was close to fifty (say between forty-six and fifty-two), then Moses could have fled Egypt when he was around 37 (closer to 40 than 30); and if the, approximately, two years of Thutmose III and Amenhotep II's co-regency do not count as part of the total, then the forty-year time frame of Moses' absence begins to better fit the window.

Of course, there is a bigger problem with the numbers associated with the reign of Thutmose III. Thutmose III claims to have ruled Egypt for fifty-four years—actually fifty-three years, ten months, and twenty-six days.[127] Nevertheless, his mummy reveals a man who died in his mid forties, making a fifty-four year reign impossible.[128] It is very likely that the obvious discrepancy was, actually, carefully calculated and was well rooted in Thutmose III's desperate effort to re-write the history of Egypt and to eradicate certain elements associated with the era of Hatshepsut. His onslaught against the monuments of Hatshepsut is notorious, and the concerted effort was probably continued by Amenhotep II after the death of Thutmose III; however, the motive behind the attack and even Thutmose III's target of *damnatio memoriae* may not be as evident.[129] Why did Thutmose III want his reign counted at precisely fifty-four years? Umberto Eco proposes the theory that superimposing a "counter-memory" is the most effective way of eclipsing a memory.[130] What fifty-four year event was Thutmose III trying to eclipse? In Hatshepsut's mortuary temple, Thutmose III clearly changed the message to reflect that he, not Hatshepsut, was the rightful heir to the throne of Thutmose I. Do the fifty-four years account for the time between the death of Thutmose I and the ascension of Amenhotep II? Perhaps.

Still, there are places in Egypt where representations of Moses/Senenmut were destroyed while adjacent images of Hatshepsut were left untouched.[131] The more consistent target of Thutmose III's rage seems to have been Moses/Senenmut. Under this theory, it was Moses/Senenmut, "the greatest of the great in the whole land," who made Thutmose III feel overshadowed for the first two decades of the young pharaoh's life; Moses/Senenmut, "that wretched foe" he pursued in vain for the next two decades; and Moses/Senenmut whose space in time and eternity Thutmose III intended to occupy and to terminate. Furthermore, Thutmose III seems to have been keenly aware of exactly how much time was needed to eclipse Moses/Senenmut. Fifty-four years plus twenty-six years (the reign of Amenhotep II) is eighty years. Moses was eighty years old in the year of the exodus (Exodus 7.7). Therefore, at the time of Thutmose III's death, Moses/Senenmut was fifty-four (fifty-three years, ten months, and twenty-six days), exactly the space in time that Thutmose III wanted to claim as his own. John Rea also concludes that "Thutmose III must be the ruler whose death is recorded in Exodus 2.23."[132] When Moses returned to Egypt, terrifying things occurred. "And the Lord said unto Moses, When thou goest to return into Egypt, see that thou do all those wonders before Pharaoh, which I have put in thine hand" (Exodus 4.21).

The first wonder was this:

> And the Lord spake unto Moses and unto Aaron, . . .Take thy rod, and cast it before Pharaoh, and
> it shall become a serpent. And Moses and Aaron went in unto Pharaoh, and they did so as the
> Lord had commanded: and Aaron cast down his rod before Pharaoh, and before his servants, and
> it became a serpent. Then Pharaoh also called the wise men and the sorcerers: now the magicians
> of Egypt, they also did in like manner with their enchantments. For they cast down every man his
> rod, and they became serpents: but Aaron's rod swallowed up their rods (Exodus 7.8-12).

Egyptians believed in "*heka*" or magic.[133] Certainly, *The Book of the Dead* was little more than a catalogue of nearly two hundred incantations believed to be of great benefit in the afterlife.[134] Magic words, magic spells, protective amulets, and various other "magical paraphernalia" were part of everyday life as well as being integral to Egyptian mythology and religion; yet it's possible that the Eighteenth Dynasty didn't really have a specific governmental office for "magicians," although the title "*Hery Seshta*" or "Chief of Mysteries" was found on a wooden box from the Middle Kingdom.[135] Instead, certain individuals were considered to be somewhat naturally gifted with "*heka*." Interestingly, the god Heka was depicted as a man holding two snakes that looked very much like rods or walking sticks.[136] In fact, if pressure is applied to the right spot, a cobra can be immobilized and made to resemble a staff.[137] Josephus identifies the magicians who opposed Moses and Aaron as "priests."[138] This is probably a likely description, and may refer to the Egyptian title "chief lector priest."[139] Priests were certainly considered to be wise men and sorcerers who could recite magic spells, interpret dreams, and perform other mystifying rituals.[140] In Amenhotep II's staff of priests there were those who held the title "Master of Secrets" as did his vizier, Rekhmire.[141]

The pharaoh that Moses and Aaron encountered was wholly unimpressed by their miraculous display, just as God had predicted (Exodus 7.13). Josephus claims that the pharaoh accused Moses of using "deceitful tricks, and wonders and magical arts."[142] It's significant to note that Amenhotep II shared a similar dubious posture concerning the magic arts in a letter that he wrote "with his own two hands" to his childhood friend, Usersatet.[143] Distrustful of magic as deceptive trickery, Amenhotep II warned Usersatet to be wary of the "machinations and magic of the Nubians."[144]

In II Timothy 3.8, Paul identifies Jannes and Jambres as men who "withstood Moses." Most biblical scholars associate these names with the Egyptian magicians who opposed Moses and Aaron, though the priests are never named in the Exodus account.[145] In *The Latin Vulgate* the magicians' names appear as Iannes and Mambres, and in the apocryphal, *Chronicles of Jerahmeel*, the Hebrew translations are Johanai and Mamre. Did any priests with names like these serve under Amenhotep II? Perhaps. "The most important high priest" in Amenhotep II's administration was a man named "Mry."[146] He was the overseer of all of the priests of Upper and Lower Egypt, was called "the god's father of the great throne," and was high priest of Amun.[147] "Mry" would likely be pronounced "Mery." With the dominant "m" at the beginning and the strong "e" sound at the end of this short name, its striking similarity to "Mamre" is noteworthy. Mry's "second in command" was another powerful priest named "Jmn-m-h3t." He, too, was considered high priest of Amun, overseer of priests of Upper and Lower Egypt, god's father, first god's father of Amun, and master of secrets in Karnak.[148] Again "J," "h," and "n" are all usual components in names that are variations of "John" as is "Jannes." These names, Jmn-m-hat and Mry, are similar enough to the names provided in II Timothy to perhaps supersede coincidence, and it is especially compelling to consider that these were the names of the two most powerful priests to serve in the time of Amenhotep II and *only* in the time of Amenhotep II.

The contest between the magic arts of the Egyptian priesthood and the miracles of God, leads to a discussion of the plagues.

The First Plague

And the Lord spake unto Moses, Say unto Aaron, Take thy rod, and stretch out thine hand upon the waters of Egypt, upon their streams, upon their rivers, and upon their ponds, and upon all their pools of water, that they may become blood; and that there may be blood throughout all the land of Egypt, both in vessels of wood, and in vessels of stone. And Moses and Aaron did so, as the Lord commanded; and he lifted up the rod, and smote the waters that were in the river, in the sight of Pharaoh, and in the sight of his servants; and all the waters that were in the river were turned to blood. And the fish that was in the river died; and the river stank, and the Egyptians could not drink of the water of the river; and there was blood throughout all the land of Egypt. And the magicians of Egypt did so with their enchantments: and Pharaoh's heart was hardened, neither did he hearken unto them; as the Lord had said. And Pharaoh turned and went into his house, neither did he set his heart to this also. And all the Egyptians digged round about the river for water to drink; for they could not drink of the water of the river. And seven days were fulfilled, after that the Lord had smitten the river. (Exodus 7.19-25)

The Second Plague

And the Lord spake unto Moses, Go unto Pharaoh, and say . . . Thus saith the Lord, Let my people go, that they may serve me. And if thou refuse to let them go, behold, I will smite all thy borders with frogs: . . . the river shall bring forth frogs abundantly, which shall . . . into thine house, and into thy bedchamber, and upon thy bed, and into the house of thy servants, and upon thy people, and into thine ovens, and into thy kneadingtroughs: And the frogs shall come up both on thee, and upon thy people, and upon all thy servants. And the Lord spake unto Moses, Say unto Aaron, Stretch forth thine hand with thy rod over the streams, over the rivers, and over the ponds, and cause frogs to come up upon the land of Egypt. And Aaron stretched out his hand over the waters . . . and the frogs came up, and covered the land of Egypt. And the magicians did so with their enchantments, and brought up frogs upon the land of Egypt. Then Pharaoh called for Moses and Aaron, and said, Entreat the Lord, that he may take away the frogs from me, and from my people; and I will let the people go, that they may do sacrifice unto the Lord. And Moses said unto Pharaoh, . . .when shall I entreat for thee . . . to destroy the frogs from thee and thy houses, that they may remain in the river only? And he said, Tomorrow. And he said, Be it according to thy word: that thou mayest know that there is none like unto the Lord our God. . . . And the frogs shall depart . . . from thy houses, and . . . .they shall remain in the river only. And Moses and Aaron went out from Pharaoh: and Moses cried unto the Lord . . . And the Lord did according to the word of Moses; and the frogs died out of the houses, out of the villages, and out of the fields. And they gathered them together upon heaps: and the land stank. But when Pharaoh saw that there was respite, he hardened his heart, and hearkened not unto them; as the Lord had said. (Exodus 8.1-15)

The Third Plague

And the Lord said unto Moses, Say unto Aaron, Stretch out thy rod, and smite the dust of the land, that it may become lice throughout all the land of Egypt. And they did so; for Aaron stretched out his hand with his rod, and smote the dust of the earth, and it became lice in man, and in beast; all the dust of the land became lice throughout all the land of Egypt. And the magicians did so with their enchantments to bring forth lice, but they could not: so there were lice upon man, and upon beast. Then the magicians said unto Pharaoh, This is the finger of God: and Pharaoh's heart was hardened, and he hearkened not unto them; as the Lord had said. (Exodus 8.16-19)

The Fourth Plague

And the Lord said unto Moses, Rise up early in the morning, and stand before Pharaoh; lo, he cometh forth to the water; and say unto him, Thus saith the Lord, Let my people go, that they may serve me. Else, if thou wilt not . . . behold, I will send swarms of flies upon thee, and upon thy servants, and upon thy people, and into thy houses: and the houses of the Egyptians shall be full of . . . flies, and also the ground whereon they are. And I will sever in that day the land of Goshen, in which my people dwell, that no swarms of flies shall be there; to the end thou mayest know that I am the Lord . . . of the earth. And I will put a division between my people and thy people: to morrow shall this sign be. And the Lord did so; and there came a grievous swarm of flies into the house of Pharaoh, and into his servants' houses, and into all the land of Egypt: the land was corrupted by reason of the swarm of flies. And Pharaoh called for Moses and for Aaron, and said, Go ye, sacrifice to your God in the land. And Moses said, It is not meet so to do; for we shall sacrifice the abomination of the Egyptians to the Lord our God: lo, shall we sacrifice the abomination of the Egyptians before their eyes, and will they not stone us? We will go three days' journey into the wilderness, and sacrifice to the Lord our God, as he shall command us. And Pharaoh said, I will let you go, that ye may sacrifice to the Lord your God in the wilderness; only ye shall not go very far away: entreat for me. And Moses said, . . . I will entreat the Lord that the swarms of flies may depart from Pharaoh, from his servants, and from his people, to morrow: but let not Pharaoh deal deceitfully any more in not letting the people go to sacrifice to the Lord. And Moses went out from Pharaoh, and entreated the Lord. And the Lord did according to the word of Moses; and he removed the swarms of flies from Pharaoh, from his servants, and from his people; there remained not one. And Pharaoh hardened his heart at this time also, neither would he let the people go. (Exodus 8.20-32)

The Fifth Plague

Then the Lord said unto Moses, Go in unto Pharaoh, and tell him, Thus saith the Lord God of the Hebrews, Let my people go, that they may serve me. For if thou refuse to let them go, . . . Behold, the hand of the Lord is upon thy cattle which is in the field, upon the horses, upon the asses, upon the camels, upon the oxen, and upon the sheep: there shall be a very grievous murrain. And the Lord shall sever between the cattle of Israel and the cattle of Egypt: and there shall nothing die of all that is the children's of Israel. And the Lord appointed a set time, saying, To morrow the Lord shall do this thing in the land. And . . . all the cattle of Egypt died: but of the cattle of the children of Israel died not one. And Pharaoh sent, and, behold, there was not one of the cattle of the Israelites dead. And the heart of Pharaoh was hardened, and he did not let the people go. (Exodus 9.1-7)

The Sixth Plague

And the Lord said unto Moses and unto Aaron, Take to you handfuls of ashes of the furnace, and . . . sprinkle it toward the heaven in the sight of Pharaoh. And it shall become small dust in all the land of Egypt, and shall be a boil breaking forth with blains upon man, and upon beast, throughout all the land of Egypt. And they took ashes of the furnace, and stood before Pharaoh; and Moses sprinkled it up toward heaven; and it became a boil breaking forth with blains upon man, and upon beast. And the magicians could not stand . . . because of the boils; for the boil was upon . . . all the Egyptians. And the Lord hardened the heart of Pharaoh, and he hearkened not unto them; as the Lord had spoken unto Moses. (Exodus 9.8-12)

The Seventh Plague

And in very deed for this cause have I raised thee up, for to show in thee my power; and that my name may be declared throughout all the earth. As yet exaltest thou thyself against my people, that thou wilt not let them go? Behold, to morrow about this time I will cause it to rain a very grievous hail, such as hath not been in Egypt since the foundation thereof even until now. Send therefore now, and gather thy cattle, and all that thou hast in the field; for upon every man and beast which shall be found in the field, and shall not be brought home, the hail shall come down upon them, and they shall die. He that feared the word of the Lord among the servants of Pharaoh made his servants and his cattle flee into the houses: And he that regarded not the word of the Lord left his servants and his cattle in the field. And the Lord said unto Moses, Stretch forth thine hand toward heaven, that there may be hail in all the land of Egypt, upon man, and upon beast, and upon every herb of the field, throughout the land of Egypt. And Moses stretched forth his rod toward heaven: and the Lord sent thunder and hail, and the fire ran along upon the ground; and the Lord rained hail upon the land of Egypt. So there was hail, and fire mingled with the hail, very grievous, such as there was none like it in all the land of Egypt since it became a nation. And the hail smote throughout all the land of Egypt all that was in the field, both man and beast; and the hail smote every herb of the field, and brake every tree of the field. Only in the land of Goshen, where the children of Israel were, was there no hail. And Pharaoh sent, and called for Moses and Aaron, and said unto them, I have sinned this time: the Lord is righteous, and I and my people are wicked. Entreat the Lord (for it is enough) that there be no more mighty thunderings and hail; and I will let you go, and ye shall stay no longer. And Moses said unto him, As soon as I am gone out of the city, I will spread abroad my hands unto the Lord; and the thunder shall cease, neither shall there be any more hail; that thou mayest know how that the earth is the Lord's. But as for thee and thy servants, I know that ye will not yet fear the Lord God. And the flax and the barley was smitten: for the barley was in the ear, and the flax was bolled. But the wheat and the rye were not smitten: for they were not grown up. And Moses went out of the city from Pharaoh, and spread abroad his hands unto the Lord: and the thunders and hail ceased, and the rain was not poured upon the earth. And when Pharaoh saw that the rain and the hail and the thunders were ceased, he sinned yet more, and hardened his heart, he and his servants. And the heart of Pharaoh was hardened, neither would he let the children of Israel go; as the Lord had spoken by Moses.(Exodus 9.16-35)

The Eighth Plague

And the Lord said unto Moses, Stretch out thine hand over the land of Egypt for the locusts, that they may come up upon the land of Egypt, and eat every herb of the land, even all that the hail hath left. And Moses stretched forth his rod over the land of Egypt, and the Lord brought an east wind upon the land all that day, and all that night; and when it was morning, the east wind brought the locusts. And the locusts went up over all the land of Egypt, and rested in all the coasts of Egypt: very grievous were they; before them there were no such locusts as they, neither after them shall be such. For they covered the face of the whole earth, so that the land was darkened; and they did eat every herb of the land, and all the fruit of the trees which the hail had left: and there remained not any green thing in the trees, or in the herbs of the field, through all the land of Egypt. Then Pharaoh called for Moses and Aaron in haste; and he said, I have sinned against the Lord your God, and against you. Now therefore forgive, I pray thee, my sin only this once, and entreat the Lord your God, that he may take away from me this death only. And he went out from Pharaoh, and entreated the Lord. And the Lord turned a mighty strong west wind, which took away the locusts, and cast them into the Red sea; there remained not one locust in all the coasts of Egypt. But the Lord hardened Pharaoh's heart, so that he would not let the children of Israel go. (Exodus 10.12-20)

The Ninth Plague

> And the Lord said unto Moses, Stretch out thine hand toward heaven, that there may be darkness over the land of Egypt, even darkness which may be felt. And Moses stretched forth his hand toward heaven; and there was a thick darkness in all the land of Egypt three days: They saw not one another, neither rose any from his place for three days: but all the children of Israel had light in their dwellings. And Pharaoh called unto Moses, and said, Go ye, serve the Lord; only let your flocks and your herds be stayed: let your little ones also go with you. And Moses said, Thou must give us also sacrifices and burnt offerings, that we may sacrifice unto the Lord our God. Our cattle also shall go with us; there shall not an hoof be left behind; for thereof must we take to serve the Lord our God; and we know not with what we must serve the Lord, until we come thither. But the Lord hardened Pharaoh's heart, and he would not let them go. (Exodus 10.21-27)

The Tenth Plague

> And the Lord said unto Moses, Yet will I bring one plague more upon Pharaoh, and upon Egypt; afterwards . . . he shall surely thrust you out hence altogether. Speak now in the ears of the people, . . . And Moses said, Thus saith the Lord, About midnight will I go out into the midst of Egypt: And all the firstborn in the land of Egypt shall die, from the firstborn of Pharaoh that sitteth upon his throne, even unto the firstborn of the maidservant that is behind the mill; and all the firstborn of beasts. And there shall be a great cry throughout all the land of Egypt, such as there was none like it, nor shall be like it any more. But against any of the children of Israel shall not a dog move his tongue, against man or beast: that ye may know how that the Lord doth put a difference between the Egyptians and Israel. And all these thy servants shall come down unto me, and bow down themselves unto me, saying, Get thee out, and all the people that follow thee: and after that I will go out. And he went out from Pharaoh in a great anger. And the Lord said unto Moses, Pharaoh shall not hearken unto you; that my wonders may be multiplied in the land of Egypt. And Moses and Aaron did all these wonders before Pharaoh: and the Lord hardened Pharaoh's heart, so that he would not let the children of Israel go out of his land. (Exodus 10.28--11.10)

> And it came to pass, that at midnight the Lord smote all the firstborn in the land of Egypt, from the firstborn of Pharaoh that sat on his throne unto the firstborn of the captive that was in the dungeon; and all the firstborn of cattle. And Pharaoh rose up in the night, he, and all his servants, and all the Egyptians; and there was a great cry in Egypt; for there was not a house where there was not one dead. And he called for Moses and Aaron by night, and said, Rise up, and get you forth from among my people, both ye and the children of Israel; and go, serve the Lord, as ye have said. Also take your flocks and your herds, as ye have said, and be gone; and bless me also. (Exodus 12.29-32)

In the scientifically oriented community, there have been those who, intrigued by the story of the exodus, are willing to concede that it may be based in at least some methodical truth. A trend in recent years has been to attempt to ascribe the plagues to a series of predictable environmental phenomena. Of course, if the plagues are "miraculous wonders," as the Bible asserts, supernatural events, by definition, cannot be explained by natural means.[149] Still, there may be a basis to help explain the order and dynamics of the plagues.

If the biblical account is read as literal, the plagues occurred within a single year because Moses was eighty years old when he came to Egypt, he wandered in the wilderness for forty years, and died at the age of 120 (Deuteronomy 34.7).[150] Unless these numbers are figurative, there is no room for the plagues to have occurred over the course of several years. In fact, since it took the Hebrews about three months to reach Sinai, it's possible that the plagues occurred over a span of only forty weeks (Exodus 19.1). If true, the year of the plagues would then have divided into two parts: forty weeks of plagues and twelve weeks of departure; both of these numbers are recurring numbers with symbolic significance in scripture—like a fingerprint of God. The observation is also analogous to nature; human gestation is forty weeks. In that comparison, that fateful year was forty weeks of a very difficult pregnancy (i.e., forty weeks of labor pains) and twelve weeks of delivery. However, while there are several instances in the Bible that are identified as lasting for forty days and even a few for forty years, forty weeks is never specified.

Of course, this forty-week time frame is based on a seven-day week as outlined in the creation account provided in Genesis (Genesis 1.1-2.2). Egyptians had a ten-day week, with three weeks to a month, and twelve months to a year.[151] Their calendar was divided into three seasons—based around the flooding of the Nile: Akhet, Peret, and Shemu.[152] Likewise, "we find a sequence of ten plagues, which (as several commentators have pointed out) divide into three threes, with the tenth as a separate climax."[153] Yet, the plundering of the

Egyptians and the destruction of their army may well be seen as twelve plagues, not ten (Exodus 12.36; 14.28).

The plagues (scripture never ascribes them a number) may apply to the Egyptian calendar, but they may not divide into three threes. The first four plagues could easily be identified as water plagues and would likely have occurred during the months of inundation. Water turning to blood and the plague of frogs are obviously tied to water, but the "lice" and "flies" are probably water related too. The Hebrew word in Exodus 8.16, "*kên*," that is translated as "lice" in the KJV, is a biting insect that could also be described as a gnat.[154] In fact, in the NASB, the English Standard, and the New International Version, *kên* is translated as "gnats." Two species of "gnats" are most common to Egypt: *Culex Pipiens* and *Aedes Aegypti*. Both of these insects are actually mosquitoes and are usually found near polluted water.[155] In a flooded land that had been "fouled" by "heaps" of dead frogs and countless dead fish, it isn't hard to imagine that there was plenty of polluted water in Egypt at that time (Exodus 7.21; 8.14). These two mosquitoes transmit the larvae of the *Wuchereria Bancrofti* nematode, which attacks the lymphatic system causing serious infections and chronic swelling. They are also known carriers of potentially life threatening diseases including encephalitis, yellow fever, dengue fever, West Nile virus, and Chikungunya.[156] Mosquitoes are more likely the insects associated with this plague for another reason as well: mosquitoes regularly bite both man and animals, whereas lice are often species specific (Exodus 8.17). The "flies" of the fourth plague, the Hebrew word "*ârôb*," is probably better translated as swarming mosquitoes.[157] The wording of Exodus 8 may imply that the fourth plague merely compounded the third plague; Psalm 78 may further support this idea. There is no indication that there was a "respite" from the third plague as was the case with the frogs in verse 15. "Divers flies" in Psalms 78.45 could mean that swarms of various flying insects, including mosquitoes, invaded Egypt during the fourth plague. At any rate, it was ruinous (Exodus 8.24). In a normal year, in Egypt, mosquitoes would likely have been especially bad in the fourth month of Akhet as the waters of inundation receded.[158] Of course, this was not a normal year!

The next four plagues would have affected Peret since they would have greatly hampered agriculture. The death of the livestock and the boils would have made planting crops, working the fields, and irrigation extremely difficult.[159] According to Heqanakhte, farming in ancient Egypt was hard physical work that required diligence. Constant plowing, hoeing, hacking, and "sieving with the sieve" were necessary to insure a proper yield.[160] Most sowing took place in the first month of Peret; however, on higher ground, planting began in the fourth month of Akhet.[161] Three kinds of grain were predominantly grown in ancient Egypt: wheat, barley, and durra.[162] Durra (a type of Sorghum) could be planted and harvested as much as three times a year. Crops that were planted at the end of Akhet were ready to harvest early in the fourth month of Peret.[163] Both red and white barley matured faster than the wheat, was planted later, but was usually ready for harvest later in the fourth month of Peret as well.[164] By the end of the first month of Shemu, wheat harvesting was mostly finished.[165] However, some late durra could still be standing in the fields well into Shemu.[166] If the hail fell late in the third month of Peret or early in the fourth month, it would have destroyed the flax and barley, but some wheat and durra could have survived (Exodus 9.31-32).[167] Rye or spelt, another late crop, might actually be the same as durra and/or millet and could also have survived.[168] Even though these crops matured later than barley, even tender shoots would not have escaped the jaws of the locusts in the fourth month of Peret.[169]

The last two plagues (or the remaining four) then would have occurred in Shemu. Darkness would be disconcerting any time of year, but it might have been especially disheartening at the equinox that would have fallen in the middle of the first month of Shemu.[170] Though Josephus says that the tenth plague occurred during the Egyptian month of "Pharmuth," this is doubtful.[171] Pharmuth was part of Peret; Passover usually follows the equinox. The tenth plague, of course, coincided with Passover, which occurs on the 14th day of Abib on the Hebrew calendar, Nisan in Babylonian, usually March or April on the western calendar, and would likely have been early in the second month of Shemu in ancient Egypt (Exodus 12.1-6; Esther 3.7).[172]

Yet, it may be that the plagues (or at least some of them) were tied to the Egyptian calendar in another way. Herodotus said, "The Egyptians are religious to excess, far beyond any other race of men."[173] Festivals were an almost constant occurrence in ancient Egypt. Most were regional; practically all were religious. To interfere with the traditional religious festivities would have made a strong statement against the power of the deity/deities being honored.[174] But beyond this, festivals were occasions when masses of people were allowed to participate and would have been gathered together to witness the inception of the plagues, therefore removing speculation about the power behind the terrible event.[175] It was God's desire for the people of Egypt to know and to fear him; that particular audience would have been amassed for the festivals (Exodus 7.5).[176]

For instance, New Year's Day (Wep-renpet) was observed when Sopdu/Sothis, known to the modern world as Sirius, rose in the eastern horizon at dawn, on the first day of Thoth, the first month of Akhet.[177] This annual astronomical event could have served to reset the Egyptian 365 day calendar each year, which did not allow for leap year. The reappearance of Sothis was considered by Egyptians to be one of their most important days. Not only was New Year's Day an annual celebration, it was a national holiday.[178] On New Year's Day, the season of Inundation began; and the Nile would literally run red, indicating a heavy rainy season further south in Africa.[179] Under normal circumstances, soon after the waters turned red, they would turn green, and then the Nile would flood its banks, filling the irrigation reservoirs with vital stores of water. To the Egyptians, this was a magical event and symbolized rejuvenation and rebirth as in the story of Osiris.[180] The Nile was crucial and central to Egyptian society. Like the marriage of the White Nile and the Blue Nile at Khartoum; the Nile that flowed through Egypt was "the Mother of all Men" and "the Father of Life."[181] In this respect, the Nile was both Isis and Osiris and was the prolific precursor of Egypt.[182] New Year's Day would have been celebrated for several days all over Egypt in temples and religious centers. Included in the celebrations that occurred at the rising of the Nile was The Night of the Tear, dedicated to Isis whose crying over her dead husband was believed to cause the Nile to flood. "The Night of the Tear honored Isis as the goddess of nurturing and mortuary powers, associating her with the basic life-giving function of the river."[183] Yet, the priests also burned incense to honor Osiris and to greet him on his return from the dead.[184] Fragrant ointments and mildly intoxicating flowers enhanced the experience.[185] Sacred singers and dancers, using clappers and sistrums, would have played a prominent role in the festivities.[186] Countless loaves of bread, fruits and vegetables, beer and wine, bouquets of flowers, geese, birds, oxen, and cattle were all offered at the rise of Sopdu/Sothis.[187] As was also ordinary to Egyptian festivals, there would have been days of feasting, intoxication, and reveling. Whether it was actual or simply art, festivals provided an extraordinary palette of anesthetisizing and "aestheticizing" pleasure.[188] But nothing was ordinary about the year of the plagues.

Imagine the terror that would have gripped the people gathered in the early morning, on the banks of the Nile, for the New Year's Day festival if they witnessed "Pharaoh in the morning; lo, [as] he goeth out unto the water," and there Moses and Aaron were standing in opposition to the king, the priests, Isis and Osiris, and to the day's festivities "by the river's brink;" and Moses "lifted up the rod, and smote the waters that were in the river, in the sight of Pharaoh, and in the sight of his servants; and all the waters that were in the river were turned"— not just red but—"to blood" (Exodus 7.15, 20).

Now, it is possible that the day of the first plague was just an ordinary day and not a festival day. After all, Pharaoh probably went regularly to the water early in the morning to bathe, as may be the indication in Exodus 8.20. He probably took some servants with him on this daily errand, as did the daughter of the pharaoh who went to the Nile specifically to bathe (Exodus 2.5). At first reading of Exodus 7.19, it may seem that the inundation had already happened because the reservoirs may have already been full and that there was water throughout the land, but this verse is stressing what *will* happen. Verse 20 clearly addresses water that is *in* the Nile. Furthermore, if the Nile had already flooded, it would have been difficult for Moses to have stood on the "*sepheth*," the "natural boundary," the bank of the Nile.[189] The KJV implies that the water was at its "brink," about to flood, and that it was after this scene that "there was blood throughout all the land of Egypt," indicating that blood—not water—flooded the land (Exodus 7.21). It was an ominous symbol of what was to come.

From an Egyptian perspective, water turning to blood had mythological significance. To prevent the destruction of mankind, a sea of red barley beer was prepared to trick a bloodthirsty monster, the Eye of Ra, Sekhmet (Hathor in a malevolent form). According to Egyptian mythology, the terrible eye roamed the earth in ravenous hunger for the blood of men and animals. Shriveled carcasses strewn in the desert were said to be the tragic result of an encounter with Sekhmet. When the Eye of Ra saw the sea of beer, she thought it was blood and proceeded to guzzle the red liquid. As a result, she fell into a drunken stupor and was rendered harmless[190]

Of course, Pharaoh's servants who accompanied him to the Nile that morning, could be understood to be just his few closest attendants, or it could be *all* of his servants, including his priests, officials, and even his subjects. The NIV translates "servants" in Exodus 7.20 as "officials," but it is doubtful that Pharaoh usually took "officials" or magicians with him when he took a bath (Exodus 7.22).[191] Even though Pharaoh's magicians "duplicated" the effect of water turning to blood, there would have been no doubt as to how the terrible event began. All of the servants of pharaoh who were gathered that day were eye witnesses to a miracle, and for a solid week, everyone in Egypt dug for water during a time when they were usually flooded with the life-giving liquid. It is ironic to consider that a festival dedicated to rejuvenation and to the giver of new life would have been turned to ruin and death, though it is important to note that, according to scripture, blood is the liquid of life and rejuvenation (Genesis 9.4; Leviticus 17.11, 14; Deuteronomy 12.23; Hebrews 9.12; 13.12).

"Religious festivals, celebrated in pomp by the pharaoh himself, must have been occasions of the greatest magnificence."[192] The day that water turned to blood was not an ordinary day. It seems likely that the first plague coincided with and completely disrupted the celebration of New Year's Day. Whether each plague corresponds to a given holiday is hard to say; yet the plagues probably ruined the ritual of several holidays, and it would be difficult to find any day on the ancient Egyptian calendar when a festival was not occurring somewhere in the Two Lands.[193]

In the New Kingdom, when Amun-Ra was preeminent, the Opet was arguably the most important festival of the year.[194] It took place in the second month of Akhet, in Thebes; crowds of Egyptians packed the city, many fashioning make-shift lean-tos for the festival that lasted nearly half of the month.[195] Opet celebrated Amun-Ra, the supreme god of Amenhotep II, but it also honored the pharaoh.[196] As the festival began, 18-24 priests conveyed golden statues of Amun-Ra, the pharaoh, Mut (Amun-Ra's wife), and Khonsu (Amun-Ra's son) from the Karnak temple to the Nile. A priest to clear the path, a priest to carry burning incense, and a priest to blow a trumpet preceded the procession. Two gilded barges waited to carry the statues to Luxor.[197] Countless people conducted the barques along the flooded river by ropes being handed from person to person lining either side of the water's edge. It was considered a great honor to be one holding the rope. Throngs of merry-makers surrounded the rope bearers, singing, playing instruments, dancing, waving standards, and prostrating themselves. In the harbor at Luxor, eight bulls were sacrificed in honor of the union of Amun-Ra and Mut.[198] Festivals such as this that celebrated the sexual life of the gods were erotic in nature. No doubt, frogs—coming forth from the waters "abundantly," in the houses, in the bedchambers, on the beds, and on the people—would have greatly interfered with the Opet, also known as the Festival of the Beautiful Harem (Exodus 8.3-4).[199] It's ironic to consider that frogs, Egyptian symbols of fertility, would usually have been welcomed at the Opet, but that day, Heket, the frog goddess, the defender of the home, became an unwelcome, invader of the home![200]

Perhaps it is possible that other festivals were meant to be hampered by the plagues. For instance, the "murrain of cattle" may have disrupted festivals dedicated to the Apis bull or to Hathor that, according to a Middle Kingdom temple calendar were identified as "day[s] of butchery for the god," occurring in the early part of Peret.[201] Meat was usually reserved for celebrations and sacrifice at festivals.[202] Amenhotep II, in particular, attributed his vitality and strength, in part, to Hathor.[203] Furthermore, "The Great Burning" on the first day of the third month of Peret could have involved a furnace, or kiln, like the one that is specified twice in the plague of boils (Exodus 9.8-10). The events of the first plague perhaps unfolded near Memphis since that is where most of the New Kingdom pharaohs lived a good part of the time. However, pharaohs spent the Opet festival season in Thebes.[204] In fact, festivals were occasion for Egyptians from every walk of life to pilgrimage to shrines and temples in other regions.[205] If other regional festivals caused the pharaoh to visit different locations across Egypt, plagues targeted to those celebrations would have demonstrated that there was no place of escape. With the exception of Goshen during certain plagues, all of Egypt was afflicted.

Another major festival was the Min Feast that usually happened in the first month of Shemu. Min, a fertility god, was carted through the streets by horses, and part of the celebration included the pharaoh harvesting the first sheaf of wheat.[206] However, this was also intended to be a sobering ritual that recognized the sorrow of killing the grain.[207] Egyptian reapers were weepers. Nevertheless, this festival symbolized the king's role "as life-sustainer of his people."[208] In the aftermath of the locusts, however, there would have been nothing left to celebrate, and pharaoh's power was seriously undermined. Weeping would not have been ceremonial. Assmann contrasts Egyptian religion to the Law of Moses, citing Deuteronomy 26.10-14, concerning the "first fruits of the land . . . I have not eaten thereof in my mourning . . . ."[209] The Hebrews were to tithe to God the first of their harvest. They were not to take away from what God was due for any reason: to comfort themselves, to satisfy any other purpose, or to appease the dead. They were not to begrudge or rob God; God has *always* loved a "cheerful giver" (Malachi 3.8; II Corinthians 9.7). Therefore, in contrast, some Ancient Egyptians feigned mourning but were actually glad for the harvest; while some Hebrews feigned cheerful giving but were actually measured (unhappy and grumbling) in their sentiment (Luke 11.42; Psalms 126.5).

Yet, in the second month of Shemu was held one of the biggest and most sacred festivals of the year: the Feast of the Beautiful Valley. This, too, was a festival that honored Amun and, more specifically, the creation myth associated with him. Since Amun was believed to have first emerged from a subterranean region as the primeval serpent Kneph, he was also seen as a god of the underworld. Therefore, the Valley Festival was a celebration of both the living and the dead.[210] As was the case in many Egyptian festivals, specific idols were removed from their temple sanctuaries and were transported to other locations as if on a holiday. Usually these statues were considered to be going to spend the night with some other god, or they were re-enacting the wedding night with their mate. In the Valley Feast, the statues of Amun-Ra, his consort Mut, and their son Khonsu were sailed across the Nile from Karnak to Deir el-Bahri where events culminated in a huge feast.[211] Amun-Ra was also conveyed to the mortuary temple of Hatshepsut, to spend the night with Hathor. Festivals that celebrated the sexual exploits of deities often involved sensual and erotic elements.[212] However, the Valley Feast was also a festival of the dead. Therefore, another part of this particular feast involved a procession of the living, carrying images of the dead from Karnak to the tombs, where families, visiting private chapels of dead relatives, would spend the entire night feasting and drinking in celebration of their ancestors. At sunrise, Amun-Ra sailed back to Karnak with great fanfare, and the crowds went home to bed.[213] In fact, "the connection between religiosity, ritual experience, and sexuality is most fully articulated in this festival."[214]

However, there was one night during the events of the exodus when it would have been especially perilous to venture out to participate in a festival or any other activity:

> And the Lord spake unto Moses and Aaron in the land of Egypt, saying, This month shall be unto you the beginning of months: it shall be the first month of the year to you. Speak ye unto all the congregation of Israel, saying, In the tenth day of this month they shall take to them every man a lamb, according to the house of their fathers, a lamb for an house: And if the household be too little for the lamb, let him and his neighbour next unto his house take it according to the number of the souls; every man according to his eating shall make your count for the lamb. Your lamb shall be without blemish, a male of the first year: ye shall take it out from the sheep, or from the goats: And ye shall keep it up until the fourteenth day of the same month: and the whole assembly of the congregation of Israel shall kill it in the evening. And they shall take of the blood, and strike it on the two side posts and on the upper door post of the houses, wherein they shall eat it. (Exodus 12.1-7)

> Then Moses called for all the elders of Israel, and said unto them, Draw out and take you a lamb according to your families, and kill the passover. And ye shall take a bunch of hyssop, and dip it in the blood that is in the bason, and strike the lintel and the two side posts with the blood that is

in the bason; and none of you shall go out at the door of his house until the morning. For the Lord will pass through to smite the Egyptians; and when he seeth the blood upon the lintel, and on the two side posts, the Lord will pass over the door, and will not suffer the destroyer to come in unto your houses to smite you. (Exodus 12.21-23)

And . . . at midnight the Lord smote all the firstborn in the land of Egypt, from the firstborn of Pharaoh that sat on his throne unto the firstborn of the captive that was in the dungeon; and all the firstborn of cattle. And Pharaoh rose up in the night, he, and all his servants, and all the Egyptians; and there was a great cry in Egypt; for there was not a house where there was not one dead (Exodus 12.29-30).

According to Tyldesley, the Valley Festival was celebrated at the full moon.[215] The Hebrew's lunar calendar began with the appearance of the (waxing crescent) New Moon.[216] Therefore, the first day of the first Hebrew month of Abib came with the New Moon. By the fourteenth day, the moon of that month would likely have been full. Therefore, Passover was celebrated at the time of the full moon as well. The tenth plague coincided with the first observance of Passover; if the tenth plague were to have coincided with the Feast of the Beautiful Valley, it might help to explain why the Hebrews had to be so strongly encouraged to remain in their homes all night. It would have been very tempting for a highly Egyptianized people to have sought to participate in the celebrations of one of the biggest festivals of the year.

"Festivals forged social links," allowing superiors and inferiors to celebrate together as a collective. Though servants are depicted as serving at festivals, anointing revelers with perfumes, work and even mundane tasks were mostly suspended.[217] In the general holiday atmosphere, sensual indulgence was universally accessible to anyone in attendance, albeit in varying degrees. Many ancient Hebrews obviously enjoyed "the fish, . . . the cucumbers, and the melons, and the leeks, and the onions, and the garlick" abundantly available in Egypt (Numbers 11.5).[218] It is probable that they enjoyed festival activities too.

In the communion of the living and the dead, during the Valley Festival, Egyptians believed that graves in the necropolis became "houses of the joy of the heart."[219] A prayer from the Valley Festival ended in a wish: "May they [the gods] grant a long life and vital old age." Interestingly, the Egyptian word "*nfrt*" that is translated into "beautiful" also means "vitality" and "completion."[220] How sad and ironic to consider that, perhaps, in the celebration of this very festival that the firstborn died. If this is true, in an instant, all the houses of "joy of heart" became the houses of a "great cry" as hopes for long life and vitality were snuffed (Exodus 12.30). In a festival to venerate their heritage—the inheritors died. It was the climax of the plagues of Egypt.

If the plagues were orchestrated to undermine Egyptian festivals and their associated ideology, God was manifesting his intimate knowledge of Egyptian culture, his utter disapproval of idols, and his own rightful supremacy. Both Hebrews and Egyptians suffered in the year of plagues. Only the plagues of the flies, the death of the livestock, the hail, the darkness, and the death of the firstborn expressly excluded the Hebrews; and the tenth plague only excluded compliant Hebrews (Exodus 8.22; 9.4, 26; 10.23; 11.4-7). Damage from the plague of hail could have been mitigated by anyone, Hebrew or Egyptian, who feared and obeyed God, whether this is true of other plagues, is not completely known (Exodus 9.19-20). Nevertheless, at the end of the year of ceremonial chaos caused by plagues, God established his own ordered festival—Passover.[221]

Perhaps it may be enlightening to submit the observation that though the tenth plague was severe, God did not allow Egyptians to suffer the death of their first-born alone; in a way, God, himself, shared this excruciating experience with them. On the same day, roughly two thousand years later, God's first-born, his only begotten son, died (Psalms 89.27; Luke 22.1-2). According to scripture, God's relationship with time is completely different from mankind's; so is his perspective (II Peter 3.8). Ancient Egyptians flocked to festivals because they believed that their attendance guaranteed the rare opportunity for participants to see a god (an idol). They also fashioned small images of themselves and presented them as votives at the temple in hopes that a god might see them too.[222] From the true God's perspective, he already saw and loved each one; he gave his son to die for Egyptians, for Hebrews, for all mankind of all time; if only they would look to him and live (John 3.16; Isaiah 45.22)! If Egyptians came to festivals to encounter a god, in the year of the plagues, they did.

Does evidence exist to suggest that the plagues occurred at the end of the reign of Amenhotep II? Perhaps yes. In the tomb of Tjanuny, who served Thutmose IV, there is a depiction of cattle and horses being restored to this Egyptian.[223] What had happened to Tjanuny's livestock that moved him to commemorate this event? The tomb wall seems to indicate some tragedy may have befallen the herds of this one man, but it hardly supports the notion that a plague destroyed the livestock of all Egypt (Exodus 9.6). However, it is curious to add to this evidence that during the short administration of Thutmose IV, the job description of the Nubian viceroy was expanded—for the first time—to include the title: "Overseer of Cattle." Some experts have speculated that perhaps Thutmose IV did this in an effort to undercut the power of the priests of Amun, however:

> This idea gains little support from the evidence. In fact there is evidence that the cattle in question were those held in Nubia, and since the viceroy was the chief representative of Egypt in the south, he controlled both Amun's goods and the King's.[224]

Why would the bulk of Egypt's cattle suddenly be in Nubia and not in Egypt? Could this redistribution of cattle be evidence of the effects of the fifth plague? Of course, some livestock was obviously restored to the Egyptians between the fifth and the seventh plague because livestock was in the fields to be susceptible to falling hail (Exodus 9.19-21). It stands to reason that Egyptians with means could have procured livestock from neighboring countries or could have demanded animals from their Hebrew slaves. Of course, after the exodus, acquiring cattle from the Hebrews would not have been easy.

Further evidence of the plagues may exist in a curious feature about the mummy of Amenhotep II that is often cited by his observers. His body is covered in strange, round papules.[225] Some ascribe these marks to the mummification process, but it is difficult to accept this theory since a chemical reaction would likely have been more uniform, involving the entire surface of the skin and not merely patches. Most medical experts believe that these scars were the result of some systemic disease, although the exact identification of the illness has yet to be diagnosed.[226] Further speculation suggests that the skin condition could have been hereditary since similar lesions also appear on the remains of Thutmose II, Thutmose III, Hatshepsut, Thutmose IV, Amenhotep III, and Tutankhamun, all of whom share a common ancestry in Thutmose I.[227] Still, there are other unrelated persons who also bear pockmarks on their bodies. The wife of Amenhotep III, Queen Tiye, whose body was discovered in the tomb of Amenhotep II, has pock marks.[228] Also, the mummy of Ramses V, another body in the cache of monarchs found in the tomb of Amenhotep II, is scarred with papules, as is the body of Ramses II who was not among the pharaohs in KV35.[229] Interestingly, the Roman historian, Pompeius Trogus, talks about a scabrous skin disease that was associated with Hebrews. Similarly, Manetho, Lysimachos, and Chaeremon associate leprosy with the time of the Hyksos, foreigners, and/or Hebrews, particularly, Moses.[230]

However, the descriptions given for lesions found on the various mummies are not always the same. For example, the doctors who examined the mummy of Ramses V felt confident enough in the "distribution and form of these eruptions" to venture no alternative diagnosis of this condition other than smallpox.[231] While, as part of the same study, the "scabrous patches" observed on the body of Thutmose II remain an enigma and, therefore, must not appear to be consistent with smallpox.[232] Only the lesions of Thutmose II are consistently described as "scabrous" though several of the pockmarks on the afflicted mummies are identified as nodules.[233] Of course, the severity, amount, and form of scarring varies from individual to individual; no two people have skin that scars in exactly the same way. There are many different injuries (even bug bites) and skin disorders that can result in scarring, and one of them is boils. Could the mysterious round, lesions that cover the body of Amenhotep II be evidence of the sixth plague, perhaps even of the third through the sixth plagues?[234] It is interesting to note that the skin condition that affected Thutmose II did not include his hands and feet, but even the feet of Amenhotep II are "covered in papules of various sizes."[235] The boils associated with the sixth plague, similar to the boils that covered Job, seemed to have involved the feet of the Egyptians because Pharaoh's magicians were unable to stand because of them (Job 2.7; Exodus 9.11).[236]

If boils are a possible explanation for the mysterious lesions on Amenhotep II, they could well explain the scars on Thutmose IV, Amenhotep III, and Queen Tiye too. All of these people would likely have been alive during the time of the plagues. As for the others, perhaps boils were not particularly uncommon in the ancient world; perhaps it was the extent of the condition, not the condition itself that constituted the sixth plague.

All ten of the plagues were potentially life threatening, especially to any individual whose health might have been already compromised before the plagues began. Josephus reports that many did die from each of the plagues.[237] Is there, then, evidence to support a great number of deaths at the end of the reign of Amenhotep II? Yes. "Thutmose IV's reign has been credited with a large number of tombs in Thebes, probably far more than it ever saw constructed."[238] If plagues wiped out scores of people in the last days of Amenhotep II's reign, it stands to reason that many of those, if not most of those, would have been buried in the early reign of Thutmose IV. Under this theory, the disproportionately large number of tombs is sadly understandable.

Further evidence from these tombs that could support the notion of an overwhelming number of dead is found in the tombs themselves. Even in the Valley of the Kings, where Egypt buried its most powerful and socially connected, "a number of" tombs believed to date to the mid Eighteenth Dynasty were left undecorated and even unfinished. Indeed, some of these uncharacteristically austere tombs had multiple chambers "intended for group burials."[239] It gives the impression that, suddenly and unexpectedly, there were so many dead, there simply was not enough time, energy, and/or manpower to sustain convention. Affluence in Egypt was not lacking during this time. Therefore, it cannot be the case that the patrons of KV 12, KV 21, KV 25, KV 27, KV 30, KV 39, KV 42 and others were not wealthy enough to pay for elaborate tombs.[240] Even Rekhmire, the vizier for both Thutmose III and Amenhotep II, was buried in a place that appears not to have been originally intended as a place for burial. Though the tomb is decorated with "elaborate paintings of his funeral procession and all the grave goods to accompany him," it's possible that the great Rekhmire had no funeral at all.[241] Some wonder what may have "disgraced the vizier" and caused him to be buried in such sad fashion.[242] The most likely explanation seems to be that death came suddenly and unexpectedly to even influential Egyptians, and that they were caught woefully unprepared for the afterlife, an almost unimaginable fate for an Egyptian, especially for an Egyptian like Rekhmire whose family had served the Great House for generations.[243] KV 25 is an another example of a tomb that was intended to be grand, even royal, but it abruptly stops before its second corridor. Either the sponsor of this tomb changed his mind, lost his fortune, or lost his life before the work was complete. Furthermore, the number of dead was so great, expedience superseded extravagance. KV 42, another unfinished tomb abandoned by its unidentified, intended occupant, was filled with the bodies of "intrusive private individuals." Obviously, tomb space was lacking, and grave goods from these improvised burials tie them to the reign of Amenhotep II.[244] Indeed, Exodus 14.11 expresses a similar idea.

Workers and workmanship were apparently also lacking because "finished" tombs from the time of the end of Amenhotep II's reign into the time of Thutmose IV demonstrate "stylistic changes."[245] Some consider this a demonstration of experimentation, throwing off the formulaic "books of models."[246] However, could the "new expression" represent a lack of manpower and/or a lack of experience? Tombs for high officials, such as Haty who served as Steward for the god's Wife (presumably Tiaa), exhibit workmanship of very low quality. The plasterwork is sub-standard, and the painting is considered "sloppy," leading to speculation that either Haty or his artisans were not the caliber of those who held similar positions in previous administrations.[247] Even the tomb of Amenhotep II is an example. Though his tomb is undeniably beautiful, it is left almost, but not quite, completed, suggesting the conclusion that Amenhotep II, also, died suddenly.[248] Furthermore, the quality of much of the artwork in the tomb of Amenhotep II is simple and flat.

> A comparison of images from the tomb of Amenophis II [sic] and the tomb of Ramses III shows the simple paint on plaster of the earlier tomb and the carved and painted relief technique of the later monument. The differing treatment of individual features: for example the mouth, ears, stomach and pupil of the eye is usually diagnostic of specific periods.[249]

Is this a correct assessment of why the artwork in Amenhotep II's tomb is substandard? During his lifetime, Amenhotep II built elaborate tombs decorated with vibrant artwork for loyal officials who served in his administration; his vizier Amenemipet, Sennefer, Sentnay (a royal wet nurse), Kenamun, Miny and Ahmose Humay, who was probably Amenhotep II's nurse are all examples.[250] Perhaps these individuals were all much older than Amenhotep II, and he expected them to precede him in death. Yet, it is not consistent with the ego of Amenhotep II to be understated in his own tomb.

As a side note, it is important to mention that Dr. Rohl believes that the first cache of mummies in the Valley of the Kings was the group relegated to KV 35. Since the rich "Nubian gold mines were lost at the end of the New Kingdom, and with them the necessary 'hard currency' for dealing with the Levantine Coast," the priests/pharaohs of the Twenty-first Dynasty "mined" the Valley of the Kings for riches. [251] If this is true, it makes sense that they would begin their treasure seeking operations in the tomb of the king of the Golden Age, Amenhotep III. Rohl thinks that after Amenhotep III's tomb was emptied of its bounty, his body was deposited in Amenhotep II's tomb; and that the tomb of the heretic, the Amarna tomb, was stripped next.[252] Then, some of the mummies from that tomb were also relocated to KV 35. If Amenhotep II was the pharaoh of the exodus, his tomb may have been relatively free of goods in comparison to other pharaohs in the Valley because of the devastation left in the wake of the plagues and because the exiting Hebrews plundered the Egyptians (Exodus 3.21-22; 11.2; 12.35-36). Since many of the burial goods entombed with a pharaoh were tributes from his subjects, it is probable that the tomb of the pharaoh of the exodus would have had more empty space than most because his subjects were left relatively empty handed.

Yet, Amenhotep II's tomb stands out for another reason: it was the first tomb to have only painting—no relief work—on the walls, a poor substitute for former craftsmanship.[253] Furthermore, while the antechambers of both Thutmose III and Thutmose IV's tombs are completely decorated, the antechamber of Amenhotep II's tomb is blank, but the sepulchral hall is painted to resemble sheets of papyrus with script of dark green. The style of the artwork is "severely simple."[254] Even to the casual observer, the paintings on the walls of Amenhotep II's burial chamber appear as little more than glorified stick figures (however such figures are common to the *Amduat*). Expedience seems to have been the order of the day. Death must have caught Amenhotep II unprepared, but Thutmose IV, though his reign barely spanned a decade and though he died young, made sure that his own tomb was ready, if not complete, by the time of his demise.[255] Thutmose IV also began the tomb where his son, Amenhotep III was later buried.[256] Thutmose IV's early preparations stand as likely testimony to his life experience: death often arrives prematurely.

Plasterers and tomb builders were not the only professions, appearing to have suffered from a lack of numbers, experience, and skill, during the reign of Thutmose IV. The work on several of his limestone stelae at Giza is "generally fair to poor," causing some to question whether these stelae represent a new "Giza style" of expression or not.[257] However, by the time of Thutmose IV's successor, the quality of art had returned to its former standards as if a new style was never the intension but the sub-standard work was a mere reflection of learning on the job.[258] Even the embalmers who prepared Thutmose IV's body for burial left work that is described as "crude" and "unprofessional."[259] What could account for this sudden ineptitude in Egyptian arts? The plagues described in Exodus blanketed Egyptian society. Every profession in Egypt would have been effected by the loss of skilled workers. Firstborn children usually received the best training, learning the trade of their fathers, who had been the firstborns of the previous generation. No doubt, the loss of the firstborns, alone, would have had a significant impact on the quality of workmanship in Egypt. However, the plagues probably exacted a heavy percentage from the elderly population as well, meaning the loss of experience and teachers.

Of course, the military was especially devastated. Hardly any position in Thutmose IV's administration was carried over from the administration of Amenhotep II, and he seems to have drawn heavily from the ranks of scribes to serve as officers in his military.[260] Nearly every position in the court of Thutmose IV was filled by a novice or by someone who was reactivated after having gone into retirement. This was certainly a stark contrast to the court of his father that drew heavily from the experienced officials who served Thutmose III.[261] The following is a (non-exhaustive) list of names, offices, and the pharaohs under whom they served:

Name	Title	Served
Rekhmire	Vizier in Thebes	Thutmose III & Amenhotep II
Menkheperrasonb	High Priest of Amun	Thutmose III & Amenhotep II
Minmose	Chief Architect	Thutmose III & Amenhotep II
Nb-wꜥwy	High Priest of Osiris	Thutmose III & Amenhotep II
Ka-m-hry-jb-sn	Third Priest of Amun	Thutmose III & Amenhotep II
Amenemhat	Scribe & Steward	Thutmose III & Amenhotep II
Sennefer	Mayor of Thebes	Thutmose III & Amenhotep II
Ddj	Overseer of West Thebes	Thutmose III & Amenhotep II
Jmn-mhb	Captain of the Army	Thutmose III & Amenhotep II
Jmn-ms	Troop Commander	Thutmose III & Amenhotep II
Nakhtmin	Career Military	Thutmose III & Amenhotep II
Pekhukher	Lieutenenant	Thutmose III & Amenhotep II
Tjenenu	Adjutant of the King	Thutmose III & Amenhotep II
Ph-sw-hr	Commander of Nubians	Thutmose III & Amenhotep II
Nb-jmn	Royal Butler	Thutmose III & Amenhotep II
Mntw-jy-wy	Overseer of Food/Wine	Thutmose III & Amenhotep II
Nfr-rnpt	Overseer of Grainary	Thutmose III & Amenhotep II
Menkheper	Overseer of Construction	Thutmose III & Amenhotep II
Bnja	Mortuary High Priest	Thutmose III & Amenhotep II
Jꜥh-ms	Mortuary Steward	Thutmose III & Amenhotep II
Jmn-m-hb	Mortuary Wab Priest	Thutmose III & Amenhotep II
Pa-wah	Mortuary Wab Priest	Thutmose III & Amenhotep II
Mry	Wab Priest	Thutmose III & Amenhotep II
Nb-jmn	Wab Priest	Thutmose III & Amenhotep II
Mn-hpr	Wab Priest	Thutmose III & Amenhotep II
Nfr-hb-f	Second Priest	Thutmose III & Amenhotep II
Hwy	Offering Bearer	Thutmose III & Amenhotep II
Hwy	Adjutant of the House	Thutmose III & Amenhotep II
Dhwty-ms	Goldworker	Thutmose III & Amenhotep II
Nfr-rnpt	Overseer of Goldsmiths	Thutmose III & Amenhotep II
Nb-Sny		

In contrast, very few officials serving under Thutmose IV had served in previous administrations:

Name	Title	Served
Hepu	Vizier of Upper Egypt	Thutmose IV
Ptahhotep	Vizier of Lower Egypt	Thutmose IV
Kha	Deir-el Medina Sculptor	Amenhotep II & Thutmose IV
Tjenuna	Chief Steward	Amenhotep II & Thutmose IV
Jpw	First King's Son of Amun	Amenhotep II & Thutmose IV
[Jmn]-wsr-hat	Butler	Amenhotep II & Thutmose IV
Nebi	Troop Commander	Amenhotep II & Thutmose IV
Tjanuni	Overseer of the Army	Thutmose III & Thutmose IV
Sobekhotep	Treasurer	Thutmose III & Thutmose IV
Horemheb	Royal Scribe of Recruits	Amenhotep II, Thutmose IV, & Amenhotep III
Any	Steward and Scribe	Amenhotep II to Akhenaten[262]

Furthermore, several of the officials in Thutmose IV's administration who had worked in previous administrations, served in new capacities. Tjenuna, for example, who served Thutmose IV as chief steward, had only served as a scribe to the chief steward during the reign of Amenhotep II; Tjenuna was promoted to the position of his former master.[263] Thutmose IV's first chief steward was a man named Merire; he must have been very old because Merire had served as a steward to Thutmose III. After Merire, Thutmose IV promoted Merire's scribe, Tjenuna, to chief steward.[264] Thutmose IV's treasurer, Sobekhotep, who was also "Mayor of Faiyum," had served his father, Min, the overseer of the treasury under Thutmose III, but there is no mention of him serving at all in the administration of Amenhotep II.[265] Another unconventional choice was Amenemhet, who served as the High Priest of Amun under Thutmose IV even though he was of "lowly birth" and at the age of 54 was still only a wab priest; "he obviously then rocketed into the pontificate of Amun, through what means we cannot say. But it would be unreasonable to suggest he served as High priest for many years at an advanced age."[266] Amenhotep si-se, another man of lowly rank, was promoted to the prestigious position of Second Prophet of Amun under Thutmose IV though there is no evidence that he came from a military background or had been "a child raised at court."[267] Nebi was a troop commander for Thutmose IV, but in the days of Amenhotep II, he was a fort commander stationed at the outpost in Wawat.[268] Tjanuni, the overseer of Thutmose IV's army, was promoted from a scribe in the court of Amenhotep II, as was Horemheb.[269]

Horemheb was the remaining "sole representative" to have served in a military capacity under Amenhotep II (and perhaps even under Thutmose III) and went on to serve in the court of Amenhotep III.[270] Thutmose IV also reinstated officers for his military from men who had already gone into retirement.[271]

Why did Thutmose IV rely on old men, former scribes, and bureaucrats to run his army? Why didn't he maintain the army under current generals and commanders, career military men with years of battle experience? In fact, "the rank of 'general' or 'military officer [was] practically unknown in the period" of Thutmose IV. However, the "office of 'scribe of recruits' was never so well attested;" yet the men who held these positions were "clearly court associates" not "hardened military men."[272] It has been suggested that Thutmose IV simply allowed "the military ranks to shrink and to bureaucratize."[273] However, this may not have been, at all, the case! It may be that there were no surviving military men for Thutmose IV to have in his army.

> And the Lord said unto Moses, Stretch out thine hand over the sea, that the waters may come again upon the Egyptians, upon their chariots, and upon their horsemen. And Moses stretched forth his hand over the sea, and the sea returned to his strength when the morning appeared; and the Egyptians fled against it; and the Lord overthrew the Egyptians in the midst of the sea. And the waters returned, and covered the chariots, and the horsemen, and all the host of Pharaoh that came into the sea after them; there remained not so much as one of them. (Exodus 14.26-28)

If Amenhotep II, "all the chariots of Egypt, and captains over every one of them" and "his army" drowned, Thutmose IV would have had little choice other than to promote scribes and bureaucrats into leadership positions, to bring old military men out of retirement, and to recruit and train a whole new army (Exodus 14.7, 9). This may also explain why there are no "lengthy tomb biographies of Thutmose's (IV) soldiers."[274] It also stands to reason that Nubia, more than any other of Egypt's neighbors, would have been keenly aware of the weakened condition of the army under Thutmose IV. After all, Nubians had almost always served in the Egyptian army. Even in the Middle Kingdom, Nubian warriors knows as Mejia were an integral fixture in the military forces of the pharaoh.[275] In Amenhotep II's army, the Nubians seemed to have constituted entire divisions with separate "Commander of the Nubian Troops" and a "Chief of the Nubians."[276] Therefore, Nubia would have had first hand knowledge of a sudden mass loss in the Egyptian army, of the compromised position of Egypt, and could very well have been emboldened to invade the Two Lands.

Still, death, as it is associated with the plagues of the biblical exodus, is not only notorious for being devastating, widespread, and sudden; it is mostly identified with the tenth plague: the death of the firstborn. Without argument, the tenth plague was the worst. One can only imagine the overwhelming grief and loss that shrouded the Two Lands as the scriptures describe, "there was a great cry in Egypt; for there was not a house where there was not one dead" (Exodus 12.30). As in many ancient cultures, in Egypt the firstborn child was especially treasured. Psalms 105.36 calls the firstborn of Egypt "the chief of all their strength."

There is some debate, however, as to whether the tenth plague claimed only the lives of firstborn sons— not daughters. In Exodus 13.12-13, God singled out Hebrew firstborn males in—even firstborn male animals, and verse 15 seems to limit those Egyptian firstborns who were sacrificed to God in the tenth plague to males— both of man and beasts. Exodus 4.23 makes it clear that God was poised to slay the firstborn *son* of Pharaoh.[277] However, this statement may be just another indication that Amenhotep II was the pharaoh of the exodus. Most experts agree that Amenhotep II, unlike most other pharaohs, may have had only one wife, Tiaa. (Although the cedar coffin of a woman named Merit-Amun is considered by some as evidence to the contrary).[278] Amenhotep II is only known to have had children with Tiaa, so it is likely that Amenhotep II was the father of only one woman's firstborn child, and though princes in the Eighteenth Dynasty had been relatively rare, Amenhotep II's firstborn child was likely a son.[279] In fact, though it is hard to determine an exact number, Amenhotep II and Tiaa may have had as many as nine sons and at least one daughter.[280]

Certainly, firstborn sons died in the tenth plague, and the loss would have been tremendous. In the ancient world, usually it was the firstborn son who carried on the family trade; and therefore, the firstborn son was trained as a skilled worker, providing, as previously discussed, an explanation for the sudden lack of experienced tradesmen and the sub-standard craftsmanship in the time of Thutmose IV.[281] The firstborn son also typically carried on the family's standing in the community. Firstborn sons were often groomed to occupy the position of their fathers. However, in Egyptian society, a son whom a father wished to inherit his authority had to pass the formality of being nominated by the king.[282]

The protocol for military service, however, may have been different. Motives behind military careers in ancient Egypt are not completely understood.[283] Of course, in many ancient cultures, second born and subsequent sons, who did not expect to benefit from the lion's share of their father's inheritance, found careers in the military as soon as they were of age to serve; therefore, when Egypt lost its army, it lost many subsequent sons who did not die in the tenth plague. It is even likely that the subsequent sons of Amenhotep II, sixteen years and older, were old enough to serve in the military, following in the legacy of their father.[284]

Still, most passages that discuss the tenth plague do not specify firstborn males, and it is hard to explain the statement, "there was not a house where there was not one dead" if only sons died (Exodus 12.30). Indeed, one can imagine many scenarios where houses may not have included a firstborn male. Firstborn daughters could have been included in the death of the tenth plague because daughters were especially valued in Egypt. Egyptian women had rights and power.[285] It has even been suggested that Egypt evolved from a matriarchal society.[286] However, though Egyptian women were not usually as powerful as men, they were not relegated to the status of mere property, as was the case in most ancient cultures. In Egyptian culture, women could own property, divide property among their heirs, be employed, divorce their husbands, and receive a sizeable portion of the estate in the event of a divorce.[287] At times in Egyptian history, royal daughters—not sons—were kept in record and did not fade into obscurity like their brothers (potential male successors were often not mentioned by a sitting pharaoh), which helped foster the "heiress' theory of ascension.[288] However, if the tenth plague occurred on the night of the Beautiful Valley Festival, families from various ancestral "houses" would have been gathered to honor the dead. In that case, it is easier to reconcile that, even if the death of the first born was gender specific, "there was not a *house* where there was not one dead."[289]

At any rate, the death of so many people in the plagues and especially the loss of the firstborns would have made a significant impact on Egyptian society. No longer could there be "business as usual." Though some have speculated that the drastic change in the composition of Thutmose IV's court could mean that he denied the sons of powerful families to follow in their fathers' footsteps (perhaps in some sort of effort to effect the balance of power or in order to appoint the king's own favored "newcomers"), others have surmised that Thutmose IV's reliance on bureaucrats and diplomats was merely a transition in style of government, moving away from the military model.[290] However, it could also be that the impromptu king had little choice.

Curiously, after the reign of Amenhotep II, high officials and whole families of those who were once powerful seem to have been extinguished. One example is Usersatet who disappeared into obscurity.[291] Kenamun, who grew up with Amenhotep II, who is called "Foster Brother of the Lord of the Two Lands," who is considered by some to be Amenhotep II's best friend, who served in an active capacity throughout Amenhotep II's reign, who fought beside him in battle, who was named Steward of Peru-nefer (an important ship yard), and who later, became Steward of the King's Household is never heard of again after the death of Amenhotep II.[292] "There is evidence that Kenamun had planned an elaborate expansion of his tomb/chapel complex, but the plans were left unfinished."[293] Another example is Amenemipet, the vizier considered to be Amenhotep II's most trusted official, yet none of his "children or other descendants obtained influential status comparable to his. Indeed, so far as we know, Amenemipet's family disappears politically with his death."[294]

Is there further evidence to suggest that the terrible tenth plague occurred at the end of the reign of Amenhotep II? If so, the most conspicuous deaths would likely have occurred within the royal family. The sitting pharaoh, at the time of the tenth plague, survived; because on the night of the tenth plague "he called for Moses and Aaron," (Exodus 12.31). Therefore, the pharaoh of the exodus could not have been a firstborn son. As already established, Amenhotep II was not the firstborn son of Thutmose III.[295] Amenhotep II's older brother, Amenemhat B, who was identified as the eldest, disappeared between years 24-35 of Thutmose III's reign.[296] Another probable older brother of Amenhotep II was Menkheperre A, who was also the son of Meryetre-Hatshepsut, making Amenhotep II unlikely to be the firstborn son of his father and not the firstborn son of his mother either.[297] Others of the royal family who survived the tenth plague are of interest. Queen Tiaa was not a first-born child.[298] Furthermore, she survived her husband, Amenhotep II, to occupy a very prominent role in the administration of her son.[299] Thutmose IV was not the first-born son of Amenhotep II and Tiaa.[300] In the tomb of Hekarnehhe, a royal tutor, Thutmose IV is twice referred to as "the eldest king's son." However, this inscription was probably written after Thutmose IV had already become acting pharaoh. Indeed, in Hekarnehhe's tomb, Thutmose IV is depicted as an adult. Therefore, a better interpretation of the writing in Hekarnehhe's tomb would probably be that Thutmose IV was the eldest "surviving" king's son.[301] Amenhotep II's oldest son, Amenhotep C, was probably born during the first five years of Amenhotep II's reign, since he was given the title of Executive at the Head of the Two Lands and "held office by the king's twentieth year"; he also may have served as Semi-Priest of Ptah at Memphis under Amenhotep II.[302] And even though Thutmose IV was very young when he became king, he had at least two wives and had already fathered more than one child. His "eldest son, Amenemhat, died young" and Amenhotep III, who was about two-years-old when his grandfather Amenhotep II died, was not proclaimed as heir apparent until year seven of Thutmose IV.[303] Could it be that both the oldest brother and the oldest son of Thutmose IV died on the same night? Though he was but a young king, Thutmose IV was buried in KV 43 "alongside two of his children," his son, Amenemhat (whose canopic jars were found in the tomb of Thutmose IV), and a daughter, Tentamun, who may have died in the same year as her father.[304]

Did the biblical plagues occur at the end of the reign of Amenhotep II? Something extraordinary did! Experts say that "we catch only glimpses" of the "conflict" that engulfed the royal family at the end of Amenhotep II's reign and that events preceding the ascension of Thutmose IV are "clouded" by "unexpected difficulties."[305] Even Amenhotep II's mother was disgraced for some unknown reason.[306] However, if such utter humiliation of any pharaoh (perhaps especially Amenhotep II) had occurred, one would hardly expect to find a whisper of it among Egyptian records.[307] Dr. Kitchen goes so far as to suggest that such evidence *cannot* exist.[308] Yet, the ominous statement left by a scribe may lend an indication of the unparalleled chaos that was experienced. Amenhotep II's scribe writes, "Nothing like it had happened 'since the time of men and gods.'"[309]

Perhaps it was the memory of the death of the firstborn from that tragic year and other Exodus-related events that the ancient Greek historian, Hecataeus of Abdera, who lived several hundred years before Manetho, was trying to record. Hecataeus wrote that Egypt was being ravaged by a plague, during a time when the Egyptians believed that the plague was the result of divine punishment and was associated with the presence of aliens in the land. "Consequently, the aliens were expelled." Some of these aliens relocated to Greece; others settled in Palestine.[310] This account sounds very like the scripture's explanation that the terrified Egyptians, after being softened by the plagues, were favorably disposed to be rid of the Hebrews (Exodus 3.21-22; 11.3; 12.36). However, if Hecataeus is referring to the exodus, his recollection may also display an indomitable hubris in Egyptian perspective—the Hebrews were not "expelled"; they were delivered.

Did the pharaoh of the exodus drown in the Red Sea? Currently, there is debate as to the correct interpretation of the word *"chald,"* the Hebrew word for "papyrus" that makes up the first part of the name that is usually interpreted as "Red Sea." Of course, papyrus was paper that was made out of the fibers of the papyrus plant (that could well be classified as a reed), which grew in the marshes along the Nile.[311] Therefore, does *chald* specify the Red Sea or the ancient Reed Sea? The New Testament offers little clarification since the Greek word *"thalassa,"* that is also usually translated to "Red Sea" in Acts 7.36 and Hebrews 11.29, in actuality only means "the sea." Certainly, parting the waters of a marshy swamp would not nearly be the miracle of parting the sizable Red Sea! Understanding *chald* as a reference to the Reed Sea makes an explanation of the parting of the waters easier to conjecture; but then, supernatural events cannot be limited to or explained by natural means—and "with God all things are possible" (Matthew 19.26). Regardless, the army of the pharaoh, according to Exodus, attempted to pursue the Hebrews through a body of water that was deep enough to completely cover scores of men, horses, and chariots; it was deep enough to be called "the depths" and for them to sink "to the bottom as a stone" (Exodus 14. 28; 15.5) Few marshy swamps could be described in such ways, yet perhaps the no-longer-remaining Sea of Reeds was such a body.[312]

There also seems to be a question as to whether pharaohs actually accompanied their men into battle and, therefore, whether the pharaoh of the exodus would have drowned with his army or not.[313] Certainly, annuls of the pharaohs' battles read as if the pharaohs were present. Depictions of countless battle scenes on temple walls provide a similar impression. Leading their army in battle seems to have been a primary function of ancient kings. Kings from many different nations, in numerous Old Testament battles, led their forces on the battlefield. In fact, that was one of the main reasons that Israel desired to have a king (I Samuel 8.20). The pharaoh of the exodus "made ready his chariot and took his people with him," "he pursued the children of Israel" (Exodus 14.6, 8). The text indicates that Pharaoh was with his army in pursuit of the escaping Hebrews.

> But lift thou up thy rod, and stretch out thine hand over the sea, and divide it: and the children of
> Israel shall go on dry ground through the midst of the sea. And I, behold, I will harden the hearts
> of the Egyptians, and they shall follow them: and I will get me honour upon Pharaoh, and upon
> all his host, upon his chariots, and upon his horsemen. And the Egyptians shall know that I am
> the Lord, when I have gotten me honour upon Pharaoh, upon his chariots, and upon his
> horsemen. (Exodus 14.16-18)

This passage makes no distinction made between "Pharaoh," "his hosts," "his chariots," and "his horsemen." God seems to consider them to be one group, and he intended to be glorified through all of them. "The horse of Pharaoh went in with his chariots and with his horsemen into the sea" (Exodus 15.19). If the horse of Pharaoh went into the sea, it stands to reason that Pharaoh went with his horse. Psalms 136.15 seems to confirm this reasoning when it says, "[God] overthrew Pharaoh *and* his host in the Red Sea." "Not so much as one of them" did not drown (Exodus 14.28). "And Israel saw the Egyptians dead upon the sea shore" (Exodus 14.30). Therefore, the scripture strongly indicates that the pharaoh of the exodus drowned; if Amenhotep II was the pharaoh of the exodus, he likely drowned with his army in pursuit of the Hebrews.

Yet, why would any pharaoh lead his army into a scene as anomalous as a divided sea? As is documented on the Westcar Papyrus, since the days of Sneferu, from the Old Kingdom, Egyptians believed in pharaoh's ability to part waters down to dry rocks; the pharaoh who led his army into the Red Sea probably thought he could do the same.[314] Though there are those who say that the pharaoh of the exodus did not die with his army, most biblical scholars believe that Pharaoh drowned in pursuit of the Hebrews.[315]

Therefore did Amenhotep II die of drowning? To date, no complete autopsy of Amenhotep II is known to have been conducted to determine cause of death, although an examination of his heart, to see if it was, literally, "hard" may have occurred.[316] Yet, clues about his burial may indicate that Amenhotep II drowned.

When archaeologist, Victor Loret, first entered the burial chamber of Amenhotep II in 1898, he was met with a strange and gruesome sight.[317] He describes:

> . . . a terrifying spectacle, a corpse lying there, resting on a boat, completely black, horrendous;
> his face contracted in a grimace, is turned toward me, he looks at me, his long brown hair tossed
> in curls around his head. In less than an instant I think it must only be an unbandaged mummy.
> The legs and arms seem to be sound. A laceration cleaves his breastbone and another one tears
> open his cranium. Was this the victim of a human sacrifice? An ancient desecrator assassinated
> by his accomplices during a bloody division of the booty, or perhaps killed by soldiers who
> appeared on the scene while the tomb was being plundered?[318]

What Loret had encountered was, in fact, the unidentified mummy of a young man. His body had been unwrapped and robbed so soon after his burial that the embalming resins used in the mummification process were still wet because the pitiless looters cast the young man aside into a funerary boat where the resins on his body subsequently hardened and permanently affixed him to the barque.[319] Over the years, some have speculated as to the identity of this desecrated mummy. Most believe that he is a son of Amenhotep II, perhaps

Prince Webensenu, while others say he is Sethnakhte, a pharaoh of the Twentieth Dynasty.[320] Yet, was the gruesome image merely happenstance, or was the funerary boat purposefully placed at the entrance of this tomb for a reason? It is ironic that the first shocking introduction to KV 35 is an image that is graphically tied to water, and perhaps even more specifically, to death and water. Were the tomb robbers or perhaps the priests of the Twenty-first Dynasty who resealed this tomb saying something about the history of the type of death associated with KV 35? Was this a comment on drowning?

Perhaps another indication of a recurring theme of drowning found in KV 35 is on the walls. The walls of Amenhotep II's sepulchral hall are decorated with the *Amduat*, a book of *That Which is in the Underworld*.[321] This volume, related to *The Book of the Dead*, was intended to be used by the deceased as a guidebook to safely navigate perils of the afterlife. Thutmose III's tomb contains (what is said to be) the first known, full copy of the *Amduat*; Amenhotep II's tomb supposedly has the second. In the *Amduat's* tenth chapter is a curious scene: "the drowned swim in a great watery rectangle, the primeval ocean, Nun. At the command of Horus, they are brought to land, where despite their not being mummified they are granted a blessed existence;" their bodies wash up on the shores of the underworld.[322] Even those whose bodies were consumed by crocodiles are protected.[323] In this text, those who drown, known in Egyptian as the *hesy*, at least those who drown in the Nile, are especially blessed by Horus; he delivers them to the Fields of the Blessed. In fact, in Egyptian theology, the souls of the dead passed over "the sea of reeds."[324] The *Amduat* presents a much brighter afterlife for the drowned than the seeming hopelessness expressed by Schetepibre of the Twelfth Dynasty, "there is no tomb for one hostile to his majesty and his body shall be thrown into the waters"; or by *The Dialogue of a Man and His Soul* that refers to victims who drowned in a flood as "oblivious ones."[325]

It is especially intriguing to observe the painting of these scenes as they appear in the tomb of Amenhotep II. The representations are little more than stick figures, in a cursive style used for writing on papyrus, such as is common to the *Amduat*.[326] The work has very little detail until the artist(s) reaches the depiction of the drowned. There, the striking block of color and the sudden attention to detail draws the eye of the observer immediately to this scene. In the depiction, the drowned are not presented as identically repeated forms. Some are on their backs, some are face down, some are on their sides; they individuals. Extra attention is also given to the depiction of the water itself; detailed zigzagging lines, to represent waves, completely cover the illustration. Perhaps this method of depicting the *Amduat* is nothing more than a template. However, artists from every time and culture tend to devote more effort and detail to embellish parts of their work that, to that artist, are important for some reason. Therefore, the meticulous attention devoted to the *Amduat* scenes of the drowned in this primary rendition indicates that these images may have been of particular interest to the artist(s) who painted them. They stand out as significant. Could it be that some of the artist(s) own families were among those individuals who drowned? Could it be that they were members of the army that pursued the Hebrews into the Red Sea? Could it be that this is the reason that the tenth chapter of the *Amduat* is given special attention in the tomb of Amenhotep II? At any rate, the artistic expression in this tomb seems to portray a preoccupation with drowning. Why? Perhaps it is nothing more than an ironic coincidence, but it is curious.

It should be noted that the *Amduat* in the tomb of Thutmose III (KV 34) is very similar in style to the rendition preserved on the walls of KV 35.[327] Stick figures that resemble a form of stylized text appear on the walls of both tombs and seem to strongly suggest ties to the same artist(s). An appreciable difference in the two versions of the *Amduat*, however, is the background. In Amenhotep II's tomb, the background is painted green and resembles sheets of papyrus; while in the tomb of Thutmose III, the *Amduat* is displayed as if on a scroll, with a light background.[328] Of course, it can only be assumed as to when the work was painted on the walls of either tomb, and since Egyptian artists did not sign their work, no one can know who painted them or, for that matter, who commissioned the *Amduat* to be depicted on the walls of these two tombs in the first place. However, there is reason to believe that the *Amduat* in the burial chamber of Amenhotep II was painted "at the sealing of the tomb," while the *Amduat* in Thutmose III's tomb was painted sometime after his funeral.[329] How long after? Though it is most likely that the work was done in the short term, could it be possible that both tombs were decorated during the reign of Thutmose IV? Could it be that Thutmose IV commissioned the painting of the entire *Amduat* on the walls of his father's tomb and afterward had the work duplicated on the walls of his grandfather's tomb as well? After all, Thutmose III had special connections to the men in Amenhotep II's army; he had led them into battle many times. If they had all drowned, the *Amduat* would have spoken comfort to Thutmose III as well as to Amenhotep II. The plasterwork in the tomb of Thutmose III supports the notion that Thutmose IV commissioned the copy of the *Amduat* that is painted there. The plaster is similar to the walls in the tomb of Tiaa's steward, Haty and is described as "substandard," reminiscent of amateur work that characterizes other arts in the time of Thutmose IV.[330]

The Amduat as Seen on the Walls of KV 35

The *Amduat*, itself, seems to be an Eighteenth Dynasty creation.[331] Although it is seen in its entirety on the walls of KV 34 and KV 35, huge panels decorated with the Amduat are stacked in the tomb of Hatshepsut. It appears that they were intended to be installed in her tomb but never were. Perhaps Thutmose IV intended to make this addition to her tomb, but if so, he left them incomplete. If that were the case, his son, Amenhotep III, would certainly have had ample time and resources to finish the task, but never did. Thutmose III and Amenhotep II were more interested in destroying the visions of Hatshepsut than completing them. Therefore, it seems most likely that Hatshepsut herself commissioned the addition of the *Amduat* to the tomb that she intended to share with her father. In that case, concern for the drowned takes on an entirely new significance. If Thutmose I was the pharaoh who ordered Hebrew baby boys to be cast into the Nile, and if Hatshepsut was the daughter of the pharaoh who showed compassion for the baby in the basket, perhaps the story of the *Amduat* (in keeping with her demonstrated affinity for narrative) was especially comforting to Hatshepsut. After all, the daughter of the pharaoh who rescued Moses was probably haunted by the thought of what had happened to countless babies who were not as fortunate. The *Amduat* would have reassured her that the innocent souls of those who drowned and/or were eaten by crocodiles were safe and blessed. Their eventual fate, as described in the *Amduat*, vindicated her beloved father of his heinous crime.

Is it possible that Amenhotep II, in his competitive desire to be "greater than any king who ever lived," neglected, not only the completion of Hatshepsut's tomb, but also failed to decorate the antechamber of his own father? Yet, perhaps he was again merely emulating Thutmose III who, from all appearances, didn't decorate the tomb of his father, Thutmose II, at all.[332] Of course, Thutmose III was likely only a baby when Thutmose II died, therefore Hatshepsut is probably more to blame for the sparse conditions of Thutmose II's burial. Could it be that Amenhotep II only began the decorations for his own tomb just shortly before his death and that he was the one who commissioned the innovative paintings on the pillars in his burial chamber? The artwork on the pillars of KV 35 is decidedly different than the renderings on the walls. The "fully drawn figures of the king" alongside Osiris, Anubis, and Hathor that occupy the pillars are stylistically very dissimilar to the scant figures of the *Amduat*. It is easy to imagine that Amenhotep II would have desired to be depicted in the company of gods, a practice that appeared on the pillars of most of the kings who followed him.[333] However, excerpts of the *Amduat* also became standard decorations in royal tombs.

In fact, the tenth chapter of the *Amduat* and the ninth chapter of the *Book of Gates* could suggest drowning as a common denominator for others selected to be part of the cache of bodies interred in KV 35. Merenptah has long been suspected of drowning, and perhaps he did, since he spent a great deal of his career in battles with Sea People, and one would assume that the name of that opponent implies some naval conflict. It is curious that an excerpt from the ninth chapter of the *Book of Gates* that depicts the drowned as deified is found in the original tomb of Ramses IV, another occupant of KV 35.[334] Furthermore, depictions of the drowned decorate the tomb of Queen Tawosret, the co-regent of Siptah. Tawosret is suspected to be the sole, unidentified woman who was sealed in the side chamber of KV 35 along with eight pharaohs, including her husband.[335] Therefore, nearly half of the bodies in KV 35, at least, could be associated in some way with death by drowning.

One last unusual feature in the burial of Amenhotep II may indicate that he drowned. As was the custom for pharaohs, Amenhotep II was originally buried in an elaborate pectoral collar. It was robbed from him, but it left an impression in his skin. From this impression, it has been determined that Amenhotep II's burial pectoral collar was made of pearls.[336] If this is correct, why, of all the precious and semi-precious stones and embellishments available in Egypt, was an ornament that can only be found in water chosen to adorn this one pharaoh? Is it coincidental that Amenhotep II was buried wearing pearls or was it a gesture that was intended to be symbolic, to have significance, to be somehow appropriate?

Pearls were extremely rare in ancient Egypt. In fact, the *Oxford Encyclopedia of Ancient Egypt* says "pearls were not known in Egypt until the time of the Ptolemaic period."[337] Therefore, it would have been highly unusual for Amenhotep II's pectoral to be pearls. Cleopatra possessed a famous set of pearl earrings, according to the first century historian, Pliny.[338] Pearls must have been fairly widespread during the first century since they are mentioned in the New Testament; but they were still rare and must have been considered quite valuable in light of Jesus' parable about the Pearl of Great Price (Matthew 13.45-46). Job 28.18 probably mentions pearls, although the Hebrew word *gabiysh* is somewhat obscure in its meaning. Saltwater pearls being used before the first millennium BCE have been discovered in regions along the Persian Gulf.[339] Nevertheless, pearls from the Persian Gulf and from the Red Sea were known, harvested, and used in the ancient world.[340] Mother-of-pearl from Red Sea oysters was regularly used to make jewelry that was worn in Egypt, albeit by Nubians.[341] Black-winged Pearl Oysters and Black-lipped Pearl Oysters are both indigenous to the Red Sea, one of the richest sources of pearls on earth.[342] Therefore, ancient Egyptians must have been aware of the oysters in the Red Sea that grow pearls and of how treacherous it was to harvest them.[343] If pearls were in fact part of Amenhotep II's burial pectoral, someone went to extreme lengths to obtain the precious gems, making it even more likely that they were meant to convey a symbolic message. Did Amenhotep II's burial attire make a comment on how and even where died—drowned in the water of the Red Sea?

In fact, apart from early rheumatoid arthritis and the mysterious pockmarks that covered his body, Amenhotep II had no apparent illness or affliction that would account for his death.[344] Even his teeth were sound.[345] From all appearances, he was strong and vigorous, the picture of a middle aged man, having most of his brown, wavy hair, distinguishedly graying at the temples.[346] Amenhotep II appears to have died suddenly. Such could certainly be the case for a victim of drowning. Perhaps at some point in the future, the appropriate medical examinations can be conducted to definitively answer the question of Amenhotep II's death. Until then, it must remain a matter of conjecture.

Yet, what of the body of the young man in the boat? Perhaps the same robbers who stole Amenhotep II's pearl collar were responsible for tossing the unwrapped mummy into the boat since, when the priests of the Twenty-first Dynasty found it, the body of Amenhotep II had also been displaced (presumably dumped out onto the dirt floor of his tomb) and all of his coffins had been destroyed.[347] It is perhaps significant that the tomb robbers were able to remove Amenhotep II's necklace. King Tut was also buried in a grand pectoral collar, jewelry that he was still wearing when Howard Carter first unwrapped the boy king's mummy. Sometime later, Tut's necklace was also stolen. However, since the embalming resins had long since hardened, Tut's magnificent pectoral was impossible to remove from his body. Therefore, the insensitive thieves cut through the boy's chest wall and took Tut's costly necklace along with his sternum and the front of his rib cage. In antiquity, Amenhotep III's body was hacked into pieces by tomb robbers similarly intent on retrieving valuable amulets and jewelry.[348] Amenhotep II's collar had been on his body long enough and securely enough to leave an indelible impression in his skin, but the embalming resins were obviously still soft enough to release the pearls into the hands of the robbers. However, an abundance of resins had been used in the mummification of Amenhotep II because, to this day, there are still pieces of "cloth soaked in resin" permanently adhered to the pharaoh's face.[349] If both the body of Amenhotep II and the body of the young man in the boat were still damp with resin when they were robbed, is it possible that they were buried at the same time? Many have speculated that the body in the boat is a son of Amenhotep II.[350] Could it be the body of his firstborn son who died in the tenth plague? If Amenhotep II drowned in the Red Sea with his army, his death would have occurred only shortly after the death of his firstborn son. It stands to reason that they would have been buried at the same time.

Many people assume that Pharaoh's son who died in the 10th plague was a child. However, the scriptures do not reveal an age of the prince. Thutmose IV, based on the estimated age at the time of his death (between 25-35) and the length of his reign (nine years, eight months), was probably between 15-20 when he became pharaoh, therefore, Amenhotep II's firstborn son was probably a young man when he died.[351] In fact, since Amenhotep II became king at 18, he probably already had children at the time of his ascension; and if he reigned for 26 years, his oldest son would have been at least in his late teens, and could have been near 30. Since the body in the boat was thought by some to be Sethnakhte, the mummy is not that of a child.

Some have speculated that the body in the boat is that of Webensenu; perhaps that is a possibility. Betsy Bryan, author of The Reign of Thutmose IV, even raises the notion that Webensenu may have been Amenhotep II's crown prince.[352] After all, Webensenu lived long enough to be named along with his brother Nedjem on a statue at Karnak.[353] Bryan believes these two were the first and second sons of Amenhotep II.[354] Perhaps the body in the boat is his second-born son, who drowned with his father's army. Nevertheless, Dodson and Dyan think it more likely that Amenhotep C was the firstborn and heir apparent of Amenhotep II.[355] Could it be that the mummy in the boat is Amenhotep C? After all, Amenhotep II's son Webensenu, according to Dodson and Dyan, died as a child, but he is believed to be buried in KV 35, since canopic jars and shabtiu bearing Webensenu's name were found in the tomb of Amenhotep II.[356] If Webensenu was not the first born, it is possible that he died of some unknown cause before the year of the plagues or as a result of one of the plagues preceding the tenth? Could Webensenu be the boy with the sidelock of a young prince and the expression described as "laughing and mischievous" who was found in KV 35, laying between the Elder Lady, Queen Tiye, and the mother of king Tut?[357] Though the mummy is estimated to be the body of a boy who was about 15 years old, could it be that, like his father's boast, he appeared to be mature beyond his years?[358]

Though it is difficult to call for certain a roll of all the children of Amenhotep II, several of his sons are named: Amenhotep C, Khaemwaset, Nedjem, Amenmopet, Webensenu, Thutmose IV, and Ahmose B.[359] It is very possible that all of these, except for Ahmose B, were older than Thutmose IV. Ahmose B was likely younger because he served as High Priest of Ra at Heliopolis during Thutmose IV's reign.[360] In fact, given the age of Thutmose IV at the time of his ascension, it is possible that all of Amenhotep II's sons between Thutmose IV and the firstborn died with the army in the Red Sea (with the possible exception of Webensenu who may have died as a child), and just because the Hebrews saw the bodies of the Egyptians washed up on the shore doesn't mean that all of the bodies of those who drowned were recovered. In fact, the bodies that the Hebrews saw were likely only those lying on the Sinai side of the sea. However, some have suggested that perhaps as many as four of Amenhotep II's sons were buried in the tomb of Amenhotep III.[361]

Giving Grace to the Humble

Over the years, several have attributed wicked ambitions to Thutmose IV. Many scholars, fueled in part by the conjecture of a woman named Dorothy Eady, believed that Thutmose IV murdered his older brother(s) in order to rule Egypt.[362] Citing the obvious damage done to the stelae of the sons of Amenhotep II in his Giza temple, Eady (better known to some as Omm Sety) surmised that Thutmose IV must have been the culprit who tried to erase his siblings' names.[363] She even indicted Thutmose IV's famous Dream Stela as an attempt to cover the usurper's guilty conscience. Interestingly, Thutmose IV's Dream Stela was placed between the front paws of the Great Sphinx, which would have positioned it directly in front of the statue that Amenhotep II

110

erected of himself under the sphinx's beard.[364] Therefore, if Thutmose IV was trying to cover something, perhaps it was that. However, most modern day scholars do not consider Thutmose IV to be a usurper.[365] Bryan goes so far as to say that if Thutmose IV was a usurper, his "usurpation was poorly effected."[366]

There is no question that significant damage was done to the Giza stelae of Thutmose IV's brothers, but there is a question as to who is responsible for the vandalism.[367] Many attribute the erasures to Thutmose IV; however, the bottom of Thutmose IV's own *Dream Stela* is damaged in a similar fashion.[368] Would Thutmose IV have defaced his own monument? If Amenhotep II was the pharaoh of the exodus, there were likely many in Egypt who blamed him for all of the tragedy that had transpired. In fact, Exodus 10.7 and 14.5 hint that the tide of public opinion was already turning against the pharaoh. Even Moses, the meekest man on earth, was greatly angry with the unrelenting pharaoh (Numbers 12.3; Exodus 11.8). That pharaoh valued his stubborn pride and his sense of power more than the lives of countless innocents; he would rather let his heart be hardened than submit to the will of God. No doubt, it was common knowledge that only a word of concession from the pharaoh could have averted the tenth plague. Therefore, if the pharaoh of the exodus was Amenhotep II, there was, surely, any number of angry, grief-stricken potential vandals. Perhaps this also explains why Amenhotep II's mother, his choice for the lofty position of "God's Wife," was dishonored.[369] Nevertheless, there could well have been many embittered Egyptians who considered themselves to be enemies of Amenhotep II, Thutmose IV, and of Amenhotep II's entire family and wanted to destroy the memory of the lot of them, "presently there is no way to demonstrate what provoked it [the Giza vandalism]."[370]

Was Thutmose IV an evil son who hated and murdered his brothers to enact his greedy designs on the throne of his father? If that were true, why would he place his only surviving brother, Ahmose B, in such a prominent office as High Priest of Ra at Heliopolis? His consideration and inclusion of Ahmose B seems to indicate that Thutmose IV valued and cared for his family. In fact, his *Dream Stela* recounts a day of hunting and target practice, attended by only two companions "unlike previous princes," and could be read as if he was accustomed to enjoying such activities in the company of a larger group and missed having his many brothers with him on such excursions—these two associates were poor substitutes for the "previous princes"; they were not like being with his brothers.[371] In fact, some of Websensenu's canopic jars were buried with Thutmose IV.[372] If Webensenu was the boy with the sidelock in KV 35, based on the estimated age of the body, Webensenu may have been the brother closest in age to Thutmose IV, perhaps just younger. Thutmose IV also looked after his younger sister, Iaret, who was born to Amenhotep II late his reign. In Year 7 of Thutmose IV, Iaret was seen at official functions; later, she became a "ritual" wife.[373] Thutmose IV obviously loved Tiaa, his mother, too. He provided for her and significantly elevated her status, proclaiming her to be "god's wife."[374] He also seems to have been very concerned about her emotional state. On the

Thutmose IV

statue he erected at Giza to commemorate Tiaa, Thutmose IV expressed his tender desire for her protection and his longing to "remove ills" and to "drive off any evils" away from his mother. It is believed that Tiaa was a woman who was troubled by great sadness.[375] If she had lived through the plagues and the loss of multiple sons, it's little wonder why.

In fact, far from being a murderous usurper, the declaration on his *Dream Stela* seems to indicate that Thutmose IV admired his father and had wanted to emulate him, that he was "shell-shocked" by unimaginable events that transpired and was attempting to somehow justify what had happened. In his *Dream Stela*, Thutmose IV identifies himself as "the king's son," as if he was proud to be known by that title. He shared with Amenhotep II a similar love of sports and training on the Giza plateau; he wanted to be like, dreamed about, and missed having his father.[376] Thutmose IV was also like his father in the strange status he gave to his mother. Amenhotep II, unlike previous pharaohs, greatly honored his own mother, Meryetre-Hatshepsut, and never shared the limelight with his wife Tiaa; Thutmose IV conducted his public image in a similar fashion, naming Tiaa to the honored position once held by his grandmother.[377] Of course, it's possible that, unlike his father, Thutmose IV's beloved wife, Nefertiry, may not have been alive to be called "god's wife."

If Thutmose IV was the first pharaoh after the exodus, extraordinary events landed him in an unanticipated and extremely difficult position; he had no idea that he would ever be pharaoh until he suddenly found himself on the throne, grasping to pick up pieces of a shattered society, maneuvering to maintain and protect Egypt. The fact that there is no evidence to suggest a co-regency of Thutmose IV and Amenhotep II may indicate that his assent to the throne was totally unexpected, and he was utterly unprepared.[378] Examiners of Thutmose IV's body concluded that though the young man had been well cared for, he was extremely emaciated before he died, and he was balding.[379] Loss of appetite and loss of hair are well-known signs of extreme stress and could indicate that Thutmose IV was under tremendous pressures that he was not prepared to handle; in fact, it may have been stress that claimed the life of this young man in a space of only about ten years. The mere fact that Thutmose IV's first wife, his chosen wife, Nefertiry, was not royal indicates that he probably never expected to be king.[380] It is unclear what happened to Nefertiry, but she probably died. Deaths were seldom recorded by ancient Egyptians.[381] Yet, besides his father, his brothers, and his infant son (Amenemhat), in the exodus, Thutmose IV may have lost Nefertiry too. Later, Thutmose IV married Nefertiry's full (and likely younger) sister, Iaret.[382] It is as though Thutmose IV missed Nefertiry and longed for the way things used to be; he, like everyone else in Egypt, was struggling to put life back in order. Thutmose IV was obviously also married to a second wife, the mother of Amenhotep III, before he became king because Amenhotep III was born to Thutmose IV in Year 24 of Amenhotep II's reign. Amenhotep III's mother's name was Mutemwia, but she was a concubine and never publicly acknowledged by Thutmose IV as his wife.[383]

If Thutmose IV was the pharaoh who followed the exodus, then subsequent to the sudden and unexpected deaths of the sitting pharaoh, the heir apparent, and any other princes who were older than Thutmose IV, he was suddenly thrust into the leadership of a nation that was reeling in the aftermath of sheer devastation. In fact, "the succession of Thutmose IV appears to have had no recognition at all by Amenhotep II, by co-regency or announced intent," supporting the understanding that the young pharaoh had neither intuition nor inclination of kingship.[384] On top of this, he was probably just a teenager, dealing with overwhelming personal grief—and fear. Egypt was tremendously weakened, vulnerable, and unprotected. Thutmose IV understood that mere men, Moses and Aaron, were not responsible for what had happened to Egypt. As the scripture says in Joshua 24.5, "I sent Moses . . . and Aaron, and *I* plagued Egypt, according to that which *I* did among them." It was a terrifying realization; Egypt had angered a god! When one examines Thutmose IV's most famous monument, the *Dream Stela*, from this perspective, a new interpretation emerges.

On the *Dream Stela*, Thutmose IV writes:

Year one, month three of Inundation, day 19, under the Majesty of the Strong Bull, perfect of diadems, the Two Ladies enduring of kingship like Atum, Golden Horus, powerful of the khepesh (scimitar) who subdues the [Nine Bows], the king of Upper and Lower Egypt Men[khepru]re, [son of Re Thutmose kha khau, beloved of Horemakhet], given life stability and dominion like Re forever.

Live the Good God, the son of Atum, the protector of Horakhty, the living image of the Lord of All, the sovereign whom Re made, the excellent inheritor of Khepri, beautiful of face like the ruler, his father, who goes forth perfectly equipped with [his forms of Horus on his head, the king of Upper and Lower Egypt beloved of the gods, lord of charm before the Ennead, who purifies Heliopolis, who propitiates Re, who embellished the House of Ptah, who presents truth to Atum, who offers it to him who is South of his Wall, who makes monuments consisting of [daily offerings] to the god who made all that exists, who seeks what is beneficial to the gods of Upper and Lower Egypt, who builds their temples [in white stone] who endows all their offerings, the son of Atum of his body Thutmose kha khau, like Re, the heir of Horus upon his throne Menkheprure, given life.

When his Majesty was an inpu, like the young Horus in Chemmis, his goodness already like the "protector of his father"; he was seen like a god himself. [Through love of him the army rejoiced (likewise) the royal children and] all [the nobles]. His might made his victories flourish, and he repeated the circuit, his powers being like the son of Nut.
Now he passed time amusing himself upon the plateau of the White Wall on its southern and northern confines, shooting copper targets and hunting [lions] and wild goats, and traveling upon his chariot, his horses being faster than the wind, together with one sole companion from his retinue; and no person knew it.

Then the hour of allowing rest for his retinue happened near the Setpet (emplacement) of Horemakhet beside Sokar in Ro-Setau (necropolis), Rennutet in Tjamut in the necropolis, [Mut (foremost) of the horns of the gods], north of the mistress of southern Sat (?), Sakhmet, foremost of the desert, of Seth, Dewa and Heka, eldest of the holy place of the first occasion in the neighborhood of the lord of Kher-Aha, and of the divine road of the gods to the western horizon of Heliopolis. Now the image of the very great Khepri rested in this place, great of fame, sacred of respect, the shade of Re resting on him. Memphis and every city on its two sides came to him, their arms in adorations to his face, bearing great offering for his ka.

One of these days it happened that the prince Thutmose came traveling at the time of midday. He rested in the shadow of this great god. [Sleep and] dream [took possession of him] at the moment the sun was at zenith. Then he found the majesty of this noble god speaking from his own mouth like a father speaks to his son, saying: "Look at me, observe me, my son Thutmose. I am your father Horemakhet-Khepri-Re-Atum. I shall give to you the kingship [upon the land before the living]. You shall wear its white crown and its red crown upon the throne of Geb, the heir. The land in its length and its breadth will be yours, and everything which the eye of the Lord of All illuminates. Good provisions will be for you from within the Two Lands, and the great produce of every foreign country, and a lifetime of time great in years. My face belongs to you; my heart belongs to you, and you belong to me. [Behold, my condition is like one in illness], all [my limbs being ruined]. The sand of the desert, upon which I used to be, faces me (aggressively); and it is in order to cause that you do what is in my heart that I have waited. For I know that you are my son and my protector. Arrive! Behold I am with you! I am [your leader." He completed this speech.

Then this prince stared because] he heard this [utterance of the Lord of All]. He understood the words of this god and he placed silence in [his] heart. [Then he said: Come, let us travel] to [our temple] of the city, that they may set aside offerings for this god. [We shall bring to him cattle, and all sorts of vegetable, and we shall give praises to those who came before] . . . a statue of Chephren made for Atum-Re-Horemakhet . . . in the festivals . . . numerous . . . for my Majesty for making to live which . . . speech of Khepri in the western horizon of Heliopolis in . . . . [385]

It's clear that Thutmose IV remembers, fondly, his childhood and speaks admiringly of his father. He even highlights the strong physical resemblance he shared with Amenhotep II, saying that he was "beautiful of face like the ruler, his father." Incidentally, examinations of the mummies of these two men confirm that they did bear a striking facial similarity.[386] Yet, in sharp contrast to the Sphinx stela of his father, Thutmose IV never mentions Amun or Amun-Ra: the king of gods, the patron deity of Thebes and of Amenhotep II. Instead, Thutmose IV pronounces himself to be the "son of Atum of his body," clearly aligning himself with the ancient theology of On, "a city of hoary antiquity, its foundations buried in the dust of prehistory."[387] Thutmose IV credits "the Lord of All" with causing him to be pharaoh. Thutmose IV's omission of Amun and his "increasing the importance of the Heliopolitan gods" seems to have been deliberate.[388] From the stela's many references to Heliopolis, it can be assumed that the Lord of All, to whom Thutmose IV refers and ties to the Sphinx, must have been considered by the young pharaoh to be an ancient deity.[389] This was a god who had been forgotten and neglected and who sought the service of Thutmose IV.

At Giza, O'Connor says Thutmose IV was attempting "to compensate for some unexpected difficulties in his succession."[390] If the *Dream Stela* was written in the wake of the exodus, this remarkable document may well have been Thutmose IV's effort to create an acceptable context for the extraordinary events that Egypt had experienced. There was no doubt that the plagues had been the supernatural actions of an angry god, but what god? By concluding that the deity of Moses was an ancient god associated with On, Atum, Ra, and with Ptah and the Sphinx, Thutmose IV suggested that the Lord of All who made him king was not a foreign god, but was one who had long been linked to Egypt. In Genesis 42.18, before he revealed his true identity to his brothers, Joseph told them that he feared "God"; the brothers didn't seem surprised to hear such admission from an Egyptian. Apion, a Greco-Egyptian historian and contemporary with Josephus, "declares Moses to be an Egyptian priest from Heliopolis," not advocating a new "religious institution" but in keeping with "Egyptian tradition."[391] Apion also may have recognized little conflict between the echoes of On and the God of the Bible, consistent with what seems to have been the case in the days of Joseph. In fact, further evidence exists to suggest a long-standing ancient Egyptian knowledge and compliance with the Lord of All, the one God, the God of the Bible:

From the Old Kingdom:
Ptahhotep writes, "It is not the intentions of men that are fulfilled, but the plan of God."
A man named Akhtoy says, "God knows him who acts for him. He knows every [man by] name." And from Egyptian moral literature: "God wishes of thee respect for the poor more than honor to the great." "God hates him who speaks falsely"
"Happy is he who walks in the way of God."[392]

Slaves making Bricks in the days of Amenhotep II

As discussed in the first chapter, the pharaoh of Joseph seemed to be familiar with the God of the Bible and went to On, to Heliopolis, to find Joseph a mate whose theology was, presumably, most comparable with the ancient God of Joseph.[393] According to Romans 1.20-23, ancient people "knew God," but they lost their connection to him through "vain imaginations." The original god of On did not originate in On.[394] In the religion of On, Thutmose IV's *Dream Stela* seems to suggest, there was a distant memory of the Lord of All, the God of the Bible. Was there also perhaps a connection between the Sphinx and God?

The Sphinx is very old. Some believe that it is the oldest man-made structure in Egypt and perhaps the oldest man-made structure on earth.[395] Even at the time of Thutmose IV, the Sphinx was an ancient relic.[396] Sphinxes are composite creatures and guardian figures.[397] It's possible that the Great Sphinx was built as a guardian for the Giza plateau.[398] Though the face and head of the Sphinx were likely modified in the Fourth Dynasty, the statue may have always been that of a Sphinx with the body of a lion and the head of some other creature. There are those who suggest that Thutmose IV mistakenly associated the Sphinx with the primeval gods of Heliopolis, but perhaps he didn't.[399] The end of Genesis chapter 3 discusses a similar entity. The Cherubim that God placed at the east of the Garden of Eden were (by definition) composite creatures, not existing in nature, who acted as guardians (Genesis 3.24; Ezekiel 1.5-10).[400] However, unlike the Great Sphinx, the Cherubim discussed in scripture are usually described with wings (Exodus 25.20; I Kings 6.23-27) Nevertheless, Cherubim would likely have been understood as formidable guardians, associated with God by ancient peoples and perhaps by the ancients who carved the Sphinx.

It has been suggested that Egyptians in the New Kingdom were less informed about the history of the Sphinx than even we are today.[401] That may be, but perhaps they also had some understanding about the Sphinx that is lost to us. Though Thutmose IV did not seem to have a complete grasp of the true identity of the Lord of All, he associated the Sphinx with an ancient, universal God, and he offered a gesture of service by removing the sand from the monument and erecting a retaining wall to help keep the desert at bay.[402] Interestingly, the Great Sphinx was also called "the Father of Terror."[403] In the plagues, Egypt certainly suffered terror. Through Thutmose IV's conscientious act, perhaps the young pharaoh believed (and the Egyptian people could also believe) that the God who had been angered was somehow appeased through the attention that was being given to the statue of this ancient image that was tied to the beginning, to Eden; but more than this, Thutmose IV was sweeping the sand off of a distant memory of the God of the Bible . By referring to the figure as "Horemakhet-Khepri-Ra-Atum," Thutmose IV was further associating the Sphinx/the cherub as a representative of an ancient universal God, echoing the all-encompassing nature of the Lord of All; he was the rising sun (Khepri), the noon-day sun (Ra), and the evening sun (Atum), lord of the whole sky, lord of everything under the sun, from horizon to horizon.[404] Thutmose IV understood that the God who was responsible for the plagues was not Amun-Ra; therefore, he was seeking the favor of a different God, a bigger God, an older God, a universal God.[405] Perhaps by extending his worship to Giza, Thutmose IV was appealing to a God whom he understood to exist beyond the confines of On.[406] Thutmose IV sought to remember, to appease, and to worship a new God, in a new place, but also an ancient God, in an ancient place, a God who had been all but forgotten by the Egyptian people and who had been angered by that neglect.

In contrast to Thutmose IV, the pharaoh of the exodus did not seem to remember God or at least had no regard for him when Moses first appeared before the king:

Moses and Aaron went in, and told Pharaoh, Thus saith the Lord God of Israel, Let my people go, that they may hold a feast unto me in the wilderness. And Pharaoh said, Who is the Lord, that I should obey his voice to let Israel go? I know not the Lord, neither will I let Israel go. And they said, The God of the Hebrews hath met with us: let us go, we pray thee, three days' journey into the desert, and sacrifice unto the Lord our God; lest he fall upon us with pestilence, or with sword. And the king of Egypt said unto them, Wherefore do ye, Moses and Aaron, let the people from their works? Get you unto your burdens. And Pharaoh said, Behold, the people of the land now are many, and ye make them rest from their burdens. And Pharaoh commanded the same day the taskmasters of the people, and their officers, saying, Ye shall no more give the people straw to make brick, as heretofore: let them go and gather straw for themselves. And the tale of the bricks which they did make heretofore, ye shall lay upon them; ye shall not diminish ought thereof: for they be idle; therefore they cry, saying, Let us go and sacrifice to our God. Let there more work be laid upon the men, that they may labour therein; and let them not regard vain words. And the taskmasters . . . spake to the people saying, Thus saith Pharaoh, I will not give you straw. Go ye, get you straw where ye can find it; yet not ought of your work shall be diminished. So the people were scattered abroad throughout all the land of Egypt to gather stubble instead of straw. And the taskmasters hasted them, saying, Fulfill your works, your daily tasks, as when there was straw. And the officers of the children of Israel, which Pharaoh's taskmasters had set over them, were beaten, and demanded, Wherefore have ye not fulfilled your task in making brick both yesterday and to day, as heretofore?

Then the officers of the children of Israel came and cried unto Pharaoh, saying, Wherefore dealest thou thus with thy servants? There is no straw given unto thy servants, and they say to us, Make brick; and, behold, thy servants are beaten; but the fault is in thine own people. But he said, Ye are idle, ye are idle; therefore ye say, Let us go and do sacrifice to the Lord. Go therefore now, and work; for there shall no straw be given you, yet shall ye deliver the tale of bricks. And the officers of the children of Israel did see that they were in evil case, after it was said, Ye shall not minish ought from your bricks of your daily task. (Exodus 5.1-19)

Is there evidence of Hebrew slaves in the time of Amenhotep II? Compellingly, in a passage from Manetho that some tie to the story of Moses, a pharaoh named "Amenophis" (a Greek alternative form of Amenhotep) pressed slaves to work in quarries.[407] Of course, this could have been a reference to Amenhotep I or III as well. Nevertheless, from the days when Ahmose subdued the Hyksos, there is evidence of "large numbers" of Asiatic slaves and other foreign slaves doing hard labor in Egypt.[408] Subsequent pharaohs, especially Thutmose III and Amenhotep II, only added to that number. It would seem that over their many campaigns into Palestine, these warrior pharaohs continued to find, capture, and enslave Hebrews, former Hyksos, who had managed to escape Ahmose. In fact, "hordes of slaves" were brought from Palestine to Egypt by Thutmose III and Amenhotep II.[409] Foreign slaves were even "registered as taxable serfs."[410] It is likely that many of these foreign captives were Hebrews because they are identified as being "'Apiru" or "Habiru," and many experts agree this word could translate as "Hebrew."[411] In TT 39, the tomb of Puyemre the Second Prophet of Amun, and in TT 155, the tomb of Intef a herald, Habiru slaves acting as wine-makers are depicted during the reign of Thutmose III.[412] Habiru captives are specified in the records of Amenhotep II's second campaign into Palestine.[413] Though most believe it to be boasting, nevertheless, on his third campaign, Amenhotep II claims to have brought back between 100,000 to 101,128 captives, of which, he says 3,600 were Habiru.[414] In the tomb of Rekhmire, Amenhotep II's vizier, Asiatic slaves are even portrayed making bricks and working under the oversight of taskmasters.[415] Thutmose III brought back captives from Palestine especially for the task of making bricks to expand his "Great House," his temple complex at Karnak.[416]

It has been suggested that the large number of captives obtained from Amenhotep II's third campaign into Palestine was perhaps not an exaggeration but was necessary to replenish the slave-base that was lost to him in the exodus.[417] In order to advance this theory, one first must be of the understanding that the pharaoh of the exodus did not drown with his army. Yet, if this premise is true, where did Amenhotep II find an army to lead on this third campaign? Furthermore, if Amenhotep II did, in fact, bring back over 100,000 captives (though some believe that this would have been more than Egypt's "agrarian economy" could have supported), what happened to all those slaves?[418] They obviously were not around in the reign of Amenhotep II's successor. Thutmose IV found it necessary to lead an attack on Katia, in the southern reaches of Nubia, in order to obtain "laborers" for his mortuary temple.[419] Furthermore, Thutmose IV used another of his very few military campaigns to "round up" captives from Giza, in Palestine.[420] Thutmose IV must have needed a workforce very badly to risk the security of Egypt by leading an army of raw recruits, bureaucrats, and old men into battle in order to acquire slaves. It is therefore more likely that he, and not Amenhotep II, was the pharaoh who was attempting to recover from the loss of Hebrew slave labor.

Beyond the circumstantial evidence, does Amenhotep II fit the profile of the pharaoh of the exodus? It is compelling to compare Amenhotep II as he described himself on his Amada and Elephantine stelae to the character of the pharaoh of the exodus:

A Side By Side Comparison of
The Pharaoh of the Exodus

Described in the Bible:

He exalted himself (Exodus 9.17)
Perhaps the most defining characteristic of the pharaoh that Moses confronted was arrogant, stubborn pride. So great was the self-confidence of this pharaoh, God warned Moses that the king of Egypt would not give in, even though the opposition against him was "mighty" (Exodus 3.19; Nehemiah 9.10)

The pharaoh of the exodus was a terrifying sight when he appeared with his army (Exodus 14.9-10)
The advisors of the pharaoh of the exodus knew that he saw himself as a formidable and shrewd opponent, standing against his enemies as the defender and protector of Egypt (Exodus 10.7)

The pharaoh of the exodus was uninterested in any terms other than what he saw as his own (Exodus 8.2, 9-10)

When confronted with any rebellion, he was immediately unreasonable and without pity. The pharaoh of the exodus was a callous tyrant (Exodus 5.6-9)

The pharaoh of the exodus must have had great confidence in the god he felt worthy of his ear and loyalty because he was completely dismissive and refused to acknowledge God (Exodus 5.2)

He must have been known for having a "strong hand" (Exodus 6.1)

When it was obvious that he would not prevail over Moses, pharaoh threatened to execute him (Exodus 10.28)

In his heart, the pharaoh of the exodus believed that there was no one comparable to himself because God was compelled to show him otherwise (Exodus 9.14)

**The Mummy of
Amenhotep II**

Described on the Amada
and Elephantine Stelae:

His strength is greater than any king who has ever existed. . . .

(He is) one who rages like a panther when he courses through the battlefield. There is none who can fight in his vicinity; (he is) a brave bowman of combat

(He is) a wall which protects Egypt, standing firm upon the battlefield in the moment of plunder,

(He is) one who tramples those who rebel against him

. . . They do not know that Amun-Ra is loyal to him.

his limbs imbibed with majesty. . . He is a king who is extolled proportionally to his arms being in the frey

(He is one) who puts an end to those who attack him

(He is) one whose equal does not exist, and whose peer has not been found."

Highly competitive and uninterested in negotiation, Amenhotep II was vain to a fault. He did not seem to care who suffered as long as he prevailed. Regardless of his assertion that "It is the god who has determined that he act to protect Egypt and that he is granted obeisance;" regardless of his boasting, it was *not* Amenhotep II's amazing athletic abilities or his imposing prowess that won him the crown of Egypt.[421] In fact, there is every indication that if something hadn't happened to his older brother, Amenemhat B, Amenhotep II would have never succeeded Thutmose III.[422] Though he prided himself as being the greatest of all kings, backed by the king of all gods, if he was the pharaoh of the exodus, it was the God of the Bible—not Amun-Ra—who elevated Amenhotep II to power "for this very cause," in order that the power and the name of God would be shown throughout the earth (Exodus 9.16; Romans 9.17). In fact, this may be the reason that in the tomb of Amenhotep si-se, the Second Prophet of Amun in the administration of Thutmose IV, the name of Amenhotep II is hacked out, twice, and the former pharaoh, once regarded as a god on earth, is identified merely as "a man."[423] It is ironic that in his jubilee hall at Karnak, on Amenhotep II's (probable) last monument to himself since he died during the making of it, he emphasizes his station of godhood over the whole world![424] Evidenced perhaps nowhere better than in the contest between the pharaoh of the exodus and Moses: "God resisteth the proud, but giveth grace unto the humble" (Psalms 138.6; Proverbs 3.34; Matthew 23.12; James 4.6; I Peter 5.5).

Another possible indication that points to Amenhotep II as the pharaoh of the exodus is found in the tomb of Sheshonq I. "An almost perfectly preserved copy" of Amenhotep II's Asian campaign in Year 7 serves as the ceiling of Sheshonq I's burial chamber.[425] Perhaps, it is possible that the use of Amenhotep II's victory stela was just a happenstance case of recycling. However, if Sheshonq I, of the Twenty-second Dynasty, is the same as Shishak, the king of Egypt mentioned in scripture, perhaps the use of Amenhotep II's stela was purposeful (I Kings 11.40; 14.25-26; II Chronicles 12.2-9). At Karnak, Sheshonq I left record of his successful campaign through Palestine, and the scriptures confirm his plundering of the temple of Solomon in Jerusalem.[426] Sheshonq I/Shishak may well have believed that he went up against the God of the Hebrews, the God who brought the plagues, but—unlike Amenhotep II—Sheshonq I (from his perspective) won! Perhaps Sheshonq I enjoyed a certain satisfaction in that thought and wished to be reminded of it for all eternity.

Nevertheless, regardless of the evidence pointing to Amenhotep II, most people, including most experts, seem certain that the pharaoh of the exodus was named Ramses—and more specifically, Ramses II.[427] Why is this? Since the scriptures make it clear that Hebrews were pressed into service, building "for Pharaoh treasure cities, Pithom and Raamses" and since one of those places was named Ramses, it is assumed that the "city" was named after the pharaoh for whom it was being built (Exodus 1.11).[428] There is little doubt that, at the time of Ramses II, Pi-Ramses (the city of Ramses) was Egypt's capitol, that Ramses II lived there, and that it was a great city.[429] However, was the great city really named after Ramses the Great, and was Pi-Ramses the city of "Raamses" to which Exodus 1.11 refers? While it has been said there is no evidence that a city of Ramses existed before the Saite Period (which was hundreds of years after Ramses II), others say that the city of Ramses far *predated* Ramses II and perhaps goes back to the Middle Kingdom.[430] The name Ramses obviously predates Ramses II; after all, there was a Ramses I. Which Ramses was the namesake of Pi-Ramses? Ramses was also the name of a vizier who served Amenhotep III, and another Ramses is listed on the *Ibi-aa Stela* from the Twelfth Dynasty.[431] For that matter, Ramose, Senenmut's father's name, was a form of Ramses. However, it would be highly unusual for a city in Egypt to have been named after a mere official and certainly not after a commoner. "The Egyptians named cities after gods, kings, cult objects, and sacred places, but not after non-royal personages."[432] There can be no doubt that the Raamses in Exodus 1.11 was a place named after a god; Ramses means, "Ra is Born" or "it is Ra who has fashioned him."[433] However, most think that the city of Raamses was named after a king, and perhaps it was. In fact, John Rea holds that the city, Pi-Ramses, was first called Ramses by the Hyksos and that "Ra" was part of some Hyksos' throne names.[434] Yet, the places specified in scripture were not ordinary "cities;" Pitholm and Raamses, the places that the Hebrew slaves were forced to build, were "treasure cities." That may mean that Pitholm and Raamses were not cities in the traditional sense but were probably more military outposts, fortresses, and/or supply stations for Pharaoh's army when he went to war against the former Hyksos allies in Canaan.[435] If that were true, it would only have added to the humiliation of the Hebrews/Hyksos building Pitholm and Raamses for Ahmose who was re-establishing the supremacy of Egyptian rule over Palestine and the re-birth of Ra and all other Egyptian gods over Seth.

Therefore, does the name of the city mentioned in Exodus 1.11 indicate that Ramses II was the pharaoh of the exodus? The first obstacle challenging that theory is the well-preserved body of Ramses II. With its striking profile and red hair, the remains of Ramses II have become an icon of Egyptian mummies. He ruled for nearly sixty-seven years, and lived about ninety.[436] His longevity alone makes it difficult for Ramses II to fit the biblical account. Moses was in Midian for forty years, fleeing a pharaoh who died while he was away (Exodus 4.19). If Ramses II was the pharaoh of the exodus, Moses would have been in Midian for much longer than forty years and would have fled Egypt when he was approaching adolescence instead of middle age. Seti I, the immediate predecessor of Ramses II, reigned a decade.[437] The Pharaoh before Seti I, Ramses I, only occupied the throne a couple of years.[438]

If Ramses II was the pharaoh of the exodus, then Moses would have been born during the reign of Ramses I or at the end of Horemheb's reign. Medical examinations suggest that, though he suffered from several age-related illnesses (Arteriosclerosis, arthritis, and dental problems), Ramses the Great probably died of great age. It is unlikely that such an aged individual would have survived the plagues, and in his feeble condition, it is highly unlikely that an elderly Ramses II could have accompanied his army in pursuit of escaping slaves while riding in a chariot. Therefore, to advance the theory of Ramses II as the pharaoh of the exodus, one must believe that pharaoh did not drown with his army.

Yet, if Ramses II didn't drown, perhaps the exodus occurred when he was a much younger man. If that were the case, then Moses' return to Egypt would, of necessity, have happened in the first forty years of Ramses II, but Moses could not have returned to Egypt during the first two decades of Ramses II's rule because the pharaoh was heavily engaged in military actions against Kadesh, Syria, and the Hittites throughout that time. Surely distress of the plagues of the exodus would have superseded Ramses II's preoccupation with far away kingdoms. Of course, in Year 21, a treaty was made between the Egyptians and the Hittites, so maybe Moses could have arrived after that time. However, Ramses II does not seem to have suffered the loss of his army because in Year 40 and in Year 44, his sons led his army with "forces available" in successful campaigns against Nubia and perhaps into Libya as well.[439]

If Ramses II was the pharaoh of the exodus, who was the daughter of the pharaoh who adopted Moses? To answer this question, the daughters of several pharaohs before Ramses II must be considered. Akhenaten had six known daughters, but suggesting one of the Amarna princesses for the adoptive mother of Moses requires a multi-concessional placement of the exodus very early in the reign of Ramses II. King Tut had no surviving children. Two mummified fetuses are his only known offspring.[440] Ay, who ruled briefly upon the death of the boy king, had one son, Nakhtmin, who died before Tut; and Ay's daughter was never known by the title "king's daughter."[441] Horemheb, the last ruler of the Eighteenth Dynasty, occupied the throne about forty years but had no known children; Horemheb's heir, Ramses I, was not his son. Ramses I's wife, Sitre, was not a pharaoh's daughter.[442] Ramses I was already an old man when Horemheb chose him as his successor. He only reigned two years, but he did have a large family.[443] Perhaps he had a daughter who could have raised Moses. The successor of Ramses I, Seti I, had a daughter named Tja; she was the sister of Ramses II, but due to the fact that the scriptures say that Moses was 80 when he stood before the pharaoh of the exodus, Tja is an unlikely candidate for Moses' adopted mother.[444]

It is equally difficult to reconcile the events following the reign of Ramses II with the history of the exodus. The

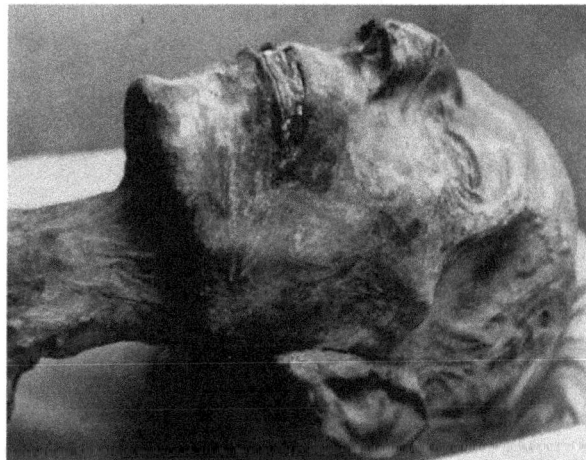

Ramses II

successor of Ramses the Great was his sixteenth son, Merenptah.[445] Merenptah was already middle-aged when he became pharaoh, and he only reigned for a decade. However, his time on the throne was fraught with conflict. Egypt was attacked by the Sea People (known to ancient Egyptians as "foreigners from the sea, northern countries, or their islands) who had formed an alliance with Libyans and others.[446] Merenptah successfully defended Egypt, but he was unable to completely put down the invasion of the Sea People that continued well into the reign of Ramses III.

The subject of the Sea People touches on another point that causes some scholars to lean toward Ramses II as the pharaoh of the exodus. When the Hebrews were leaving Egypt, scripture says:

> And it came to pass, when Pharaoh had let the people go, that God led them not through the way
> of the land of the Philistines, although that was near; for God said, Lest peradventure the people
> repent when they see war, and they return to Egypt. (Exodus 13.17)

An inscription in Thebes on the walls of Medinet Habu, a temple built by Ramses III, records the Egyptians battling with the Sea People and clearly identifies Philistines ('prw in Egyptian) as being among the pirates.[447] Though the 'prw are mentioned in Egyptian texts from as early as Thutmose III. Still, some believe that the Sea People gave rise to the Philistines, citing that there is evidence to suggest that the Philistines as a distinct people were not really established in Canaan until after the fall of the Hittites.[448] Logically, therefore, that could not have occurred before the latter reign of Ramses II since he made a treaty with the Hittites two decades into his term when Hattusa was still strong enough to fight the Egyptian army, seemingly, at least to a draw. Though men from "Sherden" were pressed into serving in the army of Thutmose III, there is little significant interaction between Egypt and the infamous seafaring marauders until Merenptah. Yet, Philistines depicted in Egyptian art from the mid-Eighteenth Dynasty are shown as Canaanite warriors or slaves. Even Merenptah's reliefs at Karnak portray Philistines wearing Canaanite clothes, not the uniform dress of the Sea People.[449] Dagon worship further ties the Philistines to early Canaan and to the sea, since Dagon was one of the oldest Canaanite gods and he was half fish (Judges 16.23). Still, Ramses II did not seem to have much trouble with Philistines when he campaigned through Palestine; of course, Ramses II had his sights set on Syria, not Canaan.[450] However, the Philistines did seem to be an obstacle in Hebrew possession of the Promised Land; "no portion of it [Philistine territory] was conquered in the lifetime of Joshua."[451] The book of Joshua says:

> Joshua was old . . . there remaineth yet very much land to be possessed. . . .all the borders of the
> Philistines, and all Geshuri, From Sihor, which is before Egypt, even unto the borders of Ekron
> northward, which is counted to the Canaanite: five lords of the Philistines; the Gazathites, and
> the Ashdothites, the Eshkalonites, the Gittites, and the Ekronites; also the Avites. (Joshua 13.1-3)

Nevertheless, most of the Philistine area in question was allotted to the tribe of Judah because Caleb, with God's help, was eager to take on the Anakim; and Caleb prevailed against the giants (Joshua 14.6-14). The boundary for the tribe of Judah was identified to the west as the Mediterranean Sea and to the south reaching all the way to "the river of Egypt," though this was likely not the Nile but rather a brook on the northern Sinai Peninsula (Joshua 15.4, 12). However, the region of Judah clearly included disputed Philistine territory. The scriptures indicate that the Philistines remained a serious threat to the Hebrews during the days of the judges and into the days of the kings of Israel (Judges 3.1-3; 10.6-8; 13.1; I Samuel 4.1-11; 7.7-8; 13.1-23; 14.52; 31.1-7). In the reign of David, however, the Philistines were significantly suppressed (II Samuel 5.17-25; 21.18-22; I Chronicles 14.8-16). Yet, there was a resurgence of Philistine aggression throughout the time of the divided kingdom (II Chronicles 26.1-7; 28.16-21). The chapter in Philistine history coinciding with the kings of Israel was perhaps introduced by Ramses III. A papyrus, composed shortly after his death, explains that after the Sea People were defeated, Ramses III placed them in cities along the Canaanite coast as Egyptian vassals.[452]

Why did God express concern about leading the Hebrews through the land of the Philistines? The Philistines are a difficult people to define, but according to the scripture, they began as an ancient race, residing in Canaan.[453] In fact, if "Philistim" named in Genesis 10.14 is the father of the Philistines, their roots can be traced all the way back to Babel, Nimrod, Cush, Ham, and Noah (Genesis 10.1-14; I Chronicles 1.12).[454] As a people, they are first mentioned in scripture during the days of Abraham beginning in Genesis 20 when he sojourned in the land of Abimelech. Abimelech was the king of an established group of people in Gerrar; a civilization advanced enough to have its own army and chain of command. In fact, Abimelech may have been the king's title and not his name.[455] This may also explain why David's Psalm 34 is titled as being presented before "Abimelech" and not before "King Achish" of the Philistine city of Gath (I Samuel 21.10).[456] Abraham and Abimelech entered into a treaty according to Genesis 21.22-32, and the latter part of this passage makes it clear that Abimelech was from the land of the Philistines. After this Abraham lived in the land of the Philistines for a time, as did Isaac (Genesis 21.34; 26.1-22). Gerrar was only 10-12 miles northeast of Sharuhen, both squarely situated within the region of Philistia.[457] Since Sharuhen was the eastern stronghold of the Hyksos in Canaan, it stands to reason that ancient Philistines and the Hebrews/Hyksos were allies. This might help explain the Philistine's mysterious connection to Greece, Cyprus, other places along the coast of the Mediterranean, and the Aegean, areas that were known trading partners with the Hyksos.[458] In fact, pottery unearthed in Philistine territory with styles reminiscent of pottery common to that of the Hyksos suggests an affiliation or at least an affinity between the Philistines and the Hyksos.[459] Certainly, the affluence of the Hebrews/Hyksos and the seafaring capabilities of their Philistine neighbors in Canaan, who had lived on the coast of the Mediterranean since before the days of Abraham, would have made an excellent partnership. The Hebrews/Hyksos had ample funds to back trading voyages, through which the Philistines/Hyksos could establish favorable contacts in multiple ports-of-call, could experience and learn from foreign cultures, and perhaps, could do a little trading of their own. Sharuhen would have been a capitol of advancement for both nations.[460]

According to the theory proposed by this book, the Hebrews lived in Egypt for over 400 years, in total, but were (physically) slaves for roughly 100-150 years before the exodus. In fact, it's possible that Moses' father was born during the days of the Hebrews/Hyksos. Though it is unlikely that any Hebrews from the days of the Hyksos were still alive at the time of the exodus, it is likely that some knowledge of those days had been passed down to subsequent generations. If God had led the Hebrews by the shortest route into Canaan, they would have come through the vicinity of Sharuhen. Under this scenario, Exodus 13.17 could be read to mean that if the Hebrews had been allowed to pass through the land of the Philistines (their old cronies), they would have repented (i.e., changed their minds about retreating from Egypt) when they saw (the chance for) war (against Egypt through consolidation with the Philistines), and they (the Hebrews and the Philistines together, as the revived Hyksos, would have wanted to) return to (take the fight back to) Egypt! After all, the Philistines had probably long wished for a revival of the prosperity they, no doubt, enjoyed during their alliance with the Hyksos and would have been eager for relief from Egyptian repression. In the very least, the Hebrews would have substantially fortified Philistine manpower against their mutual enemy—Egypt. Furthermore, the Hebrews were keenly aware of Egypt's weakened state on the heels of the plagues. Also, having just plundered the Egyptians, the Hebrews were again wealthy and could have funded the procurement of supplies and weapons. It would have been like "old times"; it would have been an *excellent* time to launch an attack on Egypt!

It really makes little sense to interpret Exodus 13.17 to mean that God did not want the Hebrews to be frightened by war, discouraged by "the Wall of Rulers" (a string of fortresses that guarded the northeaster border of Egypt)—or that somehow the Philistines were a more formidable enemy than *Egypt*—or even more ridiculous—that God could not protect the Hebrews against the Philistines![461] The Hebrews were going to be frightened by war anyway when the Egyptian army came thundering after them. As for being discouraged, there is probably little the Philistines could have done to contribute in that department; the generation of Hebrews that left Egypt in the exodus was consistently discouraged at every turn. As for wanting to return to Egypt, the Hebrews of the exodus needed little encouragement in that sentiment either—even *onions* made them want to return to Egypt (Numbers 11.5). It is more likely that God desired to teach these "stiff-necked" Hebrews to depend on him and not on the nations around them for their resources and/or their strength. After all, there is very little chance that Moses would have agreed to an alliance with the Philistines. Therefore, either the Philistines or Moses would have needed to be eliminated. If the Hebrews had decided to overthrow or kill

Moses, God would likely have destroyed them all—just as he suggested on Sinai and as he did to the families in Korah's rebellion (Exodus 32.9-10; Numbers 16.1-40).

It is perhaps more likely that during the early New Kingdom, the Philistines (along with other remnants of the Hyksos) were kept extensively subdued by the constant pharaonic campaigns through their region. After all, the most likely land route from Egypt to the land of the Hittites would have been the Via Maris, which traced the length of the Plain of Philistia and most port cities along the coast of Canaan were part of Philistine territory.[462] Therefore, it would have been difficult for the Philistines to avoid contact with the Egyptian army by land or by sea. However, though they would still have been compelled to provide tributes to Egypt during this time, the decades from Thutmose IV through Akhenaten presented a chance for regrouping of the Philistines which could account for concern about the Sea People (especially Libyans) already being expressed in the papyrus fragments found at Tell Amarna.[463] Through their ready access to the Mediterranean, it would have been relatively easy for the Philistines to rekindle old friendships forged through the extensive trade connections established during the days of the Hyksos. It is perhaps likely that the Philistines and the Libyans had been common allies before, through their association with the Hyksos, based on the reliefs carved and posted by Ahmose at the quarry of Maasara. In contrast, other former Hyksos, the Hebrews, wandering in the wilderness of Sinai, were completely cut off from their old trading partners along the coast of the Mediterranean. Still, alliance had been a strategy of the Philistines in the past; it makes sense that they would seek to form advantageous coalitions (especially with enemies of their enemies) if given any chance. In fact, evidence seems to suggest that it was through alliance with others from countries such as Greece, Libya, Phoenicia, and even as far away as the Balkans that Philistines became synonymous with the Sea People, who attacked the Hittites, Egypt, and others.[464] It is even possible that, during the days of Ramses II (or even earlier) defectors from the Hebrew tribe of Dan joined the Sea People.[465] Deborah seems to indicate a troubling affinity for seafaring—and disloyalty—among the tribe of Dan in her song of victory over Sisera and Jabin (Judges 5.17). Samson was from the tribe of Dan, and his insalubrious association with the Philistines is legendary. Israel was actually under Philistine rule for the first twenty years of Samson's term as judge (Judges 15.20). Perhaps Samson wasn't the first Danite to be enticed by a Philistine.

As depicted on the walls of Ramses III's temple, the Philistines, as the Sea People, were so fully allied with their fellow pirates, they wore uniforms: identical feathered headdresses, tasseled kilts, and quilted corsets, one would not readily surmise that the Sea People were composed of at least three different nationalities: the Philistines, the Tjekker, and the Denyen, coming from places such as "Sherdanu, Danunu, Shekelesh, Zakkala, Washasha, and Pulasati."[466] Perhaps Sherdanu is an interpretation of Sharuhen, the old Hyksos capital, and perhaps the Sea People from Danunu were actually Hebrews from the tribe of Dan. Still, the outfits worn by the Sea People were hardly as protective and/or as advanced as the armor worn by Goliath (I Samuel 17.5-7). Of course, Goliath was the Philistines' "champion"; it is highly doubtful that the entire Philistine army

Captured Sea People

122

was arrayed in such gear. Saul had armor too, but there's no indication that his troops did (I Samuel 17.38). However, it seems reasonable that, due to the use of more progressive armor, the story of David and Goliath must have happened sometime after the days of the Sea People's excursions around the Mediterranean and wars with Egypt. Furthermore, the tactic of having a battle decided by the clash of two champions, reminiscent of Achilles and Hector in the writings of Homer, seems to represent an advancement in Philistine war strategy from their earlier conflicts with the Hebrews in the days of the judges and with the Egyptians in the days of the Sea People.[467] Perhaps the Philistines acquired both combat devices during their travels as the Sea People.[468]

Due to the developing confederation and the threatening, emerging identity of the Sea People in the days of Amenhotep III and Akhenaten, as evidenced in the fragments at Tell Amarna, it is very likely that the Philistines in the days of Joshua were radically different from the culture that Abraham and Isaac encountered and different still from the oppressed residents of Philistia in the days of the warrior pharaohs. In fact, archaeological evidence from Tell Qasile suggests that the original Philistines were indigenous to Canaan and founded agrarian cities.[469] Certainly, the Philistines in the days of Abimelech seem to have advanced beyond their roots as simple farmers and had developed an organized society with a sovereign government and a distinct civilization. However, a strong alliance with the Hyksos would no doubt have represented an exponential metamorphism in Philistine culture. During the Hebrew conquest of Canaan, it is likely that displaced Canaanites (including giants, such as the family of Goliath) would have fled to Philistia since they inhabited the fringes of Hebrew aggression (Joshua 11.22).[470] In turn, the refugees would have increased Philistine strength with motivated reinforcements for the Philistine army. It only stands to reason that the Philistines would have acquired new ideas and equipment from the peoples they incorporated. It seems that the Philistines, to an extent, maintained an open-door policy, unlike other Canaanites who did not seem to trust each other and were not nearly as willing to form alliances. As witnessed even in the days of David, the Philistines were willing to provide refuge to anyone, as long as there was an understanding of loyalty (I Samuel 27-29). Indeed, study of Philistine pottery reveals that "Philistine culture was the result of a complex evident formation and integration of various influences."[471] With the Philistines' adaptive culture and access to the sea, along with continual supplies and influences from other countries, it is very understandable that they would grow more formidable over time. Therefore, by the days of the judges and the kings of Israel, it is little wonder why the Philistines were a difficult problem for the Hebrews and, as the Sea People, posed a difficult problem for Egypt and others. Though the Philistines were doubtlessly more impressive in the days of Ramses II than in the days of Amenhotep II, they were never an obstacle for God. Therefore, the fearsomeness of the Philistines, and the statement concerning them in Exodus 13.17, is not enough to justify Ramses II as the pharaoh of the exodus.

Nevertheless, the scenario posed by this book does place the Philistines acting as the Sea People against Merenptah during the most notable period of the Philistines in biblical history, corresponding to the late judges and the time of Samuel. Perhaps it also provides an explanation for the most compelling artifact from the short reign of Merenptah, a document known as the *Israel Stela*. Dated to Merenptah's fifth year, this carving is the only mention of Israel ever found in ancient Egypt.[472] It records Merenptah's successful campaign against eight nations: Libya (Tjehenu), the Hittites (Hatti), Palestine (Pa-Canaan), Ashkelon and Gezer (Philistines), Yanoam (northern Canaan in the territory of Dan), Israel, and Syria (Hurru).[473] Concerning the Hebrews, the stela says "Israel is laid waste, his seed is not."[474] It seems that during the time of Merenptah, Israel was established and recognized by the Egyptians as an autonomous nation in Canaan. Though some will only venture to place the *Israel Stela* to sometime between Joshua and Saul; several of the peoples listed by Merenptah were contemporaries of the Hebrews during the time of the judges, but Israel, in those days, was not completely separate from the nations around them culturally, religiously, and (at times) politically (Judges 3.5-7).[475] In the days of Samuel, the Hebrews declared "we will have a king over us; that we also may be like all the nations; and that our king may judge us, and go out before us, and fight our battles" (I Samuel 8.19-20). Shortly after this, Israel was established as a kingdom and would have been recognized by those around them as sovereign (I Samuel 10). Therefore, perhaps Merenptah is acknowledging the Kingdom of Israel. However, it is still possible that Merenptah could be referring to Israel as it was distinguished during the days of one of the strong judges, like Samuel, when the Hebrews were not under foreign rule; in those periods, Israel legitimized autonomy. Of course, Dan did not occupy the northern territory, (Yanoam) indicated on the *Israel Stela*, until after the death of Samson, if the book of Judges follows a chronological order (Judges 18). Therefore, the earliest placement for *The Israel Stela* of Merenptah is, perhaps, in the days between Samson and Samuel. However, the autonomy and certainly the unity of Israel in those days is questionable, and since the book of Judges makes it clear that Hebrews during that time were independent in their thinking and actions, could it be that Merenptah's stela is merely chronicling the various nationalities of individuals identified as combatants allied with the Sea People? (Judges 21.25) If not, since Egypt's struggle with the Sea People continued well after the death of Merenptah, and there is no mention of a time in the scriptures, in either the days of the judges or of the early kings, when Israel was "laid waste" by Egyptians. Therefore, Merenptah's *Israel Stela* is likely wishful thinking and boastful propaganda than fact.

Yet, there may be a clue to the timing of the *Israel Stela* in I Samuel 7.13. This intriguing passage says, "So the Philistines were subdued, and they came no more into the coast of Israel: and the hand of the Lord was against the Philistines all the days of Samuel." This indicates a period of time when the Philistines might have had motive to do battle on another coast. If they were unable to expand eastward into Hebrew territory, it makes sense for the Sea People to seek land elsewhere; this could account for their "bewildering migration around and across the Mediterranean Sea over a period of fifty years," certainly into the days of Ramses III.[476] Perhaps this verse also provides a hint as to why the Sea People are shown with their women and children with them, riding in ox carts.[477] According to I Samuel, the Philistines were "subdued" after a terrifying encounter with the Ark of the Covenant that inflicted their people with plagues of mice and tumors (I Samuel 5-6). They returned the Ark to the Hebrews (interestingly, via ox cart), but perhaps a significant portion of the Philistines were afraid to remain living anywhere near the mysterious Ark. If the Philistines were unable to advance to the east; were concerned that, in time, they too would be driven from their homeland by Hebrew incursion; and were afraid of the power of the Hebrew God, perhaps they took to the sea, seeking a new place to live.

Is Ramses II the pharaoh of the exodus? Immediately following the exodus, the Hebrews wandered in the wilderness for 40 years as punishment for their faithless behavior (Numbers 14.27-35). The conquest of Canaan, led by Joshua, took perhaps another 10-30 years, assuming that Joshua was close to the same age as Caleb (Joshua 24.29; Joshua 14.7-10). This time frame alone makes it highly unlikely that Ramses II was the pharaoh of the exodus, since at least 50 years were required, according to the Bible, for Israel to leave Egypt and to "settle" in the Promised Land. The reign of Ramses II and Merenptah *combined* do not allow enough time for the exodus, the wilderness wandering, and the conquest of Canaan, and for Israel to be recognized as a kingdom on the *Israel Stela* in the days of the late judges. Therefore, unless the biblical account is compromised at every turn, Ramses II is not the pharaoh of the exodus.

On the other hand, there is a puzzle concerning the juncture of Ramses II and the Hebrews. Although his battle focus was more outside of Canaan, in areas north and east (territories of the Hittites, Kadesh, and Syria); nevertheless, Ramses II's campaigns into Palestine are well documented and memorialized on monuments in Canaan.[478] Why then is there no mention of Egyptian military conflict with the Hebrews during the time of the judges? It is most likely that, using Canaan as a conduit for accessing nations to the north, Ramses II hardly ventured beyond the Plain of Philistia in his jaunts through the region. Furthermore, out of the over 300 years that Israel was led by elders and judges, not only were Hebrews still living with the people of Canaan, as punishment for idolatry and unfaithfulness to God, they were conquered and considered servants of other nations on at least four significant occasions (Judges 3.8; 3.14; 4.2; 6.1; 10.8; 13.1).[479] Altogether, the Hebrews were under foreign rule for nearly a third of the time of the judges. In fact, they were under the rule of the Philistines, alone, for 40 years (Judges 13.1). When one considers that Ramses II only fought with enemies to the north during the first decade of his rule (at most, until Year 21), if Ramses II had campaigned through Canaan during the days of the judges, at any of the times that the Hebrews were serving another king, Israel would have been, essentially, a non-entity, a non-combatant. If Merenptah corresponds to the days of Samuel and the crowning of Saul and if Ramses III's vassal city solution to the problem of the Sea People was enacted during the reign of Saul, it might help to explain the Egyptian and other foreign influences in the Philistine culture discovered by archaeologists Clarence Fisher and Alan Rowe at Bethshan.[480] Bethshan was a Philistine city, infamous in scripture for being the place where the bodies of Saul and his sons were hung for public display (I Samuel 31.10, 12). After the death of Ramses III, Egypt fell into the hands of a string of "ineffectual" pharaohs.[481] The Egyptian army was weak, and the gold mines in Nubia were tapped out. It is very possible that, increasingly concerned about domestic issues, Egypt was not as watchful over its vassal states in Palestine in the days following Ramses III. Under this scenario, the Philistines could easily have resumed an aggressive posture toward Israel. Furthermore, it would have been in the Philistine's best interest to maintain good relations with Egypt in case they needed help against their hostile neighbors to the east. There is mention of an Egyptian mercenary, who had been fighting as a member of the Amalekite army in the days of Saul and David, but it is doubtful that this young man had any connection to the Philistines (I Samuel 30.11-14). However, based on the disrespectful account of Egyptian authority recorded in the *Golénuscheff Papyrus*, there is a good chance that Philistine vassal cities were not too concerned about Egyptian domination.[482]

Excavations, in the early 1960s, in the ancient city of Ashdod, uncovered Philistine pottery and a scarab from Ramses III in the deepest layer. It was therefore concluded that Philistines must have arrived in Canaan around the time of Ramses III.[483] However, "Ashdothites" were contemporaries of Joshua according to Joshua 13.3. Is it possible that the Ashdod layer containing a scarab of Ramses III was part of a vassal city built to house the re-located Sea People? Could it be that an earlier Ashdod predated Ramses III? Importantly, subsequent excavations on the site have revealed Mycenaean and Cypriot pottery, causing archaeologists to hypothesize connections between more ancient residents of Ashdod and the Hyksos; subsequently, Ashdod was theorized to have been a "pre-Philistine Aegean settlement."[484] Could it not be that the residents of Ashdod during the days of the Hyksos, were actually Philistine/Hyksos who were "Aegeanized" in much the same way that the Hebrew/Hyksos were "Egyptianized" and, in the worldly gluttony that characterized the Hyksos, they essentially lost their cultural identity? (Genesis 10.14; Jeremiah 47.4; Amos 9.7)[485] The Bible ties Caphtor (Crete) to Philistines, not necessarily as an origin, but certainly as an influence and relationship. The wealth, power, and access to exotic new goods and customs that the Philistines experienced in their days as allies of the Hyksos surely would have been beguilingly transformative. Isn't similar behavior observed on the part of the Philistines when they donned the costume and culture of the Sea People? Perhaps they were "Ashdothites," but they may still have been Philistines. According to Joshua, it seems that they were (Joshua 13.3).

Yet, the question remains: why did Thutmose IV turn away from the god of his father and seek to worship a forgotten god? The religious beliefs of ancient Egypt are complex and enigmatic. "If two gods represented the same or related powers, they could exchange names or forms with one another."[486] Therefore, all manifestations of the sun were interconnected, in a sense, the same. In fact, Amun-Ra's connection to the sun deities of Heliopolis may be the only reason that Thutmose IV included him, at all, on his seventeen limestone stelae; the former "king of the gods" received no extra attention from this pharaoh.[487] Still, Thutmose IV appears to have been a young man who was torn. He wanted to venerate the gods of his ancestors (as is reflected in many of his monuments), but he seems conflicted in his reverence, as if he was afraid of failing to honor any deity.[488] As Bryan expresses, "[Thutmose IV] honored the established cult centers and was hardly an iconoclast. On the other hand, at several locations he left certain harbingers of things to come."[489] Evidence of the dawning of religious reform may be seen in the single obelisk erected by Thutmose IV to honor Thutmose III. Though he may have merely been putting the finishing touches and setting up a monument begun by an earlier pharaoh, traditionally, "obelisks were almost always erected in pairs, not singly."[490] Could it be that in this single monument, Thutmose IV was suggesting the recognition of one god, *the* Lord of all? Seemingly unsure of the validity of contemporary Theban religious convention, it seems Thutmose IV cast his religious attention north, to On, to revere an ancient god sometimes depicted in Egyptian iconography as a "human-armed sundisk."[491] Perhaps, in reality, Thutmose IV sought the favor of the God whose actual form is unknown but whose "stretched out arm" had brought "great judgments" on Egypt (Exodus 6.6; 33.20; John 1.18; 5.37).

In the religion of On, there was an amalgamation of the following concepts: life after death, a primeval, creator God, the "complete one," who existed before the creation of the world; he created all things and all beings (including man); he is also a destroying God; he is the father (even of the souls in the afterlife, in the place of the dead), the universal good God; he is hidden, and yet he is the illuminator of all things.[492] As such, this divine entity was usually represented as the sun. However, he could also be seen in the form of a man, a scarab beetle, a serpent, the mound of creation, or an obelisk.[493] He was identified with Atum, Tum, Khepri, Ra, Horus, Aten, and others.[494] Adoration of this God is exemplified in the following hymn:

Come to me, O thou Sun;
Horus of the horizon, give me help.
Thou are he that giveth help;
There is no help without thee.
Come to me, Tum; hear me, thou great God;
My heart goeth forth towards On;
Let my desires be fulfilled;
Let my heart rejoice,
My inmost heart rejoice in gladness.
Hear my vows,
My humble supplications every day,
Hear my adorations every night—
My cries of terror,
Cries that issue from my mouth
That come forth from it one by one

O Horus of the horizon,
There is none other beside thee,
Protector of millions,
Deliverer of tens of thousands,
Defender of him that calls upon thee,
Lord of On!
Reproach me not for my many sins—
I am young, and weak of body;
I am a man without a heart.
Anxiety preys upon me,
As an ox [feeds] upon grass;
If I pass the night in [sleep],
And therein find refreshment,
Anxiety nevertheless returns to me
'ere the day is done.[495]

According to the writing of the Greek biographer, Diogenes Laërtius, it was in response to a terrible plague that the Athenians erected an altar to "The Unknown God" (Acts 17.23).[496] This monument was an attempt to appease any god(s) that may have been inadvertently offended.[497] Though Thutmose IV was drawn to the ideals expressed at On, his monuments leave the impression of a man who was afraid of offending some god, therefore he made a concerted effort to leave no god dishonored. Toward that end, he erected a monument to credit "the Lord of All."[498] Similar behavior was also displayed in the throws of a violent storm, according to the book of Jonah. The terrified sailors, on the boat where the fugitive prophet had sought refuge, suspected that the raging sea that threatened to destroy their ship was the manifestation of an angry god. They were right. They began to call out to every god they knew and to those they didn't know, hoping to appease the unknown, offended deity (Jonah 1.4-6).

However, perhaps Thutmose IV was also afraid of offending the Egyptian people. His obvious attraction to the ancient religion of northern Egypt makes it relatively clear where his true loyalty was directed.[499] Yet, exclusive acknowledgement of the deity who had plagued Egypt would probably not have been well received. Nevertheless, in his purification of Heliopolis and his efforts to restore "maat to Atum," Thutmose IV, not Amenhotep II, set the stage for Atenism.[500] In fact, Amenhotep II's attachment to Heliopolis, like most other aspects of his life, may have been little more than another platform for self-aggrandizement. According to the records written on a scarab, Amenhotep II was born near Heliopolis, which may explain why, more than once, he laid claim to be "Amenophis, the God who rules in Heliopolis, in the house of his fathers, the gods."[501] It was not so much the gods of Heliopolis, including the Aten, that Amenhotep II sought to elevate; it was himself.

Thutmose IV, at first, seems to have sought to worship the gods of Heliopolis in general, but as time went on, Aten appears to have gained his more narrow focus. Thutmose IV was the first to wear a uraeus displaying Aten; he adorned himself with jewelry dedicated to Aten; and he credited his victories in battle to Aten on a large commemorative scarab.[502] Regardless of those who propose Amenhotep II as the designer of Aten worship, it is perhaps more likely that Thutmose IV constructed monuments or modified monuments depicting Amenhotep II paying homage to the Aten in an attempt to curry favor with the Lord of All on behalf of his father.[503] Perhaps Thutmose IV hoped to obtain mercy for Amenhotep II. After all, the pharaoh of the exodus had expressed such desire in the abject words, "and bless me also" (Exodus 12.32).

In the final analysis, perhaps this is why priests from the Twenty-first Dynasty treated Amenhotep II differently from any other pharaoh. Though the funerary cult of Amenhotep II kept vigil for three hundred years, an astonishingly long time, though the priests wrapped him in a sheet of fine linen and adorned his mummy with garlands of flowers, the re-organizers of the Valley of the Kings put Amenhotep II right back where he belonged.[504] In the special treatment of this one mummy is perhaps a strange mixture of reverence and fear, a desire to honor the dead pharaoh and yet not to arouse the anger of a living God. If Amenhotep II was the pharaoh of the exodus, the priests of Amun desired to pay homage to a king who refused to relinquish his faith in traditional Egyptian religion, who had remained loyal to Amun-Ra; but, at the same time, they would not have wanted to risk angering the deity who put Amun-Ra in his place and put Amenhotep II in his grave. They would have wanted to do nothing to disrupt the peace and court chaos. Rightly so, they were fearful to disturb the father of terror! In an Eighteenth Dynasty hymn, Amun-Ra is called "The lord of fear, great of dread."[505] Yet, Amun-Ra was powerless against the God of the exodus, the *real* father of terror (Jeremiah 32.21). Ultimately, even the priests of Amun-Ra feared the Lord of All, the one God, the true and living God of Egypt.

Thutmose IV's Dream Stela

127

Citations

1. qtd. in Gill 326

2. O'Connor & Cline 24
3. Rohl 78, Hawass 36, Hayes 25; Harris & Weeks 113; *Great Pharaohs of Ancient Egypt*
4. Brock 42; Reeves & Wilkinson 198; Hawass & Janot 19; Tyldesley, *Hatshepsut* 92
5. O'Connor & Cline 33; Petrovich 22; Redford, *Akhenaten* 31; Aling, *Egypt* 97
6. O'Connor & Cline 36
7. Montet 37; Fletcher 27
8. Grosvenor 106
9. Der Manuelian 210; Redford, *Akhenaten* 31
10. Grosvenor 107; Reifstahl 48
11. Riefstahl 47; Grosvenor 106, Tyldesley, *Pharaohs* 118, Dodson & Dyan 137
12. Montet 37; Breasted, *Records II* 304
13. Montet 37
14. Tyldesley, *Pharaohs* 119; Shaw 249
15. Lange & Mirmer 440
16. Tyldesley, *Pharaohs* 119
17. Lange & Mirmer 440
18. Romer 20
19. Fletcher 16; Aldred 239
20. Dodson & Dyan 137; Roehrig 261
21. Hetherington & Parke 345
22. Dodson & Dyan 132
23. Dodson & Dyan 140; O'Connor & Cline 40; Baron & Byrne 512

24. O'Connor & Cline 39
25. Dodson & Dyan 137
26. Aldred 133
27. O'Connor & Cline 32
28. Hawass & Janot 128; Davis 105; Grosvenor 226, Tyldesley, *Pharaohs* 111
29. Grosvenor 226, Riefstahl 43
30. Aldred 237
31. Hawass & Janot 39; Lange & Mirmer 438; O'Connor & Cline 32; Tyldesley 119
32. Grosvenor 107
33. O'Connor & Cline 33, 37
34. Casson 43; Hoerth, *Archaeology* 125
35. D. Stewart 51
36. O'Connor & Cline 27
37. Tyldesley 118; Dodson & Dyan 130
38. Newby 79
39. Fletcher 10
40. Grosvenor 226; Der Manuelian 52; R. Smith xiii
41.
42. Bille-De Mot 15; Tyldesley 112; Der Manuelian 52
43. Newby 93; Reifstahl 45; Tyldesley 119
44. Der Manuelian 37, 52; Hoffmeier 109,110
45. Der Manuelian 50
46. Grosvenor 226; Der Manuelian 53, 56
47. Spalinger 111
48. *Ancient Egypt Unearthed*
49. Petrovich 15
50. Fletcher 11
51. Petrovich 15
52. Newby 97; Petrovich 20
53. Tyldesley 111
54. Der Manuelian 59
55. Newby 81; Tyldesley 115
56. Der Manuelian 68
57. Petrovich 21
58. Der Manuelian 82
59. Petrovich 23
60. Newby 94
61. Der Manuelian 60
62. Spalinger 104
63. Reifstahl 177
64. Breasted, *Records II* 306-307
65. Der Manuelian 37, 68; Reifstahl 44
66. Petrovich 15, 20; Der Manuelian 69
67. Petrovich 19
68. Lange & Mirmer 440
69. Petrovich 19
70. Der Manuelian 48, 49
71. Der Manuelian 70-72
72. Newby 94
73. Tyldesley 111; Der Manuelian 77-78
74. Der Manuelian 78-80
75. Der Manuelian 83, 90, 92, 96
76. Spalinger 170; Petrovich 15
77. Der Manuelian 82; Tyldesley 118
78. Newby 72; Spalinger 49
79. Spalinger 49
80. Silverberg 115
81. A. Myers 880
82. Peloubet 32
83. Peloubet 31
84. Spalinger 51, 71; T. Stewart 188

85. Spalinger 84
86. Spalinger 23
87. Spalinger 51
88. May 51
89. Spalinger 37; Shaw 245
90. Davis 17; Kitchen, *Reliability* 246
91. Der Manuelian 69-70; Petrovich 22
92. A. Myers 881
93. Der Manuelian 210
94. Davis 105, McWhirter 1-3
95. Peloubet 382
96. Peloubet 32
97. Der Manuelian 210
98. Reifstahl 47-48; Der Manuelian 54, 157-158; O'Connor & Cline 37
99. O'Connor & Cline 32; Kemp 282
100. Der Manuelian 210
101. Der Manuelian 157; Newby 93
102. Der Manuelian 190
103. Rohl 184
104. O'Connor & Cline 33-34
105. Redford, *Akhenaten* 17
106. Janot & Hawass 110; O'Connor & Cline 46
107. Reifstahl 50
108. Bille-De Mot 15
109. Silverman 32; O'Connor & Cline 256-257; Bryan 119
110. Tyldesley 112
111. Tyldesley 112
112. Bryan 118
113. Bryan 332, 336; Aldred 143
114. O'Connor & Cline 56; Bryan 333-334
115. O'Connor & Cline 56
116. Tyldesley 114
117. Hawass 42, 122
118. Bryan 290
119. Bryan 288
120. Hawass 133
121. Hawass 40, 133; Petrovich 14, 21
122. Petrovich 2, 6; Aling, *Egypt* 97
123. Vos 54
124. Hawass 37
125. Reifstahl 33; Roehrig 261; Breasted, *Records II* 180; Aling, *Egypt* 97
126. O'Connor & Cline 31; Tyldesley 115; Fletcher 16; Petrovich 12, 13; Der Manuelian 42
127. Thomas 1676
128. Janot & Hawass 108; Tyldesley 96, 115
129. Harris & Weeks 138
130. Petrovich 29; O'Connor & Cline 31
131. Assmann 58
132. Dorman 136
133. Petrovich 6; Davis 43
134. David 182
135. Silverman 136
136. Oakes & Gahlin 440-442
137. Oakes & Gahlin 441
138. Davis 91
139. Josephus 60
140. Redford, *Oxford* 203
141. Oakes & Gahlin 442-443
142. Kemp 306; Der Manuelian 102, 104-105
143. Josephus 60
144. Der Manuelian 37
145. Reifstahl 47-48
146. A. Myers 549, 552
147. Der Manuelian 107
148. Der Manuelian 106
149. Der Manuelian 103-104
150. Hoerth, *Archaeology* 164
151. Davis 138; Greenberg 122

152. *Great Pharaohs of Ancient
     Egypt*; Reeves & Wilkinson 23
153. *Ancient Egypt Unearthed*

154. Kitchen, *Reliability* 249
155. Strong 56
156. Davis 111
157. Strouhal 74
158. Strong 91
159. Strouhal 73
160. Davis 120
161. Ray 23-35
162. Rawlinson 161, 165
163. Rawlinson 62
164. Rawlinson 165
165. Rawlinson 62
166. Rawlinson 166
167. Rawlinson 63
168. Thompson, *Handbook* 141;
     Davis 126; Beegle 112-113;
     Greenberg 129
169. Hussein 3; Zodhiates 89
170. Rawlinson 169
171. O'Connor & Cline Fig. 51
172. Josephus 62
173. Watterson 30
174. Rawlinson 320
175. Davis 137
176. El-Sabban *xii*
177. Petrovich 3; Greenberg 96, 125
178. Redford, Oxford 521; Rawlinson
     312; Bunson 50; Bauval &
     Gilbert 89; Shaw 10
179. Redford, Oxford 521; T. Stewart
     327-330

180. *Great Pharaohs of Ancient
     Egypt*; Kitchen, *Reliability* 250
181. *Great Pharaohs of Ancient
     Egypt*; Redford, *Oxford* 521
182. Hoerth, *Archaeology* 125;
     Bunson 190
183. Davis 102
184. Bunson 191
185. Bunson 91
186. Meskell 131
187. Szpakowska 140-141
188. El-Sabban 22, 88
189. Meskell 170; Hoffmeier 150
190. Strong 120
191. Oakes & Gahlin 169, 320-321
192. Davis 100
193. El-Sabban *xii*
194. Meskell 168
195. Aldred 134
196. Spalinger web; Meskell 171;
     Strouhal 228
197. Hamlyn 117
198. El-Sabban *xii*
199. Strouhal 229; Watterson 143
200. Vos 55
201. Szpakowska 29, 196; Davis 107
202. El-Sabban 10; Szpakowska 143;
     Vos 56; Hoffmeier 150
203. Szpakowska 98
204. Lange & Mirmer 437
205. Bryan 350

206. Meskell 48
207. Strouhal 228
208. Watterson 76
209. Redford, *Oxford* 521
210. Assmann 65, 68-69
211. Aldred 70; Shaw 240
212. Bunson 91; Redford, *Oxford*
     521; Ikram 199, Shaw 155
213. Meskell 131
214. Tyldesley, *Pharaohs* 110
215. Meskell 171
216. Tyldesley, *Pharaohs* 110
217. A. Myers 761
218. Meskell 176
219. David 54
220. Meskell 171
221. Meskell 172
222. Greenberg 96, 129
223. Assmann 26; Szpakowska 146
224. Hawass 122
225. Bryan 253
226. Hawass & Janot 128; Janot &
     Hawass 128' Tyldesley,
     Hatshepsut 91

227. Harris & Weeks 139
228. Janot & Hawass 108; Tyldesley,
     Hatshepsut 91; Hawass & Janot
     105, 108; *Secrets of Egypt's Lost
     Queen*
229. Booth 112; Reeves & Wilkinson
     118
230. Harris & Weeks 166; *Ancient
     Egypt Unearthed*
231. Assmann 31-37
232. Harris & Weeks 166
233. Harris & Weeks 133
234. Tyldesley, *Hatshepsut* 90
235. Harris & Weeks 139
236. Tyldesley, *Hatshepsut* 90;
     Hawass & Janot 128
237. Davis 123
238. Josephus 61-62
239. Bryan 242
240. Reeves & Wilkinson 107, 115,
     116, & 117
241. Reeves & Wilkinson 89, 115
242. Booth 102
243. Booth 95-96
244. Der Manuelian 153
245. Hayes 7
246. Bryan 242
247. Bille De Mot 92
248. Bryan 272
249. Hayes 151
250. Reeves 34
251. O'Connor & Cline 38; Reifstahl
     47
252. Hornung 47
253. Rohl 397
254. Murray 176
255. Hayes 37; Murray 177
256. Hayes 151; Tyldesley, *Pharaohs*
     120; Reifstahl 49
257. Tyldesley, *Pharaohs* 127
258. Bryan 151-152
259. Redford, *Akhenaten* 45
260. Harris & Weeks 140

261. Bryan 281-282
262. O'Connor & Cline 37; Der
     Manuelian 168; Bryan 23
263. Der Manuelian 117-148;
     O'Connor & Cline 58-59;
     Fletcher 101; Hawass 40-41;
     Bryan 288; Bille De Mot 80
264. O'Connor & Cline 58
265. O'Connor & Cline 58
266. O'Connor & Cline 58, 60
267. Bryan 267; Redford, *Akhenaten*
     160
268. Bryan 269; Redford, *Akhenaten*
     161
269. Bryan 288
270. O'Connor & Cline 58; Bryan
     281-282
271. Bryan 23
272. Bryan 279
273. O'Connor & Cline 61
274. O'Connor & Cline 58
275. Bryan 336
276. Hoerth, *Archaeology* 141; Shaw
     130
277. Spalinger 6; Gnirs & Hoffmeier
     web; Der Manuelian 122
278. Petrovich 8
279. Lange & Mirmer 439; Reeves &
     Wilkinson 105; Dodson & Dyan
     140; Tyldesley, *Pharaohs* 120
280. O'Connor & Cline 40
281. Dodson & Dyan 134, 138
282. Vols 39
283. Feucht web
284. Spalinger 73
285. Tyldesley, *Pharaohs* 114
286. Cameron & Kuhrt 77
287. Cameron & Kuhrt 69
288. Robins web; Vols 69
289. Tyldesley, *Hatshepsut* 56;
     Cameron & Kuhrt 67
290. *Great Pharaohs of Ancient
     Egypt*; Gore web
291. Feucht web, O'Connor & Cline
     61
292. Bryan 254; Der Manuelian 158
293. Reifstahl 47
294. O'Connor & Cline 38
295. Der Manuelian 154
296. Petrovich 8
297. El-Sabban 26; Manuelian 172
298. Dodson & Dyan 138
299. O'Connor & Cline 39
300. Dodson & Dyan 140
301. Reeves & Wilkinson 105;
     Dodson & Dyan 137
302. Bryan 40, 41; O'Connor & Cline
     40, 41
303. Dodson & Dyan 21, 137, 138;
     Manuelian 174
304. Bryan 52, 119; O'Connor &
     Cline 9; Fletcher 10, 28
305. Bryan 55; O'Connor & Cline 10;
     Tyldesley, *Pharaohs* 120;
     Fletcher 32
306. Der Manuelian 216; Tyldesley,
     Pharaohs 120; Dodson & Dyan
     134; Fletcher 15; Bryan 155,

336; O'Connor & Cline 49
307. Dodson & Dyan 139
308. Petrovich 22
309. Kitchen, *Reliability* 246
310. Newby 97
311. Assmann 34
312. Leach & Tait web
313. Hoerth, *Archaeology* 167; Aling,
   Egypt 102
314. Reifstahl 177; *Great Pharaohs
   of Ancient Egypt*; *Ancient Egypt
   Unearthed*; Petrovich 11-14

315. *Great Pharaohs of Ancient
   Egypt*; Parkinson, *Sinuhe* 110-
   111
316. Petrovich 11
317. Hoerth, *Archaeology* 163
318. Janot & Hawass 76; *Great
   Pharaohs of Ancient Egypt*
319. Hawass & Janot 75
320. Romer 161
321. Hawass & Janot 37, 78; Reeves
   & Wilkinson 199
322. Hornung 144; Lesko web
323. Hornung 27, 144-145
324. Hornung 138
325. Hoerth, *Archaeology* 168
326. Ikram 200; Breasted, *History*
   167; Parkinson, *Sinuhe* 157

327. Reeves 34, 98
328. Tyldesley, *Pharaohs* 115
329. Reeves 97; Hawass & Janot 123

330. Reeves 98; Hayes 37
331. Reeves 98
332. Hornung 145
333. Reeves 96
334. Reeves 102
335. Hornung 145
336. Hornung 144; Dodson & Dyan
   176; Hawass & Janot 35, 37
337. Hawass & Janot 128; Clayton
   113
338. Marowitz web
339. Landman, Mikkelsen, Bieler, &
   Bronson 42-43; Taburiaux 89;
   Ludwig 145
340. Landman, Mikkelsen, Bieler, &
   Bronson 104
341. Taburiaux 19, 39
342. Marowitz web
343. Landman, Mikkelsen, Bieler, &
   Bronson 32, 33, 107
344. Taburiaux 31-32
345. Harris & Weeks 139
346. Hawass & Janot 128
347. Harris & Weeks 138; Der
   Manuelian 13
348. Hayes 25; *Ancient Egypt
   Unearthed*; Hawass & Janot 36
349. Aldred 106
350. Hawass & Janot 128
351. Hawass & Janot 37
352. Harris & Weeks 139; Hawass &
   Janot 110; Hayes 27; Bryan 10,

43; O'Connor & Cline 9
353. Bryan 63
354. Dodson & Dyan 140
355. Bryan 49
356. Dodson & Dyan 138
357. Dodson & Dyan 141; O'Connor
   & Cline 44
358. Hawass & Janot 37; Romer 162
359. Romer 161; Janot & Hawass 86
360. Dodson & Dyan 134; Tyldesley,
   Pharaohs 120
361. Dodson & Dyan 137
362. Dodson & Dyan 134
363. Hawass 39; Bryan 39
364. Bryan 64; O'Connor & Cline 44

365. Silverman 67, 187
366. O'Connor & Cline 44
367. Bryan 153
368. Der Manuelian 175; Bryan 64
369. O'Connor & Cline 44
370. Dodson & Dyan 139
371. O'Connor & Cline 44; Der
   Manuelian 177
372. D. Stewart 50
373. Bryan 63
374. Bryan 112-113
375. O'Connor & Cline 44
376. Bryan 39, 95
377. Kemp 282; D. Stewart 50
378. Dodson & Dyan 139; O'Connor
   & Cline 40, 45
379. Der Manuelian 42

380. 379. Harris & Weeks 139-140;
   Hayes 27
381. 380. Dodson & Dyan 140; Bryan
   113
382. *Great Pharaohs of Ancient
   Egypt*

383. O'Connor & Cline 45
384. Dodson & Dyan 139; O'Connor
   & Cline 45; Silverberg 31; Shaw
   260
385. O'Connor & Cline 40;
   Tyldesley, *Pharaohs* 120
386. Bryan 145-146
387. Harris & Weeks 138
388. O'Connor & Cline 28, 49;
   Reifstahl 40, 128
389. O'Connor & Cline 50; Bryan
   155, 350; Tyldesley, *Pharaohs*
   120
390. Kemp 262; Lange & Mirmer 406

391. O'Connor & Cline 49
392. Assmann 38
393. Reifstahl 135
394. Lange & Mirmer 379
395. Lange & Mirmer 379
396. Lange & Mirmer 406; Zivie-
   Coche 23-24; "Secrets of the
   Sphinx"
397. D. Stewart 51
398. Zivie-Coche 4
399. Silverman 188

400. Reifstahl 49
401. Peloubet 116; Assmann 74
402. D. Stewart 51; Reifstahl 59
403. D. Stewart 50
404. "Secrets of the Sphinx"
405. O'Connor & Cline 49; Zivie-
   Coche 70
406. Lange & Mirmer 379
407. O'Connor & Cline 50
408. Shanks & Meinhardt 110;
   Hoffmeier 112
409. Redford, Akhenaten 27
410. Casson 142; Redford, *Joseph*
   198
411. Bille-De Mot 26
412. Casson 143
413. Petrovich 24
414. Petrovich 23; Spalinger 144
415. Der Manuelian 76; Kemp 29;
   Casson 143
416. Kitchen, *Reliability* 246
417. Breasted, *Records II* 293; D.
   Stewart 62
418. Petrovich 23
419. Der Manuelian 76
420. Bryan 333; Kemp 29
421. Bryan 334; D. Stewart 51;
   Tyldesley, *Pharaohs* 120
422. Bryan 334; D. Stewart 51;
   Tyldesley, *Pharaohs* 120
423. Lange & Mirmer 441
424. Dodson & Dyan 137
425. Bryan 269
426. O'Connor & Cline 36;
   Tyldesley, *Pharaohs* 118
427. Der Manuelian 57
428. Rohl 21; Peloubet 624
429. Redford, *Exodus* 402
430. Davis 23
431. Tyldesley, *Hatshepsut* 37;
   Redford, *Exodus* 408
432. Redford, *Exodus* 416
433. Align, *Ramses* 132
434. Aling, *Ramses* 133
435. Redford, *Exodus* 410
436. Aling, *Ramses* 129-132
437. Vos 47; Redford, *Exodus* 413; T.
   Stewart 13; Kitchen, *Reliability*
   256
438. Silverman 139
439. Stadelmann web
440. Allen web "Ramesses I"
441. Kitchen web

442. 441. *King Tut Unwrapped: Life
   and Death*
443. 442. Dodson & Dyan 153
444. 443. Silverman 35; Montet 159;
   Kitchen web
445. *Great Pharaohs of Ancient
   Egypt*, Oakes & Gahlin 199

446. Stadelmann web
447. Oakes & Gahlin 132
448. Silverman 45-46; Rohl 164;
   Sourouzian web; Bierling 52
449. Dothan & Dothan 14-18; 22;

Wiseman 4

450. A. Myers 828; Wiseman 4
451. Reifstahl 171; Hoerth, *Peoples* 238; Bierling 99
452. Leahy web
453. Peloubet 51; Wiseman 58
454. Dothan & Dothan 27; Bierling 62
455. Dothan & Dothan 10
456. Zlotowitz 57: Hoerth, *Peoples* 158, 232, 247; Peloubet 134
457. Peloubet 4; Wiseman 56
458. Macalister 38
459. May 63
460. Dothan & Dothan 87
461. Dothan & Dothan 193; Hoerth, *Peoples* 244
462. Leahy web; Reifstahl 171
463. Hoerth, *Archaeology* 166; Van Seters 18
464. May 49; Bierling 37
465. Leahy web
466. Dothan & Dothan 51
467. Dothan & Dothan 117, 217; Bierling 99
468. Dothan & Dothan 18, Macalister 24; Hoerth, *Peoples* 233; Wiseman 57; Kitchen, *Reliability* 163
469. Dothan & Dothan 29-31;

Wiseman 67

470. Dothan & Dothan 48; Bierling 149
471. Dothan & Dothan 82; Bierling 36, 38, 43
472. Macalister 68
473. Dothan & Dothan 94; Hoerth, *Peoples* 231, 232, 237; Wiseman 42, 57, 60
474. Rohl 164; Bierling 99
475. May 61-63
476. Vos 54; Aling, *Egypt* 79
477. Vos 123; Van Seters 1-4; Lewy, *Origin* 3; Gray 180, 187, 188
478. Leahy web
479. Dothan & Dothan 21; Macalister 20, 22; Shaw 328; Hoerth, *Peoples* 235; Bierling 53, 62
480. Kitchen web; Hoerth, *Peoples* 324
481. Smith 1693
482. Dothan & Dothan 59
483. Rohl 21; Macalister 24
484. Macalister 31-33
485. Dothan & Dothan 150
486. Dothan & Dothan 162, 164; Bierling 61; Hoerth, *Peoples* 244

487. A. Myers 191; Hoerth, *Peoples* 232; Wiseman 53, 54, 56;

Bierling 61, 62, 65-67, 76; Kitchen, *Reliability* 339
488. Lange & Mirmer 377
489. Bryan 150; Hamlyn 89; Aling, *Egypt* 82, 88ff
490. Bryan 150, 206
491. Bryan 141
492. Redford, Akhenaten 74
493. Bryan 154-155
494. Hamlyn 28, 30; Lange & Mirmer 379; Rawlinson 335, 358, 359; Breasted, *History* 34
495. Lange & Mirmer 379; Hamlyn 28, 30
496. Lange & Mirmer 379, Hamlyn 30, Watterson 170
497. Rawlinson 362-363
498. Vos 557
499. Bryan 156
500. Reifstahl 49; Bryan 154-155
501. Davis 33
502. O'Connor & Cline 51, D. Stewart 51, Newby 93
503. Fletcher 15; Booth 112
504. Hawass & Janot 181, 200; Reifstahl 45
505. Silverberg 16

Akhenaten

Chapter 5
Living in Truth

Dawning

The days of Thutmose IV's successor, Amenhotep III, also known as Amenhotep the Magnificent, were a golden age in Egypt.[1] Peace between Egypt and Mitanni was secure; diplomacy and good relations prevailed among the world powers; Egypt's empire was intact; Nubia was subdued; the harvests were plentiful; gold, tributes, and "trade goods" poured into the land.[2] It was a good time to be an Egyptian!

> . . . everywhere were fine tunics of pleated linen, sandals of gilded and glazed leather, bracelets, necklaces and rings of gold and silver set with turquoise, cornelian, and lapis lazuli, ostrich-plume fans. . . . Festivals and entertainments were held one after the other, the days passed in the delight and charm of an ideal existence. . . . Thebes was the Versailles of the ancient world and Amenophis III [sic] was styled by his subjects, as later Louis XIV, the Sun King.[3]

The economy of Egypt was strong; wealth was well distributed; unemployment wasn't an issue; the government was stable; and the king was satiated. Unlike the warrior pharaohs in his ancestry, Amenhotep III showed little interest in expanding the borders of Egypt. It seems that he was more interested in expanding his waistline.

Amenhotep III was a man who enjoyed the good life. Tushratta, the king of Mitanni, said of him, "He rejoiced very, very much!"[4] Besides eating, Amenhotep III loved charioteering, hunting, and cats as evidenced by the tiny, limestone sarcophagi he had fashioned for two pet cats, Tamyt and Miu.[5] He also liked women—his harem held a thousand wives.[6] Yet, one woman in particular facilitated Amenhotep III's hedonistic lifestyle: his head wife, Queen Tiye. Amenhotep III may have been enjoying the ride, but there are many who believe that it was Queen Tiye who was driving.[7] Perhaps this is why his administration is sometimes compared to the governing style of Hatshepsut.[8] Also reminiscent of Hatshepsut's supervision were the numerous, ambitious building projects that "transformed" the Nile Valley during Amenhotep III's tenure.[9]

Though Queen Tiye's parents, Yuya and Tuya, were buried like royalty, they actually were commoners.[10] Tuya, Queen Tiye's mother, oversaw the harems and was the Superior of both the *Harim of Amun* and *Min of Akhmim*.[11] It's possible that Queen Tiye's father, a celebrated military man, was a foreigner, perhaps Nubian.[12] Regardless of these conspicuous irregularities, Amenhotep III was not only happy to marry Tiye, he was extraordinarily proud to make her his queen, as the joyful event is recorded on a commemorative wedding scarab. Some believe that "disregard of tradition is evidence of the strength and confidence of the Egyptian state, which was now in its zenith. . . . nobody seemed to care."[13]

Of course, if the exodus had occurred only a few years prior, the population of Egypt would probably not have yet recovered to a point that "qualified" candidates to arrange for marriage were readily available.[14] Nevertheless, Amenhotep III viewed Tiye as his partner and, if the scale of his monuments is credible witness, his equal.[15] Only with her did Amenhotep III have children, at least three sons and eight daughters.[16] Based on correspondence between Tiye and other heads of state, it seems that Amenhotep III was perfectly happy to delegate to his wife and to let Tiye represent him and Egypt.[17] He was much more interested in jubilees than jurisdiction. Perhaps too much is read into the rather sour expression preserved on "the small green-steatite head" and the similarly carved wooden representation of Queen Tiye, but it does seem that she was more sober-minded than her husband.[18]

However, if Tiye was a driving force in Egypt's golden age, that characteristic was magnified in Amenhotep IV/Akhenaten, her son.[19]

Queen Tiye

James Breasted once referred to him as "the first individual in history."[20] He was completely determined to drive Egypt in a new direction, toward a new horizon, and to a destination of vision. He was not to be detoured or deterred; for him, it was Aten or bust. This was a spiritual journey. Yet, according to Egyptian oral tradition, bad things happened after "King Amenophis [Amenhotep IV/Akhenaten] wanted to see the gods."[21]

Amenhotep III

Like many monarchs before him, Amenhotep IV was not the first in line to be king, but that is where the similarity ends.[22] Other New Kingdom pharaohs were steeped in the mythology and tradition of Egyptian culture, although the purpose and focus of each administration was somewhat different. For instance, Ahmose was determined to restore Egyptian autonomy; Amenhotep I desired to continue his father's legacy; Thutmose I sought to complete the mission of his superior; Thutmose II just hoped to live; Hatshepsut wanted better relations for Egypt; Thutmose III craved undisputed authority; Amenhotep II demanded personal respect; Thutmose IV wished to appease; Amenhotep III wanted everybody to be happy, but Amenhotep IV/Akhenaten was only interested in the happiness of a single entity: Aten.

However, Amenhotep IV/Akhenaten may not have begun his reign with a radical, single-minded agenda. Though it is a matter of some debate, it seems likely that Akhenaten served for some time as co-regent with his father.[23] And, although he was always drawn to the Aten, during the first few years of his regency, Amenhotep IV seemed content to rule from Thebes, building monuments and augmenting the temples of accepted and widely venerated cultural orthodoxy, and is depicted as the picture of convention.[24] For instance, though he is seen standing beneath a winged sun-disk, a remarkable stela carved into the cliffs at *Gebel es Silsila* shows Amenhotep IV making an offering to Amun-Ra.[25] Significantly, though, on this same monument (perhaps added later), the young pharaoh, likely only around sixteen years old at the time, identifies himself as "the Chief Prophet of Re-Herakhte [Harakhte] Rejoicing in the Horizon in his Aspect of the Light which is in the Aten."[26] Ramose, the vizier, preserves an image of Amenhotep IV's coronation where the crowned prince receives "bouquets and temple-staves in the names of the gods of Thebes."[27] Evidence also exists to suggest that, in those early years, Amenhotep IV oversaw the decorating of blocks in Thebes with images of Re-Harakhte shown, not as a disk, but as a falcon-headed man.[28] In fact, early on, Amenhotep IV was a clear continuation of Amenhotep III. Amenhotep III promoted the elevated position of the Aten as commended by his father, Thutmose IV, but Amenhotep III's religious attitude was much more ecumenical.[29] In fact, it was said he made "monuments for Amun, the like of which has never occurred."[30]

Thutmose IV turned his apologetic gaze to On, seeking to appease an offended deity. Amenhotep III, though he was called "Egypt's Dazzling Sun" and named his opulent palace: "Palace of the Dazzling Sun Disk (Aten)," his ship: "Rising in Truth," his royal barge: "Splendor of The Aten," and even named a daughter "Beketaten" after the Aten, Amenhotep III paid dutiful service to all gods—not just Aten—his true heart was more secular than sacred.[31] In fact, for most of his reign, though he called himself "Son of the Sun" and erected a giant scarab in honor of Atum-Khepri-Ra, Amenhotep III's interest and attitude seems more human than divine.[32] Still, at the sed-festival to celebrate his thirtieth year (as determined from the Rosetta Stone),

134

Amenhotep III apparently allowed himself to be worshiped and inducted into full godhood. Some even propose that it was really Amenhotep III, who was the Aten, the father, that was the object of Akhenaten's worship all along.[33] Besides this, there are even images in which Amenhotep III appears to be worshiping himself.[34]

Nevertheless, something profound occurred between year three and year six of Amenhotep IV's reign. As though provoked by some sudden epiphany, Amenhotep IV denounced the religion of his fathers, "declared Amun anathema," pronounced the foundation of a new capital—Akhet-Aten (Akhetaten), held a jubilee to the Aten, and even rejected his own name.[35] No longer would he be known as Amenhotep (Amun is satisfied); he now was Akhenaten (One Who is Beneficial for the Aten). What happened?

If the biblical exodus ushered in the reign of Thutmose IV, then for a little more than thirty years into the reign of Amenhotep III, the Hebrews were wandering in the wilderness (Joshua 5.6). Therefore, at just about the time for Amenhotep III's sed-festival, Joshua began the conquest of Canaan (Acts 13.18).[36] Around the thirty-fifth year of Amenhotep III, Caleb would have asked Joshua for the challenging area of Hebron as an inheritance for the tribe of Judah (Joshua 14.7-13). However, some time prior to that, the Bible records this extraordinary occurrence:

> Now it came to pass, when Adonizedec king of Jerusalem had heard how Joshua had taken Ai, and had utterly destroyed it; as he had done to Jericho and her king, so he had done to Ai and her king; and how the inhabitants of Gibeon had made peace with Israel, and were among them; that they feared greatly, because Gibeon was a great city, as one of the royal cities, and because it was greater than Ai, and all the men thereof were mighty. Wherefore Adonizedec king of Jerusalem sent unto Hoham king of Hebron, and unto Piram king of Jarmuth, and unto Japhia king of Lachish, and unto Debir king of Eglon, saying, Come up unto me, and help me, that we may smite Gibeon: for it hath made peace with Joshua and with the children of Israel. Therefore the five kings of the Amorites, the king of Jerusalem, the king of Hebron, the king of Jarmuth, the king of Lachish, the king of Eglon, gathered themselves together, and went up, they and all their hosts, and encamped before Gibeon, and made war against it. And the men of Gibeon sent unto Joshua to the camp to Gilgal, saying, Slack not thy hand from thy servants; come up to us quickly, and save us, and help us: for all the kings of the Amorites that dwell in the mountains are gathered together against us. So Joshua ascended from Gilgal, he, and all the people of war with him, and all the mighty men of valour.
>
> And the Lord said unto Joshua, Fear them not: for I have delivered them into thine hand; there shall not a man of them stand before thee. Joshua therefore came unto them suddenly, and went up from Gilgal all night. And the Lord discomfited them before Israel, and slew them with a great slaughter at Gibeon, and chased them along the way that goeth up to Bethhoron, and smote them to Azekah, and unto Makkedah. And it came to pass, as they fled from before Israel, and were in the going down to Bethhoron, that the Lord cast down great stones from heaven upon them unto Azekah, and they died: they were more which died with hailstones than they whom the children of Israel slew with the sword.
>
> Then spake Joshua to the Lord . . . Sun, stand thou still upon Gibeon; and thou, Moon, in the valley of Ajalon. And the sun stood still, and the moon stayed, until the people had avenged themselves upon their enemies. Is not this written in the book of Jasher? So the sun stood still in the midst of heaven, and hasted not to go down about a whole day. And there was no day like that before it or after it. (Joshua 10.1-14)

If this event is read as history and not mythology, then according to the theory in this book, it happened sometime between year thirty and year thirty-five of Amenhotep III. Amenhotep III's tenure lasted between thirty-seven and thirty-nine years, but perhaps two to as many as twelve of those years were shared in co-regency with his son, beginning, perhaps, from Amenhotep III's jubilee.[37] Could it be that the sun stood still for an entire day sometime in the first five years of Amenhotep IV's co regency? If the sun literally stood still in Canaan, it would have stood still in Egypt too and would have been a powerful and frightening image. It shouldn't be surprising, then, that Akhenaten would direct the attention of the Egyptian people toward the sun.[38]

Yet, if the sun stood still, some deity greater than the sun had demonstrated power over the sun. That intangible deity was the true focus of Akhenaten's devotion. Could it be that the sun standing still was the pivotal event that convinced Akhenaten that a real God had demonstrated real power and had chosen the sun as a symbol of that power? Akhenaten said, "Thou hast made heaven afar off to shine in, in order to see everything that thou hast made from afar, shining in thy form of living Disc [Disk], arisen, resplendent, far-off!"[39]

Could it also be that the intimidating, highly public, and unprecedented phenomenon of the sun standing still sufficiently stymied any delusions of grandeur conjured in Amenhotep III's jubilee and prevented the senior pharaoh and/or high officials from preventing Akhenaten's radical proposals? No one could deny that the sun stood still; no one could explain the spectacle; and no one could refuse Akhenaten's fervor.[40] Could it be that the day the sun stood still marked the dawning of Amarna? Just as Joshua proclaimed that there was no day like it, reaction to it may also have launched "one of the most astonishing periods in world history."[41]

Yet the Egyptians recognized many solar deities; why was the Aten singled out? From the biblical account, "the sun stood still in the midst of heaven," likely midday. Aten, "Aten of the Day," was usually associated with midday.[42] However, this may not have been the only reason that Aten was selected. Though the Aten is considered to be domestic to Egypt, recognized as an ancient deity of On, Thutmose IV demonstrated a significant resurgence in fascination with the Aten, or, as the deity was more fully known in Akhenaten's ninth year: "Re-Harakhte/Horus, he-who-rejoices-in-the-horizon-in-his-name, Shu 'light' which-is-in/from-the-Sun-disc."[43] Why this sudden interest?

Many commentators would answer that Thutmose IV's sudden fascination with the religion of On was purely political. They suggest that Thutmose IV and perhaps even Akhenaten felt threatened by the ever-increasing power of the priests of Amun-Ra.[44] However, Thutmose IV completed the Theban temple to Amun-Ra that was begun by Thutmose III. Perhaps he was bypassing the powerful priesthood by giving common people more direct access to Amun-Ra, after all, his vision was a temple intended to be used by the public as "a place of the ear."[45] Still, Thutmose IV does not appear to have had particular interest in limiting the influence, access, and/or devotion to Amun-Ra, *per se*. He is even depicted making offerings to Amun-Ra on two stelae at Giza.[46] Of course, his completion of temples and conventional representations of various deities may say more about Thutmose IV's reverence for his ancestors than it does about his regard for Amun.[47] After all, he also completed and erected the tallest obelisk in Egypt to mark thirty-five years since the death of Thutmose III, but it too had been started by Thutmose III; and Thutmose IV also finished a temple to Amun-Ra in Nubia that Amenhotep II failed to complete.[48] Thutmose IV decorated columns at Alexandria that were dedicated to Amenhotep II.[49] Therefore, Thutmose IV's monuments to Amun-Ra were not necessarily indicative of a desire to challenge the cult's authority, but neither were they a comment on the pharaoh's own religious preference.

On the contrary, Thutmose IV definitely magnified Aten and was the first pharaoh to wear the Aten symbol as part of his dress.[50] He wore jewelry that identified him with the solar disk: a collar of gold rings and gold armlets. Usually these were reserved for funerary adornments, but Thutmose IV appeared with them on his stela and on his chariots.[51] He often depicted the sun disk above his head and referred to himself as the offspring of the sun god.[52] Daring contrast to his father, Amenhotep II, who had boastfully traced his heritage from numerous gods—especially Amun-Ra, Thutmose IV only claimed to be the "son of Atum of his body," who some believe may have been the first God of Heliopolis.[53] Furthermore, though he may not have had much confidence in his army, Thutmose IV seems to have had great confidence in Aten, the Lord of All, because he led his troops into battle "with the Aten before him" and vowed "to make the foreigners to be like the [Egyptian] people, in order to serve the Aten forever."[54] Being sentimental over his ancestors did not seem to prevent Thutmose IV's own sentiments/convictions. Amenhotep IV/Akhenaten, on the other hand, did not show the least fear of retaliation from ancestors, Amun-Ra, or the priesthood when he "sent them packing." In fact, Amenhotep IV/Akhenaten could not have made his sentiments more clear. Neither of these brave pharaohs seemed concerned about the power of Amun-Ra or of the priests of Amun-Ra. Perhaps other explanations for the sudden elevation of Aten should be considered.

When Moses encountered the burning bush, he asked God to reveal his name. "And God said unto Moses, I AM THAT I AM . . . Thus shalt thou say unto the children of Israel, I AM hath sent me unto you" (Exodus 3.14). "I am" or "I shall be what I shall be" in this passage translates into a curious word, *YHWH,* sometimes pronounced "Yahweh".[55] However, the truth is, no one knows its exact pronunciation. All we know is that it is a short word that seems to have two syllables and begins with a "y," an "iee," or an "eea" sound. If that is the case, the name *YHWH* would probably have been written in Egyptian hieroglyph beginning with what looks like a feather but is more probably the head of a reed (such as is seen at the bottom of page 1). "Aten" is also a short word that seems to have two syllables and, in its hieroglyphic form, begins with that same sound. However, no one living today knows for certain the exact pronunciation of the word "Aten" either.[56] Alternative pronunciations for Aten include (among others): "Aton," "Atonu," "Yati," and "Yata."[57] Furthermore, neither *YHWH* nor the hieroglyphs for Aten contain an "A". Yet, obviously, experts in ancient languages believe it most likely that an "A" sound was present and prevalent in both names. Could it, therefore, be possible that "Yahweh," spoken in ancient Hebrew, and "Aten," pronounced in ancient Egyptian, sounded similar? Religious words in Amarna were carefully written phonetically. Of course, these wary phonetic spellings may have been merely an exercise in accurate pronunciation and distinction from any false religious or non-religious terms. [58]

However, could it also be that the sound was significant, that it was an attempt to mimic the pronunciation of *YHWH*? In fact, if Moses had some sort of speech impediment, it's possible that the actual pronunciation of *YHWH* could have been even more obscure. Could it be that Thutmose IV believed that "Aten" was the name of the God, *YHWH,* who Moses said had plagued Egypt? That *YHWH*/Aten was the name of the God who was angered and who his father, Amenhotep II, had greatly offended? It is curious to note that, according to Dr. Bryan, representations of "Aten" in the time of Thutmose IV were distinctive: "a pair of undulating horns" were added, for some unknown reason, to the figure of the winged sun-disk.[59] Could it be that this odd addition was an attempt to slightly modify the pronunciation of the word Aten, to make it sound more like Yahweh? Names were incredibly important in Egyptian culture, especially the names of gods.[60] To know the name was to know the character of an individual.[61]

However, Aten may not have been mistakenly understood as a name for the God of the Bible. Exodus 3 is the first time in scripture that God is identified by the name Yahweh, although Yahweh is considered an acceptable substitute for Adonay or Lord.[62] Throughout the book of Genesis, God is called "Elohiym," which is the plural form of El or El Ahaddai (God of the Mountain or God Almighty),

except for three instances when God is called "Yhovah."[63] According to Exodus 6.3, God did not make himself known to the patriarchs as Yahweh. Yet, a form of Yahweh, Adonay, and/or Aten may have been a name for God in ancient times, used by ancient peoples, perhaps even beyond Egypt, before the days of Moses.[64]

It is important to re-visit the Egyptian name that was given to Joseph by the pharaoh he served. "Zaphenat-Pa'aneah," as the name is translated and presented in the KJV, would more likely have been "Zatenaph-Ipi-ankh(u)" in its original Egyptian form according to Dr. Kitchen (Genesis 41.45). One can't help but notice the name "Aten" at the start of Zatenaph. Egyptians were often named after a god, and it sure seems that the pharaoh of Joseph named him after Aten. According to Kitchen, the first half of Zatenaph is "Joseph," and the second half, "aph" means, "who is named." However, since Egyptian names more usually incorporated the name of a god, it seems more likely that Zatenaph would actually mean "Aten named." Making Joseph's full Egyptian name to be "Aten who called Ipi, life" or, perhaps, "May Aten who has distinguished Ipi grant him long life." Mentuhotep II knew Aten; engraved into the massive stone slab that served as the lintel above the entrance to Mentuhotep II's mortuary temple was the sun disk and double uraeus that symbolized sovereignty.[65] At any rate, "life" and "Aten" seem associated in Zatenaph-Ipi-ankh(u); and if Kitchen is right, to Egyptians, Joseph would have been known as Ipi.

A further curiosity is observed in the name of Joseph's wife, Asenath. It is not hard to see that "Asen" could easily have been translated into Hebrew from "Aten" in the original Egyptian. If that is the case, then Potipherah, the priest of On, named his daughter, "Aten belongs to you," "Aten is to you," or simply, "Aten is," which is hauntingly similar to "I AM." Both names pay tribute to the incomparable power and eternal nature of God (Deuteronomy 33.27; Revelation 1.8).[66]

This also means that when the pharaoh of Joseph went looking for a suitable bride for his Hebrew vizier, he chose the daughter—not just of a priest of On, but, more specifically, a priest of Aten—a very high office indeed. In fact, in the Old Kingdom, only a king was allowed to be the priest of Aten, which is another consistency with the order of Melchizedek, both in On and in Akhet-Aten.[67] Melchizedek was a priest and a king (Genesis 14.18; Hebrews 7.1). Jesus, who is a priest according to the order of Melchizedek, is also a king (Psalms 110.4; Hebrews 6.20; Jeremiah 23.5; Daniel 7.14; John 1.49, 18.37; Revelation 1.5). It has already been suggested that Pharaoh sought a wife for Joseph who shared similar religious beliefs with the faithful Hebrew. Perhaps this is also why Pharaoh named Joseph after the same God whose name was part of the name of Joseph's bride. Pharaoh was aware of the deity that had spoken to him in dreams, and based on this understanding, he associated God with Aten. It may well be that Atum/Aton/Aten was an ancient Egyptian name for the God of the Bible. It is also intriguing to note that a poem from the time of Amenhotep III refers to Aten as "the valiant herdman driving his herds."[68] This is certainly reminiscent of the observation made by the Middle Kingdom poet, Ipuwer.

Of course, Aten may not have been the only ancient Egyptian name for the God of the Bible. Just as the Hebrews referred to God by different names, other Egyptian names may have originally been ascribed to God too. Perhaps it is not incidental that when God changed the name of Abraham, he kept "ra" as part of that name (Genesis 17.5). For instance, it is compelling to consider Potiphar/Potipherah which are versions of the same name. Though Dr. Kitchen keys in on the god name "Ra" that is incorporated at the end of these names, one can also hear the striking similarity between "Poti" and "Ptah".[69] If that is the case, then the names could be read "Ptahfera" or "Ptahnefera," perhaps meaning "Ptah perfect/beautiful Ra." It is strange to consider that a priest of Aten would be named after Ptah. However, the two names—actually the three names "Aten," "Ptah," and "Ra" may originally have referred to the same God. Much as "Yahweh," "Yhovah," "Elohiym," and "Adonay" were all ancient names referring to the God of the Bible. Significantly, a strong connection has been made between "Adonay" and "Aton," which is just another form of "Aten".[70] Under this scenario, the haunting similarity between both the Ptah creation myth and the creation myth of On with the Genesis account is probably not coincidental. They hearken back to the same story and retain elements of truth.[71]

138

Jan Assmann, in his thought provoking book, *Moses the Egyptian,* quotes the Roman theologian, Marcus Terentius Varro, *"nibil interesse censens quo nomine nuncupetur, dum eadem res intelligatur"*; the idea being, that from an ancient perspective, the name of the god didn't matter as long as the intent was to worship the same deity. One can certainly understand this perception from an ancient Roman perspective since they, essentially, appropriated and renamed the Greek pantheon. However, for the God of the Bible, Varro's statement is only true to a point. God is God. His integrity is absolute, and his name is holy (Isaiah 57.15). However, since even in scripture, he is called by various names (and even calls himself several different names), the God of the Bible, obviously, is willing to tolerate a variety of names for himself and in different languages; after all, according to Genesis 11.7, he purposefully confused the languages of men. Also, according to Acts 17.30, in ancient times God was willing to overlook a certain amount of ignorance; but he has never been willing to overlook sin. He will not tolerate confusing concepts and teachings or lies about his nature, his being, or his will that would cause people to behave in disrespectful, disobedient, or degenerate ways. Therefore, to God, the message on the lips matters more than the name that is called. Truth is truth. Respectful integrity in handling his message and humble obedience to his instruction is the only intent that God esteems. As Isaiah says:

> For thus saith the high and lofty One that inhabiteth eternity, whose name is Holy; I dwell in the high and holy place, with him also that is of a contrite and humble spirit, to revive the spirit of the humble, and to revive the heart of the contrite ones. (Isaiah 57.15)

Further illustrating the importance of humble obedience to the message of God, Jesus said:

> A good tree cannot bring forth evil fruit, neither can a corrupt tree bring forth good fruit. Every tree that bringeth not forth good fruit is hewn down, and cast into the fire. Wherefore by their fruits ye shall know them. Not every one that saith unto me, Lord, Lord, shall enter into the kingdom of heaven; but he that doeth the will of my Father which is in heaven. Many will say to me in that day, Lord, Lord, have we not prophesied in thy name? and in thy name have cast out devils? and in thy name done many wonderful works? And then will I profess unto them, I never knew you: depart from me, ye that work iniquity. (Matthew 7.18-23)

God has never been pleased with people who place their own will above his. Even in ancient times, when ancient peoples began to place their own ideas above God and to believe and follow their own mythology and to devise their own methods of worship, God would no longer accept their worship no matter their intent or what they called him. The story of Cain and Abel is one example that illustrates this point.

> And in process of time it came to pass, that Cain brought of the fruit of the ground an offering unto the Lord. And Abel, he also brought of the firstlings of his flock and of the fat thereof. And the Lord had respect unto Abel and to his offering: But unto Cain and to his offering he had not respect. And Cain was very wroth, and his countenance fell. And the Lord said unto Cain, Why art thou wroth? And why is thy countenance fallen? If thou doest well, shalt thou not be accepted? And if thou doest not well, sin lieth at the door. (Genesis 4.3-7)

Both boys intended to call upon the name of/to worship the same God, the God of the Bible, yet God only accepted the worship of Abel (Genesis 4.26). Why? Is God arbitrarily pleased? No, God is consistent. In Hebrews 11.4, the scriptures explain, "By faith Abel offered unto God a more excellent sacrifice than Cain, by which he obtained witness that he was righteous, God testifying of his gifts." And the book of Romans expounds further, "So then faith cometh by hearing, and hearing by the word of God" (Romans 10.17). Therefore, if Abel offered his sacrifice by faith, he did so by hearing and obeying what God had said to do. Abel humbled himself to the will of God; Cain followed his own way. Much as God observes in the book of Judges, Cain "did that which was right in his own eyes" (Judges 21.25). Indeed, religious error, rebellion, and not being careful to follow God's instructions may be "the way of Cain" that Jude talks about in Jude 11. As the scriptures say, "to obey is better than sacrifice" (I Samuel 15.22).

Akhenaten either was following the way of Abel or the way of Cain; there really is no other choice. The fanatical pharaoh was either implementing instructions that he was receiving from deity, or he was pridefully following the imaginations of his own heart. If he wasn't crazy, he was either "living in truth," or he was lying. If Aten was the name by which Akhenaten knew the God of the Bible, then Akhenaten was either seeking to obey the will of God, to glorify God, and to build a city to honor God; or he was glorifying himself, because God will not share his glory or look favorably upon pride (Isaiah 42.8; Proverbs 6.16-19).

In similar fashion, the Tower of Babel offers a second example. On the plain of Shinar, the clan of Nimrod said, "Go to, let us build us a city and a tower, whose top may reach unto heaven; and let us make us a name, lest we be scattered abroad upon the face of the whole earth" (Genesis 10.8-10; 11.4). In essence, the people of Shinar were devising their own way to heaven. God thwarted their plans. There is only one way to God (Matthew 7.14; John 14.6). In ancient times, God had not fully revealed that way, but that fact did not give Nimrod or anyone else the right to invent his or her own way of salvation. It is important to consider that, instead of humbling themselves, the people at Babel were elevating themselves—figuratively and literally. They were, at that point, their own god, and it seems that they may have even intended to name themselves as their own god. It is also remarkable to consider that, a handful of generations past the universal flood, man's plan of salvation involved building a tower, reaching to higher ground. If they were trying to build a tower to survive another flood, it would have needed to be at least fifteen cubits taller than the highest mountain, according to Genesis 7.20. That was certainly a "tall" order for mud bricks and slime mortar, but even that is puny in comparison to their stated objective (Genesis 11.3). Still, the message is the same: "God resisteth the proud, and giveth grace to the humble" (I Peter 5.5).

While considering the Tower of Babel, an observation can be made that may parallel that structure to the pyramids and perhaps provide a better understanding of the intention on the plain of Shinar. According to theory, Imhotep's design, the Great Pyramid, was built as a conduit to direct the soul of the monarch to the heavens. In fact, a shaft leading upward from the king's burial chamber inside the largest pyramid at Giza creates a direct line of sight to the belt of the constellation Orion.[72] Of course, ancient Egyptians knew that constellation as Osiris, and they believed that souls of the pharaohs lived there forever.[73] It has even been proposed that the three pyramids at Giza were purposefully arranged to mirror the stars in the belt of that same constellation.[74] Significantly, the constellation of Orion was also known by ancient cultures as Nimrod, the Mighty Hunter, son of Cush who is long associated with Africa (Genesis 10.8). Could it be that the Tower of Babel was never intended to physically reach to heaven, but to serve as a platform to direct the souls of the dead to join/"reach unto" the same constellation? In fact, could it be that the mysterious Shinar (perhaps *Shnayim naah*, in Hebrew, "two pleasant places/pastures ") has been Egypt, "the two lands", all along? (Amos 6.1-6)

If the true identity of Aten was lost in the accumulation of false ideas and false images between pre-historic times and the Old Kingdom, certainly by the time of Akhenaten, such error would not stand alone.[75] In other words, it wouldn't be the only time that the identity of God and true worship was confused with mythology and polytheism. Of course, the identity of Aten was sufficiently smudged again, probably, before the resins had hardened in Akhenaten's coffin. Yet, a terra cotta altar found in Taanach of Palestine shows that apostasy and religious confusion was on going and not limited to Egypt. This crude Canaanite altar displays a winged sun-disk riding on the back of a four-footed beast, atop the open doors of a temple, atop a winged lion-cherub (perhaps like the cherubim associated with Solomon's temple), all atop images of Asherah, the mother-goddess of Canaan.[76] Since all of these images were mingled on the same offering stand, Asherah in this place, was wrongly considered to be appropriately connected with the temple of God and with the Aten. The sovereignty, the identity of Yahweh was lost, was sacrificed, on this blasphemous altar. Obviously, the integrity and the identity of the Aten and Yahweh was also confused in the Assyrian and Babylonian cultures as well:

> . . . quadrupeds with Sun-discs on their heads have been connected with biblical references to Josiah cleansing the Jerusalem Temple of the 'horses . . . dedicated to the sun' and 'chariots of the sun' (2 Kings 23:11). This is an obvious allusion to Assyrian and Babylonian solar and astral cults, which probably made serious inroads into Israelite and Judahite religion in the eighth to sixth centuries BCE and which met with strong prophetic condemnation.[77]

Yet, God honors humble efforts to maintain and to submit to the truth of his sovereignty. There may have been a persistent flicker of truth surviving in On from pre-history. Furthermore, because of that, it may be that God purposefully identified himself with On and with the religion of On. In the exodus, God manifested himself as "a pillar of cloud" and "a pillar of fire" (Exodus 13.21). Clearly, this was an apparition that was visible, not only to the Hebrews, but to the Egyptians as well (Exodus 14.20, 24). God could have chosen any form to represent his presence; he chose a pillar. Perhaps it is not a coincidence that On, "*Iwnw*" means, in ancient Egyptian, "Pillar Town." The primary pillar of Pillar Town was manifest in a pillar of fire and cloud; the God of *Iwnw* was real!

Therefore, it isn't really surprising that Thutmose IV would turn his attention to Pillar Town, even though he may have been relatively unfamiliar with the religion of Lower Egypt. Thutmose IV made definite concessions to On when he sought to make a drastic correction in his religious loyalties and sought to give due pre-eminence to an overlooked God, a God who had come to the pharaoh's attention, the Lord of All.[78] The young pharaoh's obvious efforts to distance himself from Amun-Ra, especially from Amun, may have been sharply influenced by what he saw and what he heard—he may very well have seen God in the shape of a pillar—a shape associated with On, and he may very well have heard a name for that God that sounded like a name associated with On, perhaps sounding like "Aten" and/or perhaps even like "*Iwnw*."

Of course, Ra was also anciently associated with On. Ra far predated Amun, and was the supreme god of the Old Kingdom.[79] In fact, originally, Ra was completely *un*associated with Amun; their concepts were diametrically opposed to one another.[80] Thutmose IV was reaching to the distant past and making an appeal to an ancient God, but one who was new to him. The young pharaoh intended to restore an unadulterated understanding of Ra, the Ra of Heliopolis, not the Ra of Thebes.[81] For his part, Thutmose IV wanted to be understood as having "purified Heliopolis and propitiated Re" and having "presented maat [good justice] to Atum." It is, therefore, probably not a coincidence that Aten was elevated and specifically recognized by Thutmose IV and was even more prolifically publicized by his son, Amenhotep III, although perhaps not as devoutly revered by the intemperate pharaoh.[82]

Under the theory of this book, Thutmose IV *was* drawn to On out of fear, but not fear of the supposed strength of the Amun-Ra priesthood. Thutmose IV was afraid of incurring any further vengeance from God Almighty who had proven Amun-Ra (and his priests) completely ineffectual. Similarly, Akhenaten's confrontation with the priests of Amun-Ra wasn't motivated by fear or politics either. Akhenaten wasn't a man who was particularly moved by politics; he was driven by religion; his obsession was truth.

Perhaps the best way to understand the administration of Akhenaten, the art of Akhenaten, and Akhenaten as a person is to examine the Amarna period through the eyes of faith, guided by the Bible. Akhenaten has been described as a "God intoxicated man."[83] Faith was the force that drove Amarna. If both Thutmose IV and Akhenaten were witness to the miraculous power of God as described in the Bible, their actions have new motive. Thutmose IV responded by posturing so as not to be seen as God's antagonist, but Akhenaten boldly sought to be God's ally!

Akhenaten set about this ambitious task by clearly stating his intentions and then acting on them. On a monument that was later recycled by Horemheb to use as part of a pylon at Karnak, Akhenaten explained that "all of the other gods have failed and 'ceased' to be effective"; the writing goes on to say that there is only one God who had not "ceased."[84] This God was without "another of thy kind"; he was located in the heavens, "exalted" and "radiant."[85] Under Akhenaten's rule, no longer would the worship of gods who had failed to protect the Egyptian people be acceptable in Egypt.[86] No longer would Egypt waste its time serving gods who, through the entire chaotic year of the exodus, had proven themselves to be completely impotent. (II Chronicles 25.15).[87] There was only one God who had demonstrated power, and as far as the king was concerned, it made no sense to worship any other God. To that end, Akhenaten closed temples and sent out crews of people to erase the names of false Egyptian gods wherever the names were found, "from the tops of obelisks to the depths of sepulcure vaults" —even if the offensive names were part of the name of a pharaoh.[88] Not even the name of his own father was spared; however, rather than just erase Amenhotep III, Akhenaten replaced his father's name with "the old king's coronation name, Neb-maat-re, because it contained the names of Maat, the goddess of truth and justice and of Re, still thought to be an aspect of Aten."[89] *Damnatio memoriae* was not new in Egypt, but never had the names of gods been eradicated.[90] Even the plural form of the word "god" was chiseled out.[91] Akhenaten was seeking to cleanse Egypt of the detestable apostasy of polytheism.

Akhenaten's actions were actually very similar to those of King Josiah:

Josiah was eight years old when he began to reign, and he reigned thirty and one years in Jerusalem. . . And he did that which was right in the sight of the Lord, and walked in all the way of David his father, and turned not aside to the right hand or to the left.

And it came to pass in the eighteenth year of king Josiah, that the king sent Shaphan the son of Azaliah, the son of Meshullam, the scribe, to the house of the Lord, saying, Go up to Hilkiah the high priest, that he may sum the silver which is brought into the house of the Lord, which the keepers of the door have gathered of the people: And let them deliver it into the hand of the doers of the work, that have the oversight of the house of the Lord: and let them give it to the doers of the work which is in the house of the Lord, to repair the breaches of the house, Unto carpenters, and builders, and masons, and to buy timber and hewn stone to repair the house. . . .

And Hilkiah the high priest said unto Shaphan the scribe, I have found the book of the law in the house of the Lord. . . Hilkiah gave the book to Shaphan, and he read it. . . . And Shaphan read it before the king. And it came to pass, when the king had heard the words of the book of the law, that he rent his clothes. And the king commanded Hilkiah the priest, and Ahikam the son of Shaphan, and Achbor the son of Michaiah, and Shaphan the scribe, and Asahiah a servant of the king's, saying, Go ye, enquire of the Lord for me, and for the people, and for all Judah, concerning the words of this book that is found: for great is the wrath of the Lord that is kindled against us, because our fathers have not hearkened unto the words of this book, to do according unto all that which is written concerning us.

So Hilkiah the priest, and Ahikam, and Achbor, and Shaphan, and Asahiah, went unto Huldah the prophetess, . . . Thus saith the Lord, Behold, I will bring evil upon this place, and upon the inhabitants thereof, even all the words of the book which the king of Judah hath read: Because they have forsaken me, and have burned incense unto other gods, that they might provoke me to anger with all the works of their hands; therefore my wrath shall be kindled against this place, and shall not be quenched. But to the king of Judah . . . Thus saith the Lord God of Israel, . . . Because thine heart was tender, and thou hast humbled thyself before the Lord, when thou heardest what I spake against this place . . . and hast rent thy clothes, and wept before me; I also have heard thee, saith the Lord. . .

And the king sent, and they gathered unto him all the elders of Judah and of Jerusalem. . . . all the men of Judah and all the inhabitants of Jerusalem with him, and the priests, and the prophets, and all the people, both small and great: and he read in their ears all the words of the book of the covenant which was found in the house of the Lord. And the king stood by a pillar, and made a covenant before the Lord, to walk after the Lord, and to keep his commandments and his testimonies and his statutes with all their heart and all their soul, to perform the words of this covenant that were written in this book. And all the people stood to the covenant.

And the king commanded Hilkiah the high priest, and the priests of the second order, and the keepers of the door, to bring forth out of the temple of the Lord all the vessels that were made for Baal, and for the grove, and for all the host of heaven: and he burned them without Jerusalem in the fields of Kidron, and carried the ashes of them unto Bethel. And he put down the idolatrous priests, whom the kings of Judah had ordained to burn incense in the high places in the cities of Judah, and in the places round about Jerusalem; them also that burned incense unto

Baal, to the sun, and to the moon, and to the planets, and to all the host of heaven. And he brought out the grove from the house of the Lord, without Jerusalem, unto the brook Kidron, and burned it at the brook Kidron, and stamped it small to powder, and cast the powder thereof upon the graves of the children of the people. And he brake down the houses of the sodomites, that were by the house of the Lord, where the women wove hangings for the grove.

And he brought all the priests out of the cities of Judah, and defiled the high places where the priests had burned incense, from Geba to Beersheba, and brake down the high places of the gates . . . . And he defiled Topheth, which is in the valley of the children of Hinnom, that no man might make his son or his daughter to pass through the fire to Molech. And he took away the horses that the kings of Judah had given to the sun, at the entering in of the house of the Lord . . . and burned the chariots of the sun with fire. And the altars that were on the top of the upper chamber of Ahaz, which the kings of Judah had made, and the altars which Manasseh had made in the two courts of the house of the Lord, did the king beat down, and brake them down from thence, and cast the dust of them into the brook Kidron. And the high places that were before Jerusalem, which were on the right hand of the mount of corruption, which Solomon the king of Israel had builded for Ashtoreth the abomination of the Zidonians, and for Chemosh the abomination of the Moabites, and for Milcom the abomination of the children of Ammon, did the king defile. And he brake in pieces the images, and cut down the groves, and filled their places with the bones of men. Moreover the altar that was at Bethel, and the high place which Jeroboam the son of Nebat, who made Israel to sin, had made, both that altar and the high place he brake down, and burned the high place, and stamped it small to powder, and burned the grove. And as Josiah turned himself, he spied the sepulchres that were there in the mount, and sent, and took the bones out of the sepulchres, and burned them upon the altar, and polluted it, according to the word of the Lord which the man of God proclaimed, who proclaimed these words. . . And all the houses also of the high places that were in the cities of Samaria, which the kings of Israel had made to provoke the Lord to anger, Josiah took away, and did to them according to all the acts that he had done in Bethel. And he slew all the priests of the high places that were there upon the altars, and burned men's bones upon them . . . .

And the king commanded all the people, saying, Keep the passover unto the Lord your God, as it is written in the book of this covenant. Surely there was not holden such a passover from the days of the judges, . . . nor in all the days of the kings . . . Moreover the workers with familiar spirits, and the wizards, and the images, and the idols, and all the abominations that were spied in the land of Judah and in Jerusalem, did Josiah put away, that he might perform the words of the law which were written in the book that Hilkiah the priest found in the house of the Lord. And like unto him was there no king before him, that turned to the Lord with all his heart, and with all his soul, and with all his might, according to all the law of Moses; neither after him arose there any like him. (II Kings 22.1-23.25)

**Ruins of Small Temple
in Akhet-Aten**

Both kings, Josiah and Akhenaten, began their tenures involved in benign building projects that gave a nod to religious reform; but that, essentially, maintained the status quo. Both men met an epiphany that sparked a fanatical "house-cleaning" religious frenzy. Both went to war against idols, priests of idols, mythology, mysticism, and polytheism. Both led their people in revival of a neglected/forgotten worship. Yet, Josiah was arguably more fanatical than Akhenaten; he ventured into territory beyond his jurisdiction, beyond Jerusalem, beyond Judah—into the northern kingdom of Israel—to implement his righteous vengeance and religious reform, and he put dissenters to death!

However, Akhenaten, unlike Josiah, was not a Hebrew and was not bound by the Hebrew covenant with God. Hundreds of years before Jerusalem was established as the acceptable center of Hebrew worship, Akhenaten set about establishing an acceptable place for acceptable Egyptian worship of the acceptable God. Along the Nile, a hundred miles north of Thebes and about one hundred sixty miles south of Cairo, at a place now known as Amarna (sometimes called Tell el- Amarna, a mistaken translation of the Bedouin names for the area that now lies in ruins "el-Till and Beni Amran"), Akhenaten chose a plot of virgin soil.[92] This detail, confirmed by archaeologists in the 1920's, was obviously important to the king, presumably because he did not want the land that he was dedicating to the Aten to have been previously defiled by the worship of false gods.[93] Though he built temples to Aten in other places, such as On—even On was corrupted in its theology.[94] Though the worshipers in Pillar Town were never really in favor of combining Amun and Ra, over the years, the doctrine of On had strayed further from the original religion.[95] Akhenaten wanted truth to be separated from tradition and mythology.[96] In much the same way, he wanted God/Aten separated from the gods of Thebes. Cyril Aldred finds it appropriate that to the east of the city, a notch in the cliffs cradles the rising sun in a configuration that mimics the Egyptian hieroglyph for *akhet,* meaning horizon.[97] He also wonders if this natural occurrence may have inspired the name of the city, Akhet-Aten, "Horizon [or habitation] of the Aten."[98] If the sun stood still at precisely the right angle to form the word *akhet*, it certainly would have marked that particular vista as special. Akhenaten insisted, "it was the Aten alone who brought him to [the] spot." In the king's vision, the desolate location was the right place, not just to build a temple, but to build an entire city dedicated only to Aten. Aten should not have to share his billing, his space, his story, or his devotion with any other deity. Compellingly, Akhenaten's reasoning in this regard was very much in keeping with the spirit expressed in the first commandment delivered to the Hebrews through Moses: "Thou shalt have no other gods before me" (Exodus 20.3).[99] Akhenaten seemed to grasp and to appreciate the exclusivity of God.[100]

Furthermore, in keeping with the second commandment, "Thou shalt not make unto thee any graven image, or any likeness of anything that is in heaven above, or that is in the earth beneath, or that is in the water under the earth," Aten was not really representable by any earthly graven image (Exodus 20.4).[101] "*Aten*" was just a common word in ancient Egyptian, meaning "circle, round, or disk."[102] Although some ancient suggestions of Aten depict him as a man with a falcon's head, no idols, or graven images of the Aten, "the circle," had really ever existed. Unlike every other deity in ancient Egypt, the genderless Aten, though he could appear as a man, had no true anthropomorphic representation.[103] In a fragment found at Karnak, Akhenaten "seems to denounce graven images as futile, and remarks on the impossibility of creating one's creator."[104] Of course, Akhenaten did seem to adopt the likeness of the sun in his disk with emanating rays, something "that is in heaven above," to represent Aten. Perhaps he was using this symbol to remind people of the extraordinary power demonstrated by Aten/Yahweh on the day the sun stood still, to remind worshipers of what God had done. Crosses and menorahs are also religious symbols meant to remind worshipers of what God has done, but they do not portray a likeness of God. God looks nothing like a menorah or a cross; neither did Aten look like the sun. The true Aten was a pure abstract, symbolized by a simple circle. Aten, therefore, might have been represented by a sun-disk—but Aten was not the sun. Aten was the unseen and unrepresentable form, the great and powerful continuum that had shaped the sun, the source and creator of light and life.[105] "This sole god was a supernal lord of light."[106] "[Aten] the solar disk itself was not God, but only a symbol of God . . . a life- giving, intangible essence; not the sun or even the face of the sun, but the heat which is in the sun."[107]

Of course, the God of the Bible appeared to Moses as a burning fire; he also appeared in Egypt as a pillar of fire; and both Moses and the writer of Hebrews describe God as "a consuming fire" (Exodus 3.2-4; 13.21; Deuteronomy 4.24; Hebrews 12.29). Yet, God is not literally fire or heat. Furthermore, it wasn't the heat or the light of the sun that Akhenaten was worshiping; Aten was a conceptual entity much greater than that. Desmond Stewart points out that Akhenaten never mentions the heat of the sun in his famous *Hymn to the Aten*.[108] In fact, Akhenaten prohibited worship to Aten during the heat of the day because he was concerned that "the blazing orb might distract his followers from the true deity."[109]

The light of the biblical God is also far greater than the sun and should not be confused with mere sunlight. The light that God spoke into existence pre-dates the sun. According to the Bible, light was made on the first day, but the sun was not made until the fourth day (Genesis 1:3, 14-19). The presence of God, of other heavenly beings, and even things associated with the spiritual realm are often described in the Bible as emanating a bright light (Genesis 3.24; Exodus 34.29; II Kings 6.17; Matthew 17.2, 28.3; Acts 12.7; II Corinthians 11.4; Revelation 1.16). However, throughout the Bible, the actual heavenly appearance of God is a mystery. Therefore, God is unrepresentable by any known image. Religious symbols and icons, like crosses, menorahs, stars, and the Ichthus merely signify doctrinal concepts; they don't represent God's likeness.[110]

Significantly, in art, a circle is considered to be the most perfect shape, likewise a sphere is the most perfect form—balanced, ordered, the same in every direction, holding points at equal distance, yet drawing the eye to an inexorable, single, central point.[111] What better symbol to represent God, without beginning or end, perfect in every dimension, drawing all men unto himself (John 12.32). The beautiful symbol that God himself chose to represent his covenant with all living creatures on Earth is a rainbow, which in its complete form is a circle (Genesis 9.12-13). Ezekiel saw God as a series of concentric circles (Ezekiel 1). Could it be that the simple circle might have been an ancient symbol for God, perhaps used by the order of Melchizedek? This mysterious being was also described as without beginning or end (Genesis 14.18; Psalms 110.4; Hebrews 5.6).

Though some say that the Amarna representation of the Sun-disk pre-dated Akhenaten, he depicted Aten as a circle with multiple, downward rays, many terminating with human hands, holding royal symbols.[112] This picturesque representation, Breasted observed, was universal and easily understandable to all mankind.[113] In his numerous hands, Aten actively offered life and other blessings to all creation.[114] Clearly, however, this representation of Aten is only symbolic and not literal since on the boundary stelae, Akhenaten says that the Aten fashions "with his *two* hands."[115] Yet, even this should probably be understood as figurative language describing a non-corporeal being. The iconic sun-disk with rays merely symbolized Aten, a being who was impossible to visually portray.

Intriguingly, circles and cycles are recurring themes in God's creation. In fact, the circle is so characteristic of the work of the God of the Bible, a circle could almost be considered to be God's brushstroke, or God's signature. Circles and cycles compose every level of creation, from the atom to the cosmos. God set all cycles, orbits, seasons, and "the circle of life" in motion. Recent research of Theoretical Physicist Dr. Garrett Lisi suggests that a collection of "twisted circles," mathematical shapes called "Lies," combine into what he calls the E8 Lie Group, and may provide the overarching mathematical scaffold that explains the design of nature from Quantum Physics to Astrophysics, i.e., the "Theory of Everything."[116] In other words, in the language of Mathematics, a circle represents God—or at least his handiwork.

Akhenaten set about building Akhet-Aten (Horizon of the Aten), the city named for his God.[117] It went up rapidly partly because it was built of stones quarried into a manageable, standard size. These "*talatat*" stones are characteristic of Amarna. Akhenaten, himself, oversaw the establishment of the city's borders and the setting of "immovable" boundary stelae, sculpted into cliffs surrounding the site.[118] The first boundary stelae was probably dedicated sometime in Year 5.[119] The city had a harbor, subdivisions, administrative offices, and workshops all arranged around a grand, 130 foot-wide, central boulevard, the *Sikket es Sultan* or "Kingsway," that connected the main royal living quarters and the worship centers.[120] Magnificent temples, 730 altars (two for each day of the year), palaces, gardens, roads, man-made lakes, and houses were included in the city planning. All buildings were oriented to face to the east.[121] Two groups of tombs were carved into the cliffs on the eastern side of Akhet-Aten, nineteen tombs were south of the city and six were north.[122] Traditionally, the celebrated dead in Egypt were buried to the west, following the setting sun. Perhaps Akhenaten intended to begin a new Valley of the Kings toward the rising sun. Yet, if the tomb openings "overlooked" the city, the literal light of the rising sun never shined a glimmer into the Amarna tombs (though several tomb inscriptions illustrate the dead awakening with the rising of the sun). In fact, no sunlight at all would have illuminated the portals until the setting sun, when the angle of the sun's rays eventually strike the western face of Akhet-Aten's eastern cliffs.[123] Therefore, perhaps the rising sun was not the focus or orientation of Akhet-Aten; after all, beyond the eastern horizon was also Canaan. Of course, God instructed Israel to orient the Tabernacle to face east (Exodus 27.13), and numerous passages in the Old Testament indicate that the Temple in Jerusalem also faced east. Perhaps the same God instructed Akhenaten to orient his buildings to the same direction according to some religious significance. But it could also be that an eastern face was desirable purely for illumination.

Vividly described by Breasted as "a lovely idealist . . . ecstatic in his sense of the beauty of the eternal and universal light," perhaps Akhenaten was so passionately involved in directing the various building projects or perhaps his enthusiasm was such that he was too impatient, but for whatever reason, Akhenaten and his young family left the comforts of Luxor and lived in Akhet-Aten, in a "tent of apartments," called "The Aten is Content," while waiting to occupy a palace.[124] By that time, Akhenaten, likely in his mid twenties, already had quite a sizeable family. Based on the estimated age of Smenkhkare at his time of death, the young prince would probably have been around eight years old when his father moved the family into these temporary living quarters. Three of the daughters Meritaten, Meketaten, and Neferneferure, depicted on the boundary stelae, were like stair steps, all less than five years old.[125] Kiya, Akhenaten's second wife would also have likely accompanied the expedition to Akhet-Aten since year six is the last time she is mentioned as "the favorite."[126] Nefertiti, of course, would have been there too. Though, the young prince was likely being tutored and raised by nurses elsewhere, Smenkhkare, if he was typical of most little boys, probably would have thought that "camping" in a tent was great fun. Yet, perhaps the tender ages of the children explain why it seems that palaces were the first buildings completed in Akhet-Aten.[127] Speaking of the royal palace:

> Separated . . . by a large court, [were] . . . the six night-nurseries of the princesses. [Not only] a royal palace but . . . a simple-home, undoubtedly rather luxurious, though domestic in its conception, . . . where the life of a closely united family was passed.[128]

Not long after moving into the palace in Akhet-Aten, the royal family grew. Over the next seven years, four more children were born: three daughters, Nefernefuaten, Sotepenre, and Ankhesenpaaten, and one son, Tutankhaten.[129] Correct parentage of all of these children is debated. It seems quite certain that the daughters were all born to Nefertiti, but the identity of the mother(s) of Smenkhkare and Tut remains a mystery. Though DNA evidence has positively identified Tut's mother as the mummy known as "the younger lady" found in KV35, her actual identity remains a mystery. There are those who have long believed that Kiya may have been the mother of Tutankhaten (though DNA evidence seems to be drawing a different conclusion); and that she may have died in childbirth. However, DNA also reveals that Tut's mother and Akhenaten were brother and sister.[130] Since Kiya may have been a Mitanni bride, perhaps also known as Tadukhepa, originally intended as a wife for Amenhotep III but given to Akhenaten instead, she was not likely Akhenaten's sister. A letter to Akhenaten from Dushratta, king of Mitanni, refers to "Tadukhepa, my daughter, thy wife."[131]

"The middle years of his reign were tranquil ones for Akhenaten. He dwelled in the City of the Horizon, in a round of ceremonies and festivities, ..."[132] The "lovely and beautiful city" was intended to be a "glimpse of heaven."[133] Not only was it the only city dedicated solely to Aten, but many buildings were completely without roofs.[134] Akhet-Aten was intended to be a place founded on truth, a place of full disclosure.[135] Furthermore, in keeping with religious ties to On, the design of The Great House of the Aten in Akhet-Aten was perhaps based on the original temple of Heliopolis:[136]

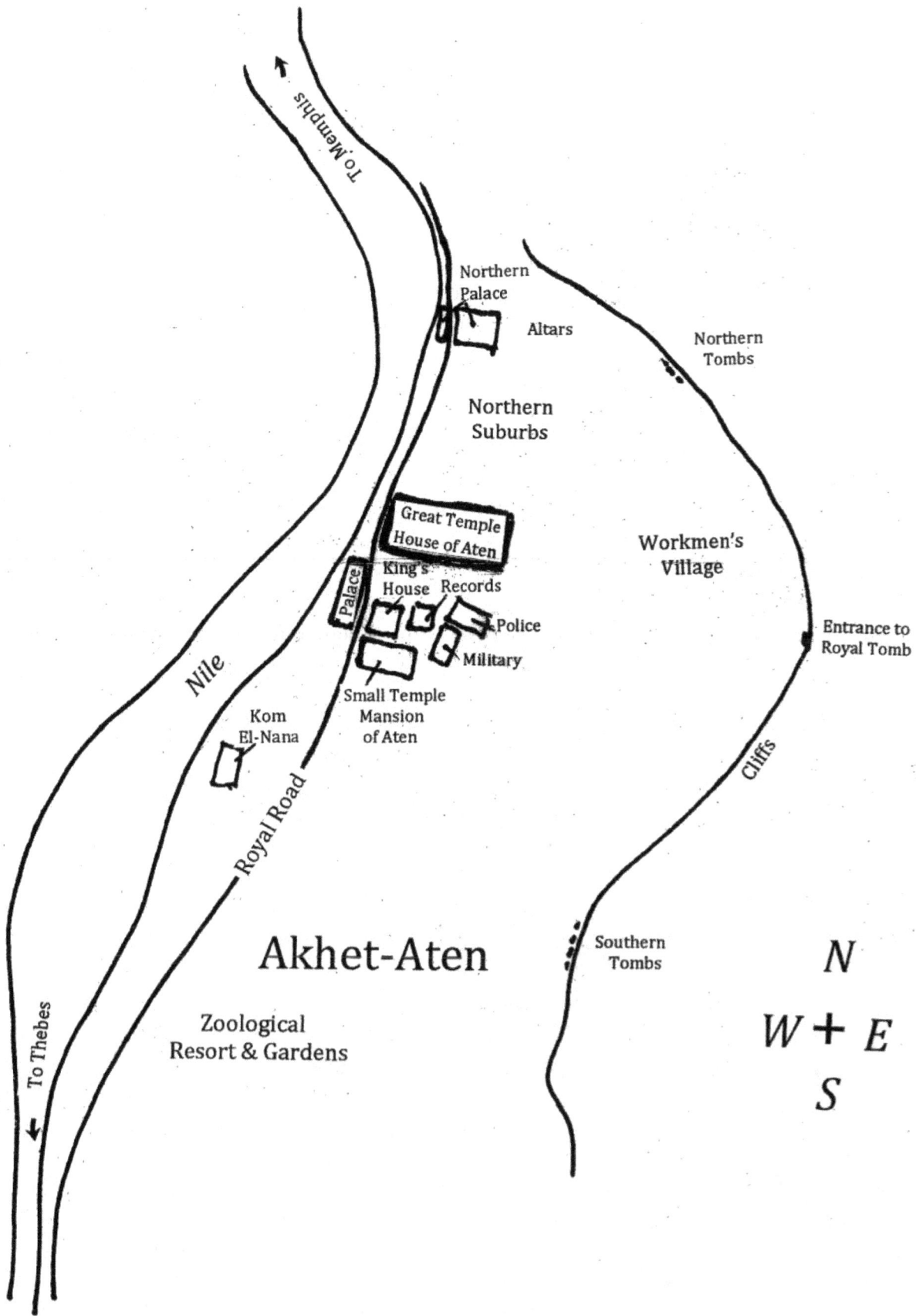

To Memphis

Northern
Palace

Altars

Northern
Tombs

Northern
Suburbs

Workmen's
Village

Great Temple
House of Aten

King's
House

Records

Palace

Police

Military

Nile

Entrance to
Royal Tomb

Small Temple
Mansion
of Aten

Kom
El-Nana

Cliffs

Royal Road

Akhet-Aten

Southern
Tombs

To Thebes

Zoological
Resort & Gardens

N

W + E

S

The "House of Tum" at Heliopolis was one of the grandest of the Egyptian temples. In front of it stood a number of granite obelisks, . . . one that which has been recently erected on the Thames Embankment, and which is the second Egyptian obelisk that has been brought to England. The temple itself was resplendent with gold, and so celebrated for its magnificence, that to say a building was 'like the house of Tum' came to be regarded as the highest conceivable eulogy. Large tracts of land were assigned to it by the munificence of the Egyptian monarchs; its sacred slaves . . . were reckoned by thousands; and its furniture was of the richest and most costly character, comprising vessels and ornaments of gold, silver, lapis lazuli, turquoise, crystal, jasper, alabaster, green feldspar, and hematite.[137]

The temple in Akhet-Aten was open and inviting; nothing was hidden from the eyes of the worshipers or from the gaze of God.[138] Akhenaten's sentiment in this architectural statement seems echoed in Psalms 139.23, "Search me, O God, and know my heart . . ." This was a sharp contrast to conventional Egyptian temples and worship where statues of the gods were sequestered in dark, inaccessible recesses of restricted temples, attended only by priests and shrouded in secret rituals.[139] Such was especially true of Amun, known as the hidden one.[140]

Not only the use of space and light was new in Akhet-Aten, but even the colors and decorations adorning Amarna were distinctive. Coral, gold, and teal were a novel, signature color theme. In fact, apart from religious reform, it was perhaps art that was the most innovative element in Akhet-Aten.[141] Realism and natural beauty replaced static, formulaic art at every level and in every medium to achieve an unprecedented purity and delicacy.[142] The city was adorned with beautiful naturalistic murals, featuring birds and plants and other organic elements, capturing life and emotion with a freedom rarely expressed in Egyptian paintings, and "reliefs of this period are perhaps the most perfect in Egyptian art."[143]

Everywhere there was movement, in the cantering of the royal cavalcade, in the plucking of strings by the expressive fingers of the musicians who were so much in evidence, in the dances of jubilation by onlookers, and the waving of palm fronds and olive branches in the hands of those welcoming the subjects whom royalty had honoured.[144]

Depictions of the city's citizens also seem to be honest. Mahu, Akhet-Aten's chief of police, for instance, was a man who was overweight. In former times, that abnormality would likely have been obscured by

Nefertiti

the accepted template to depict a man of such office.[145] Even royalty was naturalized. It seems that the king wished to be depicted exactly as he was seen and as he was seen expressing himself.

This was a new skill for artists who had been taught to trust grids, rigid proportions, and convention more than their own eyes.[146] Significant evidence suggests that Akhenaten, himself, was the innovative, creative force behind the dramatic evolution of art in the Amarna period, causing some to propose "genius" as an apt description for the unique pharaoh.[147] In fact, "The King's Hand," a relief donated to the Metropolitan Museum of Art in 1985, rivals Michelangelo's hand of Adam in the Sistine Chapel.[148] One Amarna artist, the Chief Sculptor, Bek, considered himself to be merely "the pupil whom His Majesty taught."[149] So did the Chief Architect, Ma'nakhtuf, who was perhaps also the vizier and chancellor linked to Amarna Tomb 12.[150] Prior to Amarna, an Egyptian artist "sculpted or painted his ruler less as he appeared to the studio eye than as he ought to appear to the eye of faith. The artist aimed at abstracting the majesty of the pharaoh from mortal man. . . . [To Akhenaten] maat involved fidelity to fact as much as to justice and order."[151]

Akhenaten was in no way conventional; his appearance alone is evidence of that fact. Far from standard features that resembled his ancestors, Akhenaten's facial features were extreme and sometimes described as grotesque. Some believe that his odd presentation was meant to convey some symbolic message.[152] Indeed, a mold of Akhenaten's face was found, along with several such plaster casts, in the Amarna studio of Thutmosis. The replica, that was probably made in the interest of preserving realism, does not appear to have facial features quite as irregular as artists' renderings of the pharaoh imply.[153] Perhaps his distorted image was meant to suggest a distorted mind.[154] Some believe that Akhenaten's unattractive features mean that the artists in Akhet-Aten were striving to present some "inner truth" and not necessarily a truth as seen by the eye.[155]

In many depictions, Akhenaten's skull is oddly elongated, and his hips are unusually broad. These obtuse characteristics coupled with excess weight in his abdomen and thighs have led to speculation that Akhenaten suffered from some deforming malady.[156] However, loincloths buried with Tutankhamun reveal that Akhenaten's son also had unusually wide hips. Furthermore, Tutankhamun's similarly shaped skull, although extreme, is, nonetheless, within the scale of "normal." Akhenaten's other son, Smenkhkare, shared similar anatomical features.[157] Therefore, the remarkable renditions of Akhenaten are probably more accurate than not.

For his part, Akhenaten didn't seem to suffer concern over his appearance. He considered himself one "whose beauty Aten created," and likely would have agreed with the Psalmist who said, "the Lord is righteous in all his ways, and holy in all his works" (Psalms 145.17).[158] It has been suggested that truth was the ultimate objective of art in Amarna and that understanding the art he commissioned may be key to understanding Akhenaten himself.[159] Perhaps the art in Akhet-Aten sought to capture both inner and outer truth.

Yet, Akhenaten's strange figure was translated into artists' depictions of other residents in Amarna. It is difficult to believe that many Egyptians had long "spindly necks and heavy legs."[160] However, rhythm is a common element in Egyptian art. Therefore, perhaps the repeated forms should not be surprising. Also, it isn't uncommon human behavior to emulate the style and appearance of a celebrity. Perhaps, people living in Amarna cultivated an image that imitated the king's appearance. However, it could also be possible that artists were making a statement about the rampant hypocrisy that existed in citizens of Akhet-Aten, likely including the artists themselves. Many residents of the city outwardly presented an image that mirrored the king and his ideology; but that was probably not the real picture. Pretense of allegiance to Aten evaporated almost immediately following the death of Akhenaten.[161] Truth is always truth, but truth is not always pleasing.

In truth, however, this was not the case with Nefertiti, Akhenaten's queen. The famous limestone bust of Nefertiti, also discovered in the ruins of the sculptor Tuthmosis' studio in Amarna, presents the face of one of the greatest beauties of all time.[162] "The beautiful one is come," Nefertiti was aptly named.[163] Her ubiquitous image was prominent in Amarna art.[164] Beautiful women have long been favorite muses for artists.

It has been suggested that Nefertiti's exquisite beauty was perhaps the main reason Akhenaten was so interested in realistic art. He wanted to preserve the queen's true likeness for posterity. Indeed, he did, literally, from head to toe. A voluptuous statue of Nefertiti, inscribed with the glowing tributes, "Fair of Face, Mistress of Joy, Endowed with Favor, Great of Love," has been interpreted by some to represent the queen as "a love goddess."[165] Yet, such assessment is aberrant. Though Nefertiti was undeniably beautiful, her figure was distorted by excess weight, carried especially in her thighs. Nevertheless, the truth of her irregular figure was not concealed, and neither were her less-than-perfect flat feet. Preserved in delicate, pink limestone, Nefertiti's long-toed, flat feet are perhaps the world's "first examples of accurate foot anatomy."[166] It's probably safe to assume that to Nefertiti's truth-obsessed husband, who no doubt commissioned the above statue, the queen was, honestly, fair of face; she was his mistress of joy; she was endowed with favor for him and by him, and was great of love. After all, Akhenaten said, "How happy is my heart in the queen and her children."[167] The expressions on this statue, like the representations, were simply true; from Akhenaten's singular perspective, nothing more and nothing less would have pleased the king "(whose) heart is satisfied with truth."[168]

In fact, the truthfulness of the vivid art in the tombs of Akhet-Aten has been of great help to modern-day excavators.[169] "The artists' renditions of the palaces, temples, and even the harems as they were depicted in

[the] tombs" outside the city are so accurate, they help bring the ruins to life.[170] If what is painted in Amarna has proven to be accurate and true, could it be that what was said was also true?

Akhenaten's obsession with truth was much, much deeper than the tracing of a sculptor's chisel. He called himself, "the king who lives on Truth."[171] The overarching and fundamental truth for Akhenaten was the nature of the divine being: an eternal being who was not an invention of man's imaginings (II Peter 1.21). He did not live in temples, or need to be carted about on feast days (Acts 17.24-25).[172] He was not married to a consort; he was not human in his constitution (Isaiah 55.8; Job 9.32).[173] To Akhenaten, God was real! He was the Lord of All, and he was one.[174]

To some, the idea of a universal God was the most novel concept proposed by Akhenaten; however, Thutmose IV clearly addressed the Lord of All, and though some would contend that Thutmose IV really meant the Lord of All Egypt, Ipuwer included "all," presumably mankind, as the herd of the deity, "the shepherd," and, from ancient times, Ra and Atum were considered to be universal gods of both barbarians and Egyptians.[175] Therefore, it seems that Akhenaten was not the first to propose the idea of a universal God.

Akhenaten's God was the creator and giver of all things.[176] He was the giver of life, and in the God of Akhenaten, the highest aspiration of Egyptian culture was truly attainable—eternal life! In fact, Akhenaten recognized no other source for life. He said, Aten is "he who decrees life, the lord of sunbeams, maker of brightness'; he 'causes everyone [to live]."[177] The pharaoh, likely, would have heartily agreed with Paul on Mars Hill, ". . . in him we live, and move, and have our being" (Acts 17.28).[178]

Akhenaten recognized that God is not a human being, but in simple keeping with reality, the pharaoh *was* a human being, and he had every intention of living and of being depicted as living consistent to that truth. Nowhere in Egyptian history or "anywhere in antique art" are depictions of royalty as intimate and as human as they are in Amarna (Numbers 23.19).[179] Akhenaten and Nefertiti are routinely seen humbling themselves in conspicuous ways: prostrating themselves in worship, bestowing gifts to their subjects, lovingly parenting their children, tenderly displaying affection for each other, eating, and grieving.[180] The king was a man! In Akhenaten, Egyptians were being offered a new way of seeing God and of seeing the king. The pharaoh was authoritative and deserving of proper respect and obedience from his subjects; the pharaoh was important and was a visionary administrator; but the pharaoh was not a god.

There are those who disagree with this assessment of Akhenaten and believe that he demanded more than respect, that he demanded to be worshiped in keeping with Egyptian tradition. For centuries, Egyptians had desired a god to be their ruler and had envisioned their ruler to be a god. Akhenaten agreed. The king should be a God, so the radical pharaoh—far from upholding traditional perceptions—essentially abdicated his throne to God/Aten, the King of Kings (Revelation 19.16).[181] Akhenaten stepped aside, handed over the throne, the deed to Akhet-Aten, and even the entire empire to God/Aten:

> Now, as for the width of Akhetaton [Akhet-Aten] mountain to mountain from its eastern horizon
> to its western horizon, it shall belong to my father, Aton [Aten], given life, forever and ever;
> whether its mountains, or its cliffs, . . . or all its people, or all its cattle, or anything which Aton
> causes to exist, upon which his rays shine, . . . They shall belong to my father, the living Aton[182]

Akhenaten was Aten's co regent. Aten's name appears in cartouches with the same treatment as a king.[183] Aten is the only God (other than deified pharaohs) who ever had throne years counted for him and jubilees celebrated to him.[184] However, Amarna may not have been the first time that Aten was considered to be the great king of Egypt. Some of the earliest depictions of Atum portray him as a pharaoh wearing the double crown of Upper and Lower Egypt and holding the royal ankh and scepter and adorned with other symbols of a phraoh'.[185] There was "no rival to the regality and omnipotence of the Aten."[186] Akhenaten was subject to Aten, gladly and completely; he said, "[The king] is upon the throne of the Sun-disk that created [him]," and "thou [the Disk/Aten] hast installed him in thine office of king of Upper and Lower Egypt."[187]

Upon coronation, a pharaoh was assigned a series of five ascension names that comprised the full title of that king. The list of names were assigned in a specific pattern:

1. the Horus name
2. the Nebty name (of the Two Ladies)
3. the Horus of Gold name
4. the Throne name (the praenomen)
5. the Given name (the nomen)

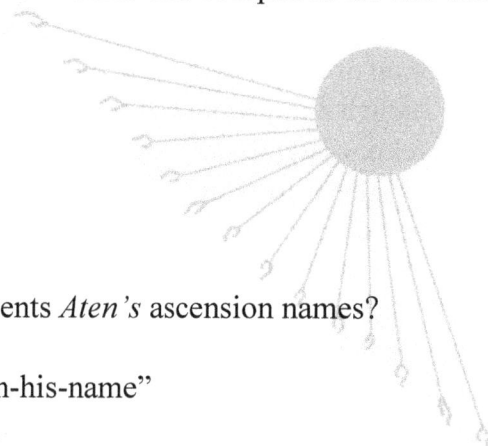

Could it be that the expanded name: "Re-Harakhte/Horus, He-who-rejoices-in-the-horizon-in-his-name, Shu, Aten" represents *Aten's* ascension names?

1. the Horus name is Re-Harakhte
2. the Nebty name is "He-who-rejoices-in-the-horizon-in-his-name"
    because Aten's two lands were heaven and earth
3. the Horus of Gold name is Shu ("light")
    because Egyptians likened gold to the skin of the gods,
    but Aten's "skin" wasn't gold; it was light/Shu
4. the praenomen is Aten
5. the nomen: there is none, no Given name because Aten was never born

Perhaps, Aten—not Akhenaten—is "the king" in confusing statements such as when Ay refers to *the king* as "my god who fashioned me"; when Pentu, in Amarna Tomb 5, says *the king* is "the god who fashions mankind, and makes the Two Lands live"; or when Tutu hails *the king* as his "god who fashioned and fostered him"[188]

So, if Aten was the sole object of worship in Akhet-Aten, why did people appear to grovel in the presence of Akhenaten? Why were there gigantic statues of Akhenaten and Nefertiti adorning the entrance to the temple in Amarna?[189] Why did houses in Akhet-Aten contain shrines adorned with red-painted door jams framing stelae of members of the royal family engaged in worship?[190] Why did Akhenaten not say, like Peter said to Cornelius, "Stand up; I myself also am a man"? (Acts 10.26). Why did Akhenaten allow people to "pray" to him, to praise him, and to make statements indicating that he and Nefertiti were responsible for them receiving eternal life, as if the king and queen were gods? Why did he call himself "the good god" and Aten's son?[191] Was Akhenaten actually advocating the worship of himself, and the Sun-disk was really only a heavenly reflection of the king?[192] Why did he say:

Ho all living upon the earth, and those who shall be young men someday! I shall tell you the way of life . . . . Offer praises to the living Disc and you shall have a prosperous life; say to him 'Grant the ruler health exceedingly!' then he shall double favors for you . . . . Adore the king who is unique like the Disc, for there is none other beside him![193]

Unlike Peter, Akhenaten was a king. A certain amount of decorum was appropriate for a monarch; it was considered acceptable for people to bow to royalty. It had been a custom in Egypt for centuries before Akhenaten.[194] Respect for the throne was good for the people and good for the social order. When courtiers addressed Akhenaten as "the incarnation of the sole god the Aten," perhaps it was just grandiose language meant to suggest that Akhenaten hoped, one day, to "be like" Aten, in much the same way as John said to Christians in I John 3.2: "Beloved, now are we the sons of God, and it doth not yet appear what we shall be: but we know that, when he shall appear, we shall be like him; for we shall see him as he is."[195]

Akhenaten, clearly, aligned himself with Aten. The king believed that honoring Aten was best for him and best for the people. Therefore, he imparted the teaching that he claimed to have received from Aten, and he hoped that all Egyptians would hear, accept, and follow that teaching. As far as we know, most of Akhenaten's teachings were given orally, aside from hymns, stelae, some correspondence, and incidental statements there is no written "Law of Akhenaten."[196] However, what does remain of his teaching is remarkable for its common language, written in a "lyrical style that clearly distinguishes his compositions from other pharaonic

151

announcements."[197] The teachings were presented in the vernacular of everyday life, not in the high language of the scribes.[198] Easy to understand, easy to repeat, easy to remember, Akhenaten's hymns were intended for the consumption of everyday people, many of whom were likely illiterate.[199]

Though many would disagree, Akhenaten wanted what was good for his people. In an Amarna tomb one official acknowledged Akhenaten's intention, "We see the good things which the Good Ruler hath done."[200] Akhenaten meant to restore *maat*, the "harmony" that existed between God and creation in the beginning.[201] "The ethics of the new religion still look to Maat for their basis, but the Truth now acclaimed is that of the king."[202] Some claim that Akhenaten did not consider himself to be a prophet; however, he called himself the "Chief Prophet." A true prophet, a prophet of God, is due highly honored status and ought to be heard and obeyed (Deuteronomy 18.18-22).[203] Could a non-Hebrew be a prophet of God? Enoch was; even Balaam spoke the truth (Jude 14). Petrie once said of Akhenaten, "His affection is the truth, and as the truth he proclaims it." Akhenaten also, clearly, served as a high priest, and curiously, he even removed his shoes when serving in that capacity. This peculiar practice is consistent with the instructions God gave to Moses in Exodus 3.5.[204] Like the order of Melchizedek, Akhenaten was a king, a high priest, and a prophet (Hebrews 7.1).

If Akhenaten was right, if there is only one God, then he was absolutely leading his people in the only right way.[205] He needed their respect in order for them to follow him, but ultimately, it was not Akhenaten and Nefertiti that the people were following; it was Aten. Much as Paul said to the Corinthians, "Be ye followers of me, even as I also am of Christ," Akhenaten wanted the people to follow his teaching and example, even as he was following the Aten—not for the good of Akhenaten, but for the good of the people (I Corinthians 11.1). He acted as their prophet, as their liaison between the will of Aten and the behavior of the people. Just as the Hebrews begged Moses, "Speak thou with us, and we will hear: but let not God speak with us, lest we die" (Exodus 20.19). Moses was much more approachable than God; such would also have been the case for Akhenaten. Perhaps this is why "prayers" such as the one in Ay's tomb say things like:

> May thou [Akhenaten] grant to me a good old age as thy favorite; may thou grant to me a goodly
> burial by the command of thy ka in my house . . . . May I hear thy sweet voice in the sanctuary
> when thou performest that which pleases thy father, the living Aten.[206]

Ay wanted Akhenaten to speak to him and he would listen, but he didn't want Aten to speak to him directly. Perhaps this is similar to the words in Psalms, "Now know I that the Lord saveth his anointed; he will hear him from his holy heaven with the saving strength of his right hand. . . . Save, Lord: let the king hear us when we call," was the king, David, to be called upon as the Lord, as God? (Psalms 20.6, 9). No, God was the ultimate king of Israel; however, in the afterlife, the earthly king, David, to whom God would grant eternal life, would still have the ability to hear. However, these verses were probably also prophetic of Christ who is also a king and the Lord's anointed (Isaiah 9.7; 61.1; Luke 4.14-20; John 1.49).

Even though Ay, as vizier, was one of the closest confidants of Akhenaten and was likely Akhenaten's uncle, perhaps Ay did not feel worthy to address Aten directly; but it is more likely that Ay was feigning humility, and didn't believe in Aten at all.[207] He only wanted to please Akhenaten and, to that end, was willing to say anything he believed the king would like to hear. It was the king's rewards that Ay sought, and as soon as Akhenaten was dead, Ay no longer had any desire to worship Aten or to live out his life in Akhet-Aten. He built himself a new tomb in the Valley of the Kings, KV 23, and that's where he was buried.[208] Nevertheless, Ay's fawning over Akhenaten isn't surprising. Pleasing a pharaoh to the point of worshiping the pharaoh was nothing new in Egypt. Even if it may not have been what Akhenaten wanted, it was what the people knew.[209]

So much did Akhenaten want people to follow the teaching of Aten, he generously rewarded—some have even suggested that he bribed—those who did: "Let the Superintendent of the Treasury of Golden Rings, take the High Priest of Aten in Akhenaten and put gold around his neck to the top of it, and gold around his ankles because of his obedience to the Teaching."[210] Therefore, if encouraging others to obey the teaching of Aten was Akhenaten's goal, could it be that shrines in Amarna homes were not identifying members of the royal family as objects of worship but merely as examples in worship?[211] According to scripture there is only one source of eternal life and of every good blessing; Akhenaten was doing everything in his power to draw everyone's attention to that one divine source (I Corinthians 9.25; II Timothy 4.8; James 1.12).

In fact, though the color red held different meanings in Egyptian tradition, if Akhenaten intended to worship the God of the Bible, the God of Moses and the exodus, could it be that the red paint on the door jams surrounding the shrines that displayed images of acceptable worship, was intended to be reminiscent of the tenth plague? On the night of the first Passover, those inside of door jams painted red with blood were preserved and served as examples of acceptable worship. Not that Akhenaten was advocating the observance of Passover in Amarna, but, perhaps, he was advocating that obedience to the instructions of Yahweh/Aten resulted in life.

Midday

In 1887-88, in the ruins of Akhet-Aten, the 382 Tell-Amarna Tablets were discovered, by a peasant woman.[212] 350 of the tablets are letters, yet it's possible that they only represent about a dozen to perhaps fifteen years of correspondence, and may be only about a fifth of the original number.[213] The small, clay treasures, at first dismissed as forgeries, are covered front and back in cuneiform writing, in good, formal Middle Babylonian language, diplomatic Akkydian. They contain correspondence that falls into, basically, two categories: diplomatic letters to pharaoh from comparable, foreign heads of state, and impassioned pleas from subordinate government officials in Syrio-Palestine requesting immediate military aid from Egypt.[214]

The body of work presents a clear picture of unrest. Though the heads of state call each other "brother" (and several were relations by marriage), still the language is often tense and mistrustful. Gifts were carefully measured.[215] Balance of power in the world was shifting, and footholds were being gained and lost.[216] Ten of the Amarna letters were probably addressed to Amenhotep III, ten to Akhenaten, one may be to Tutankhamun, and one is to Queen Tiye. Some originated in Egypt. Two are likely from Amenhotep III to the king of Babylon; a third correspondence is really nothing more than a long inventory of gifts also sent from the pharaoh to the king of Babylon.[217] A fourth letter, perhaps from Amenhotep III, is addressed to the king of the Hittites.[218] Most of the rest of the letters written by the pharaohs are letters to vassals; but some of these letters may never have been sent.[219] Sadly, agreement about the correct chronology and sequence of the Tell el-Amarna tablets is illusive. The correct author and recipient of each letter is sometimes difficult as well.[220] However, the bulk of the tablets contain frantic letters written to Amenhotep III and Akhenaten from governors in Canaan, seeking immediate aid to help them

Habiru Man

defend their cities or else "the land of my lord the King will be lost." Sometimes, the writer makes a plea directly to the vizier or to a scribe, "Tell the King frankly that his land is being lost."[221] Could the Tell-Amarna letters be decrying the Hebrew conquest of Canaan?

A major obstacle in placing the conquest of Canaan to coincide with the Amarna tablets has been a satisfactory placement of the Hebrew exodus in Egyptian history.[222] If the exodus occurred in the Hyksos era or during the reign of Ramses II, of course the Amarna letters are not concerned with the exploits of Joshua. Yet, if the Hebrews' forty years of wilderness wandering began in the reign of Thutmose IV, then the timing for a convergence with Joshua and the turmoil in Palestine expressed in the Amarna tablets is reasonable. Under this theory, Joshua crossed the Jordan and began the conquest of Canaan in about year thirty of Amenhotep III (depending on the length of the reign of Thutmose IV); and based on the scribbled words of a scribe who was visiting the pyramid temple of Medum at the time of Amenhotep III's jubilee, the fall of Jericho probably occurred near the beginning of Amenhotep IV's co-regency with his father.[223] Indeed, the region of Palestine was already in conflict by the time Akhenaten came to the throne.[224]

153

One wonders, then, why Amenhotep III doesn't share more blame in the eyes of history for the fall of the Egyptian empire. After all, the senior pharaoh didn't send significant troops to address the threat to territories in the Levant either.[225] EA 132 (El Amarna letter number 132) certainly seems to indicate that Amenhotep III was petitioned for help.[226] Of course, poor health may have contributed to Amenhotep III's lack of engagement during the last several years of his reign, or, perhaps, Amenhotep III and Amenhotep IV were in complete agreement on the issue of Palestine.

Though -Addi (Rib-Hadda), an old man of Byblos/Gubla/biblical Gebal, was most concerned with the peril of his own city, he warned the pharaoh of a larger problem, "If the king holds back in respect to the city, all the cities of Canaan will be lost to him."[227] In several Amarna letters, Rib-Addi and others like Abdi-Heba of Jerusalem, Milkilu of Gezer, Biridiya the Prince of Megiddo, Abi-milki the King of Tyre; Pirywaza of Damascus, etc., wrote to Amenhotep III and Akhenaten, pleading for immediate assistance in defense against the encroaching "'Apiru," Egyptian for "Habiru," a forgotten word until the discovery of the Amarna Letters.

Those who do not believe that the Amarna letters were written during the conquest of Canaan by the Hebrews sometimes cite Rib-Addi, who said, "Like a bird that is caught in a snare, so am I in this city of Gebal . . . if no help comes, then am I a dead man."(Numbers 24.21-22)[228] Gebal/Byblos is an area located well outside of the traditional borders of Israel and, therefore, is usually considered by critics to transcend the conquest of Joshua. However, though it is usually associated with Lebanon and Phoenicia, Gebal was, nevertheless, part of the territory that Joshua was originally instructed to conquer:

. . . the Giblites [Gebal], and all Lebanon, . . . from Baalgad under mount Hermon unto . . .
Hamath. All the inhabitants of the hill country from Lebanon unto Misrephothmaim, and all the
Sidonians, them will I drive out from before the children of Israel . . . (Joshua 13.5-6)

Although the term Habiru also appears on the tablets, 'Apiru is the word usually used in the Amarna letters to describe the enigmatic aggressors who were taking possession of pharaoh's land in Palestine.[229] "Most scholars allow that Habiru and Hebrew are etymologically equal, but there is little agreement beyond that point."[230] 'Apiru/Habiru was more or less a pejorative term for "enemy."[231] However, some experts are willing to concede that the Tell el-Amarna Tablets may have been written during the conquest of Canaan and may provide insight into Canaanite reactions to the conquering Hebrews.[232]

No less than 53 of the tablets mention the mysterious 'Apiru/Habiru.[233] In EA letter 68, Rib-Addi said, "The war, however, of the 'Apiru forces against me is extremely severe, and so may the king, my lord, not neglect Sumur (Zemar?) lest everyone be joined to the 'Apiru forces."[234] Later on he said, "Why are you negligent so that your land is being taken? Let it not be said in the days of the commissioners, 'The 'Apiru have taken the entire country!'"[235] It seems that the 'Apiru/Habiru were more occupiers than looters because Rib-Addi warned in letter 118, "Look, if the peasantry goes off, the 'Apiru will seize the city."[236]

In letter 144, Zimreddi of Sidon reported, "May the king, my lord, know that the war against me is very severe. All the cities that the king put in my charge, have been joined to the 'Apiru" (Joshua 13.6).[237] One letter to the pharaoh from Milkilu said that the city of Gezer had allied with Askelon, Lachish, and Megiddo specifically to fight against the 'Apiru/Habiru who were decimating everyone in their path (Joshua 10.33).[238]

This would tend to corroborate alliances like the one described in Joshua 10.5. Abdi-Heba, the mayor of Jerusalem, who wrote several letters, said:

". . . the 'Apiru are taking the cities of the king. There is not a single governor remaining to the
king, my lord. All have perished." and "Behold the territory of Seir, as far as Carmel; its princes
are wholly lost; . . . the 'Apiru are occupying the king's cities." (Joshua 11.17)[239]

He "becries [sic] the defeat of Gaza, Gath-Carmel, Beth-Shan, Shechem, and many others." Abdi-Heba falls silent after Akhenaten's Year 15 or 16 (Joshua 10.41, 20.1-7).[240] Yet, the report of Mayarzana is no better:

The 'Apiru captured Mahzibtu (possibly En-Mishpat/Mizpat), a city of the king, my lord, and
plundered it and sent it up in flames, and then the 'Apiru took refuge with Amanhatpe (perhaps

the ruler of Tyre). And the 'Apiru captured Gilunu (likely near Hasi, southwest of Baalbek, between Sidon and Damascus) . . . plundered it, sent it up in flames, and hardly one family escaped from Gilunu. Then the 'Apiru took refuge with Amanhatpe. And the 'Apiru captured Magdalu (possibly Migdol, an Egyptian fortress city), a city of the king, my lord, my god, my Sun, plundered it, sent it up in flames, and hardly one family escaped from Magdalu. Then the 'Apiru took refuge with Amanhatpe. And Ustu (another town in the region near Gilunu), a city of the king, my lord, the 'Apiru captured, plundered it, and sent it up in flames. Then the 'Apiru took refuge with Amanhatpe. (Genesis 14.7; Joshua 19.24-29) [241]

Others testify:

EA 207, Ipte??? (the rest of the name is missing) says, "Lost to the 'Apiru . . . from my control are all the cities of the king" [242]

EA 215, from Bayawa, says, "all the lands are lost to the 'Apiru" [243]

EA 243, from Biridiya, says, "And as the warring of the 'Apiru in the land is severe, may the king, my lord, take cognizance of his land" [244]

EA 271, from Milkilu, says, "May the king, my lord, know that the war against me and against Suwardata is severe. So may the king, my lord, save his land from the power of the 'Apiru. Otherwise, may the king, my lord, send chariots to fetch us lest our servants kill us" [245]

EA 272, from Sum??? (the rest of the name is missing) says, "the mayors that were in the major cities of my lord are gone, and the entire land of the king, my lord, has deserted to the 'Apiru" [246]

EA 273 and 274 were written by Ninurmah, a woman, likely a queen. In both letters she urges the king to save his land from the 'Apiru. In the second letter, she reports the fall of Sapuma (perhaps Saphon, a city in the Jordan Valley or Baal-zephon, near Migdol) (Exodus 14.2) [247]

EA 318, by Dagantakala, says, "Save me from the powerful enemies, from the hand of the 'Apiru, robbers, and Suteans. And save me, Great King, my lord. And behold! I have written to you! Moreover, you Great King, my lord, save me or I will be lost" [248]

EA 305, from Subandu, says, "the 'Apiru are more powerful than we" [249]

EA 299, Yapahu, the ruler of Gazru (likely Gezer) says, "Since the 'Apiru are stronger than we, may the king, my lord, give me his help, and may the king, my lord, get me away from the 'Apiru lest the 'Apiru destroy us" (Joshua 21.21) [250]

EA 287, Abdi-Heba says, "Consider Jerusalem! This neither my father or my mother gave to me. The strong hand of the king gave it to me. Consider the deed! . . . As the king has placed his name in Jerusalem forever, he cannot abandon it—the land of Jerusalem."

Tell el-Amarna Tablet

155

EA 288, "The 'Apiru have taken the very cities of the king. Not a single mayor remains to the king, my lord; all are lost. Behold, Turbazu was slain in the city gate of Silu (a city that borders Goshen on the Sinai Peninsula). The king did nothing. Behold, servants who were joined to the 'Apiru smote Zimredda of Lakisu (probably Lachish), and Yaptih-Hadda was slain in the city gate of Silu. The king did nothing. Why has he not called them to account? May the king provide for his land. If there are no archers this year, all the lands of the king, my lord, are lost. . . . If there are no archers this year, may the king send a commissioner to fetch me [and] my brothers, and then we will die near the king, our lord."

EA 290, "May the king give heed . . . and send archers to restore the land of the king to the king. If there are no archers, the land of the king will desert to the Hapiru." (Joshua 10.32) [251]

Suwardata, a ruler in Hebron, wrote about the Habiru:

> The king, my lord, should know that the 'Apiru have arisen in the land which the god of the king, my lord, has given me, and they have attacked it, and the king my lord, should know that all my brothers have abandoned me.[252] If the Habiru were the Hebrews, Suwardata in Hebron, was fighting against Caleb—a formidable opponent indeed (Joshua 14.13).

Clearly, all of these voices, all of these witnesses testify that something unusual was happening in Palestine. A difficult to identify group of people was seeking to conquer and to occupy Canaan. Unlike established world powers in the region, this group of nomads had no fortified cities, no capital, and no king; yet they were nearly unstoppable, greatly feared, and amazingly successful. What other such disenfranchised, disconnected group of people in history came out of nowhere to sweep through and conquer Canaan other than the Hebrews? Under the theory in this book, there is no other candidate for the identity of the 'Apiru/Habiru in the Amarna letters. The impassioned pleas are those of the unfortunate residents of Canaan during the Hebrew possession of the land that God, according to the Bible, had promised to give Abraham.

However, were the 'Apiru/Khabiri/Habiru the Hebrews? Much as the term Hyksos was more of a generic description rather than a true identity, the words used to describe the alien forces at work in Canaan at the time of the Amarna tablets are equally vague. In fact, since the days of the Hyksos, "The Egyptian phantasm of the religious enemy first became associated with the Asiatics in general and then with the Jews in particular."[253] This further connects the Hyksos/Hebrews with the conflict expressed in the Amarna letters and ties to the oral tradition espoused by Manetho that had long associated the Hyksos and the Amarna period.[254] But then, the earliest Egyptologists that studied Akhenaten, or "Atinre-Bakhan" as J. Gardner Wilkinson called him, suspected that Amarna was somehow connected with the Hyksos.[255] "Enemies," "outlaws," "immigrants," "fugitives," and "refugees" are all words that can translate from 'Apiru. Habiru can mean "dusty" or "person from beyond or across," i.e., "a foreigner."[256] Ancient texts seem to categorize the 'Apiru as a social class of people "between freedmen and slaves." For that measure, even the word "Hebrew" is more of a description than a name. Perhaps the best interpretation of the word "hebrew" is "alien."[257] Certainly, the Hebrews under Joshua could have been described in exactly those ways.

The fact that these "enemies" were referred to in such vague terms may indicate that, as in the days of the Hyksos, no one was really certain who these people were. After 430 years in Egypt, Hebrews had no doubt adopted many Egyptian characteristics; but they were not Egyptian. Though they had ancestors from Mesopotamia, Syria, and Canaan, they were not an army backed by any of those places either. They had no home, no land, no cities, no distinct culture, clothing, utensils, weapons, and/or perhaps not even a distinct language or writing at that time.[258] Joshua marked the monument that he placed in the Jordan River, but no one knows with what language (Joshua 8.32). For forty years, according to scripture, the Hebrews had wandered in the wilderness, still wearing the clothing and shoes that they brought out of Egypt (Deuteronomy 29.5). Beegle says that eventually the Habiru are largely considered to have become the Hebrews; but aside from religious objects they had been instructed to make while they were in the desert, there was really nothing to identify the Hebrews as a culture or a nation as they entered Canaan (Exodus 25.1-9).[259] To the world around them, they were a confusing mass of conquering strangers. They were still in the process of becoming the nation of Israel.

Nevertheless, the above observation seems to fit with the biblical account in Numbers. When Balak the son of Zippor, the king of the Moabites, first called Balaam, the prophet, to curse the Hebrews, he didn't seem to know who they were. Balak described the Hebrews like this:

> Behold, there is a people come out from Egypt: behold, they cover the face of the earth, and they abide over against me. Now shall this company lick up all that are round about us, as the ox licketh up the grass of the field. (Numbers 22. 5, 4)

The scriptures say that Balak was distressed because he was well aware of what these unidentified people had done to the Amorites; and Balak's people, the Moabites, were "sore afraid" (Numbers 22.2-3). At first, Balaam didn't seem to clearly know the identity of the Hebrews either because he, restating Balak's observation, said "unto *God*" that "Behold, there is a people come out of Egypt, which covereth the face of the earth" (Numbers 22.10-11). However, three times, while being moved by the Lord who, according to the text, put the words in Balaam's mouth, the reluctant prophet identified the mysterious people to Balak as the descendants of Jacob and as Israel (Numbers 23.5, 7, 21; 24.5). Nevertheless, even after being told their proper name, Balak continued to refer to the former Egyptian slaves as his "enemies"/'Apiru (Numbers 23.11; 24.10). Therefore, it may be that writers of the Amarna letters knew the name of their assailants (or at least a name that they would be called), but preferring not to call them by the name of Israel, used the moniker 'Apiru instead. It is noteworthy that in this account in Numbers, Balak was in league with "the elders of Midian" who, one would think, would well know the identity of the Hebrews (Numbers 22.4, 7). However, perhaps this was a different tribe of Midian than the Midianites with whom Moses was associated for forty years (Exodus 3.1).

Nevertheless, the 'Apiru/Habiru in the Amarna letters may well have been the Hebrews who left Egypt in the exodus—they had come from beyond the Red Sea and had crossed the Jordan River; they were likely dusty from forty years in the desert, they were not quite established as freedmen with lands and houses of their own, but they were no longer slaves; since they were taking homes that they had not built and were eating from vineyards that they did not plant, they were likely seen as outlaws and bandits; and since they were putting thousands of people to the sword, they were, no doubt, feared and considered enemies (Deuteronomy 6.11).

The labels used in the Amarna letters to identify this group of displaced wanderers make sense. However, the indistinct classification does not mean that the Habiru/'Apiru at work in Canaan were not a distinct people. In other words, just because 'Apiru and Habiru can be used as vague descriptions does not mean that 'Apiru/Habiru was not considered to be an appropriate designation and was not, in fact, being used as a proper noun. According to Newby, "The word 'Habiru' is the same as the word 'Hebrew.'"[260] Therefore, "when the Bible calls Abraham 'the Hebrew,' it is designating him as one of the Hapiru [Habiru]"(Genesis 14.13).[261] Significantly, in EA 288, Abdi-Heba uses the term 'Apiru to refer to his assailants, yet in EA 290, he identifies them as the Habiru.[262] Indeed, the letter of Biryawaza references the 'Apiru as if they are a distinct group of people that he considered to be his "brothers"; the 'Apiru were Biryawaza's allies, not his "enemies."[263] Therefore, 'Apiru/Habiru was not necessarily always used as a term of derision.

It seems that Akhenaten, like Biryawaza, did not share the opinion that the 'Apiru/Habiru were enemies. The God of the Bible was the Hebrews' ally (Deuteronomy 9.1-5). Therefore, if Akhenaten was the ally of the God of the Bible, then the ally of Akhenaten was doing great things in Canaan; according to the promise that he made in scripture, God was preparing a place to bless all nations on earth, including Egypt (Genesis 12.3; Acts 3.25; Micah 5.2; Matthew 2.1; Luke 2.10-11). Akhenaten had no intention of impeding that work. Traditionally, it has been hard for people to understand why Akhenaten seemed unconcerned about the loss of Egyptian territory in Canaan. However, it may be that Akhenaten believed Egypt would be stronger than ever by submitting to the guidance, blessing, and protection of an almighty God.

Akhenaten in His Chariot
(image likely erased by order of Horemheb)

Akhenaten was not a pacifist. Karnak is decorated with Akhenaten depicted as a warrior, executing his enemies.[264] In the Amarna tombs of Huya and Meryre II, Akhenaten is seen being awarded victories in battle.[265] He did conduct successful military campaigns. His dealings with Nubia have been described as "determined and intelligent."[266] Even Nefertiti is shown in the traditional head-smiting pose and donning the war helmet of a pharaoh.[267] Akhenaten evidently wanted his queen to appear formidable. He was not interested in weakening Egypt. If the theory in this book is correct, to Akhenaten the battle in Canaan belonged to the Lord; and pharaoh supported whatever God chose to do.

Egyptian gods "from time and immemorial . . . had traveled over the waters of heaven in ships." Yet, Akhenaten said Aten was, "mounted in a great chariot of electrum like the sun-god when he rises on the horizon and fills the land with his beneficence." Chariots were a mode of transportation traditionally associated in Egypt with Canaan and with war. Perhaps this is why a chariot on the Royal Road and not a barque upon the Nile was Akhenaten's vehicle of choice as he traversed Akhet-Aten, wearing his war helmet. Indeed, before relocating to Akhet-Aten, the royal family's preferred mode of transportation was palanquin.[268] Electing to ride in a chariot was a statement of solidarity. Because his God was at war, Akhenaten was propagating a war footing. Akhenaten's divine ally was at work in Canaan; he had mounted his war chariot, and his people were serving as his foot soldiers. Akhenaten, in fact, was doing his part in that effort by simply obeying the last known orders that the God of the Bible gave to the pharaoh of Egypt, "Let my people go, that they may serve me" (Exodus 10.3). When Akhenaten set the border stelae for his city, he made an oath not to venture beyond his boundaries. Akhenaten wrote:

> Grant him, O Living Aten, whatever thy heart loves to the extent that there is sand on the shore,
> that fishes in the river have scales, and cattle, hair. Let him reside here until the egret turns black
> and the crow turns white; until the hills rise up to depart, and water flows upstream, while I
> continue . . . following of the Good God, ...[269]

Akhenaten knew his place. Perhaps it should be suggested that, as in nearly every aspect of his life, Akhenaten's pledge was spiritual, not physical; in essence, it was an act of worship. Evidence suggests that Akhenaten breached the limits of Akhet-Aten to bury his father in the Valley of the Kings.[270] Therefore, his vow was either frivolous or figurative.[271] Perhaps Akhenaten meant that he would not venture outside his "place." He promised, "that he would never encroach on land beyond these boundaries, nor move to another site." Another reading of the boundary stelae suggests that the king would not go past the boundaries of Aket-Aten "to the Orient forever and ever."[272] In other words, the king of Egypt would not seek to trespass on the will of God and/or to inject himself into the conflict in Canaan. Unlike his great-grandfather, Amenhotep II, Akhenaten humbled himself to the will of God and did not seek to recover what God was claiming for his own.

If the theory espoused in this book is true, if Akhenaten's God was Yahweh, the Great I AM, the God of the Bible, then the radical pharaoh's baffling foreign (and domestic) policies begin to make sense. For decades, modern observers have puzzled over Akhenaten's laissez-faire attitude toward the impassioned pleas preserved in the Tell-Amarna Tablets, begging for help in maintaining Egyptian interests in Palestine, and his similar indolent indifference to the unrest between Mitanni and the Hittites.[273] Accusations of reckless inattention, foolish negligence, timorous stamina, and blind obsession have been raised.[274] Of course, the ancient voices of those governors in Canaan who considered themselves to be faithful servants of the king and who found themselves in peril were especially bewildered at the pharaoh's unwillingness to send troops and to maintain control of his territories in the Levant. Akhenaten's inaction seems inexplicable.[275]

However, there are also those who believe that vital information concerning events in the Levant was purposefully kept from Akhenaten by Egyptian bureaucrats who may have been seeking to undermine his power, perhaps even by men such as Ay, Akhenaten's most trusted official and Tutu, his secretary of state.[276] EA 32, for instance, may indicate that Akhenaten wasn't completely aware of correspondence—even that which was supposedly sent from Akhenaten himself. EA 32 appears to be a response from the pharaoh to the tedious petition of Tushratta, king of Mitanni, concerning his distress over the "unacceptable" amount of gold he was receiving from Egypt. Yet, in EA 32, the blessings of Nabu and Istanus are sought to be bestowed upon the scribe who reads the pharaoh's letter. It is highly unlikely that Akhenaten would have recognized or would have asked blessings of these foreign deities, nor is it likely that he would have approved of such. Therefore, it calls into question the true authorship of EA 32. Furthermore, the fact that EA 32 ends speaking directly to Tushratta's scribe and requesting his name may indicate that the author of this letter was interested in elevating the status of scribes. Perhaps the author of EA 32 was a scribe also; perhaps Tutu wrote EA 32 and other letters on behalf of Akhenaten sight unseen. It also calls into question whether Akhenaten or Queen Tiye were even aware of the inferior golden statues about which Tushratta complained. Could it be that the wooden statutes covered in gold leaf that were sent to Tushratta were commissioned by someone other than the crown? Could that be the reason Tushratta's requests were not generously met? Could it also be that these same anarchists didn't want Tushratta to receive a truthful report from his messengers? Could this be why Tushratta's messengers were being detained? Perhaps high officials in Akhet-Aten didn't want the Mitanni messengers to tell Tushratta that they had been denied access to pharaoh and didn't know if Akhenaten was even aware of Tushratta's concerns. Could it be that there were forces in Akhenaten's administration that were hoping to force Egypt into the conflict in Asia by ruining Egypt's relationship with Mitanni? EA 42 adds to this impression because someone seems to have intentionally insulted Tushratta by exalting the name of the pharaoh over the name of the king of Mitanni. This was not an act of peace.[277]

If information was being kept from Akhenaten, it was against his wishes. In EA 151, Abi-Milku reminds the pharaoh that Akhenaten had asked him, "Write to me what you have heard in Canaan."[278] Akhenaten was, no doubt, aware of Hebrew activities in Canaan, but he was letting them go, and under the capable leadership of Joshua, was letting the 'Apiru/Habiru/Hebrews serve God by doing whatever they were being led by God to do. Yet, just because Akhenaten chose a non-interference position does not mean that he was indifferent to the plight of those who were in harm's way. He also was not indifferent to hostilities in the greater region of Asia. His dealings with Aziru, alone, are enough to quiet that allegation. Akhenaten wrote EA 162, accusing Aziru of not "having always told the truth," and ordering him to report to the king's court in Akhet-Aten to give an account of himself.[279] Aziru disregarded the pharaoh's letter, so Akhenaten had the untrustworthy, designing scoundrel arrested and dragged to Egypt "to face justice."[280] Akhenaten seems to have been especially concerned about Aziru's activities outside of Canaan, consorting with Hittites. Aziru was playing a dangerous game with forces more powerful than he understood. Akhenaten warned Aziru:

> Consider the people that are training you for their own advantage. They want to throw you into
> the fire. They have lit the fire, and still you love everything so very much! . . . If . . . you plot
> evil, treacherous things, then you, [and] your entire family, shall die by the axe of the king.[281]

Aziru's father, Abdi-Ashirta, wrote to Akhenaten's press secretary, Tutu, asking him to defend Aziru and to facilitate his release.[282] Indeed, in short order, Aziru was back in Syria, and Tutu is his suspected supporter.[283] Tutu was on especially friendly terms with Aziru because Aziru addressed letters directly to the secretary, even referring to Tutu as "father."[284] Perhaps the treachery of Aziru found a sympathetic ear in the highest reaches of Akhenaten's court. Indeed, Aziru identified Tutu as his personal representative before the king.[285] However, following the release of Aziru from Egypt, the rogue became a tribute-paying vassal of Suppiluliumas and broke all ties with Egypt.[286] Akhenaten's assessment of Aziru was, therefore, astute.

It would be a mistake to think that Akhenaten was completely unaware or unconcerned about the goings on in Asia. Akhenaten was concerned about Rib-Addi, and asked him to be on guard for himself.[287] Akhenaten also cared about the region. Events unfolding in Asia were not being orchestrated by the will, the plan, or the governing of Akhenaten. The pharaoh was submitting to the will of his superior, God. If the Amarna letters are describing the Hebrew conquest of Canaan, it was out of Akhenaten's hands. He said, in EA 162, to the wayward Aziru, "you (Aziru) know that the king does not wish to be hard with the land of Canaan."[288]

Yet, in light of the pleading letters written from Canaan and the events described in Joshua and Judges, why did God wish to be hard with the land of Canaan? If "God is no respecter of persons," why did he help the "stiff necked" Hebrews and seem to have no mercy for those living in Palestine? (Deuteronomy 9.6; 10.17; II Chronicles 19.7; Jeremiah 9.25; Romans 2.1-11; Colossians 3.25) In the conquest of Canaan, the God of Joshua was fulfilling a promise that he had made centuries before to his friend Abraham (Genesis 12.5-7). God always keeps his promises! Even though Hebrews, according to the scriptures, rejected God many times and turned to worshiping idols, Abraham had remained faithful to God. Therefore, God was keeping his promises to Abraham (specifically to the line of Abraham's descendants through Isaac and Jacob) because Abraham was obedient, and God remembered (Genesis 22.18; 26.5; 35.9-12). To walk humbly before God was Abraham's choice (Micah 6.8; Hebrews 11.8-10). However, obedience and giving exclusive honor to the God of the Bible, according to scripture, was not—was never—the choice of the indigenous peoples of Canaan. They had been given ample opportunity. God had made the ability to worship and to serve him easily available to the peoples of Canaan. In fact, in the days that God made his promises with Abraham, Melchizedek was practicing as "a priest of God Most High" in Jerusalem, *in Canaan* (Genesis 14.18). The Canaanites, no doubt, were aware of Melchizedek and of the God he served. Like Abraham, they could have chosen to acknowledge Melchizedek and to pay alms to his God. Yet, there is nothing to indicate that many residents of Canaan did.

There is no mention in scripture of any ancient, indigenous nation in Canaan repenting of idolatry, becoming monotheistic, and/or seeking to worship the God of the Bible; neither is there any record of such behavior left behind in artifacts. Canaanites continually insisted on rejecting God, making their own gods and their own religions; and ancient Canaanites are infamous for their wickedness, especially those Canaanites who lived among the cities of Sodom and Gomorrah (Genesis 19; Deuteronomy 9.4). However, sin is universal (Genesis 6.5; I Kings 8.46; Romans 3.23). Therefore, the inhabitants of Canaan were more likely overthrown by Joshua—not simply because they were sinful but because they were occupying land that God had earmarked for another purpose. There were plenty of unrepentant, idolatrous people in the ancient world, but they didn't insist on holding land that the God of the Bible had promised to give to someone else.

Even as the Hebrews were on the "doorstep" of Canaan, Balak, according to the Bible, preferred to curse when he could have chosen to bless. Even though it was made as difficult as possible for Balak to achieve his wicked objective, Balak utterly refused to choose any position other than opposing God. How different the plight of Canaanites, especially the plight of his own people, could have been if Balak had just acknowledged his own sinfulness and had appealed to God for mercy? (Deuteronomy 7 and 8) The God of the Bible delights in mercy! (Exodus 20.4-6; 33.19; 34.6-7; Psalms 103.8; Matthew 9.13; 12.7; Romans 9.15; Ephesians 2.2-4; James 3.17; 5.11) If the Amarna letters are describing the biblical conquest of Canaan, the people of that region chose to continue in their foolish rejection of God. In fact, with the possible exception of EA 250 and EA 337, where both writers use a monotheistic-sounding phrase, "the god of the king," in their petition, the writers of the Amarna letters cried out to every other source for help—Egypt, archers, horses, chariots, riches, local gods, foreign gods, etc.—but they refused to acknowledge the God of the Bible.[289] Perhaps they were blinded by the Sun, or at least could not see beyond their own interpretation of the sun; for example, see EA 147.[290]

160

It is hard to understand such blindness because God continued to demonstrate his power and his presence to the peoples of Canaan. According to the scriptures, God—not Egypt, pharaoh, horses, archers, chariots, etc.—made the sun stand still for a whole day. Yet, not even that incredible phenomenon moved the Canaanites to repentance or to reverence. Instead, they, to their own destruction, continued to oppose God. Why is there no mention of the sun standing still in the Amarna letters? Perhaps the writers shared a superstition similar to the Egyptian belief system. Perhaps they were afraid that if they recorded the terrifying event, it would happen again. The scriptures also seem to indicate that Canaanites would rather *not* talk about it (Joshua 10.21). At any rate, it seems that ancient Canaanites would rather ignore the power of God than submit to it.

If the Amarna tablets document actions recorded in Joshua and Judges, it would have been incredibly foolish for Akhenaten to have responded to the beseeching letters by sending troops to stand in God's way. Surely, Egyptian history of the half-century before Amarna was witness to that fact. On the other hand, even though EA 109 seems to indicate that Egypt "no longer struck fear into the Canaanite rulers," if Akhenaten had taken his army and swooped in to help Joshua in the conquest of Canaan, credit for the victories, in the eyes of the surrounding nations, would probably have been attributed to Egypt, not to God.[291] Besides, the God of the Bible didn't need help from Egypt; the last fifty years had proven that God's power was vastly superior to anything Egypt had to offer (Exodus 14.13-14; 23.27). It's small wonder that Canaanites were no longer afraid of Egypt; they were in the grip of a power that was redefining fear!

All lands belong to one God according to the Bible and also according to the teachings of Akhenaten (Psalms 24.1).[292] The lands of the Levant were *always* God's; they were God's to give to Mentuhotep II in the days of Joseph, and they were God's to reclaim in the days of Amenhotep III and Akhenaten. In fact, God retained ownership of the land even after he allowed Israel to posses it (Leviticus 25.23). As Job said, "the Lord gave, and the Lord hath taken away; blessed be the name of the Lord" (Job 1.21). Akhenaten's position concerning Canaan was prudent, although his exact reasoning and level of understanding is left to speculation.

Yet, Joshua was not the only force at work in Asia. Some of the Amarna letters can be explained by the hostile actions of greedy opportunists and "treacherous fellows" who took advantage of the general unrest to advance their own aggressive agendas.[293] Some writers of Amarna letters seemed to view the 'Apiru as merely "auxiliary forces" who were working for expedient anarchists, men like Itakama, who was in league with the Hittites; Aziru and his father, Abdi-Ashirta, of the Amurru; Zimrida, from Sidon; Namyawaza, a local prince; Labayu, a Canaanite of Shechem; and even Iankhamu, an Egyptian commissioner. Each sought to carve for themselves as large a piece of the crumbling pie as they could pilfer.[294] Furthermore, each did their best to deflect attention away f rom their own, apparently, treacherous and treasonous actions; to feign innocence; to proclaim their undying loyalty to Egypt, and, sometimes, to blame the marauding 'Apiru/Habiru for all the turmoil in the land.[295] For instance, Abdi-Ashirta says in EA 62:

> What do your words, my lord, . . . mean? . . . "You are an enemy of Egypt, and you committed a crime against Egyptians." May my lord listen. There were no men in Sumur to guard it . . . and Sumur was afraid of the troops of Shelal . . . So I myself hastened to the rescue . . .[296]

This, of course, was a matter of opinion—Ashirta's opinion. Clearly, however, the 'Apiru/Habiru were a convenient scapegoat for some of those who were quick to cry slander. Labayu, for one, immediately distanced himself from the actions of his own sons who had been accused of "consorting with the 'Apiru."[297] Nevertheless, letters from the governor of Qatna, the prince of Megiddo, the regent of Gezer, and others often named names, pointedly implicating Ashirta, Aziru, Labayu, and the like in violent behavior. For instance, in EA 244, Biridiya stated in his complaint:

> . . . Labayu has carried on hostilities against me, and we are not able to pluck the wool, and we are not able to go outside the gate in the presence of Labayu since he has learned that you have not given archers, and now his face is set to take Megiddo . . . .[298]

Interestingly, Labayu and his sons were accused of being in league with the Habiru. The Canaanite "guerilla chief" from Shechem flatly denied the allegation, although he was aware of the Habiru advancement because Labayu wrote to Amenhotep III, promising to put an end to 'Apiru/Habiru activities.[299] However, Biridiya, for one, didn't believe Labayu's contrition. Capturing Labayu at Megiddo, Biridiya handed him over to Zurata, the prince of Acre (Accho), and charged Zurata to transport Labayu to Egypt for trial; but Zurata's distrust of Labayu was obviously greater than Biridiya's because Zurata killed Labayu (Judges1.31).[300] Still, the accusations against Labayu's sons may have been true. More than one letter says that they handed land over to the Habiru.[301] Of course, Shechem, in the hill country of Ephraim, was an important region during the conquest of Canaan. The bones of Joseph were buried there, and Joshua lived there (Joshua 19.50; 24.32).

Itakama is another Canaanite who wrote to Amenhotep III offering to take care of the Habiru problem. He intended to drive out the marauding desert nomads that he called the Khabiri, which may have been a variation of "Hapiru," the Mesopotamian word for Habiru.[302]

Obviously, some Canaanites did aid the Hebrews. Rahab the harlot is remembered in scripture for her role in the capture of Jericho (Joshua 6.25). In EA 298, a man named Yapahu, reports that his own brother had "pledged himself to the 'Apiru."[303] Others, such as Biridiya and Milkilu were also accused of aiding the 'Apiru.[304] On the other hand, another writer, Biryawaza, seemed to brag about the alliance he had formed with the 'Apiru/Habiru. In EA 195, Biryawaza informs the king:

> I am, indeed, together with my troops and chariots, together with my brothers, my 'Apiru and my
> Suteans [a Semitic people who often worked as mercenaries], at the disposition of the archers,
> wheresoever the king, my lord, shall order me to go.[305]

Could it be that Biryawaza had a greater understanding of the position of Akhenaten concerning the unrest in Canaan? Indeed, even Rib-Addi seemed to reach a rather sardonic conclusion that the conquering of the territories must be "pleasing in the sight of the king."[306] Furthermore, in EA 286, Abdi-Heba makes a curious statement, "As truly as the king, my lord, lives, I say to the commissioner of the king, my lord, 'Why do you love the 'Apiru but hate the mayors?'"[307] Though his words are carefully couched as a criticism of the pharaoh's commissioner, one wonders if this mayor suspected that Akhenaten held similar sentiments.

Was Akhenaten sympathetic to the 'Apiru/the enemies? Did Akhenaten comprehend that God was in the process of establishing Israel according to his promises? Did he perceive that God was teaching "a stiff necked people" to rely on the Lord of All and not to turn to any other helper? (II Chronicles 30.8; Leviticus 26.12; Hebrews 13.6) Did he understand that God was demonstrating his power to all people on earth? (Joshua 4.24) But more than this, is it possible that Akhenaten understood that the God of the Bible was implementing a new phase in his plan to bless *all* nations? (Genesis 12.3) Ultimately, through the seed of Abraham, in the land of Canaan, the Bible says that God would send the greatest gift that mankind (and Egypt) would ever receive (Luke 2.10-11). By submitting to the will of God/Aten, Akhenaten was contributing to that plan. Actually, Akhenaten could not have made his motivation more clear. The greatest motivating factor in this pharaoh's life was to please Aten. If he had an inkling of an idea that Aten desired to occupy the Egyptian territories in Canaan, Akhenaten would have sought to please the Aten. Akhenaten recognized that God is God; he owns everything under the sun! Whatever God desired and/or required, Egypt, under Akhenaten, would give—even if it meant sacrificing the *entire* empire. Akhenaten's devotion was absolute!

Furthermore, perhaps other combatants named in the Amarna letters and accused of being in league with the 'Apiru, in fact, were; but, arguably, their intentions may not have been as admirable as Akhenaten's. Abdi-Ashirta, for instance, is heavily mentioned in the correspondence of Rib-Addi. In EA 71, he says:

> What is Abdi-Ashirta, servant and dog, that he takes the land of the king for himself? What is his
> auxiliary force that it is strong? Through the 'Apiru his auxiliary force is strong! . . . Let him not
> gather together all the 'Apiru so he can take Sigata and Ampi, and seize . . .[308]

Rib-Addi, seems to have been stationed in Gubla (Gebal in the Bible), well into the region of Lebanon. However, in EA 89, he reports about events as far south as Tyre.[309] In the conquest of Canaan, Tyre was part of the land that was allotted to Asher. Their tribe's inheritance was the northwestern-most region of Canaan:

> And their border was Helkath, and Hali, and Beten, and Achshaph, And Alammelech, and Amad, and Misheal; and reacheth to Carmel westward, and to Shihorlibnath; And turneth toward the sunrising to Bethdagon, and reacheth to Zebulun, and to the valley of Jiphthahel toward the north side of Bethemek, and Neiel, and goeth out to Cabul on the left hand, And Hebron, and Rehob, and Hammon, and Kanah, even unto great Zidon; And then the coast turneth to Ramah, and to the strong city Tyre; and the coast turneth to Hosah; and the outgoings thereof are at the sea from the coast to Achzib: Ummah also, and Aphek, and Rehob: twenty and two cities with their villages. This is the inheritance of the tribe of the children of Asher according to their families, these cities with their villages. (Joshua 19.25-31)

Though Joshua 13.5 includes "the land of the Giblites [Gebal], and all Lebanon" in the conquest area, the designated northern border of Asher seems to have terminated with Sidon.

In Joshua 23, after the land of Canaan had been divided and assigned to each of the tribes, Joshua charged the heads of each tribe to continue the campaign to drive out the people who were living in their inheritance and to possess the land. Therefore, a time came when each tribe was responsible for leading its own men into battle. Of course, the forces of a single tribe could still be quite formidable. The sons of Asher, for instance, may have numbered 53,400 (Numbers 26.47). Could it be that "*Ashir*ta" is so named because he was a man of "Asher," and was the leader of the 'Apiru from that tribe, much like the "chief of Asher," an office acknowledged in the days of Ramses II?[310]

If that could be the case, why then was Ashirta's son, Aziru (perhaps not coincidentally: 'Apiru with a "z"), arrested and brought to Egypt for questioning? Just because they might have been Hebrews, sadly, does not mean that Ashirta and Aziru were necessarily loyal to Joshua or to the God of the Bible. It does not mean they were doing as they ought to do or were the caliber of characters they should have been. In fact, in a letter addressed to Tutu, Aziru urged pharaoh to swear an "oath to my gods and to Aman [Amun]." Akhenaten, probably, would not have received such a request well, and neither would the God of the Bible, especially if Ashirta and Aziru were Hebrews. Furthermore, Aziru extolled that the king of Egypt was like Baal and like the Sun.[311] If he was a man of Asher, this statement alone, shows that Aziru was not a man of God. The veracity of Ashirta and Aziru is also questionable. Though Ashirta proclaimed loyalty to Egypt, Rib-Addi testifies against him. Aziru also said to the king of Egypt, "I am your servant forever, and my sons are your servants."[312] Yet, in EA 117, Rib-Addi warns Akhenaten, "The cities are in Aziru's service. May the king not enter their cities. They are not at peace with you."[313] Still, Akhenaten was not naïve, he had a good sense of when he was being lied to and was highly suspect of the motives of men like Ashirta and his sons.

Although it was certainly not the only tribe to fall short of God's objective for the Hebrews in Canaan, the tribe of Asher did not do a good job of obeying what Joshua instructed them to do:

> Neither did Asher drive out the inhabitants of Accho, nor the inhabitants of Zidon, nor of Ahlab,
> nor of Achzib, nor of Helbah, nor of Aphik, nor of Rehob: But the Asherites dwelt among the
> Canaanites, the inhabitants of the land: for they did not drive them out. (Judges 1.31-32)

EA 67 and EA 137 seem to indicate that the brother of Rib-Addi made a treaty with Aziru so that the 'Apiru dwelt among the Canaanites.[314] EA 114 says, "Everyone in the land of Amurru is at peace with them [Aziru and the 'Apiru]."[315] Ashirta, in EA 60, far from driving out the inhabitants of the land as God had instructed, seems to have appointed himself as guard of all the pharaoh's lands in Amurru.[316] EA 73, 74, and 81 seem to indicate that, contrary to his authority, Ashirta was calling for the assassination of the leaders of the cities in Amurru. Then instead of driving the peasantry out of their lands, he was establishing himself as their leader. Perhaps that is why God did not protect Abdi-Ashirta against the king of Mitanni.[317] If he was a man of Asher, he had not been obedient to the instructions of God concerning the conquest of the land.

In like manner, Aziru does not seem to have been particularly loyal to anyone other than to himself. In EA 162, pharaoh accused Aziru of being a drinking buddy with the ruler of Kadesh on the Orontes.[318] All the while, in EA 157, Aziru indicates to the pharaoh that he would stand against an advancement of the king of Hatti.[319] However, Rib-Addi testifies against Aziru's statement of solidarity with Egypt, in EA 126, reporting that the Hittites were actively allied with Aziru:

> the Hittite troops and they have set fire to the country. . . . Now they are mobilizing the troops of
> the Hittite countries to seize Gubla. . . . They give all the silver and gold of the king to the sons
> of Abdi-Ashirta, and the sons of Abdi-Ashirta give this to the strong king."[320]

Such behavior would seem to indicate that Aziru was much more loyal to the king of the Hittites than he was to the king of Egypt. Yet, in EA 170, Aziru, himself, is addressed as "king" and "lord," and there seems to be no question that he is allied with the Hittites for the purposes of capturing more territory. The power-hungry Aziru and his brothers were also active as far east as Damascus.[321] If Aziru was Hebrew, he was operating far outside the boundaries defined for Asher and even for Israel, but others were too (Numbers 24.22-24; Judges 4.11; I Chronicles 2.55). EA 185, for one, describes 'Apiru military activity north of Damascus. In fact, none of the places discussed in this message to Egypt from Mayarzana fall within the land that God promised to give the Hebrews.[322] Imperialism and avarice, unfortunately, are human characteristics.

Further evidence that the Amarna letters are addressing the Hebrew conquest of Canaan can be seen in the records of refugees. In EA 187, Satiya the mayor of Enisasi, a city near Hazor, says, "I am guarding the palace of the king, my lord, my god, my Sun, where I am. . . . And I herewith send my daughter to the palace, to the king, my lord, my god, my Sun." Satiya, doubted his ability to protect his daughter, and he was sending her to Egypt in hopes of saving her life. Perhaps Satiya's daughter faired better than the nieces and sister of Rib-Addi, discussed in EA 89, who he sent as refugees to Tyre.[323] In the days of Horemheb, not long after the Amarna period, desperate refugees fleeing Palestine sought asylum in Egypt. Inscriptions from the time record:

> The barbarians have taken their land, their dwellings have been destroyed, their town devastated
> and their crops burnt. Their country has been so hungry that they lived in the mountains like
> goats. Now they come to beg the Powerful [Horemheb] to send his victorious sword to protect
> them saying, "We few Asians who do not know how we may survive, have come to seek refuge
> in the land of Pharaohs as we did in the time of the fathers of his father, since the beginning."[324]

Indeed, hundreds of years later, the escapades of the Sea People, the displaced Philistines, can be seen as an aftermath of the conquest of Canaan and of the events recorded in the Amarna letters. The Hebrews as described in scripture entered Canaan to stay.[325] Unlike other invaders in history, they were not in Canaan just to plunder, conquer, and go home. They had no other home. Those who were living in Palestine at the time of the Hebrew conquest either died, became the sworn enemies of the Hebrews, made alliances with them, or surrendered their homes and left. No one defeats God.

Akhenaten had no desire to test the power of God by sending archers and troops to fight a loosing battle, defending territories against the Hebrew conquest in Canaan. After all, according to the biblical account, God had not only demonstrated his power and ability to destroy Egypt, over the last few decades before Akhenaten, he had also shown his ability to protect and bless Egypt. Throughout the reigns of Akhenaten's father and grandfather, Egypt had—for the most part—been at peace, which is remarkable because, if the compromised condition of Egypt and its army at the rise of Thutmose IV had become common knowledge, Egypt might easily have been conquered. Egypt in the wake of the biblical exodus was essentially defenseless and reeling from loss and grief. Perhaps the God of the Bible was moved by Thutmose IV's contrite gestures and groping petitions, immediately offered in the first year of his reign. It is an astonishing contrast to consider: while the young pharaoh of the land that God had devastated was seeking to please God, the people that God had gone to extraordinary lengths to rescue seemed to have been seeking to anger him.[326] Perhaps the God who was greatly disappointed by the foolishness of the "stiff-necked" Hebrews was touched by the fearful wisdom back in Egypt. The Psalmist confesses, "We have sinned with our fathers, we have committed iniquity, we have done wickedly. Our fathers understood not thy wonders in Egypt; they remembered not the multitude of thy mercies; but provoked him at the sea, even at the Red sea" (Psalms 106.6-7). It is incredible to consider the behavior of young Thutmose IV. If he was the pharaoh in the aftermath of the exodus, it seems that he didn't have to understand God's wonders to seek ways to prevent further provoking of God's wrath. In spite of unthinkable devastation and loss, in his *Dream Stela* Thutmose IV praises the Lord of All and calls him the "good God."

Perhaps, moved with compassion by the reverence of the young king, the God of the Bible/the Lord of All protected Egypt in the days of Thutmose IV. After all, the military of Egypt in those days seems to have been of little use beyond police actions.[327] Moreover, it is highly unusual that peace would have prevailed during the transition period between Thutmose IV and Amenhotep III. Just at the time when Egypt was perhaps most vulnerable, there were not the usual "uprisings in the empire, as generally happened at each change of reign."[328] According to the book of James, the God of the Bible, the Father of Lights, is the giver of *every* good gift (James 1.17). If this is true, then under the theory of this book, during the days of Amenhotep III, God not only provided peace for Egypt, but amazing prosperity![329] "Amenhotep III had little need to fight. He already ruled the whole world. He is therefore credited with just one or two Nubian campaigns."[330] Yet, from out of riches obtained from the gold mines in Nubia alone, any plunder that the Egyptians had been favorably disposed to give to the exiting Hebrews in the biblical account was certainly repaid by God many times over—in short order, during the golden age of Amenhotep III. At that time gold was said to be as dust in the Two Lands.[331] However, the "affluent economy" of Egypt that, to some, makes Amenhotep III comparable to Louis XIV, "The Sun King," actually began in the short reign of Thutmose IV.[332] The material comfort of Egypt's golden age is probably wrongly attributed to any shrewd governmental policies of Amenhotep III; neither is the decline rightly charged to the account of Akhenaten as a failure in his ability to administrate. Akhenaten, for one, professed a keen awareness of the ultimate source of Egypt's blessings. Even Egyptian literature expresses the belief that a god (albeit, in this instance, the god was the pharaoh) ". . . will not fail to do good for a country that will be loyal to him."[333] Far from having no effective foreign or domestic policy, Akhenaten may well have believed that governing Egypt to turn in devoted obedience to the God of the Bible would eventually translate into strength in Egypt's foreign footing and into sustained domestic prosperity as well.

Zenith of Enlightenment

"Aten is light and life; he creates the world in all its glory. He lives in the heart of the worshipper, and in the mind of Akhenaten, his son."[334] How did Akhenaten seem to have such insight into God and his will? According to Freud, Akhenaten knew so much about *YHWH* because the radical pharaoh was the mentor of Moses and invented both God and the religion that later gave rise to the Law of Moses.[335] Others have postulated that Akhenaten *was* Moses. Manetho, of course writing hundreds of years after the Amarna time period, seems to have confused Akhenaten with Moses.[336] However, if the momentous events of the Exodus account happened at the end of the reign of Amenhotep II, then they likely occurred fifteen to twenty years before Akhenaten was even born. Certainly, Akhenaten would have had no recollection of Moses or the plagues. Neither is it likely that Akhenaten's parents were old enough to effectively remember the distress of Egypt in the exodus without assistance either; but such would not have been the case for Akhenaten's surviving grandparents.[337] It is probable that Akhenaten knew Yuya and Tuya, Mutemwia, and, perhaps, even his great-grandmother Tiaa.[338] Whether the young prince was raised in the harem or in the palace, in Memphis or Luxor, one can only imagine the fearsome, hushed, sobering testimony that survived the ordeal of the exodus.[339] If nothing else, Any, who appears in relief in Amarna as a toothless old man and who was the only official from Akhenaten's court to actually be buried in the cliff-tombs above Akhet-Aten, had served as a steward to Amenhotep II and, no doubt, could have given account as an eye-witness to the events that happened at the end of that infamous pharaoh's career.[340] Akhenaten's grandfather, Thutmose IV, if he was the first pharaoh after the exodus, advocated a contrite return to the religion of On as the wisest course of response to the series of tragic events. Akhenaten's father, Amenhotep III, didn't seem to disagree with that logic. However, Amenhotep III was not particularly pious, perhaps it was Tiye who held the greater devotion and "carried the torch" for Aten. There are those who believe that Tiye may have encouraged Akhenaten in his religious rebellion.[341] Yet, Tiye's sentiments and interests were probably more pragmatic. On the other hand, Akhenaten's relationship with the Aten seems to have been "intensely personal."[342] He swore not to be turned away from following the Aten no matter who may try to sway him; if a nobleman or even if Nefertiti were to say, "This other place is a good place to build a city to God," he would not listen.[343]

However, Akhenaten may have learned about God directly from tutelage that he received in On.[344] After all, though there was a definite leaning toward the Aten, there is no indication that anyone in Akhenaten's family was decidedly monotheistic in their theology; although, one of Akhenaten's uncles was a priest of Aten, and in the early years, Amenhotep IV/Akhenaten maintained a palace in Heliopolis.[345] The high priest of On, Pawah, and his wife were close personal friends of Akhenaten.[346] Further tying Atenism to On is the fact that the pharaoh arranged to have the sacred Apis bull, that died during Akhenaten's tenure, buried in Akhet-Aten.[347] Nevertheless, Akhenaten has been called the world's—certainly Egypt's—first monotheist; yet, an undercurrent of monotheism had always existed in Egyptian thinking.[348] In fact, some contend that the worship of Amun-Ra, who incorporated all other gods and who was considered to be "the sole god," was practically monotheistic.[349] And though the Hyksos assertion of the uniqueness of Seth and an anti-polytheistic movement called the 'New Solar Theology' both predated Amarna, echoes of monotheism trace all the way back to the beginnings of Heliopolis.[350]

It is therefore possible that the original, primeval religion of On was monotheistic, believing in the God of the Bible, "God (with a capital G)," and did not originate in Egypt.[351] Neo-Platonist writers, such as the Syrian, Iamblichus Chalcidensis, of the third century, stated as fact that ancient Egyptians worshiped one God, of course such assertion was made thousands of years afterward and was not without agenda.[352] Nevertheless, there are Old Kingdom texts that discuss a deity who had no name; this was an ethereal being referred to as *neter*, simply, "the God."[353] Akhenaten, himself, from inscriptions in the tomb of Ramose the vizier, says "The words of Re are before thee . . . in order to exalt me since the time of the God."[354] In fact, Ray proposes, if posed the question, "'Do you think that there is one principle behind the multiplicity of gods you worship?' [many ancient Egyptians would likely have answered] with an affirmative."[355] Some similarity between the God of the Bible and the deity worshiped at On is seen in this Old Kingdom hymn:

> Thou art the lord of heaven, thou art the lord of earth:
> Thou art the creator of those who dwell in the heights,
>   and of those who dwell in the depths.
> Thou are the One God who came into being in the beginning of time.
> Thou didst create the earth, thou didst fashion man,
> Thou didst make the watery abyss of the sky,
> Thou didst form the Nile,
> Thou didst create the great deep,
>   and thou dost give life unto all that therein is.
> Thou hast knit together the mountains,
> Thou hast made mankind and the beasts of the field to come into being,
> Thou hast made the heavens and the earth.
> Worshipped be thou whom the goddess Maat embraceth at morn and at eve . . .
> Hail, thou mighty being, of myriad forms and aspects,
> Thou king of the world, prince of On, lord of eternity,
>   and ruler of everlastingness!
> The company of the gods rejoice when thou risest and dost sail across the sky![356]

However, though the concept of "One God," the supreme deity who created all things is intact, a hint of polytheistic error and idolatry may already have been shading the theology of On by the time of this hymn. Certainly, phrases such as "the goddess Maat," "myriad forms and aspects," "the company of gods" and "when thou risest and dost sail across the sky" give pause to a student of the Bible. Of course, the references to a goddess of any kind, myriad forms, and gods smack of polytheism. Yet, "the goddess Maat" may be nothing more than a poetic trope. Personification of an attribute such as *maat*/order is also seen in the Bible. One of the earliest examples of personification of an attribute is found in Genesis 4 when God says to Cain, "sin lieth at the door. And unto thee shall be his desire, and thou shalt rule over him" (Genesis 4.7). The favorable attribute, wisdom, is personified as a female entity in the book of Proverbs. "She" is highly prized and greatly honored, and even though wisdom is an inherent attribute of God (as are order, truth, and righteousness), Proverbs does not seem to deify wisdom in the way that maat seems to have been presented at On (Proverbs 1.20ff). The rejoicing of the "goddess Maat" does seem to be a concept that is drifting from monotheism, yet Akhenaten, a monotheist, never rejected the "goddess" Maat, though he also never built temples to her or is known to have worshipped her as a deity.[357] Perhaps a similar poetic device is implemented by God in Job: "Whereupon are the foundations thereof fastened? Or who laid the corner stone thereof; when the morning stars sang together, and all the sons of God shouted for joy?" (Job 38.6-7) This passage is not only another example of personification, but also could suggest some sort of parallel between "all the sons of God" and "the company of gods." Still, "when thou risest and dost sail across the sky" does sound as if the sun itself was being ensconced as an idol, a representation of deity. If this is not just poetic language, it could indicate the dawning of apostasy in the theology of *Iwnw*. Yet, similar poetic language in the Bible describes God as one "who maketh the clouds his chariot: who walketh upon the wings of the wind" (Psalms 104.3).

Iwnw, the Egyptian name for On, may have been derived from the Sumerian word "*unu(g)*"—important, since the Tower of Babel has long been associated with that same region; and, according to the Bible, that's where all languages originated (Genesis 11.1-9).[358] Aten, "the complete one," was recognized at On as the creator God, and the temple to Aten was built at *Iwnw* atop the mythical "mound of creation."[359] In the creation myth of On, Atum says, "I was alone. I took courage in my heart. I laid a foundation. I made every form. Many were the forms coming from my mouth."[360] Aten/Atum existed before anything else.[361] Furthermore, reminiscent of Genesis 6.6, "it repented the Lord that he had made man on the earth, and it grieved him at his heart," according to the mythology of On, tears from the eye of Atum made men.[362] Atum was also credited with creating the first couple, Shu and Tefnut, who became personifications of air and moisture and were also associated with a pair of lions that lived near *Iwnw*.[363] Aten was always understood to be a universal God, the God of all men, omnipresent, omnipotent, omniscient, and good.[364] Hymns sung to Aten from the beginning of On were intended to break language barriers and to be comprehensible to foreigners.[365]

In fact, even more closely related to an understanding of the God of the Bible, the early religion of On espoused that the one God of Egypt was manifested in a unit of three deities: Atum, Ra, and Khepri.[366] Aten, Aton, Atum, Tum, Ra, and Khepri were all represented by the sun as it appeared at different times of the day.[367] Significantly, unlike the "family unit" relationship, thematic in many ancient religions; the godhead of On was not a husband, a consort, and a son.[368] Instead, Atum, Ra, and Khepri were more like different "faces," different aspects of the same entity the same creator God.[369] However, Ra appeared in the form of Atum at Heliopolis, making Atum the actual first in the triad.[370]

The God of the Bible is also believed to be and seems to be presented in scripture as a unified entity composed of three personalities. All three of them, working together as one God, orchestrated creation. Genesis 1.2 makes it clear that the Holy Spirit was involved at the very beginning, John 1.3 includes Jesus in creation, and the very identity of God the Father implies his role as creator/progenitor. In fact, Genesis 1.26 alone, "And God said, Let us make man in our image," seems to settle the question of the collective nature of God. Nevertheless, over time, probably embellished by mythology and expanded by demands from popular culture's polytheism, the gods of Heliopolis developed into an ennead, plus Horus making ten *Iwnw* deities altogether.[371]

In an explanation of the God of the Bible's view of polytheism as provided to the Romans, the Bible describes the process of religious entropy in the ancient world in this way:

> For the wrath of God is revealed from heaven against all . . . who hold the truth in
> unrighteousness; Because that which may be known of God is manifest in them; for God hath
> shewed it unto them. For the invisible things of him from the creation of the world are clearly

seen, being understood by the things that are made, even his eternal power and Godhead; so that they are without excuse: Because that, when they knew God, they glorified him not as God, neither were thankful; but became vain in their imaginations, and their foolish heart was darkened. Professing themselves to be wise, they became fools, And changed the glory of the uncorruptible God into an image made like to corruptible man, and to birds, and fourfooted beasts, and creeping things. . . . Who changed the truth of God into a lie, and worshipped and served the creature more than the Creator, who is blessed for ever. Amen. (Romans 1.18-25)

One can only imagine how many times and in how many different cultures the above scenario unfolded.[372] Certainly by the time of the Old Kingdom, popular religion in ancient Egypt embraced all kinds of images of men, birds, beasts, and "creeping things."[373] Every nome, every town had its own pet deities.[374] Most Egyptians obviously preferred the dynamic sensationalism of evolving mythology to unyielding truth and preferred polytheism to monotheism.[375] However, fable is usually a poor replacement for fact. Romans 1 says, "they [ancient people] knew God." If that is the case, a certain fundamental "faith," as defined by scripture, was not required in the Patriarchal Age. "Now faith is the substance of things hoped for, the evidence of things not seen" (Hebrews 1.1). In the earliest time, as in the days of Eden, God is recorded as interacting directly with people, removing any doubt of his existence (Genesis 3.8-10). According to the Bible, there were those, especially living in the time of the patriarchs, who didn't hope that there is a God; they *knew* him! Therefore, if the process of developing polytheism as provided in Romans 1 is accurate, the thought that ancient peoples would reject the God that they *knew* to embrace things that they only imagined to be deities does seem to make "their foolish heart" indefensible.[376] It is widely believed in the academic world that ancient peoples first believed in superstition, *numina*/spirits, local gods, and many gods. Yet, if Redford is correct, Egyptians in pre-history understood God as *the* "Supernatural," an "infinite plurality," but, still, a single entity.[377] "This One was 'in every body, of all living things, animating them by thinking and enunciating [His] will.'"[378] This idea seems consistent with Paul's explanation to the Romans; and, if what the Bible says is true, all ancient cultures originated from a monotheistic religious understanding. Obviously other nations understood the concept of God. In the tomb of Tutankhamun, inscriptions from "the chiefs of Upper Retjenu" say that they have not had diplomatic representatives in Egypt, i.e., having "been ignorant of Egypt since the time of *the* God . . ."[379]

Of course, the popular religion of Egypt at large was polytheistic, superstitious, and compartmentalized. Much like modern Americans recognize all religions and, in the name of religious freedom, encourage individuals to worship in the church of their choice (whether they, personally, agree with the doctrine of another's religion or not); ancient Egyptians recognized all gods and, in the spirit of religious tolerance, encouraged individuals to patron the god of their choice, or the god of their immediate desire.[380] However, in Akhenaten's monotheism, he rejected that ecumenical reasoning.[381] Not only Amun was abandoned; so was the ennead of On.[382] The only reasonable choice was truth, and any individual's preference was irrelevant. Placing the predilection of the individual as supreme essentially places the will of man above the will of God. Such was out of the question to Akhenaten.

It's been suggested that monotheism arises at the rejection of all other gods, and monotheism destroys polytheism.[383] This may not be the case. In actuality, it was the introduction of new gods that supplanted monotheism. If that is true, Akhenaten was merely returning Egypt to its religious origin. Amarna was not a reformation; it was a restoration. Akhenaten sought to peel away centuries of religious reforms and rubble and to re-establish Egypt's original relationship with the Almighty—not on man's terms (perhaps not even on Akhenaten's terms) but on God's.[384]

According to the Bible, there is only one God. The God of the Bible declares himself to be unique. He is the creator; therefore, from the beginning of the world, in truth, there was only one God. Akhenaten did not invent truth or the concept of monotheism. He was merely a champion of both. Indeed, monotheism is the original religion according to scripture. All other beliefs, by biblical standards, are erroneous and apostasy.

Though many of his contemporaries and his critics across time have considered Akhenaten to be a heretic, an accusation that Tyldesley says "is easy but lazy," to Akhenaten's way of thinking, he was "*Ankh em maet* /Living in truth."[385] Akhenaten was singularly interested in truth and saw himself as rectifying heresy—mending apostasy, correcting the mythological teaching that had changed the truth of his God into a lie.[386] As a lie grows over time, it becomes more and more evil. Though it's impossible to say for certain what Akhenaten meant, the lie, the teaching that there were many, many gods and other false religious ideas that were being promoted in Egypt at the time of Akhenaten were likely worse than in the days of his father and grandfather and were growing worse all the time. As Akhenaten said, "By the life of my father Re, (the words) of the priests are more perverse than the things I heard in the fourth year . . . more perverse than the [evil] things that my father and grandfather ever [were "obliged" to hear]."[387] Ay once said of Akhenaten that his "abomination is lying."[388]

If the theory in this book is correct, perhaps the priests of Amun-Ra were scrambling in an ongoing effort to work damage control and were spinning the events of the exodus to restore the standing of their defeated god(s). No doubt, the tale that they were weaving was becoming more and more perverse and farther and farther from the truth. The priests of Amun-Ra would have liked nothing more than to cover-up the truth and have the people believe a lie that would rewrite the story of the exodus in their favor and in the favor of their god. One can only imagine how the priests may have tried to explain the sun standing still. Of course, the priests of Amun-Ra weren't the only priests in Egypt. It is, therefore, ironic to consider that, from the days of Thutmose IV and his renewed interest in the Aten, the priests of On had probably been busily sweeping away the sands of error, foolishness, and unrighteousness that had buried the true God of Egypt whom they once had known. Certainly, "his wrath [was] revealed from heaven against all ungodliness" in Egypt during the exodus. By the days of Akhenaten, the priests of On were likely more familiar with the foundational beliefs than they had been fifty years prior, yet it is still hard to believe that they possessed the clarity of Akhenaten.[389]

Nevertheless, there are those who suggest that Akhenaten was never a monotheist or wasn't always a monotheist. Even the expanded name that he used for Aten: Re-Harakhte/Horus, he-who-rejoices-in-the-horizon-in-his-name, Shu 'light' which-is-in/from-the-Sun-disk, incorporated the god names Re, Horus (Harakhte), and Shu.[390] Did Akhenaten worship multiple gods? It's clear that Akhenaten's religious convictions changed over time. There is little doubt that he was less loyal to Aten in the first few years of his reign; in fact, he gave honor to Amun-Ra and others in Egypt's traditional pantheon.[391] Around year five, his persuasion crystallized into absolute devotion to Aten, but some say that his religious fervor waned later on. Perhaps as early as year nine, Akhenaten seems to have changed the name of his God again. Though still written inside a double cartouche, the new name leaves aside Harakhte and Shu but seems to emphasize Ra. This "late name" for Aten is: "Live Re, Ruler of the Horizon, Rejoicing in the Horizon in His Name 'Re, the Father, who has come as the Sun-disk."[392] What could account for this? Perhaps sinister influences in Akhet-Aten persuaded Akhenaten to soften his monotheistic convictions; perhaps Akhenaten was ill and shadowy voices were speaking on his behalf. However, an increase in Akhenaten's understanding could also account for these adjustments. For instance, at the beginning of his reign, his belief in Aten was somewhat academic, but if the sun stood still, Akhenaten would have been confronted with a new reality. And if new revelations were added to Akhenaten over time, it stands to reason that his vernacular would reflect that deeper understanding.

The greater evidence seems to suggest that after his epiphany, around year five, Akhenaten remained an unwavering monotheist. From all appearances, he continued to promote a strict intolerance to traditional Egyptian orthodoxy, even forbidding the plural form of the noun "god," all superstitious and polytheistic religious expressions were denied—this included idols, amulets, and magic spells. At the same time, an urgent iconoclasm was imposed, complete with doctrinal and ethical stipulations, intended to please a universal god and to effect a favorable standing in the afterlife.[393] It's true that Akhenaten made references to certain names of solar deities that he considered to be aspects of Aten, but Aten remained as one God.[394]

Akhenaten's clarity even penetrated time-honored burial myths, fundamental to Egyptian beliefs. Though some traditions persisted in the Amarna period, such as: mummification, anthropoid coffins, canopic jars, and personal grave goods to accompany the deceased in the afterlife—no longer were references to traditional funerary deities or the mythologies surrounding them allowed.[395] Magic spells and the *Book of the Dead* were also forbidden. The *Amduat* was replaced by a "scene on the eastern wall of [the burial] chamber . . . of the rising of the Aten and the awakening of the temple and its royal worshippers to life and joy."[396]

The notion that Osiris would judge the righteousness of an individual in the afterlife, weighing the heart against the weight of a feather, was deemed false. There was, therefore, no longer need of burial that included a heart scarab intended to testify favorably on behalf of the deceased. Heart scarabs from the Amarna period were engraved with simple praises to Aten.[397] Shabtiu figures were still allowed, but devoid of any references to other gods or magic. In the teaching of Akhenaten, magic would not bring the dead back to life, Aten would.[398] However, dispatching with the mythological superstitions about the afterlife did not mean that the afterlife itself did not exist. Eternal life for everyone who put his or her trust in Aten was anticipated. It was believed of Aten that, "Infinite life is in thee to quicken them, and the breath of life for (their) nostrils."[399] On a stone from the tomb of Bek, purchased at a Cairo marketplace just prior to the Twentieth Century, the Akhet-Aten artist expresses the prospect: "That his soul may appear, that his body may live, that his foot may march out to all places . . . grant me to drink wine and milk."[400] Others express similar hopes that they will receive, "a gift of loaves in the temple of the Aten, a site of the Aten in the necropolis, and departure in the morning from the underworld to [see] the Aten as he rises every day."[401] The footboard of Kiya's coffin preserves similar expectations for the afterlife:

> May I breathe the sweet air that issues from thy mouth? May I behold thy beauty every day—
> that is my prayer? May I hear thy sweet voice in the North Wind? May my body grow vigorous
> with life through thy love. Mayest thou give me thy two hands bearing thy sustenance, and I
> receive it and live by it. Mayest thou ever call upon my name and it shall not fail on thy lips.[402]

Akhenaten has also been called the world's *only* monotheist, arguing that even the Bible is a book that recognizes multiple gods. However, the Bible consistently only recognizes one true God; anything else that may be elevated to godhood by anyone else, according to scripture, is a false god, and is no god at all (II Kings 19.18; Jeremiah 2.11, 5.7, 16.20; Acts 19.26; Galatians 4.8). Some say that the God who spoke to Moses out of the burning bush was a different God than the God of Abraham. The argument suggests that the God in the burning bush was a fire god of a desolate mountain, while the God of Abraham was a desert god, that Elohiym and Yahweh are two different entities.[403] Freud even went so far as to suggest that the Yahweh in the burning bush was "an uncanny, bloodthirsty demon who walks by night and shuns the light of day."[404] This is certainly an odd assessment since there is nothing in scripture to indicate that Moses encountered the phenomenon of the burning bush at night. On the contrary, he was in the act of leading his father-in-law's sheep when he came across the bush (Exodus 3.1-2). Due to predators and other dangers, one would probably not drive sheep except by the light of day. Furthermore, the scriptures identify the being in the bush as an angel, not a demon. However, God, himself, seems to clarify this discrepancy when, speaking through this apparition, "Moreover he said, I am the God of thy father, the God of Abraham, the God of Isaac, and the God of Jacob" (Exodus 3.6; Mark 12. 26-27; Luke 20.37-38). Different places, different people, different names, different times, same God! Still, there are those who propose that the God of the Old Testament is a different God than that of the New Testament. The God of the Old Testament, they contend, is wrathful, vengeful, exclusive, and destroying; while the God of the New Testament is gentle, forgiving, accepting, and loving.[405] Others believe that the concept of a loving, abstract, universal God only eventually evolved among the writers of the scriptures.[406]

Perhaps a different perspective should be applied. Perhaps it isn't the God of the Bible who changes with the Old and New Testament; it's the audience that's different. The Old Testament is largely written to a people who, in God's own estimation, were a "stiff-necked people." God loved the ancient Hebrews, but, according to the scriptures, they were often obstinate, rebellious, and unfaithful. However, the New Testament is largely written to people who, of their own free will, choose to obey God and actively seek to more closely follow his will. The tone and behavior of a loving parent toward a defiant child would be very different from the tone and behavior of the same loving parent toward a compliant child. God, as revealed throughout the Bible, is a being with a full range of emotion. In both the Old Testament and the New Testament, he is wrathful and gentle, vengeful and merciful, rejecting and accepting, destroying and preserving (II Kings 22.13; Romans 1.18; Psalms 2.12; John 3.36; Psalms 18.35; Romans 2.4; Micah 5.15; Hebrews 10.30; Joel 2.13; Titus 3.5; I Samuel 15.23; Matthew 25.12; Ezekiel 20.40; Acts 10.34-35; Genesis 6.6-7; Revelation 20.11-15; Isaiah 25.9; II Peter 3.9). The common denominator is always sin. God is consistently opposed to those who persist in sin and is consistently embracing of those who don't. According to the Bible, there is one God, and he does not change (Malachi 3.6; Hebrews 13.8). He is the Lord of all, loving, complex, and incomprehensible from Genesis through Revelation (Job 5.9; 11.7; Isaiah 40.28; 55.9; Romans 11.33; I Corinthians 2.16).

Experts do not seem to agree on the basic nature of Aten either. Some say that Aten is nothing like the God of the Bible because Yahweh was jealous, demanding, and pitiless.[407] Yet, in much the same way, to some, Aten and Atenism was cruel, overbearing, and unyielding. Atenism would not tolerate any other deity; therefore, it was closed to any dissenting opinions. To these critics, Atenism was an extremely demanding religion. The offering tables were piled high with sacrificial gifts, collected from people who were supposedly given little other choice.[408] Worship services at the temples in Akhet-Aten were held more than once a day, especially at sunrise and sunset. However, all business in Akhet-Aten was considered to be the business of Aten as well and was, therefore, conducted in the open, during the day, and in Egypt, that generally means, in the sun. Foreign heads of state, such as Assuruballit, the king of Assyria, wrote in EA 16, complaining about the fanatical demands that were being imposed on his representatives. Some kings expressed concern that their ambassadors might die of heat stroke from being made to constantly stand in the sun.[409] Many have despised the religion that Akhenaten taught. On the other hand, some say that Aten was total love and goodness, compassion and kindness. Aten was not jealous of other gods.[410] He hated no one. He was the giver of every good thing. The estimation of Aten also changes with the audience.

Some say that monotheism, polytheism, and henotheism are all concepts derived from Judeo-Christian ideology.[411] Perhaps it is never wrong to question convention, but convention isn't always wrong. Though the Roman historian and senator, Tacitus, even perceived and described the Jewish religion as monotheistic and aniconic (devoid of images for God), it's argued that monotheism is a concept not correctly understood by Bible students and/or not emphatically upheld in scripture because ancient Hebrews almost never worshiped one God exclusively; they often feared and worshiped idols, and the Bible speaks of "gods".[412] For example:

Who is like unto thee, O Lord, among the gods? (Exodus 15.11) God standeth in the congregation of the mighty; he judgeth among the gods. (Psalms 82.1) Among the gods there is none like unto thee, O Lord; (Psalms 86.8)

However, most Bible students understand that instructive verses such as these simply acknowledge the fact that a belief in multiple gods was rampant among ancient nations, sadly, including Israel. Regardless of how many people believe in a falsehood, it remains false. Popular opinion cannot/does not have the power to make any error correct; it can only make error popular. Belief in multiple gods was popular for thousands of years in cultures worldwide, but that never made polytheism a correct belief system. To a student of the Bible, the above verses, and others like them, were meant to appeal to reason, to remind people who were being tempted to believe in false gods that there is a real God, to urge them to compare "apples to oranges," to apply logic to superstition, and to choose to accept that only one God was not like the others, only one God is real and deserves worship. Isaiah argued the foolishness of superstition and idolatry in this way:

The carpenter stretcheth out his rule; he marketh it out with a line; he fitteth it with planes, and he marketh it out with the compass, and maketh it after the figure of a man, according to the beauty of a man; that it may remain in the house. He heweth him down cedars, and taketh the cypress and the oak, which he strengtheneth for himself among the trees of the forest: he planteth an ash, and the rain doth nourish it. Then shall it be for a man to burn: for he will take thereof, and warm himself; yea, he kindleth it, and baketh bread; yea, he maketh a god, and worshippeth it; he maketh it a graven image, and falleth down thereto. He burneth part thereof in the fire; with

171

part thereof he eateth flesh; he roasteth roast, and is satisfied: yea, he warmeth himself, and saith, Aha, I am warm, I have seen the fire: And the residue thereof he maketh a god, even his graven image: he falleth down unto it, and worshippeth it, and prayeth unto it, and saith, Deliver me; for thou art my god. (Isaiah 44.13-17)

What profited the graven image that the maker thereof hath graven it; the molten image, and a teacher of lies, that the maker of his work trusteth therein, to make dumb idols? Woe unto him that saith to the wood, Awake; to the dumb stone, Arise, it shall teach! Behold, it is laid over with gold and silver, and there is no breath at all in the midst of it. (Habakkuk 2.18-19)

According to the monotheistic teaching of scripture, that upholds the autonomy of one God, it is wrong to consider anything to be a deity like God (I Corinthians 8.5-6). Error should never be mistaken for truth; and sin should never be mistaken for righteousness (Isaiah 5.20). The Bible defines sin in this way: "Sin is the transgression of the law" (I John 3.4). The Law of Moses said, "Thou shalt have no other gods before me" (Exodus 20.3). Therefore, certainly for the Hebrews, having other gods was sin. Exodus 20.3, however, should not be taken to mean that other gods existed, were ever real, and/or that God was demanding preeminence among them, but rather that God refuses to be insulted by being held in the company of figments of imagination. From a biblical perspective, I AM *is*; he refuses to share his glory with that which is not (Leviticus 26.30). Just because some Hebrews of the Old Testament sinned by following after the false gods of the peoples around them does not mean that those deities were ever real or deserving of anyone's worship.

A prime example that clarifies the Bible's position on the difference between false gods and the one real God is found in I Kings 18. In this chapter, Elijah poses a contest between Baal and the God of the Bible to settle the question: which god is deserving of worship and obedience? According to scripture, Hebrews needed to be shown that Baal did not exist; he was the product of myth and superstition; Baal was a false god.

And Elijah came unto all the people, and said, How long halt ye between two opinions? if the Lord be God, follow him: but if Baal, then follow him. And the people answered him not a word. Then said Elijah unto the people, I, even I only, remain a prophet of the Lord; but Baal's prophets are four hundred and fifty men. Let them therefore give us two bullocks; and let them choose one bullock for themselves, and cut it in pieces, and lay it on wood, and put no fire under: and I will dress the other bullock, and lay it on wood, and put no fire under: And call ye on the name of your gods, and I will call on the name of the Lord: and the God that answereth by fire, let him be God. And all the people answered and said, It is well spoken. And Elijah said unto the prophets of Baal, Choose you one bullock for yourselves, and dress it first; for ye are many; and call on the name of your gods, but put no fire under.

And they took the bullock which was given them, and they dressed it, and called on the name of Baal from morning even until noon, saying, O Baal, hear us. But there was no voice, nor any that answered. And they leaped upon the altar which was made.

And it came to pass at noon, that Elijah mocked them, and said, Cry aloud: for he is a god; either he is talking, or he is pursuing, or he is in a journey, or peradventure he sleepeth, and must be awaked.

And they cried aloud, and cut themselves . . . with knives and lancets, till the blood gushed out upon them. And it came to pass, when midday was past, and they prophesied until the time of the offering of the evening sacrifice, that there was neither voice, nor any to answer, nor any that regarded.

And Elijah said unto all the people, Come near unto me. And all the people came near unto him. And he repaired the altar of the Lord that was broken down. And Elijah took twelve stones, according to the number of the tribes of the sons of Jacob, unto whom the word of the Lord came, saying, Israel shall be thy name: And with the stones he built an altar in the name of the Lord: and he made a trench about the altar, as great as would contain two measures of seed.

And he put the wood in order, and cut the bullock in pieces, and laid him on the wood, and said, Fill four barrels with water, and pour it on the burnt sacrifice, and on the wood. And he said, Do it the second time. And they did it the second time. And he said, Do it the third time. And they did it the third time. And the water ran round about the altar; and he filled the trench also with water. And it came to pass at the time of the offering of the evening sacrifice, that Elijah the prophet came near, and said, Lord God of Abraham, Isaac, and of Israel, let it be known this day that thou art God in Israel, and that I am thy servant, and that I have done all these things at thy word. Hear me, O Lord, hear me, that this people may know that thou art the Lord God, and that thou hast turned their heart back again.

Then the fire of the Lord fell, and consumed the burnt sacrifice, and the wood, and the stones, and the dust, and licked up the water that was in the trench. And when all the people saw it, they fell on their faces: and they said, The Lord, he is the God; the Lord, he is the God.

And Elijah said unto them, Take the prophets of Baal; let not one of them escape. . . Elijah brought them down to the brook Kishon, and slew them there. (I Kings 18.21-40)

It is important to note that a generally accepted polytheistic convention of recognizing, honoring, and worshiping both Baal and Yahweh was not an option that was offered by Elijah. His was an "either/or" choice. Elijah was a monotheist. This passage also makes it clear that the God of Elijah was the same God as the God of Abraham, Isaac, and Israel/Jacob. Therefore, this was also the same God of the Bible who was the God of Joseph, of Moses, and of Christ (Matthew 17.2-3).

In this contest, the Bible maintains, Baal did not respond because Baal did not exist. He had never existed, and regardless of the fervor or sincerity or volume of his worshipers, no amount of frenzy would/could make Baal real. He was a false god, and his worshipers were worshipping him in vain (Matthew 15.9).

Similarly, in Ephesus, the worshippers of Diana/Artemis worked themselves into a religious frenzy. Paul had been living in Ephesus and teaching in the School of Tyrannus for two years (Acts 19.9-10). Obviously, Paul's teaching was having a negative effect on the profits of idol-makers in that great city.

. . . there arose no small stir about that way. For a certain man named Demetrius, a silversmith, which made silver shrines for Diana, brought no small gain unto the craftsmen; Whom he called together with the workmen of like occupation, and said, Sirs, ye know that by this craft we have our wealth. Moreover ye see and hear, that . . . throughout all Asia, this Paul hath persuaded and turned away much people, saying that they be no gods, which are made with hands: So that not only this our craft is in danger to be set at nought; but also that the temple of the great goddess Diana should be despised, and her magnificence should be destroyed, whom all Asia and the world worshippeth. And when they heard these sayings, they were full of wrath, and cried out, saying, Great is Diana of the Ephesians.

And the whole city was filled with confusion: and having caught Gaius and Aristarchus, men of Macedonia, Paul's companions in travel, they rushed with one accord into the theatre. . . . Some therefore cried one thing, and some another: for the assembly was confused; and the more part knew not wherefore they were come together . . . all with one voice about the space of two hours cried out, Great is Diana of the Ephesians. (Acts 19.23-34)

According to his accusers, Paul was teaching that idols and the gods they represent, not just Diana/Artemis, but the entire polytheistic Greco-Roman pantheon were "no gods." Paul's adversaries were likely telling the truth because this was much the same message that Paul wrote in Galatians 4.8. No amount of shouting or anger or force of emotion would/could make Diana exist. According to the Bible, Diana was no god; she was never real. Matthew 15.9 advises that worshipping Diana was a waste of time and tribute.

Paul's message was effective, but it was far from popular it upset the Ephesians' economy, their power scaffold, their mythology, and their patriotism. Like Egyptians in the days of Akhenaten, the Ephesians were greatly opposed to changing their commerce, their culture, or their religion even if it meant turning away from false ideas, embracing truth, and turning to the one God who is real. Ephesians 4 makes it clear that Paul, like Akhenaten, taught that there is one God (Ephesians 4.4-6). Furthermore, Paul taught salvation through the God of the Bible, the God of Abraham (Acts 13.26).

However, unlike Elijah, the apostle Paul didn't take a sword to those in Ephesus or in other places where people were opposed to his message. Yet, it was not God who was different; it was the circumstance. Elijah was upholding a contract that the Hebrew people had already entered with God (Exodus 19.4-8). They were in violation of that contract, and the consequences were severe. Paul and Akhenaten, on the other hand, were inviting people to form a relationship with God. According to scripture, people in both ancient Egypt and in Ephesus were alienated from God; they did not have a mutual understanding with God (Ephesians 4.18).[413] A means of attaining a level of righteousness was being made available to both Egyptians in Akhet-Aten and to Gentiles living in Ephesus. Both groups were being called to obey a teaching; however, the specifics of the teaching in the two places were inherently different. Paul explained in Athens:

> God that made the world and all things therein, seeing that he . . . giveth to all life, and breath, and all things; And hath made of one blood all nations of men for to dwell on all the face of the earth, and hath determined the times before appointed, and the bounds of their habitation; That they should seek the Lord, if haply they might feel after him, and find him, . . . [for] we ought not to think that the Godhead is like unto gold, or silver, or stone, graven by art and man's device. And the times of this ignorance God winked at; but now commandeth all men every where to repent: Because he hath appointed a day, in the which he will judge the world in righteousness by that man whom he hath ordained; whereof he hath given assurance unto all men, in that he hath raised him from the dead. (Acts 17.24-31)

There was a different set of expectations from the universal God for non-Hebrews who lived in the days of the Old Covenant. God did not expect Egyptians living in Akhet-Aten to keep the Law of Moses. In "the times before appointed," God, just as Akhenaten was advocating, expected men to look beyond graven images and the "ignorance" of superstitions, in order to discover the one true and living God. Neither did God expect Gentiles, living in Ephesus or Athens, to obey the Law of Moses either. By the time of Paul, Christ's death had fulfilled the contract of the Law of Moses, "For where a testament is, there must also of necessity be the death of the testator" (Hebrews 9.16). Therefore, since the contract was satisfied, the Law of Moses was no longer binding on anyone, Jew or Greek (Romans 8.2). Upon Christ's resurrection, a new testament was validated (Hebrews 9.15). The same God issued a new contract; its scope was new—including both Hebrews and non-Hebrews, and its commandments were new. It was this new, universal covenant, this New Testament that Paul taught; but since Christ had not yet come, died, or resurrected, Akhenaten's teaching could not have been the same message as Paul's (Zechariah 9.10).

This idea makes understanding the teaching of Akhenaten especially compelling. If Akhenaten was brokering a relationship between Egyptians and the God of the Bible, then in Amarna may be found extra-biblical instruction in righteousness provided to non-Hebrews, living outside the Law of Moses, in the days of the Old Testament. Of course, Akhenaten's teaching would have been nullified in the death of Christ because the promise, fulfilled in Christ, was to all people (Genesis 22.18; Luke 2.10-11). Unlike the limited teaching of Akhenaten, which would not have superseded the Law of Moses, especially in the case of Hebrews; Paul's message applied to all men everywhere (Acts 17.30). Still, the thought that extra insight into God's relationship with non-Hebrews in the days of the Law of Moses makes the study of the Amarna period beyond compelling!

Incidentally, also like Ephesus, much of the objection to religious reform among Egyptians in the days of Akhenaten was financial. The priesthoods of the vast number of deities recognized and worshiped in ancient Egypt represented a significant percentage of the workforce. When Akhenaten enacted his one-god religion, suddenly a good number of people were out of a job. Likewise, the military was idle. Akhenaten's answer to these economic issues was restructuring taxes to include taxes on temples and reassigning duty to those unemployed segments of Egyptian domestic society. Akhenaten set the priests to work in other occupations, including working in quarries, and he employed the military in the building of Akhet-Aten.[414] Of course, Akhenaten, as pharaoh, was well within his rights to make such assignments. The authority of the pharaoh was absolute. Therefore, if the pharaoh *was* the law, it is difficult to understand why Akhenaten was ever called a criminal.[415] Every person in Egyptian society, regardless of status, was merely a servant of the king. Beyond their livelihoods, their very lives were held at the whim of a pharaoh's resolution. Though he certainly held the power not to be, Akhenaten was much more merciful to false prophets and priests than was Elijah or Josiah.

Consistently, according to the Bible, righteousness recognizes one God only. Referring back to Paul's discussion in Romans, even people outside the Law of Moses were "without excuse" for the "unrighteousness" of "their vain imaginings." Exchanging the glory of God and the Godhead for any other concept was considered universally sinful by the God of the Bible. Moses said in the Deuteronomy, "Know therefore this day, and consider it in thine heart, that the Lord he is God in heaven above, and upon the earth beneath: there is none else" (Deuteronomy 4.39). God presents as fact that he is the only God and there is no other (Isaiah 45.22). Satan may have introduced the notion that there are "gods;" but God defines monotheism, polytheism, and henotheism (Genesis 3.5).

Yet, there are also those who contend that, in the Bible, there is not one God, but three: the Father, the Son, and the Holy Spirit. God cannot be quantified by fleshly limitations; he is not a human being; he is a heavenly being (Deuteronomy 32.40; Isaiah 55.8-9). God is a spirit and, to a point, he is incomprehensible to our understanding (John 4.24; Job 11.7; Ecclesiastes 3.11; Isaiah 40.28; I Corinthians 2.16). Nevertheless, in the Bible, God seems to reveal himself as a multifaceted entity. One of the earliest names for God, Elohiym, is a plural name.[416] From the very beginning, "God (one God/singular) said, Let us (plural) make man (plural and singular) in our (plural) image (singular), after our (plural) likeness (singular)" (Genesis 1.26). Many ancient peoples, including the Egyptians, believed that God was infinitely faceted; perhaps he is.[417] However, most students of the Bible recognize three personalities that comprise God; these three are completely separate but completely united. The New Testament puts it this way:

> There is one body, and one Spirit [the Holy Spirit], even as ye are called in one hope of your
> calling; One Lord [Jesus], one faith, one baptism, One God and Father of all, who is above all,
> and through all, and in you all. (Ephesians 4.4-6)

They (the Father, Jesus, and the Holy Spirit), together and individually, are one God; they are the Godhead (Deuteronomy 6.4; John 10.30; Acts 17.29; Colossians 2.9). They cannot be divided. There is only one God. The Old Testament agrees: "Have we not all one father? Hath not one God created us?" (Malachi 2.10).

On the other hand, there are those who argue that Aten is not like Yahweh, the God of the Bible, because Aten is completely abstract while the God in Genesis has an image. After all, he created man in his own image (Genesis 1.27). He also walked in the Garden of Eden, walked with Enoch, Noah, Abraham, Moses, and others; therefore, he must have had "face and form" (Genesis 3.8; 5.24; 6.9; Deuteronomy 34.10).[418] However, close examination of scriptures suggests a figurative interpretation for such conceptions of God. For instance, most Bible students would contend that man is not literally made in the image of God in the sense that our physical bodies reflect the form of God. If that were the case, whose image is the correct image? Every human being's image is unique. Jesus explained that "God is a spirit" (John 4.24). God also has a soul (Leviticus 26.11-12, 30; Isaiah 1.14; 42.1; Jeremiah 5.9, 29; 6.8; Matthew 12.18; Hebrews 10.38). Therefore, man probably took on "the image of God," became a being like God, when God "breathed into his nostrils the breath of life, and man became a living soul" (Genesis 2.7). We are eternal beings—like God; ancient Egyptians, perhaps more than any other people, embraced this understanding. Furthermore, Adam and Eve heard "the *voice* of the Lord God walking in the garden in the cool of the day"; this is odd phrasing if God routinely, physically walked in the garden. However, God did speak to Adam and Eve (Genesis 3.9-13). In much the same way, "walking with God" is not taken as a literal concept either. It is a way of saying that the faithful patriarchs were careful to conduct themselves in accordance with God's will. Both God and Abraham perhaps clarified the expression when it was explained that Abraham walked "before" God; aware of the observance of God,

Abraham carefully chose his steps (Genesis 17.1; 24.40). Akhenaten was also keenly aware of God's observing eye. As for Moses speaking to God "face to face," this too is probably figurative. On the one occasion when Moses specifically asked to see God, God made it clear that, "Thou canst not see my face: for there shall no man see me, and live" (Exodus 33.20).

Yet, perhaps Akhenaten did "see" God or an angel representing God. Often in scripture heavenly beings are described as shining with an otherworldly bright light. The seraphim that Isaiah and Ezekiel saw in their visions of God were creatures made of fire; the angel in the burning bush was likely this same type of being (Isaiah 6.2-6; Ezekiel 1.5-13; Exodus 3.2). "His countenance was like lightning," is the description given of the angel who was sent to the tomb of Jesus (Matthew 28.3). The face of Moses, reportedly, "shone" after his close encounter with God (Exodus 34.29-30). Jesus' "face did shine as the sun, and his raiment was white as the light," is the wording given for the occasion when a glimpse of Christ's heavenly glory was revealed during his transfiguration (Matthew 17.2). A blinding light was also part of Paul's convergence with Christ (Acts 9.3-8). In that bright light that shone at midday (at the Aten of the day) on the road to Damascus, the Lord also spoke to Paul (Acts 26.12-14). Likewise, if Akhenaten encountered such a heavenly being, his many references to the light of the Aten would have further context.

How did Akhenaten come to his uncanny understanding of God? Perhaps his knowledge came from God himself. After all, Akhenaten claimed to have heard the voice of God, "I am strengthened at the sound of thy voice!"[419] Furthermore, his description of the experience as a "sweet, breezelike voice" is very like that of Elijah who said the voice of God was a "still small voice" (I Kings 19.12).[420] Some dismiss such assertions as lies or madness.[421] However, Akhenaten lived in a transitional age between the Patriarchal Dispensation and the days of the prophets. According to the Bible, during the Patriarchal Age, God spoke directly to individuals, especially to patriarchs, the father figures of their families. Even in the days when God usually communicated his messages through prophets, there were exceptions.[422] If God spoke to Akhenaten, it would not have been the first time that God communicated with a pharaoh.[423] Sometimes God sent prophetic dreams and visions. Perhaps it was through such method that it was revealed to Akhenaten where to build Akhet-Aten. After all, "his courtiers proclaimed that 'it was the Aten which had put such thoughts into the king's mind.'"[424] God also got his message across to pharaohs in the days of Abraham, Joseph, and Moses (Genesis 12.17-19; 41.1-16; Exodus 5-14). Nor would it be the last time that God would speak to a king of Egypt:

> Necho king of Egypt came up to fight against Charchemish by Euphrates: and Josiah went out against him. But he sent ambassadors to him, saying, What have I to do with thee, thou king of Judah? I come not against thee this day, . . . for God commanded me to make haste: forbear thee from meddling with God, who is with me, that he destroy thee not.

> Nevertheless Josiah would not turn his face from him, but disguised himself, that he might fight with him, and hearkened not unto the words of Necho from the mouth of God, and came to fight in the valley of Megiddo. (I Chronicles 35.20-22)

It is highly unlikely that Akhenaten had access to the Law of Moses, which was delivered to Hebrews on Mount Sinai. Furthermore, under the theory in this book, the notion espoused by various philosophers over the last two centuries who claim that Akhenaten was the source of the Mosaical Law is just not possible.[425] Even if Akhenaten possessed a copy of the laws from Mount Sinai, the Law of Moses would not have applied to Akhenaten or to Egypt. The old covenant was strictly an agreement between God and Israel (Jeremiah 34.13). However, that does not mean that God did not have any kind of expectations for, or relationship with, non-Hebrews or "Gentiles." Again, the book of Romans says, "when the Gentiles, which have not the law, do by nature the things contained in the law, these, having not the law, are a law unto themselves"; and God " . . . in times past suffered all nations to walk in their own ways" (Romans 2.14; Acts 14.16).

Nevertheless, from the day that Adam and Eve ate fruit from the tree of the knowledge of good and evil, human beings have possessed an innate sense of good and bad (Genesis 3). Therefore, God has always expected and required a certain level of knowledge, behavior, and respect from all mankind (Genesis 6.5-6, 11).

Certainly, aspects of the Adamic and Noahic Covenants were universal and perpetual (Genesis 1.26-30; 2.16-17, 24; 9.4-17). In fact, certain stipulations of the Noahic Covenant were specified and still considered "necessary" in Acts 15.28-29.[426] It has always been expected of man to position God and his will in the proper place of honor that is deserved, to live civilly with fellow human beings, and to revere blood.

This is part of why God was so angry with Job's friends. God said to Eliphaz the Temanite:

> My wrath is kindled against thee, and against thy two friends: for ye have not spoken of me the thing that is right, as my servant Job hath. Therefore take unto you now seven bullocks and seven rams, and go to my servant Job, and offer up for yourselves a burnt offering; and my servant Job shall pray for you: for him will I accept: lest I deal with you after your folly, in that ye have not spoken of me the thing which is right, like my servant Job. (Job 42.7-8)

God was highly displeased by the ignorance of this Temanite, who was probably from Edom and not truly Hebrew. God was also unhappy with Bildad the Shuhite and with Zophar the Naamathite (Job 2.11; Genesis 36.11, 16). God expected better of these non-Hebrews who professed to believe in him. God also sent Jonah to preach repentance to Ninevites (Jonah 1.2). Ninevites were not Hebrews; God didn't subject them to the Law of Moses. Yet, God was so displeased with the Ninevites' behavior, he was ready to destroy them. Obviously, they were not living up to an acceptable standard. They must have known better! The contrition of Nineveh was tantamount to admission of guilt (Jonah 3.5). All of these offered "acts worthy of repentance" (Luke 3.8).

Some concede that Akhenaten's God had much in common with the God of the Bible yet wonder how this can be since Akhenaten lived hundreds of years before some experts place the earliest copies of the scriptures.[427] What did Akhenaten seem to understand about God that the scriptures also indicate?

Akhenaten marked his city with numerous imposing boundary stelae; some are twenty-six feet tall! Most are severely weathered and barely legible.[428] However, just from the proclamation on one surviving boundary stela, much can still be learned about Akhenaten's understanding of the God he worshiped.

Boundary Stelae of Akhet-Aten

Top of a Boundary Stela

Year 5, Month 8, Day 13

(Salutation to God:)

May the Good God live who delights in Truth,

Lord of Heaven and Lord of Earth,

Aten, the Living, the Great, Illuminating the Two Lands!

May the Father live, divine and royal,

Re-Harakhte, Rejoicing in the Horizon in his aspect of the Light which is in the sundisk

Who lives for ever and ever Aten, the Great,

Who is in jubilee within the temple of the Aten in Akhetaten [Akhet-Aten]!

(Address to the pharaoh:)

And May the Horus live, Strong Bull beloved of Aten;

He of the Two Ladies, Great of kingship in Akhetaten;

Horus of Gold, Upholding the Name of the Aten;

The King of Upper and Lower Egypt, Living in Truth, Lord of the Two Lands,

Neferkheperure, Wa'enre (Good like the Forms of Re, the Only One of Re)

The Son of Re Living in Truth,

Lord of Crowns, Akhenaten (the Glorified Spirit of the Aten),

Great in his Duration, Living for Ever and Always.

The Good God,

Unique one of Re, whose beauty the Aten created,

Truly excellent in mind to his Maker,

Contenting Him with what his spirit desires,

Doing service to Him who begot him,

Administering the land for Him who put him upon his throne,

Provisioning his eternal home with very many things,

Upholding the Aten and magnifying His name,

Causing the Earth to belong to its Maker . . .

(Address to Nefertiti:)

And the Heiress,

Great in the Palace,

Fair of Face,

Adorned with the Double Plumes,

Mistress of Happiness,

Endowed with Favours [sic],

At hearing whose voice the King rejoices,

The Chief Wife of the King,

His beloved,

Lady of the Two Lands,

Neferneferuaten-Nefertiti (Good like the Beauty of the Aten: A Beautiful Woman Comes)

May she live for Ever and Always.

(Description of the event:)

His Majesty mounted a great chariot of electrum, like the Aten when He rises on the horizon and fills the land with His love, and took a goodly road to Akhetaten (Akhet-Aten), a place of origin which [the Aten] had created for Himself that he might be happy therein. It was His son Wa'enre who founded it for Him as His monument when His Father commanded him to make it. Heaven was joyful, the earth was glad, every heart was filled with delight when they beheld him.

(Further down:)

The great and living Aten . . . ordaining life, vigorously alive, my Father . . . my wall of millions of cubits, my reminder of Eternity, my witness of what is eternal, who fashions Himself with His two hands, whom no craftsman has devised, who is established in rising and setting each day ceaselessly. Whether He is in heaven or earth, every eye beholds Him without [hindrance] while He fills the land with His rays and makes everyone to live. With seeing whom my eyes are satisfied daily when He rises in this temple of the Aten at Akhetaten and fills it with His own self by means of His rays, beauteous with love, and embraces me with them in life and power for ever and ever.[429]

From just the salutation we learn that goodness and truth are integral components of Akhenaten's God. He is universal, the only Lord of Heaven and Earth. He is living and great. He gives light to people. He is a father who is God and King. In a distant, yet perpetually just-beyond-reach place, he rejoices. He is brightness, like the sun. He is eternal. Akhenaten is overjoyed to think that his God accepts the worship offered to him in the temple at Akhet-Aten. Can the same attributes describe the God of the Bible?

Is God good? David thought so. In Psalms 25, he says:

Good and upright is the Lord: therefore will he teach sinners in the way. . . . All the paths of the Lord are mercy and truth . . . (Psalms 25.8-10).

Here, like Akhenaten, David praises God for his goodness and for his commitment to truth. Also similar to Akhenaten is language that encourages listeners to hear the teaching and be guided by it into the way of truth. Other passages such as Psalms 33.5; Psalms 34.8; Nahum 1.7; and Romans 2.4 stress the overwhelming goodness of the God of the Bible; and Jesus, in Matthew 19.17, went so far as to identify God as the only good being, "there is none good but one, that is, God."

Is the God of the Bible defined by truth? In Deuteronomy 32.3-4, Moses said, "I will publish the name of the Lord: ascribe ye greatness unto our God. He is the Rock, his work is perfect: for all his ways are judgment: a God of truth and without iniquity, just and right is he." God characterized himself in this way:

. . . The Lord, The Lord God, merciful and gracious, longsuffering, and abundant in goodness and truth, Keeping mercy for thousands, forgiving iniquity and transgression and sin, and that will by no means clear the guilty; visiting the iniquity of the fathers upon the children, and upon the children's children, unto the third and . . . fourth generation. (Exodus 34.6-7)

And thus, the scripture is true, "Behold therefore the goodness and severity of God" (Romans 11.22). If a more complete concept of God is a being who is both good and severe, why would Akhenaten disproportionately proclaim the goodness of God? Was Aten a different personality than Yahweh?[430]

If Aten was the God of the Bible, Akhenaten's audience knew well the severity of God. They were still recovering from the blows of the exodus. Akhenaten, then, didn't need to tell them what they already knew; he needed to help them realize the rest of God. Ancient Egyptians needed to understand that they had also experienced, and were experiencing, the ongoing blessings of God. As the Bible teaches, God's blessings are constant, like waves on the shore or rays of the sun; they continually allow life, breath, comfort, love, food, etc. God deserves to be acknowledged for the perpetual blessings he shines (John 1.16). Akhenaten hoped to help the Egyptian people to realize the same understanding that Job had of God when he said, "What? Shall we receive good at the hand of God, and shall we not receive evil?" (Job 2.10) Of course, unlike Job, ancient Egyptians had suffered "evil" at the hand of God as punishment for failing to give him the honor that he is due, for replacing him with false gods, and for their disobedience when he commanded them to let the Hebrews go.

It is significant to notice that, in his teaching, Akhenaten equated God's goodness with his truthfulness. In the exodus, ancient Egyptians had also learned, first hand, that God spoke the truth. Each plague announced by Moses materialized in just the way that God had said. God is a God who does what he says he will do. In fact, the God of the Bible is a being who cannot lie (Titus 1.2). Akhenaten, who claimed to be "living in Truth," was likely telling the truth as best as he understood it to be. If Akhenaten was a truthful prophet, then it was also true that his God was good.

Is the God of the Bible "the Lord of Heaven and Earth?" He created them (Genesis 1.1; Isaiah 45.18; Nehemiah 9.6-7). Jesus addressed God in this same way, "I thank thee, O Father, Lord of heaven and earth (Matthew 11.25; Luke 10.21). Paul, also, wanted the Athenians to recognize God in that way (Acts 17.24).

Akhenaten addressed his God as "Living;" is the God of the Bible a living God? According to Joshua, he is (Joshua 3.10). According to Jeremiah as well (Jeremiah 10.10). Paul and Barnabas wanted the Lycaonians to understand that, unlike Jupiter, God is a living God (Acts 14.15). It is a fearful thing to fall into his hands, according to the writer of Hebrews (Hebrews 10.31). Furthermore, according to I Timothy 3.15, the living God is "the pillar and ground of the truth," an intriguing correlation to both *Iwnw* and to the "holy ground" upon which Moses was instructed to remove his sandals (Exodus 3.5).

Is the God of the Bible "Great"? Yes. (Psalms 77.13; 95.3; 135.5; 145.3; Isaiah 12.6; Jeremiah 32.18)

However, is the God of the Bible "Illuminating"? Absolutely! He *is* light: "God is light, and in him is no darkness at all" (I John 1.5). He is the original source of all light. Akhenaten once said, "Your light makes eyes for everything you create"; in fact, God is light that creates.[431] According to the Bible, his creating light existed before the sun, and his supernatural light will endure forever (Genesis 1.3; 1.14; Isaiah 60.19; Revelation 22.5). Yet, God's teaching is also illuminating. David said in Psalms 119.105, "Thy word is a lamp unto my feet, and a light unto my path." Akhenaten hoped to illuminate the Two Lands with the teachings of his God. According to John, Jesus had a similar mission; the God of the Bible sent light into the world to fill the whole earth with his teachings when he sent his son to enlighten everyone who will comprehend what he has said (John 1.1-9).

Is the God of the Bible both divine and royal? David says, "For the Lord is a great God, and a great King above all gods" (Psalms 95.3). Moses says, "The Lord shall reign for ever and ever" (Exodus 15.18). I Timothy 1.17 says, "unto the King eternal, immortal, invisible, the only wise God, be honor and glory for ever and ever. Amen." And Revelation proclaims, ". . . the Lord God omnipotent reigneth" (Revelation 19.6).

Is the God of the Bible eternal, one "Who lives for ever and ever"? According to Moses he is (Deuteronomy 33.27). Other verses that point to the eternal nature of God are Romans 1.20; II Corinthians 4.18; 5.1; I Timothy 1.17; Hebrews 9.14; I Peter 5.10; and Revelation 1.8.

In fact, the God of the Bible has so much in common with the God of Akhenaten, perhaps it would be more instructive to look for ways in which they differ. For instance, is the God of the Bible an entity "Rejoicing in the Horizon"? Not literally, no, God does not live on the horizon. However, Akhenaten did not limit the existence of Aten to the horizon either. Certain language used by Akhenaten suggests that Aten was omnipresent; he "fills the land" and inhabits both heaven and earth. Jesus described God expressing joy in a similar way in Luke 15.10, "Likewise, I say unto you, there is joy in the presence of the angels of God over one sinner that repenteth." Though many have misinterpreted this verse to mean that the angels in heaven rejoice when a sinner repents; perhaps they do, but that is probably not the correct picture. There is rejoicing "in the *presence* of the angels"; angels compose the audience, but it is God who is "rejoicing in the horizon"—in that distant place just beyond our reach but that, through the eyes of faith, we see.

Is the God of the Bible the sun; does he have rays? Of course not. According to the Bible, the sun is nothing more than a created thing, a "great light" that God made "to divide the day from the night" and to mark time (Genesis 1.14). Perhaps in that sense, God has rays; the rays of the sun that we see and enjoy are his rays because they belong to God; he made them. Intriguingly, Akhenaten referred to the high priest in his Aten priesthood as "He who sees the Great One."[432] However, anyone who isn't blind sees the sun, therefore "the Great One" must not, literally, be the sun because only certain people could "see" Aten. Nevertheless, in the same poetic sense that Akhenaten identifies his God with the sun, so does scripture:

"The Lord is my light and my salvation" (Psalms 27.1)

"For the Lord God is a sun and shield" (Psalms 84.11)

"Arise, shine; for thy light is come, and the glory of the Lord is risen upon thee" (Isaiah 60.1)

" . . . Sun of righteousness arise. . .;" (Malachi 4.2) "[God dwells] in the light which no man can approach unto; whom no man hath seen, nor can see" (I Timothy 6.16)

Moses even used metaphor to depict God as the sun with hands:

> And he said, The Lord came from Sinai, and rose up from Seir unto them; he shined forth from
> mount Paran, and . . . from his right hand went a fiery law for them. (Deuteronomy 33.2)

Likewise, Akhenaten did not literally believe that his God was the sun in the sky any more than he literally believed that Aten had "two hands." Scriptures often speak of God's hands and arms, and the famous benediction in Numbers beseeches God's face, like the sun, to "shine upon thee" (Exodus 6.6; Isaiah 40.10; Deuteronomy 33.27; II Chronicles 6.4; Job 5.18; 34.19; Psalms 95.5; 111.7; Numbers 6.25). Like the biblical writers, Akhenaten understood metaphor. He used the device again on this same stela when he referred to Aten as a "wall of millions of cubits," reminiscent of metaphors in scripture comparing God to a fortress or a mighty tower (Psalms 18.2; 144.2; Jeremiah 16.19). It is readily understood that writers of scripture didn't literally consider God to be a rock, a wall, a tower, etc. Why, then, is Akhenaten not granted the same benefit?

It would be easy to understand how the sun standing still would have made a nearly irresistible focal point for Akhenaten's expression. Nevertheless, in his many references to the sun, the pharaoh was speaking figuratively. In fact, the sun had been one of the earliest, if not the earliest, symbols for deity in Egypt.[433] Therefore, if Akhenaten was rejecting traditional Egyptian religion, why would he embrace the sun, Egypt's most traditional god? Significantly, however, the example set by Akhenaten's intentions and his sentiments sounds very much like those expressed by Malachi:

> For from the rising of the sun even unto the going down of the same my name shall be great
> among the Gentiles; and in every place incense shall be offered unto my name, and a pure
> offering: for my name shall be great among the heathen, saith the Lord of hosts. (Malachi 1.11)

According to the prophecy of this passage, a day would come when people in many nations would recognize the God of the Bible as God. The fulfillment of these words begins in the book of Acts and can be seen throughout the rest of the New Testament. Akhenaten was not alone.

Furthermore, other poets have personified the sun to represent God:

> Sun of my soul, Thou savior dear,
> It is not night if Thou be near
> O may no earth-born cloud arise
> To hide Thee from Thy servant's eyes.

John Keble is not accused of worshiping the sun in his metaphorical lyrics. Neither is Anna Barbauld:

> Again the Lord of light and life awakes the kindling ray,
> Unseals the eyelids of the morn, and pours increasing day.
> O what a night was that which wrapt the heathen world in gloom!
> O what a Sun which rose this day triumphant from the tomb!
> This day be grateful homage paid, and loud hosannas sung;
> Let gladness dwell in every heart,
> And praise on ev'ry tongue.
> Ten thousand different lips shall join
> To hail this welcome morn,
> Which scatters blessings from its wings
> To nations yet unborn.

"There Is Sunshine in My Soul," by E. E. Hewitt, and "Heavenly Sunlight," by H. J. Zelley are just a couple more examples of poetic expression that, hundreds of years from now, might be taken to suggest that modern-day worshippers were worshipping the sun.[434] However, that would not be a correct assumption.

Yet, what about the second part of the salutation on Akhet-Aten's boundary stela, the part that addresses Akhenaten himself? Many have believed that in these inscriptions the pharaoh is glorifying himself, certainly phrases such as "The Son of Re . . . who begot him," "The Good God," and "Unique one of Re," add to this impression. However, compare the words of David, another king:

. . . The kings of the earth set themselves,

> and the rulers take counsel together, against the Lord, and against his anointed,

. . . the Lord hath said unto me,

Thou art my Son; this day have I begotten thee.

Ask of me, and I shall give thee the heathen

> for thine inheritance, and the uttermost parts of the earth for thy possession.

Thou shalt break them with a rod of iron;

> thou shalt dash them in pieces like a potter's vessel.

Be wise now therefore, O ye kings: be instructed, ye judges of the earth.

Serve the Lord with fear, and rejoice with trembling.

Kiss the Son, lest he be angry, and ye perish from the way, when his wrath is kindled but a little.

Blessed are all they that put their trust in him. (Psalms 2)

Did David, the Lord's anointed (an expression used to identify a king), consider himself to be, literally, the begotten Son of God? (I Samuel 16.13; Psalms 2.7). Did David expect his subjects to kiss him and to consider themselves blessed just because they had put their trust in him? No, David was a king and he expected a certain amount of decorum, but he was also a poet and a prophet. Though he may have used poetic phrases like these to loosely describe himself, they were more intended as statements prophesying Christ as is made clear in Acts 13.33 and in Hebrews 1.5 and again in 5.5. David may have been a son of God, in a general sense, but he is not the begotten son of God because Jesus was the *only* begotten son (John 1.14, 18; 3.16). However, it is doubtful that David may have completely understood what he was prophesying. It seems that prophecy is often not completely understood until it is fulfilled.

Is it possible that Akhenaten was also prophesying about things he didn't completely understand either? Is it possible that, like David, while Akhenaten was loosely describing himself, through poetic language he, too, was prophesying about Christ? Christ, the Messiah, was never promised to the Hebrews alone. He was always intended to be a blessing to all nations.

Christ is the Son of "Re," of God the Father (Mark 1.1).

Christ is full of truth, not only living in truth; he *is* "Truth" (John 1.14; 14.6).

Christ is the "Lord of Crowns" (Revelation 19.12).

Like the "Glorified Spirit of the Aten/Yahweh," in John 13.31, Jesus considered himself glorified on that particular occasion because he had been selected as the ultimate Passover lamb, worthy of sacrifice; but Jesus was glorified before the world was made, and his glory continues forever and ever (John 17.5; Galatians 1.3-5; Hebrews 13.21; Revelation 5.11-14). Acts 10.38 also speaks of God endowing Christ with his Holy Spirit. According to Romans15.12, the Spirit of the Lord was prophesied to glorify Christ in Isaiah, hundreds of years before he was even born: "And there shall come forth a rod out of the stem of Jesse, and a Branch shall grow out of his roots: And the spirit of the Lord shall rest upon him, the spirit of wisdom and understanding, the spirit of counsel and might, the spirit of knowledge and of the fear of the Lord" (Isaiah 11.1-2).

Christ is "Great in his Duration, Living for Ever and Always"; he is eternal and the giver of eternal life (Isaiah 9.6; Micah 5.2; John 8.58; Hebrews 13.8; Revelation 22.13; John 1.4; 3.16; 10.10; 14.6; Romans 6.22-23; Titus 1.2; 3.7; I John 2.25).

Christ is "The Good God": "As ye have therefore received Christ Jesus the Lord, so walk ye in him . . . for in him dwelleth all the fullness of the Godhead, bodily" (Colossians 2.6-9; John 1.1; 10.30; I Timothy 3.16).

Christ is "Unique" and beautiful (John 6.68,12.32; Acts 4.12; Hebrews 1.13; Song of Solomon 5.10-16).

Christ is "excellent in mind" (Isaiah 11.2; Matthew 13.54; Colossians 2.3). On numerous occasions, academic and religious leaders tried to outwit Jesus and failed (Matthew 22.34-46; Mark 10.2; Luke 10.25-37; 11.15-20; 20.22-25; John 8.3-8).

His "Maker" was contented with Christ, and so was the Spirit (Mark 1.9-11; Luke 3.21-22).

Jesus came to do the will of the Father (Matthew 20.28; Luke 2.49; 22.42; John 4.34).

Christ administers justice for God, "who put him upon his throne" (Isaiah 9.6-7; Zechariah 9.10; Matthew 28.18; John 18.36; Ephesians 1.19-22; I Peter 3.22; Hebrews 2.8, Philippians 2.9-11; Matthew 25. 31-46; John 5.22; Romans 14.10-11; II Timothy 4.1).

Christ is "provisioning his eternal home" (Psalms 23.5; John 14.1-3).

Christ magnifies God and his followers magnify Christ (Malachi 1.5-6; Philippians 1.19-21).

And, in Christ, the Earth is reconciled to its "Maker" (Daniel 9.24; II Corinthians 5.18; Ephesians 2.13-17; Colossians 1.16-20).

Furthermore, statements such as "thou art the Only One of Aten" from the tomb of Ramose the vizier, "the radiant child of Aten" from the tomb of Parennefer, a courtier, and "fair child of the Sun-disc [Sun-disk]" are possibly re-quoted prophetic observations of Christ more than they are observations about Akhenaten.[435] In the tomb of Tutu, the inscription says,

> Grant me that my eye may see him, that [my] hands may adore him, that my ear may hear his voice, that his ka may be before me without ceasing . . . .May I be one who may adore his majesty; may I be his follower. Grant that I may be satisfied with seeing thee . . . .[436]

Surely, Tutu had seen Akhenaten; he was his secretary. Could it be that he is making a petition to see someone he has never seen and yet seeks to follow?

Also, in Akhenaten's many references to rising, arising, and the resurrection of the dead, it's possible that he was speaking beyond metaphor.[437] Perhaps he, though prophecy, was given some understanding of the promise of Jesus' coming as the Christ, the Son of God, and of Christ's resurrection, which, perhaps not coincidentally coincided with the rising of the sun on that great day (Matthew 28.1-6; Mark 16.2-6; Luke 24.1-6). Perhaps he even had some insight into the day of judgment (Daniel 12.2; John 5.28-29; Acts 24.15). Consider, for instance, the following inscription from the Amarna tomb of Ay. Though, granted, Ay—based on his later words and behavior—probably did not personally subscribe to any of what he said in this tomb, the inscriptions are, nevertheless, evidence of what Akhenaten taught. In the following inscription, most consider Ay to be speaking only of the pharaoh, however, if the possibility of a broader interpretation is also allowed, as in the words of David that are both about the king and the Messiah, the resemblance to Christ is uncanny, especially when compared to Psalms 19.4-6:

> . . . thy child who came forth from thy rays. Thou assignest to him thy lifetime and thy years. Thou hearest for him that which is in his heart. He is thy beloved, thou makest him like Aten. When thou riseth, eternity is given him, when thou settest, thou givest him everlastingness. Thou begettest him in the morning like thine own forms; thou formest him as thy emanation, like Aten, ruler of truth, who came forth from eternity, son of Re, wearing his beauty, who offers to him the product of his rays . . . . Thy beloved son presents truth before thy beautiful face; thou rejoicest when thou seest him, (for) he came forth from thee; son of eternity, who came forth from Aten, spirit of his spirit, gratifying the heart of Aten. When he rises in heaven, he rejoices in his son; he embraces him with his rays; he gives to him eternity as king, like the Aten.[438]

Furthermore, the godhead that seems to have been represented in the original expanded name that Akhenaten attributed to Aten: Re-Harakhte/Horus, he-who-rejoices-in-the-horizon-in-his-name, Shu 'light' which-is-in/from-the-Sun-Disk, seems to be composed of Ra/Aten, Harakhte/Horus, and Shu. Aten, *yati* or *yata*, can be interpreted in ancient Egyptian as "father;" in fact he was referred to as "Father Aten."[439] Ra, of course, was also called "father." This is made especially clear in the expanded late name given by Akhenaten to Aten.[440] Traditionally, Horus was considered to be a son. Therefore, in Re-Harakhte, father and son are seen as one. Khepri, of the original trinity of On, was also known as "he who comes"; he was represented by a scarab which also symbolized Ra-Atum.[441] Finishing out the triad, is Shu, also called, "god of the luminous void" (Genesis 1.2).[442] Therefore, it may be that Ra-Aten (God the father), Khepri, he who comes (God the son), and Shu, (God the spirit) are all represented in this early name; they are one in Aten. The early name used by Akhenaten to designate Aten reflects a basic understanding of the nature of the God of the Bible. Nevertheless, the late name for Aten: Live Re, Ruler of the Horizon, Rejoicing in the Horizon in His Name Re, the Father, who has come as the Sun-Disk, seems to be more specific, as if Akhenaten had gained a deeper understanding of God and of his intentions. God was coming, to live as the everlasting Father, he was coming as a ruler in the name of the Father, and there would be rejoicing in the horizon. Compare this understanding to the prophecy of Isaiah, "For unto us a child is born, unto us a son is given: and the government shall be upon his shoulder: and his name shall be called Wonderful, Counselor, The mighty God, The everlasting Father, The Prince of Peace" (Isaiah 9.6). Was there rejoicing in the horizon when this verse was fulfilled? Oh yes!

> And there were in the same country shepherds abiding in the field, keeping watch over their flock by night. And, lo, the angel of the Lord came upon them, and the glory of the Lord shone round about them: and they were sore afraid. And the angel said unto them, Fear not: for, behold, I bring you good tidings of great joy, which shall be to all people. For unto you is born this day in the city of David a Saviour, which is Christ the Lord. And this shall be a sign unto you; Ye shall find the babe wrapped in swaddling clothes, lying in a manger. And suddenly there was with the angel a multitude of the heavenly host praising God, and saying, Glory to God in the highest, and on earth peace, good will toward men. (Luke 2.8-14)

To Akhenaten the late name for Aten was probably considered to be a better understanding, a better translation because in this name was a prophecy that held great hope for Akhenaten's people. Christ was coming to bring great joy to all people! He was bringing the hope of eternal life! This was a hope that ancient Egyptians, as a culture, had longed for more than any! Yet, the prophecy of God coming as Lord and bringing the hope of eternal life—as remarkable as that was—may not have been all that Akhenaten understood.

In the third section of the Akhet-Aten boundary stela, Nefertiti is addressed, leading some to speculate that Nefertiti was intended to be seen as a female deity. Yet, just as Akhenaten, on this stela, may represent a prophecy of Christ, could it be that Nefertiti also represents a prophecy of something else? Could it be that, like the beautiful relationship described between the king and his bride in the Song of Solomon, the bride of the pharaoh, Nefertiti, is prophetic of the church? Understanding Nefertiti in this symbolic way could explain curious images and references to Nefertiti on offering tables and in other religious spaces. In fact, it has been suggested that Nefertiti had an "elevated religious stature" that "should be constantly born in mind." She was not overly emphasized in her physical role as queen, but was in religious significance.[443] Numerous passages of scripture refer to the church as a bride (Isaiah 62.5; II Corinthians 11.2; Ephesians 5.22-32; Revelation 19.7; 21.2; 22.17). She is the bride of Christ, his "Chief Wife."

> The church is "the Heiress"; she is composed of heirs who will inherit salvation, eternal life with Christ (Romans 8.16-17; Galatians 3.26-29; Titus 3.3-7; Hebrews 1.13-14; 6.17-20).
> The church is "Great in the Palace," she is the holy building/palace/temple (Matthew 16.16-19; I Corinthians 3.9-16; Ephesians 2.19-22; I Peter 2.4-6 Revelation 21.3).
> The church is "Fair of Face"; in fact, she is beautiful/perfect/without spot or blemish (Psalms 149.4; Song of Solomon 4.7; 6.10; Ephesians 5.25-27; Revelation 21.2)
> The church is "Adorned with the Double Plumes," she is royal, priestly, and authoritative (Isaiah 62.1-3; I Peter 2.9-10)
> The church is the "Mistress of Happiness," she causes the bridegroom to rejoice (Psalms 19.4-5; Isaiah 61.10; Isaiah 62.5)
> She is joyful even in suffering (Acts 5.41; 16.23-25; II Corinthians 6.3-10; Philippians 4.4; I Peter 1.1-9)
> The church is "Endowed with Favours"[sic]; she has been clothed in royal garments (Psalms 132.16; Isaiah 61.10; Revelation 2.10; 3.5; 4.4; 7.9; 19.8)
> She is endowed with strength, dignity, glory, and praise (Proverbs 31.25-29; Matthew 13.43)
> She is given an everlasting name (Isaiah 56.5)
> She is given the gift of the Holy Spirit, forgiveness of sins and eternal life (Acts 2.38; Ephesians 1.7; John 10.28; Romans 2.7; Titus 1.2; I John 2.25)

The church's voice is a source of joy to God (Psalms 34.15; Song of Solomon 2.14; Isaiah 65.24; Matthew 6.8; Ephesians 5.17-20; Colossians 3.15-17; James 5.13; I Thessalonians 2.4; I Peter 3.12; Revelation 5.8; 8.3-4)

The church is Christ's beloved (John 15.9-13; Romans 1.7; 8.35; Ephesians 5.25; Colossians 3.12; II Thessalonians 2.13)

The church is "Lady of the Two Lands," "lovely lady" of heaven and earth (Ephesians 3.15; II John 1)

The church is good and beautiful, glorifying God

(Psalms 149.4; II Corinthians 3.18; Ephesians 5.27; Song of Solomon 6.10; Isaiah 62.3; Matthew 5.16; I Peter 2.12; I John 3.2; Revelation 21.2)

The church will live forever (Isaiah 9.7; Daniel 2.44; 7.14; Luke 1.33)

There is a very compelling inscription in Amarna Tomb 14, the tomb of May, concerning Nefertiti:

... great in loveliness, mistress of pleasant ceremonies, rich in possessions, the offerings to Ra in her midst; at the sight of her beauty there is rejoicing. She is lovely and beautiful; when one sees her, it is like a glimpse at heaven; her number cannot be calculated.[444]

Surely, the number of Nefertitis could be calculated; there was only one Nefertiti. These words, therefore, must be speaking about something that Nefertiti represents, something that is like heaven on earth and whose number of members is great. In Acts 2.47, the scriptures say "And the Lord added to the church daily such as should be saved." The word that is interpreted in the King James Version of the Bible as, "the church," the *ekklesia* literally means, the "called out" or the "assembly." The church is an assembly, the group of the saved, the community of saints, and in the NASB, "the church" in Acts 2.47 is translated as "their number." Furthermore, the church is described in John's glimpse of heaven as:

a great multitude, which no man could number, of all nations, and kindreds, and people, and tongues, . . . before the throne, and before the Lamb, clothed with white robes, and palms in their hands; (Revelation 7.9)

Perhaps Akhenaten had understanding that a group would one day exist to welcome faithful Egyptians among all of the world's faithful into the family of God. In fact, his boundary stelae, refer to a mysterious group of mortal rulers who stand between God and all people.[445] Could this group be the "royal priesthood," the church, described by Peter? (I Peter 2.9) Prophecy of the church was important to Akhenaten and to his people because, unlike the Law of Moses, the church would be equally open to everyone as Peter explained on the day that the church began, "the promise is unto you, and to your children, and to all that are afar off" (Acts 2.39). In the church, all are sons of God (John 1.12; Romans 8.14; Philippians 2.15; I John 3.1-20), thus, Akhenaten could eventually realize the title "Son of Atum/Son of Ra." If Akhenaten prophesied about Christ and the church, perhaps it is beyond ironic that, in light of Akhenaten's teachings, "the Lord's day," "the first day of the week," the day when Christians gather is *Sun*day, which in the original Latin was the day of the sun god (Revelation 1.10; Mark 16.2; Acts 20.7).

Akhenaten's Defaced Coffin

Silverberg said, "Inscriptions at Akhetaten speak of the religion as 'the teaching'—but the teaching, whatever it was, has not survived." Redford estimates that, in Thebes, perhaps only 15-20 percent of Akhenaten's writings remain, while in Amarna, it could be that only one percent of the inscriptions survived.[446] Yet, from the etchings on this one Amarna boundary stela, a compelling gist of the teaching is still discernable. Of course, more of Akhenaten's religion is revealed in his poems. Nevertheless, if God was instructing Akhenaten, it is intriguing to discern from the actions of the pharaoh what God may have expected of non-

Hebrews, living before Christ, who were not part of the Law of Moses. Based on the example of Akhenaten, it seems that it would have pleased God for the nations of the earth to acknowledge him and to place him in the place of honor that he deserves. It would have pleased God to be thanked and praised for the countless blessings that he pours out on all people. It would have pleased God for people to make free will offerings to express their sincerity and dedication. It would have pleased God for idols and false gods to be seen for what they truly are and to be put away. It would have pleased God for nations and individuals to treat each other civilly and fairly, and it would have pleased him if they did not interfere with the covenant that he was fulfilling with the Hebrews.

It may or may not be that God would have desired a special city and temples to be built for him in every nation. Even though Solomon's Temple was called "the house of the Lord," the God of the Bible does not live in any particular city or in "temples made with hands" (I Kings 3.1; Acts 17.24). Nevertheless, perhaps God did instruct Akhenaten to build a city. God didn't always give the same instructions to everyone. Only Noah, for instance, was instructed to build an ark (Genesis 6.14). Only Adam was expected to tend Eden (Genesis 2.15). Only Hebrew males were required physical circumcision (Genesis 17.10-14).

In other writings of Akhenaten and some of his contemporaries (probably trying to impress the king by spouting his teachings back to him), more similarities between the God of the Bible and the God of Akhenaten can be determined.

Aten	Yahweh

Created All Things

"Thou art he who createst the man-child in woman, Who makest seed in man" (Breasted, *History* 373)	". . . thou hast covered me in my mother's womb. . . . I am fearfully and wonderfully made:" (Psalms 139.13-14)
"O living Aten, . . . the maker of all things that are" (Breasted, *Records II* 405)	". . . the living God, . . . made heaven, and earth, and the sea, and all things that are the therein" (Acts 14.15)
"Thou art the maker of that which is not, maker of all things that come forth from thy mouth" (Breasted, *Records II* 415)	"For the invisible things . . . from the creation of the world are clearly seen, being understood by the things that are made" (Romans 1:20)
"Thou didst create the earth according to thy desire (Breasted, *History* 374)	"In the beginning, God created the heaven and the earth" (Genesis 1.1)

Is the Only God

"the living Sun-Disk [Aten] — there is none other than he!" (Redford, *Akhenaten* 176)	". . . the Lord he is God; there is none else beside him" (Deuteronomy 4.35)
"O living Aten, beside whom there is no other" (Breasted, *Records II* 405)	"Hear, O Israel: The Lord our God is one Lord"(Deuteronomy 6.4) "... thou art God alone" (Psalms 86.10)
"I am come with praise to Aten, the living, the only God" (Breasted, *Records II* 416)	"... there is no God else beside me; a just God and a Saviour; there is none beside me thou .
"O sole god, whose powers no other possesseth" (Breasted, *History* 374)	Look to me, and be saved, all ends of the earth: for I am God, and there is none else"

186

". . . O Lord God: for there is none like thee,
neither is there any God beside thee," (II Samuel 7.22; I Chronicles 17.20)

"There is . . . One God and Father of all, who is above all, and
through all, and in you all" (Ephesians 4.4-6)

". . . there is one God" (I Timothy 2.5)

Idols Are Nothing Like Him

"the one who built himself by himself
with his [own] hands—no craftsman
knows him!" (Redford, *Akhenaten* 175)

" . . . their graven image [is]
. . . a god that cannot save"
(Isaiah 45.20)

" . . . every founder is confounded by
the graven image: for his molten image
is falsehood, and there is no breath in
them. They are vanity, the work of
errors . . . they shall perish"
(Jeremiah 51.17-18)

" . . . we ought not to think that the
Godhead is like unto gold, or silver, or
stone, graven by art and man's device"
(Acts 17.29)

Is the Universal God

"Whether he is in heaven or in earth,
every eye seeth him without failing,
while he fills the land with his beams
and makes every face to live" (Silverberg 63)

"O sun of day, the fear of every distant
land. Thou makest [also] their life"
(Breasted, *History* 374)

"Behold he cometh with clouds;
and every eye shall see him" (Revelation 1.7)

"All nations . . . shall come and
worship before thee, O Lord" (Psalms 86.9)

". . . all the people of the earth may
know that the Lord is God, and that
there is none else" (I Kings 8.60)

"The world is in thy hand" (Breasted, *History* 328)

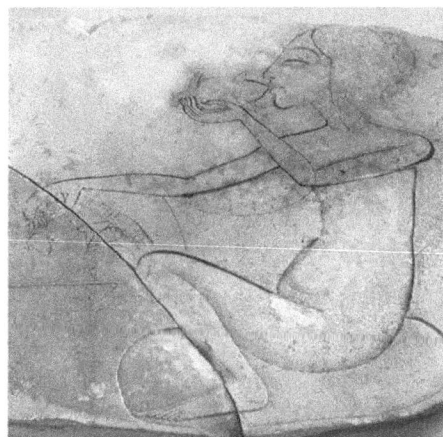

187

"Thy rays, they encompass all lands, even all thou hast made" (Silverberg 197) All [lands], all countries, . . . [come] bearing their impost, their tribute upon their backs, [for] him who bemakes their life" (Breasted, *History* 393)

"For from the rising of the sun even unto going down of the same my name shall be great among the Gentiles; and in every place incense shall be offered unto my name, and a pure offering: for my name shall be great among the heathen, saith the Lord of hosts" (Malachi 1.11)

Is the Giver of Life

"he who decrees life, the lord of sunbeams, maker of brightness'; he 'causes everyone [to live], and people are never sated with seeing him" (Redford, *Akhenaten* 176)

"And the Lord God formed man of the dust of the ground, and breathed into his nostrils the breath of life; and man became a living soul" (Genesis 2.7)

"By thee man liveth" (Breasted, *History* 375)

"he giveth to all life, and breath and all things;" (Acts 17.25)

Will Resurrect the Dead

"Thy rising is beautiful, O Living-Sun . . . who is given life, forever and ever. When thou risest in the eastern horizon of heaven, to make live all that thou hast made, even men, cattle, them that fly and them that (only) flutter, and all reptiles that are in the earth, they live when they see thee, they sleep when thou settest"
(Breasted, *Records II* 405-406)

"See now that I, even I, am he, and there is no god with me: I kill, and I make alive;" (Deuteronomy 32.39)

"The Lord killeth, and maketh alive: he bringeth down to the grave, and bringeth up" (I Samuel 2.6)

"Everyone lifts himself up because thou risest: they have seen their lord (when) he appears
(Breasted, *Records II* 416)

"all they that go down to the dust shall bow before him: and none can keep alive his own soul" (Psalms 22.29)

"Praise to thee, O living Aten, lord of rays, Creator of light. When he dawns all men live."
(Breasted, *Records II* 406)

"O Lord, thou hast brought up my soul from the grave: thou hast kept me alive, that I should not go down to the pit"
(Psalms 30.3)

"Praise to thee, O living Aten, lord of duration, who givest repetition (of Life)" (Breasted, *Records II* 406)

"But God will redeem my soul from the power of the grave" (Psalms 49.15)

" . . . even God, who quickeneth the dead"
(Romans 4.17)

188

Either Akhenaten was crazy or he wasn't. If he was sane, he was either telling the truth, or he was lying. If he was telling the truth, he was either worshiping the real God or a false god because, according to the Bible, there is only one real God. Yet, perhaps the best evidence that Akhenaten's God was the God of the Bible is Psalm 104. Many experts have commented on the striking similarity between this Psalm and Akhenaten's *Hymn to the Aten*.[447] If these two poems represent the same work, or even significantly the same work, then perhaps the question of Akhenaten's urgent devotion is settled.

Though some believe that the Bible "was written and edited exclusively by men," the Bible says of itself: "prophecy came not in old time by the will of man: but holy men of God spake as they were moved by the Holy Ghost," and "All scripture is given by inspiration of God . . ."(II Timothy 3.16; II Peter 1.21).[448] If God is responsible for *all* scripture, then the Holy Spirit inspired Psalm 104. If Psalm 104 is essentially Akhenaten's *Hymn to the Aten*, then his poem was actually a hymn to *YHWY*; Akhenaten *was* worshipping the God of the Bible, and the God of the Bible inspired Akhenaten's writing and accepted Akhenaten's worship. Otherwise, God would not have allowed Akhenaten's expression to be part of the praises in his book. Nor would God have further validated Akhenaten's worship by re-quoting his hymn in Hebrews 1.7 (Psalms 104.4).

Other explanations for the similarity between Psalm 104 and the *Hymn to the Aten* have been proposed. Some believe that the words of the psalm were "handed down through the generations of the Hebrews until the Psalms were finally written down, some six or seven hundred years after the time of Akhenaten." Others say Psalm 104 came to the Bible via other cultures, that Akhenaten's hymn was probably preserved in a Syrian Atenist temple and found its way into the Hebrew text via Phoenicians and/or Canaanites.[449] Since there were copies of the hymn in various tombs in Amarna, perhaps a copy of Akhenaten's hymn remained in On and was shared with the writers of the Psalms through Egypt.[450] After all, there were certainly favorable relations between Israel and Egypt (at least with Lower Egypt) during the days of Solomon (I Kings 3.1). Still others suggest that Akhenaten's poem is merely generic religious language common to devout writings throughout the ancient world or that both the *Hymn to the Aten* and Psalm 104 were inspired by a common, much earlier source, perhaps Chaldean.[451] Bille-De Mot cites similarities in language and concepts expressed in the *Hymn to the Aten* with passages from some other ancient religious texts.[452] Perhaps some other ancient religious texts besides the *Hymn to the Aten* and Psalm 104 were also meant to address the God of the Bible—the ancient of days (Daniel 7.9). Perhaps the *Hymn to the Aten* was not original to Akhenaten; perhaps it echoes back to early *Iwnw*. Perhaps it and other similar ancient verses were sung by priests in the order of Melchizedeck. However, the fact remains that, according to scripture, God claims *sole* responsibility for the contents of the Bible. Therefore, if what the Bible says is true, Akhenaten's words would not/could not have been preserved in the biblical text without divine approval.

In what ways do Akhenaten's *Hymn to the Aten* and Psalm 104 compare? Though many of the ideas expressed in the beginning of Psalm 104 are consistent with things Akhenaten said about God in other writings, it is more in the second half of the psalm that the strongest similarities with the *Hymn to the Aten* occur.

Psalm 104	**Hymn to the Aten**
1 Bless the Lord, O my soul	O living Aten, Beginning of life!
O Lord my God, thou art very great;	
thou are clothed with honour and majesty.	When thou riseth . . . thou fillest the land with thy beauty
2 Who coverest thyself with light	For thou are beautiful, great,
as with a garment:	
who stretchest out the heavens like a curtain:	glittering, high over the earth
3 Who layeth the beams of his chambers in the waters:	Thy rays are in the midst of the Great Sea
Who maketh the clouds his chariot:	
Who walketh upon the wings of the wind	
4 Who maketh his angels spirits;	
his ministers a flaming fire:	

189

5 Who laid the foundations of the earth,
that it should not be removed for ever.

6 Thou coveredst it with the deep as with a garment:
the waters stood above the mountains.

7 At thy rebuke they fled;
at the voice of thy thunder they hasted away.

8 They go up by the mountains;
they go down by the valleys unto the place
which thou hast founded for them.

9 Thou hast set a bound that they may not pass over;
that they turn not again to cover the earth.

10 He sendeth the springs into the valleys,
which run among the hills.

11 They give drink to every beast of the field:
the wild asses quench their thirst.

12 By them shall the fowls of the heaven
have their habitation which sing among the branches.

13 He watereth the hills from his chambers:
the earth is satisfied with the fruit of thy works.

14 He causeth the grass to grow for the cattle,
and herb for the service of man:
that he may bring forth food out of the earth;

15 And wine that maketh glad the heart of man,
and oil to make his face to shine,
and bread which strengtheneth man's heart.

16 The trees of the Lord are full of sap;
the cedars of Lebanon, which he hath planted;

17 Where the birds make their nests:
as for the stork, the fir trees are her house.

18 The high hills are a refuge for the wild goats;
and the rocks for the conies.

Thou hast set a Nile in heaven,
Making floods upon the mountains
And watering their fields among their towns

All trees and plants flourish,

The birds flutter in their marshes,

All the sheep dance upon their feet

19 He appointed the moon for seasons:
the sun knoweth his going down.

Thou makest the seasons,
. . . Dawning, shining afar, and returning

20 Thou makest darkness, and it is night:
wherein all the beasts of the forest do creep forth.

When thou settest in the western horizon of heaven,
the world is in darkness like the dead

21 The young lions roar after their prey,
and seek their meat from God.

Every lion cometh forth from his den

22 The sun ariseth, they gather themselves together,
and lay them down in their dens.

When thou risest in the horizon
The darkness is banished

23 Man goeth forth unto his work
and to his labour until the evening.

Then in all the world, they do their work

24 O Lord, how manifold are thy works!
in wisdom hast thou made them all:
the earth is full of thy riches.

How manifold are all thy works!
Thou didst create the earth
according to thy desire

25 So is this great and wide sea,
wherein are things creeping innumerable,
both small and great beasts.

26 There go the ships: there is that leviathan,
whom thou hast made to play therein.

The barques sail upstream and downstream alike,
The fish in the river leap up before thee

27 These wait all upon thee;
that thou mayest give them their meat in due season.

28 That thou givest them they gather:
thou openest thine hand, they are filled with good.

The world is in thy hand, as thou hast made them
When thou hast risen, they live

29 Thou hidest thy face, they are troubled:
thou takest away their breath,
they die, and return to their dust.

When thou settest, they die
By thee man liveth[453]

30 Thou sendest forth thy spirit, they are created:
and thou renewest the face of the earth.

31 The glory of the Lord shall endure for ever:
the Lord shall rejoice in his works.

32 He looketh on the earth, and it trembleth:
he toucheth the hills, and they smoke.

33 I will sing unto the Lord as long as I live:
I will sing praise to my God while I have my being.

34 My meditation of him shall be sweet:
I will be glad in the Lord.

35 Let the sinners be consumed out of the earth, and let
the wicked be no more. Bless thou the Lord,
O my soul. Praise ye the Lord.

Perhaps as further evidence of its divine origin, Raymaekers observes about Akhenaten's famous psalm:

> The hymn culminates in a remarkable aerial view of the Nile valley, as it must appear from the sun's globe itself, from the viewpoint of the god. It deserves to be called a masterpiece of literature, and it is difficult not to feel that we are dealing with a writer of genius; even parallels from earlier Egyptian literature, which certainly exist, do not erase this impression.[454]

Akhenaten believed in this God! Therefore, his behavior is perhaps not as radical as he has been portrayed. Historian E.A. Wallis Budge said, "He [Akhenaten] possessed a determined will and very definite religious convictions and fearless nature, but . . . [he was] earnest and sincere in his seeking after God."[455] If any king was convinced that his people were foolishly worshiping gods that had no power and were, simultaneously, angering a God who did have the power and the right to destroy them for their lack of reverence, a good king would do much the same as Akhenaten.

In fact, there were four world powers at the time of Akhenaten: Egypt, Mitanni/Syria, Babylon, and the Hittites; each of these nations had rulers who claimed the right to be called "Great King."[456] These nations also had kings who, at different times in history, according to scripture, reached similar conclusions as Akhenaten when confronted with the reality of God, and each of those rulers required similar behavior of their subjects.

Nineveh at one time was the capitol of Mitanni. In fact in Amenhotep III's Year 35, Tushratta, the king of Mitanni sent an image of Ishtar of Nineveh as a gesture to aid the ailing pharaoh in his recovery.[457] Incidentally, Amenhotep III seems to have been reluctant to part with the statue of Ishtar because Tushratta wrote multiple times asking for its return.[458] During the reign of Akhenaten, Mitanni was divided and overtaken by Suppiluliumas of the Hittites.[459] Later, Nineveh was also a capitol in the Assyrian Empire, composed of descendants of the Mitanni, the Hittites, Syrians, and others.[460]

It was likely in the days of the Assyrian Empire that Jonah, according to the Bible, was sent as a reluctant prophet to preach repentance in Nineveh (Jonah 1.1-2). Jonah was obviously a powerful speaker because, after only one day into his tour across the great city, people began to be convinced that Jonah's message was true—the God of the Bible was on the verge of destroying Nineveh; they had forty days to repent (Jonah 3.4-5). When the king in Nineveh believed Jonah's teaching, here was his response:

> . . . he arose from his throne, and he laid his robe from him, and covered him with sackcloth, and sat in ashes. And he caused it to be proclaimed and published through Nineveh by the decree of the king and his nobles, saying, Let neither man nor beast, herd nor flock, taste any thing: let them not feed, nor drink water: But let man and beast be covered with sackcloth, and cry mightily unto God: yea, let them turn every one from his evil way, and from the violence that is in their hands. Who can tell if God will turn and repent, and turn away from his fierce anger, that we perish not? (Jonah 3.6-9)

The king of Nineveh ordered worship—not of Ishtar, but of the God of the Bible! His decree extended even to animals in his jurisdiction. He forbade eating and drinking! Yet, unlike Akhenaten, this king is not charged with being oppressive or evil.[461] On the contrary, according to scripture, he saved his people from annihilation.

As another example, perhaps the greatest king that Babylon ever knew was Nebuchadnezzar. He is remembered mostly for his fabled Hanging Gardens, one of the Seven Wonders of the Ancient World. Akhenaten, too, designed and built exotic gardens, aviaries, and even zoos.[462] However, Akhenaten isn't remembered for his inventive landscaping but for his "lawlessness." Yet, sounding very like Akhenaten, according to scripture, Nebuchadnezzar issued the following *universal* decree:

> . . . every people . . . which speak any thing amiss against the God of Shadrach, Meshach, and Abednego [the God of the Bible], shall be cut in pieces, and their houses shall be made a dunghill: because there is no other God that can deliver after this sort. (Daniel 3.29)

Nebuchadnezzar is not maligned for "totalitarian thinking . . . inflicting a uniform religious policy."[463] Later, when the Biblical record reports that Nebuchadnezzar was humbled to fully believe in God and to fear his power, he made similar monotheistic inferences to that of Akhenaten:

> . . . I Nebuchadnezzar lifted up mine eyes unto heaven, . . . and I blessed the most High, and I praised and honoured him that liveth for ever, whose dominion is an everlasting dominion, and his kingdom is from generation to generation: And all the inhabitants of the earth are reputed as nothing: and he doeth according to his will in the army of heaven, and among the inhabitants of the earth: and none can stay his hand, or say unto him, What doest thou? . . . Now I Nebuchadnezzar praise and extol and honour the King of heaven, all whose works are truth, and his ways judgment: and those that walk in pride he is able to abase. (Daniel 4.34-35, 37)

Why is Nebuchadnezzar not branded as a crazy monotheist? After all, there is no indication that, after making this statement, he ever reverted back to worshiping Marduk, Ishtar, Sin, Nanna/Nebu, and other deities of Babylon.[464] However, unlike Akhenaten, there is no indication that Nebuchadnezzar ever changed his name to reflect his change of heart; Nebu, the first part of his name, was the name of a Babylonian god.[465]

The next empire to command the world stage was Syria/Persia. One of their great kings, Darius, according to the Bible, came to believe in the God of Daniel and made a proclamation with several similar conclusions to those of Akhenaten:

> . . . unto all people, nations, and languages, that dwell in all the earth . . . I make a decree, that in every dominion of my kingdom men tremble and fear before the God of Daniel [the God of the Bible]: for he is the living God, and steadfast for ever, and his kingdom that which shall not be destroyed, and his dominion shall be even unto the end. He delivereth and rescueth, and he worketh signs and wonders in heaven and in earth. . . . (Daniel 6.25-27)

John Ray says, "An admirer would say that the religious ideas which he [Akhenaten] tried to implant were too lofty for the ancients to comprehend. . . . A skeptic could respond by saying that all religious fanatics are unbearable, and the Egyptians showed a healthy dislike for the Aten."[466] Yet, none of these other rulers have been maligned in the vicious manner that Akhenaten has been.

Amarna Sunset

Horemheb certainly did everything in his power to make history forget the entire Amarna period.[467] By the time of Ramses II, Akhenaten was known only as "the rebel" or "the damned one."[468] For thousands of years, he was forgotten, his name was not even allowed to be spoken; he was only called "the criminal."[469] This type of destruction was particularly cruel from an Egyptian perspective, since to wipe out one's name was to deny eternal life to that individual.[470] Both the names of the Hyksos kings and the name of Akhenaten are absent on the Kings List in Seti I's Temple to Osiris at Abydos and on the Table of Sakkara, and though the famous Turin List even includes some of the Hyksos pharaohs, it still excludes Akhenaten.[471]

Yet, based on the above decrees issued by his peers who were monarchs of other strong nations, Akhenaten's actions were reasonable, prudent, and justified. Furthermore, though Josiah, the king of Nineveh, and Nebuchadnezzar represent distinct cultures that were proponents of diverse pantheons and religious beliefs, none of these rulers, after experiencing their own epiphanies, would likely have debarred Akhenaten. They would not have viewed him as a heretic or as overreaching his authority.

Another monotheistic leader who likely would not have considered Akhenaten to be a heretic is Joshua. Near the end of Joshua's life, he made the following observation:

> . . . choose you this day whom ye will serve; whether the gods which your fathers served that were on the other side of the flood, or the gods of the Amorites, in whose land ye dwell: but as for me and my house, we will serve the Lord. (Joshua 24.15)

Expressing a similar sentiment, by year six of Akhenaten's reign, each of the fourteen boundary stelae, marking the territory of Akhet-Aten, depicted Akhenaten, Nefertiti, and their daughters worshiping Aten. [472] Akhenaten carved in stone that, no matter where they might happen to die, all of his family were to be buried in cliffs above Akhet-Aten. [473] Like Joshua, Akhenaten boldly declared who he and his house would serve.

In his city, there was no official worship other than to Aten. Services and sacrifices were offered on the elevated altar to Aten more than once a day. The offering tables were always filled with bread, beer, and sacrificial animals. [474] Akhenaten proclaimed the sole deity of Aten throughout Egypt and strongly encouraged all Egyptians to acknowledge Aten as the only God. By closing temples, destroying monuments, and prohibiting traditional beliefs and celebrations, Akhenaten made it as difficult as possible for anyone to choose to worship other gods in Egypt. [475] He strongly encouraged Egyptians to change their names if their names included the names of other gods. [476] Yet there's no record of anyone being put to death for worshiping another god. Not even the priests of Amun were put to death; they were given another line of work—albeit oppressive and probably punitive. Nevertheless, some modern observers still suggest that Ay's statement: "Offer praises to the living Disk [Aten] and you shall have a prosperous life," implies an ominous negative: fail to worship Aten and you die! [477] On the other hand, J. Raymaekers observes, "grounds for disapproval [of Akhenaten and Atenism] vary from author to author, [and] are not always convincing." [478]

Why was Akhenaten so opposed to other gods and even seemed to be at war with their names? If they were false gods who never existed, why bother to erase them? [479] It wasn't the powerless, false deities that Akhenaten was trying to eradicate as if they would continue to exist if he did not utterly destroy them—it was the persistent, useless fear and worship of them that he was trying to eliminate. [480] Akhenaten had no fear of false gods. He had no fear of gods who had proven themselves completely useless against turning the Nile into blood, hoards of frogs, choking swarms of insects, the utter devastation of livestock and crops, disease, violent weather, darkness, and death. He had no use for gods who could not protect the Egyptian army or the pharaoh himself. He did, on the other hand, greatly fear the God who was capable of all these punishments, who had made that fact excruciatingly clear, and who made the sun stand still! Yet, in turning to this deity, Akhenaten realized another side of him. "Thy love is great and mighty, . . . Thy glowing hue brings life to hearts, When thou hast filled the Two Lands with thy love." [481] This God was loving to those who seek him. [482] To honor Aten was life; to reject him was destruction, but not because of Akhenaten. This was a basic truth that Akhenaten went to drastic lengths to teach his subjects in an effort to turn them away from the disfavor of the one God.

However, Akhenaten could not stop the worship of the traditional Egyptian gods. Though it has been suggested that there is no overt evidence of disloyalty to the king and his radical ideas, throughout the reign of Akhenaten, the further away from Amarna, the more it seems the old religion was business as usual. [483] In Memphis, for example, the temple of Ptah said, "all is well"; of course, the correspondence that includes this statement was probably written before Amenhotep IV announced his radical religious reforms; therefore, tolerance of this temple may be understandable. [484] However, even in Akhet-Aten, there were those who kept statues of the traditional gods, magic amulets, prayers to forbidden deities, and laments to Amun hidden within their homes. [485] Even in the residence of the High Priest of Aten, votive objects and figures to traditional gods were found. In the workmen's section of the town many houses had murals of Bes painted on the walls. In fact, it is probable that most residents of Akhet-Aten were unfaithful in their devotion to the Aten. [486]

It is also likely that Akhenaten was keenly aware of the hypocrisy and the "convenient lip-service" of most of his subjects. [487] "It was a time when what seemed to be was not really so. And the contrary." [488] Akhenaten knew that many Egyptians were not in favor of abandoning the traditional gods. [489] Furthermore, he knew that there was an element of the population that was violently opposed to his teachings.[490] Shockingly disrespectful figurines of monkeys with features and poses caricaturizing and satirizing Akhenaten have been found as evidence of contemptuous sedition. Chariots were used as regular transportation by Akhenaten and his family inside Akhet-Aten.[491] Akhenaten was especially known for driving his chariot down the central road of the city that led from the palace to the temple of Aten. One monkey figurine is riding in a chariot with the horses rearing out of control; the implication is obvious.[492] Ominous fragments of literature that discuss assassination were also found in the ruins of Amarna.[493] In fact, Akhenaten seems to have been concerned for his family's safety—not from outside forces, because Akhet-Aten was an unfortified city, but from his own people.[494] Pharaohs had been known to be assassinated.[495] Inside its boundaries, Akhet-Aten was like an armed camp; "policemen and soldiers accompany almost every ritual scene on the walls."[496] Wherever they went, the royal family was surrounded by a detail of guards.

> *Rwd-mnw*, armed troops surround Amenophis IV when he leaves his palace, run behind his chariot as he proceeds down the avenue, or bow low, their swords reversed and their spears to the ground, as he enters the temple. There are Egyptian spearmen and shocktroops, auxiliaries from Syria and Nubia, feather- wearing Libyans with throw-sticks, and everywhere the regimental sergeant majors with the standards of their companies.[497]

Given the unpopularity of Akhenaten and his religious movement among Egyptians, it's not really surprising that he would look to other parts of the Empire for his bodyguards.[498] Yet, beyond this reasoning, since Akhenaten held that Aten was the Lord of All, the multi-national guard may have been a captive audience intended for indoctrination with his world religion.[499] Through these men, perhaps Akhenaten hoped to spread Atenism throughout the Empire, perhaps throughout the entire world.[500] "Every heart is happy at sight of thee, for thou are risen as their lord."[501]

It has been suggested that Akhenaten was elitist in his religion, proclaiming that only he and his family would be granted eternal life by the Aten, or that perhaps only those who the king looked favorably upon— certainly not the poor—would be extended similar privilege, or that only the king could grant eternal life. The idea being proposed is that Aten selectively provided for his creation "in a rather perfunctory way," insensitive to the cries of the poor, the sick, or the sinful. Exclusivity of favor has also been interpreted from images where rays of the disk selectively seem to caress Akhenaten.[502] However, these may not be a correct assessments. Akhenaten describes Aten as a "Good God," a "kindly" God.[503] He is also described as "a god of love and warmth."[504] Far from ambivalent, in his *Hymn to the Aten*, Akhenaten describes a compassionate Aten as a "lover of mankind" who sustains and cherishes all creation.[505] "A formless essence, a loving force, invading all of time and space—this, the hymns say clearly, is Aten."[506] On one of the boundary stelae, Akhenaten states:

> I shall build Akhet-Aten in this place for Aten, my Father. . . . It belongs to the Aten my Father (like) the mountains, the deserts, the fields, the isles, the upper lands and the lower lands, the water, the villages, the men, the animals, and all those things to which Aten my father will give life eternally, I shall not neglect the oath which I have made to Aten my Father for eternity.[507]

Clearly, Akhenaten believed that Aten is the giver of "life eternally," life abundantly to all creatures. Akhenaten fully anticipated serving Aten "for eternity." He also believed that all things belonged to Aten—not to Akhenaten; and, in the pharaoh's opinion, eternal life was possible not only for all people, but even for animals!

Any, a faithful servant of the Great House for four generations seemed to have believed in the prospect of attaining eternal life. In his tomb, Any references "thy house of eternity"; and he prays, "May he [the Aten] give to me breezes [breath]."[508] In the entrance to Any's Amarna tomb, the inscription reads:

> The intimate of the King, whom his lord loves, the favourite [sic] whom the Lord of the Two Lands (?) created by his bounty, who has reached the blessed reward by the favour of the King, the acting scribe of the King beloved by him, Scribe of the Altar of the Lord of the Two Lands, Scribe of the Offering Table of Aten for the Aten in the temple of Aten in Akhetaten, Steward of the house of King Aa-kheperu-ra [Amenhotep II], Any, blessed with a good burial, says it.[509]

Obviously, Any understood that it was Aten who had the power to grant the breath of eternal life. Yet, perhaps, he came to that understanding through the favor of Akhenaten's teachings. Without the prophecy of Akhenaten, Any might not have known how to reach the blessed reward. Perhaps it was Akhenaten's unique role as a prophet that is being illustrated in images where the rays of the disk light upon him. Aten chose to speak to Akhenaten; only in that distinction was the king elevated above anyone else.

Far from being elitist, Akhenaten married Nefertiti, long suspected of being a commoner. Those holding this belief would have a hard time suggesting that that Akhenaten was intolerant of commoners. Yet Nefertiti's true pedigree is really more of a mystery. Though some believe she may have been the daughter of Ay and his wife, Tiy (which may have made Queen Tiye Nefertiti's aunt), Tiy only claimed to be Nefertiti's nurse.[510] Still, an inscription found by the French archaeologist Georges Legrain identifies Nefertiti as the probable daughter of Queen Tiye, and therefore, Akhenaten's sister.[511] It is known that Nefertiti had a sister, Mutnodjmet, who was the wife of Horemheb, the origins of whom are also unknown.[512] There are those who contend that Nefertiti was a foreigner, perhaps a princess from Mitanni, but Redford finds no evidence to support that she was anything other than Egyptian.[513] Though it's possible Akhenaten married Nefertiti before he even became king, he never looked in condescension upon his choice; Akhenaten consistently portrayed Nefertiti as his equal.[514]

Though many residents of Akhet-Aten were elites living in grand villas, the royal couple did not look down on the lowly inhabitants of Amarna.[515] At its height, the city was believed to house 100,000 people. In Akhet-Aten, there are depictions of "onlookers expressing excitement and even ecstasy in the presence of their rulers, and joy and pride in the awards that were bestowed upon them" by the king and queen. Though some modern observers see it differently, Akhenaten was recognized by some of the lowliest people of Egypt who he not only welcomed to join the pharaoh in worship and to live in his city, but allowed to hold office and to be buried in tombs.[516] In Amarna Tomb 14, May, Akhenaten's royal chancellor says:

> I was a man of low origin both on my father's and on my mother's side, but the king established
> me . . . . He caused me to grow . . . . by his bounty when I was a man of no property . . . . He
> gave me food and provisions every day. I who had been one that begged bread.[517]

It is noteworthy that at some time, the likeness of May was plastered over and his name was chiseled out.[518] Similarly, Panehesy, a priest of Aten testifies in Amarna Tomb 6: "When I knew not the companionship of princes I was made an intimate of the king . . . who maketh princes and foreth the humble."[519] The walls of the tombs of these commoners testify: "I was a servant of Waenre the Ruler who lives by Truth. I followed him and he rose up early to reward me because I did his behests."[520]

Mahu, of Amarna Tomb 9, the chubby policeman, who is depicted having difficulty keeping up with the pharaoh's chariot, might have been considered "an undesirable" in other administrations, but Akhenaten not only accepted the lowly Mahu, he made him chief.[521] In tomb after tomb, dignitaries praised themselves for the favored status they held with the king. They praised the generosity of the royal family and bragged about the collars of gold, great religious ceremonies, and feasts that they had been privileged to enjoy. In fact, Akhenaten was so generous, it has been suggested that he cheapened "the gold of bravery" by presenting such honor to even lowly subjects.[522] However, it may be that gold was given to reward the bravery of devotion and obedience to the will of Aten. After all, it was a time of war; Aten was at war in Canaan. It could be suggested that gifts of gold were actually from Aten, not Akhenaten: "Numerous as the things the Disc is able to give." Even before the completion of Akhet-Aten, Ramose, the old vizier and perhaps one of the first converts to Atenism, remodeled his Theban tomb to reflect his new devotion. Prayers to Aten adorn the walls, and a relief of Amenhotep IV says, "The words of Re are before thee . . . My august father [meaning Aten] taught me their essence and revealed them to me . . . They were known in my heart, opened to my face. I understood . . . "[523]

In Year 12, sadness visited Akhet-Aten: Amenhotep III, at around 51, died. Much of his affliction and ultimate demise was, probably, due to overindulgence.[524] The old king was very overweight and though he only had a few teeth left, at the end of his life, he still suffered a great deal from tooth decay and abscesses.[525] Based on the study of his remains, it's clear that Amenhotep III had been ailing and had "greatly suffered with dental disease for years."[526] "Our last glimpse of Amenhotep [III] is of a bloated king dressed in loose and flimsy robes, slumped in a chair."[527] The unflattering image is painted on a damaged limestone stela that was found in the ruins of Panehesy's house in Akhet-Aten. It shows Amenhotep III and Queen Tiye sitting beside each other on thrones draped with rugs, facing an altar heaped with offerings, all bathed in the rays of Aten.

Due to the fact that, in this relief, the couple appears to be living, Amenhotep III is identified by the late version of his name, which did not include "Amun," and the senior royals are obviously in Akhet-Aten; it appears that Amenhotep III probably lived out his last days serving in Akhet-Aten as co-regent with his son. Among other indications, it appears that the old royal couple lived in the city dedicated to Aten because wine and correspondence were delivered to both Amenhotep III and to Queen Tiye in that location.[528] Since Amenhotep III had probably suffered poor health for years and may not have been fit or inclined to serve as monarch, it is likely that the co-regency had also been prolonged.[529] Amenhotep III never seemed to relish ruling. Some observers have suggested that the old king may have even taken to wearing women's clothing, at the end of his life, specifically to avoid the duties of his office.[530]

However, perhaps the best indication of co-regency and that Amenhotep III was in Akhet-Aten when he died is the pharaoh's own death mask. Though experts disagree as to whether these clay casts, found in the studio of Thutmosis, were made from living or dead faces, the agonized expression on Amenhotep III's mask indicates that it likely marks the end of his life.[531] The fact that Amenhotep III's death mask was in Akhet-Aten is a good indication that he lived and died in that city.

Also in year twelve, a durbar, a grand festival, was held in Akhet-Aten. Dignitaries and tributes from throughout the empire—and beyond—poured into the city to honor and to congratulate Akhenaten.[532] Cyril Aldred builds a compelling argument, quite certain that the occasion marked the death of Amenhotep III and thus the end of a long co-regency.[533]

The Durbar

197

In the tomb of Queen Tiye's chamberlain, Huya, Amarna Tomb 1, and in the tomb of the high priest of Aten, Merire, Amarna Tomb 4, a parade of emissaries from the Hittites, Naharin, Cyprus, Syria, Palestine, Nubia, Libya, Punt, and Mitanni are depicted lining the streets of the city.[534] In fact, some think that the durbar feast was held in Akhet-Aten to honor Queen Tiye.[535] However, others have questioned the timing and purpose of the pretentious gala, suggesting that it was nothing more than a diversion meant to quiet domestic discontent and to assert to foreign nations Egypt's abiding strength and vitality.[536] Yet, perhaps Akhenaten hoped to impress more than this upon the foreign lands. Perhaps he hoped that this durbar would affect a favorable interaction and facilitate a positive re-introduction of Aten to foreign representatives and might help to spread Atenism to all people. At any rate, this durbar marks the last time that the royal family is depicted as intact. It is the last known event where Nefertiti and all six princesses were in attendance.[537]

Regardless of the celebratory atmosphere in Akhet-Aten, an undeniable climate of dis-ease was stirring in the world. The distress was not only political, but also physical. A terrible plague, known as the Asiatic Illness, was sweeping through the Near East and some have speculated that carriers of the disease were among the contingency attending Akhenaten's durbar.[538] Others believe the sickness accompanied prisoners to Amarna, perhaps even in the arrest of Aziru.[539] Nevertheless, for a quarter of a century, the illness raged, making it the worst epidemic known in antiquity. The pestilence is well documented and was perhaps first mentioned in EA 35 as "the hand of Nergal," an Alasian god of the underworld.[540] The effected area covered a region that stretched from Sumura to Cyprus and into Egypt. It seems to have struck the Hittites especially hard and ended the life of Suppiluliumas.[541]

Curiously, by the time of Manetho, Egyptian popular belief had tied plague and the Asiatic Illness to the Hyksos. According to Egyptian oral tradition, the story of "the lepers" distorted and confused elements that may be attributed to the time of Akhenaten, the Hyksos, the exodus, and the entire Hebrew sojourn in Egypt, all conglomerated into a singular tale of dread.[542] In fact, in Egyptian culture, "leper" became a metaphor to characterize "iconoclast."[543] Whether or not the Asiatic Illness involved symptoms reminiscent of leprosy, it is significant that it was connected with Akhenaten and with the Hebrews of the exodus (Exodus 15.26).

Leviticus 13 and 14 seem to link plague with leprosy, but perhaps these chapters are better understood as discussing a wide variety of disorders. The scriptures record several plagues that Hebrews suffered during the forty years of wandering in the wilderness. In Exodus 32.35, God punished the Hebrews with a plague for worshiping the golden calf. In Numbers 11.31-34, God sent a plague along with quail as a punishment for Hebrew longing for pleasures back in Egypt. The ten spies who gave an evil report about the land of Canaan died of plague according to Numbers 14.37. In Numbers 16, a plague was sent on the Hebrews following Korah's rebellion. In Numbers 25, plague was the response to sins that Hebrews committed with the Moabites, and again in Numbers 31.16. All of these plagues (among other penalties) were sent by God as punishment for sin, "And if ye walk contrary unto me, and will not hearken unto me; I will bring seven times more plagues upon you according to your sins" (Leviticus 26.21). Therefore, during this time in history, Hebrews were responsible for the plagues that they suffered, but only for the plagues that *they* suffered. Hebrews were not, necessarily, responsible for the pestilence of any other people unless the maladies that were sent to punish the Hebrews' sins were transmittable to other nations and were not event specific. The scriptures do not stipulate.

If the Hebrews were God's chosen people, why did they suffer so? (Jude 5) Jesus explained, "that servant, which knew his lord's will, and prepared not himself, neither did according to his will, shall be beaten with many stripes. But he that knew not, and did commit things worthy of stripes, shall be beaten with few stripes. For unto whomsoever much is given, of him shall be much required" (Luke 12.47-48). By the time of Moses, much had been given to the Hebrews. According to the Bible, the Hebrews had been given promises through their patriarchs: promises that they would be numerous, that they would be given the land of Canaan as a place to live, and that all nations on earth would be blessed because of a messiah who would be born of their race. The Hebrews had been given special treatment above all other people during the famine in the days of Joseph. The Hebrews had been given deliverance from slavery in Egypt. They had been given food and water in the desert. However, most importantly, they had been given the written Law of Moses. Because of this, they knew the Lord's will specified for them; therefore, God required obedience of them. The Law of Moses was the Hebrews' contract with God: if they obeyed the law, God would send blessings on them; if they sinned against God's law, he would send punishments (Deuteronomy 28.1-47ff). That was the agreement.

So, were the Hebrews responsible for the Asiatic Illness? Probably not. Was the Asiatic Illness sent by God as a punishment for the sins of the Hebrews or any other people in the Near East? The scriptures do not indicate that it was. Did God not care about the sins of other nations?

The God of the Bible hates sin. He loves all people but hates all sin. As seen throughout scripture, he has *always* loved all people but hated all sin. Still, "He maketh his sun to rise on the evil and on the good, and sendeth rain on the just and on the unjust" (Matthew 5.45). Other nations in the days of the Old Testament were not held to standards of behavior that were as high as those imposed upon the Hebrews because other nations were not bound by the Law of Moses. Nevertheless, worshipping false gods is an egregious sin in God's eyes, and according to Romans, it is a sin that is "without excuse." Other nations were punished for their abominable idolatry. Some nations were utterly destroyed. If not for the amazing contrition of Thutmose IV, Egypt, too, may very well have been annihilated in the wake of the exodus.

After the durbar, tragedy after tragedy befell Amarna. Remarkable reliefs, carved into the walls of Akhenaten's own tomb, record what most believe to have been the death of Meketaten, the second daughter of Akhenaten and Nefertiti.[544] The little princess was probably only around eleven years old.[545] Since she is mentioned by name in a wine docket from Year 11 and is pictured with the royal family at the festivities in Year 12, most believe Meketaten was alive at that time.[546] Some say she died in the year of the durbar, yet some evidence suggests that she may have been buried in Year 14.[547] Therefore, perhaps pestilence was not among the ambassadors visiting Egypt.

Nevertheless, in the heart wrenching reliefs, Nefertiti is wearing the same tall, oddly shaped headdress that adorns her lovely countenance in the famous bust of her elegant head; the queen is standing behind her husband, peering over his shoulder. Akhenaten, pictured in the pharaoh's war helmet, reaches behind with his left hand and clasps Nefertiti's left forearm as if to protect, steady, and support his wife. With their right hands, both royals beat their brows in anguish and are transfixed in abject disbelief at the horrible spectacle of the small female "figure on the bier."[548] Further behind the royal couple, two of their daughters stand, weak-kneed, as if they might collapse. One sister (probably Neferneferure) clutches the other and tightly leans against her with both arms wrapped around her mid-section. The foremost sister (probably Meritaten) raises her hands as if forlorn and beseeching comfort in prayer. The grief expressed in these four figures is palpable. Immediately behind Nefertiti, a woman (probably a nurse) and a fan-bearer whisk a child away from the dreadful scene, leading some to think that the female on the bier may have died in childbirth; but this seems unlikely.[549] It is, perhaps, more likely that Nefertiti, herself, is the mother of this mysterious child, whom most agree is probably Tutankhaten.[550] This relief, at the death of Meketaten, is the last time that Nefertiti is ever depicted.[551]

No one knows why Meketaten died. Perhaps it was the Asiatic Illness that killed her.[552] Nevertheless, her passing ushered a steady string of untimely deaths into the "glimpse of heaven" that Akhenaten built on earth. In short order, Queen Tiye, Nefertiti, Meritaten, Neferneferure, two of the three youngest daughters, Kiya, Meritaten-minor, Beketaten (the last child of Queen Tiye and Amenhotep III), Smenkhkare, and Akhenaten would all be dead.[553] If a pestilence had entered Akhet-Aten, perhaps that is the reason that the nurse is seen quickly removing the baby from the contaminated area. Though most ancient Egyptian medical texts seem to implicate demons as the main cause of disease, perhaps there was a rudimentary sense that illness is contagious and that being in close proximity to an infected person is ill advised.[554]

Although some contend that she may have outlived her husband, Nefertiti essentially disappeared from the record after Year 13, and most believe that by Year 14 she had died.[555] Part of the reason for controversy concerning the death of Nefertiti lies in the fact that mystery marks the time before her death. Perhaps she changed her name to Neferneferuaten, perhaps she and/or Akhenaten lay very ill, perhaps she fell out of favor, perhaps there was a power struggle between Nefertiti and Queen Tiye, perhaps she was severely depressed after the death of Meketaten, perhaps she was in quarantine; but for whatever reason, shortly after the death of the young princess(s), Nefertiti retreated into seclusion in her own palace in the northern part of the city. With her, she took Ankhesenpaaten and Tutankhaten, who some believe, were only about a year apart in age and who, by that time, were the youngest of her four surviving children; only Ay was granted regular contact. [556]

Many have posed a marital rift in the royal couple, but evidence to the contrary seems to indicate that Nefertiti remained fiercely loyal to her husband and to Aten until the end. In her palace, called "The House of Aten," Nefertiti kept "inscriptions linking herself and Akhenaten as though no break had occurred."[557] Furthermore, strong evidence supports that Nefertiti was buried by Akhenaten and was "mourned as a great queen, loyal to his teachings."[558] Indeed, all indications are that Nefertiti was genuinely indoctrinated with her husband's teachings and "sustained the pharaoh's religious fervor without allowing the least falling-away."[559] Like the virtuous wife, praised in the writing of Solomon, and like the church/the bride of Christ, so it could be said of Nefertiti, "She will do him [her husband] good and not evil all the days of her life" (Proverbs 31.12).

Although wine dockets labeled "House of the King's Mother" were dated to Year 14, by the end of that same year, Queen Tiye was also dead.[560] The matriarch queen obviously lived in Akhet-Aten since correspondence and goods were delivered to her there.[561] She is also pictured in reliefs visiting the temple in Akhet-Aten with her son.[562] When she died, she was probably buried in the cliffs east of the city, in Akhenaten's own tomb; however, her mummy was later relocated: first to KV 22, the tomb of her late husband, since Amenhotep III had designated space in his tomb for both Queen Tiye and for Gilukhepa, the daughter of Shuttarna king of Mitanni, but eventually Queen Tiye's mummy was moved to KV 35.[563]

Also in Year 14, Meritaten assumed the title of "Great Royal Wife."[564] All over Akhet-Aten, Nefertiti's name was replaced with Meritaten.[565] Some believe that Meritaten was briefly married to Akhenaten, and correspondence from the time contributes to the confusion. However, it is perhaps more likely that when Nefertiti left with the two younger children, Smenkhkare and Meritaten stayed with their father, were married, and the young prince took his place as coregent.[566] Smenkhkare was probably in his mid to late teens when he was crowned.[567] Wine dockets, believed to be associated with Meritaten, from Year 14 read "House of the King's Wife," an understandable title if her husband, Smenkhkare, was co-regent.[568] Around Year 15, a daughter, Meritaten-minor, was born to Smenkhkare and Meritaten.[569] It's possible that Nefertiti lived long enough to know she had a grandchild. Within a year of becoming queen, however, Meritaten was dead. Not

long after, little Meritaten-minor was dead too. Some think that Ankhesenpaaten took her sister's place as wife to Smenkhkare although it hardly seems likely since she was probably between five and seven years old, at the time.[570] Dodson and Dyan think that someone named Neferneferuaten (whom some speculate was a new name for Nefertiti) took the place of Meritaten, but Dodson and Dyan also concede that there is a lot of disagreement on the matter.[571] Kiya is mentioned in Year 16, appearing on a talatat from Hermopolis along with Akhenaten and two of his daughters; Nefertiti is conspicuously absent.[572] Nevertheless, by Year 17, Kiya was almost certainly dead.[573]

In Year 17, sometime after the grape harvest, around July, Akhenaten died.[574] He was likely in his thirties.[575] No one knows his cause of death.[576] The poor condition of his remains, positively identified in 2009, leaves little more than bones for examination.[577] He was buried in the tomb that he prepared, in the cliffs to the east of Akhet-Aten and was laid beside those family members who had preceded him in death.[578]

Plaster Mask of Akhenaten

And that is where his body remained. His stone sarcophagus that was tenderly decorated on each corner by the image of a winged Nefertiti, his beloved, was smashed to pieces and his likeness and his name were completely chiseled off of his coffin.[579] While other members of the royal family were eventually relocated to various caches, Akhenaten was left unattended, faceless, and nameless.[580] Perhaps James Breasted said it best:

> . . . there died with him such a spirit as the world had never seen before—a brave soul, undauntedly facing the momentum of immemorial tradition, and thereby stepping out from the long line of conventional and colourless [sic] Pharaohs, that he might disseminate ideas far beyond and above the capacity of his age to understand. . . . the modern world has yet adequately to value or even acquaint itself with this man who, in an age so remote and under conditions so adverse, became not only the world's first idealist and the world's first individual, but. . . the most remarkable figure of the Ancient World.[581]

In short order, Smenkhkare died too.[582] He was hastily mummified and buried in KV 55, "a small, crude tomb."[583] He only ruled for three years.[584] In the end, only Ankhesenpaaten and Tutankhaten survived.

What happened? Do all these deaths indicate plague? If so, it would have been an unusual plague, taking five years to wipe out such a close family. Furthermore, it was certainly selective for an epidemic, killing mostly those individuals in the prime of life; and it's timing is significant as well. The Egyptian custom of relinquishing the care of royal infants to a wet-nurse would likely have made very young children more susceptible to disease because they were denied the advantage of tailor-made antibodies that would have been provided in their own mother's milk. Therefore, one would think that Ankhesenpaaten and Tutankhaten would have been among the most vulnerable to the ravages of pestilence. Indeed, in most epidemics the very young and the very old usually succumb at a disproportionate rate. Yet that is not what happened in Akhet-Aten. Sequestered in a palace with their mother, Ankhesenpaaten and Tutankhaten survived while Nefertiti, a seemingly healthy young woman, probably in her mid-thirties, died. Also of note, Ay, an old man, survived.[585]

It was certainly convenient that the royal couple best suited to carry on the pharaonic tradition, Smenkhkare and Meritaten, were well and stepped on to the royal stage, just as their parents were sufficiently silenced and/or incapacitated.[586] Evidence exists to suggest that Smenkhkare was being influenced and strongly encouraged to re-establish the traditional Egyptian religion. Someone was using Smenkhkare as "an olive branch" reaching out to Thebes. His name is written on the wall inside a Theban tomb, indicating that he had visited there during his last year; also, several images of Smenkhkare being portrayed as Osiris exist.[587] The Horus name for the young king was "Propitiating the gods," and early in the co-regency of Smenkhkare, new building activity began in Thebes. It is hard to imagine that Akhenaten would have approved of such actions, either Akhenaten had softened in his beliefs or, perhaps, he was too sick to be aware of what was happening.[588]

However, after the death of Akhenaten, when Smenkhkare became sole pharaoh, there is reason to believe that the young ruler was reluctant to leave Akhet-Aten and that he retained "rigors of the old monotheism" and devotion to Aten.[589] How ironically convenient, then, that Meritaten and Smenkhkare suddenly died; but, reserved in the wings, was another young couple to take the throne—too young to assert their own will, even over the changing of their names to Ankhesenamun and Tutankhamun.[590]

Over the years, several have speculated that ominous forces conspired against Akhenaten and Nefertiti.[591] Many believe that, if there was foul play against the royal family, Ay and Horemheb are the most likely suspects.[592] Certainly when Aziru was arrested, officials in Akhenaten's court gained a new appreciation for the respect that Egypt had lost in the furthest reaches of the empire.[593] Egyptian retaliation was no longer feared or even expected. It's possible that Horemheb implicated himself in the destruction of Akhenaten when the general said "that he was called in to calm down the Palace when it fell into a rage," although this statement could also refer to events that transpired later.[594] Ay was unquestionably the more senior of the two shadowy figures, and he had unfettered access to the king and queen.[595] After all, as the husband of Nefertiti's nurse, he had all but raised the queen, and she, no doubt, trusted him implicitly. Furthermore, honored with many titles: Master of the Horse (general of chariotry), King's Secretary (king's scribe), battalion commander, Divine Father, and fan-bearer of the king's right hand, Ay was perhaps the closest advisor of Akhenaten.[596]

It seems almost impossible to believe that someone who was so trusted may have been so treacherous. Nevertheless, could it be that Ay advised Nefertiti to take the children to the northern palace, perhaps suggesting that it was for their own safety, all the while intending to divide the royal couple so each would be unaware of the condition of the other. Once Akhenaten and Nefertiti were separated, could it be that Ay employed "a poisoned chalice" in both residences, carefully orchestrated to render those in authority essentially incapacitated while inducing symptoms that mimicked a prolonged illness, eventually resulting in murder?[597] Was it Ay who was grooming the teenaged Smenkhkare to forsake the teaching of his father and turn Egypt back to Amun-Ra; and when the young pharaoh gave resistance, he was killed too? If so:

> Ay was playing a double game at that point, outwardly loyal to . . . Aten, but quietly scheming with the Thebans for a restoration of the old religion. After the mysterious series of events that removed both co-regents and their wives . . . Ay stepped forward as the king-maker of Egypt.[598]

Yet Ay, himself, polishes the glass and allows a clearer glimpse of his true nature. In his Amarna Tomb, the grandest of all in Akhenaten's court, a tomb in which he was never buried, Ay hypocritically boasts:[599]

> I was eminent, possessing character, successful in opportunities, contented of disposition, kindly . . . . I was the first of the officials at the head of the people . . . I am a true witness, devoid of evil, my name has penetrated into the palace, because of my usefulness to the king, because of my hearing his teaching. I was one favored by his lord daily. My favors increased year by year inasmuch as I was extremely competent in His Majesty's opinion, so he doubled my perquisites for me, like the number of the sands. I was at the head of both the princes and the common people . . . I was a truly correct person, one in whom was no greed. My name [i.e., reputation] reached the palace because I was useful to the king and obeyed his teaching, and performed his laws . . . I was competent and a man of good character . . . contented and patient . . . who followed the *ku* of His Majesty as he had commanded, as I listened unceasing to his voice.[600]

Furthermore, Ay disingenuously displayed the finest copy of Akhenaten's masterpiece, *Hymn to the Aten*. Yet, an observation of Ay's true nature can be asserted with confidence, since Ay later expressed his nefarious sentiments in a poem of his own—a hymn to Amun that heartlessly mocked Aten and Akhenaten:

> The sun of him who knew thee not has set, O Amon,
> But as for him who knows thee, he shines.
> The temple of him who assailed thee is in darkness
> While the whole earth is in sunlight.
> Whoso putteth thee in his heart, O Amon,
> Lo, his sun hath risen![601]

"And history, knowing that Ay ultimately placed himself upon the royal throne under mysterious and perhaps dishonorable circumstances, frowns."[602]

Of course, perhaps there are other explanations for all the tragedy that befell Amarna at the end. Some say that there was a lack of food in the last days of Akhet-Aten, perhaps that accounts for some of the deaths.[603] The remains of Akhenaten's dogs, found still in their kennels, and his oxen, still in their sheds, show that the animals starved to death. However, this probably happened, not as a result of famine, but in the wake of the departure. When Ay moved king Tut and Ankhesenamun back to Thebes and eventually to the ancestral palace of Thutmose I in Memphis, he simply abandoned the royal animals, something he probably would not have done if there was famine and the animals could have been used for food.[604] The poor were also left in Akhet-Aten, while the Amarna elites quickly built new tombs devoid of Atenism and re-established themselves in the good graces of Amun-Ra, the sun god, who had "chosen to appear" in the form of a boy king.[605]

It is possible, even likely, that members of Akhenaten's family died of various causes. Perhaps some did die of disease, perhaps some died in childbirth, perhaps there were deadly accidents, and perhaps some were murdered. Until definitive tests can be conducted on the remains of the mummies from the last days of Amarna, questions will remain. But mysterious deaths continued to haunt this family. It has long been speculated that king Tut was murdered. Most are satisfied that his cause of death is no longer a question; he died from a compound fracture of his knee, probably the result of a chariot accident. The break had begun to heal before he died, but subsequent infection and sepsis, further complicated by chronic malaria, resulted in the death of the boy king. However, was the severe injury really an accident? Did someone who wanted the young king dead sabotage Tut's chariot? Was he accidentally or purposefully run over? One person stood to gain: Ay.

Tut was only about eight years old when he was crowned.[606] He died a young man, around nineteen. Could it be that when he reached an age to begin asserting his own will, he opposed Ay? Aten was emblazoned on Tut's throne, although it was probably recycled from Akhet-Aten.[607] Jars of wine from the vineyard in the "Domain of Aten" were buried with Tut.[608] Could it be that he was eliminated for much the same reasons as his brother Smenkhkare? Akhenaten's offspring didn't make good puppets.[609] If Tut and his sister remembered anything about their parents, it would have been love for family, devotion to Aten, and fierce independence.

Ay is depicted in Tut's tomb conducting the "opening of the mouth" ceremony for the young king. This role of honor was usually reserved for the son and heir. Indeed, Ay, an old man, had assumed the title "eldest king's son" during the reign of Tutankhamun; how did Ay seem to know that Tut would never have a son? Did he expect the boy king to die young?[610]

Intriguingly, shortly after Tut's death, Ankhesenamun wrote to Suppiluliumas, the king of the Hittites:
My husband has died. A son I have not. But to thee, they say, the sons are many. If thou wouldst give me one son of thine, he would become my husband. Never shall I pick out a servant of mine and make him my husband.
Then, ominously, she added: I am afraid.[611]

Suppiluliumas, unsure that this might not be a hoax, sent an ambassador to Egypt. Ankhesenamun successfully entertained her Hittite guest, assured him that she was earnest in her request, and sent him back to his master along with an Egyptian representative, Hania, who carried another pleading letter from the queen.[612] In response, the Hittite king sent his son, Zannanza. However, the prince was ambushed and killed before he ever reached Memphis.[613] Most believe that Ay and Horemheb were both involved in the assassination of Zannanza.[614] Military actions ensued between Egypt and the Hittites after news of his son's demise reached Suppiluliumas, which resulted in Ay laying claim to the title, "Smiter of the Asiatics."[615]

Ankhesenamun, as the last living link to the royal bloodline, was probably forced to marry Ay when he ascended to the throne. A blue ring, now in the West Berlin Museum, likely testifies to that sad fact, as it is inscribed with both the names of Ankhesenamun and Ay.[616] However, that is the last that is ever heard of her. Four years later, Ay died and was succeeded by Horemheb, who surely would have married Ankhesenamun as well, if she had been alive.[617]

Why would Ankhesenamun send to Suppiluliumas for a husband? Was she seeking to hand Egypt over into the hands of its greatest enemy? Why did Ankhesenamun perceive herself as desperate? Of whom was she afraid? Perhaps the young woman was more aware than anyone of what had become of her parents, her siblings, and her husband. It seems that she had very good reason to be afraid. None of her family had been able to save themselves, and there was no one left for her to turn to. Perhaps she was turning to a place that Ay and Horemheb would fear; "the enemy of my enemy is my friend."

Of course, the official answer in ancient times for all the tragedy that befell Akhet-Aten was retaliation by the gods for abandoning the venerated religion of Egypt.[618] Tutankhamun posted a restoration stela that said:
Now His Majesty appeared as king at a time when the temples of gods and goddesses from Elephantine as far as the Delta marshes had fallen into ruin, and their shrines become dilapidated. They had turned into mounds overgrown with [weeds], and it seemed that their sanctuaries had never existed: their *enceintes* [houses] were (crisscrossed) with footpaths. This land had been struck by catastrophe: the gods had turned their backs upon it. If (ever) the army

was dispatched to the Levant [Syria] to extend the borders of Egypt, they had no success. If (ever) one prayed to a god to ask something of him, he never would come at all; if (ever) one supplicated any goddess likewise, she would never come at all. Their hearts were weakened in their bodies, (for) they had destroyed what had been made.[619]

Hardly anyone believes that, Tut, a mere child, issued the above decree by himself.[620] The obvious author, the obvious ruler was Ay; and "the reins of government were picked up from the point where Amenophis III had dropped them."[621] It's significant that the official excuse for what had happened, like all propaganda, was blown out of proportion; and it's even more chilling to consider that the document may have been used by a murderer to deflect attention away from his own culpability.[622] After all, the one person who stood to gain from the deaths of Akhenaten, Smenkhkare, and Tutankhamun was Ay. In actuality, Ay may have been running Egypt for a long, long time.[623]

If Meketaten died of an illness that appeared to be plague, it might have been relatively easy to convince her grief stricken parents and grandmother to retreat into seclusion. With Queen Tiye, Akhenaten, and Nefertiti living in different residences, it would have been much easier to begin the process of slowly poisoning the monarchs without them being aware that the others were sick with similar symptoms. Likely, Queen Tiye succumbed first, having outlived her husband, but probably not by more than two years.[624] In short order, Nefertiti followed. Having Kiya alive would have given too much potential power to a foreign kingdom, so she was eliminated. Meritaten may have died in childbirth, but that is purely speculation. Akhenaten, the largest and strongest, would have taken the longest to poison. However, when Smenkhkare and Tut showed any sign of independence from Ay's puppet strings, they too were killed. Ay stepped into the limelight, but the light of truth may be yet to shine on either him or on his successor, Horemheb. Although, after his short time as pharaoh, there seems to have been little regard for Ay at the time of his death.[625] To what extent and just how much Ay and Horemheb worked together to bring down the Amarna administration is unknown, but the fact that they were collaborators is nearly certain.[626] As it turns out, Ay buried the players, and Horemheb cleared the board.[627] Between them, they successfully erased the memory of Amarna for thousands of years.[628]

Ray contends that Horemheb's actions were "reactionary," restorative, and righteous; he was reacting to the chaos of Amarna, was restoring Egypt to the way it had been, and was seeking justice.[629] Shortly after the death of Tut, Horemheb launched a Syrian campaign. However, restoring the empire proved to be more than Horemheb could muster. The days of Thutmose III and his army were long gone. It was all that Horemheb could do to maintain the borders of Egypt itself.[630]

Why do the eyes of history not view Akhenaten in the same way as Horemheb? If the theory espoused in this book is true, Akhenaten, too, was three thrones removed from chaos—the chaos of the exodus, and his actions were merely reactionary to the failure of the gods during that time. Akhenaten, too, believed that he was restoring Egypt—to the way it had been before the lies of polytheism. Furthermore, Akhenaten, perhaps more than any pharaoh, perhaps more than any man in ancient times, sought righteousness. He sought to do what was right in the eyes of his God and he sought justice for the one God who deserved to be honored. It is compelling to reconsider God's statement to Moses, "I will be honoured [sic] upon Pharaoh, and upon all his host; that the Egyptians may know that I am the Lord" (Exodus 14.4). Most, even most Bible scholars, would likely deem this verse to be only talking about the pharaoh who drowned in the sea with his army. Surely, the Egyptians knew that a God had been responsible for that tragic event, and there was probably fear added to the fear that they had already experienced in the plagues (Exodus 14.31). However, that is not exactly the same dynamic as honoring God. Amenhotep IV honored a new God, but no pharaoh ever heaped honor for God upon himself like Akhenaten did! He did his best to bring honor to God through all his hosts: all his family, all his people, all his empire; and he wanted more than anything for the Egyptians to know who the one true God is. Perhaps Exodus 14.4 was truly fulfilled in Amarna.

It is true that the size of the Egyptian empire suffered during the days of Amenhotep III and Akhenaten. Clearly, most of Canaan was lost. However, since Joshua acknowledges that the land of the Philistines and other areas along the coastlands were not successfully "possessed" during the Hebrew conquest, it may be that regions along the Via Maris maintained ties and tributes to Egypt (Joshua 13.1-5). Still, it is puzzling to consider why subsequent pharaohs did not immediately seek to recapture areas lost in the Levant that had been part of the empire since the Middle Kingdom. Certainly, the warrior pharaohs of the early New Kingdom would have acted swiftly and decisively to reclaim territory and valuable Levantine overland trade routes facilitating access to the Euphrates. Of course, the excuse given in Tut's restoration stela was that campaigns launched into the Levant failed because of the pitiful condition of Egypt's neglected deities. Was this really the reason? Numerous campaigns into Nubia, Syria, Libya, and engaging the Hittites were vigorously conducted from the days of Tut through Ramses II. Why were the pharaohs of the waning 18th Dynasty and the early 19th Dynasty more interested in recapturing Kadesh on the Orantes than the Jordan Valley, the Transjordan, the hill country of Hebron, etc? Were they seriously less concerned about engaging Syria and the Hittites, two of the four most powerful nations in the region, than they were about challenging the rag-tag, coming-out-of-nowhere Habiru? Or, could it be that the post-Amarna, bombastic pharaohs feared the God of the Habiru and knew better than to court disaster. They doubted the protection of even the "reinvigorated" gods of Egyptian devotion.[631]

Nevertheless, one would think that Egyptians would have become accustomed to the inaction of their traditional gods. After all, how many prayers to Amun, Hathor, Isis, and/or Osiris were answered during the plagues? For that matter, where were the gods during the famine of Joseph, or in the rise of the Hyksos?

Yet, perhaps the greater question is, where was Aten? Why did Aten not protect Akhenaten, his family, or his city? It seems that "Aten did not offer protection against illness, injustice, or death."[632] Certainly, if Aten was Yahweh, the God of the Bible, he was strong enough and was able to keep tragedy at bay. Was he not pleased with Akhenaten? Did he not see all the sacrifices that Akhenaten made in order to worship him?

Many people across time have held the conception that God blesses the righteous by protecting them from all harm and by showering them with rich physical rewards. However, this is a perception that is not completely supported in scripture. Righteous Abel still died even though his worship was acceptable in the eyes of God. Job's friends were convinced that God was punishing him for unrighteousness and that was why terrible physical tragedy after tragedy had entered Job's life. However, God was never under obligation, especially with non-Hebrews, to grant physical blessings and protection for righteousness. The book of Hebrews speaks of righteous people in the days of the Old Testament those who:

> . . . were tortured, not accepting deliverance; that they might obtain a better resurrection: And others had trial of cruel mockings and scourgings, yea, moreover of bonds and imprisonment: They were stoned, they were sawn asunder, were tempted, were slain with the sword: they wandered about in sheepskins and goatskins; being destitute, afflicted, tormented; (Of whom the world was not worthy:) they wandered in deserts, and in mountains, and in dens and caves of the earth. And these all, having obtained a good report through faith, . . . (Hebrews 11.35-39)

According to the Bible, God promised Hebrews, living under the Law of Moses, physical blessings in return for their obedience, according to the terms of the covenant that they entered with God, but that agreement was exclusive and time specific (Deuteronomy 7.6-16). The terms of that covenant did not even extend to Christians living under the new covenant in the New Testament. Though they had responded in obedience to the gospel message, at peril of life, livelihood, and property, God still allowed a terrible famine to cause suffering even for Jewish Christians living in Jerusalem during the first century (Acts 2-4; 11.27-29). Though Christians throughout the Roman Empire converted under threat of terrible persecution, God didn't stop the mouths of lions in the coliseum as he did for Daniel in the lion's den (I Corinthians 15.32; Daniel 6).

Nevertheless, the misconception that physical blessings are always the reward for devotion to God has persisted from ancient times to present day. Job's friends were certainly of that mindset. It is possible that Akhenaten also believed that Egypt's dedication to God would eventually result in peace and prosperity. Perhaps it would have, but God's greater blessings are spiritual. Bad things do happen to good people! Even obeying the Lord's instructions doesn't always mean smooth sailing; after all, a terrible storm still threatened to capsize their boat though Jesus, himself, told his disciples to go to the other side of the Sea of Galilee (Luke 8.22-24). God *is* the giver of every good gift, but he gives good gifts to everyone—righteous and unrighteous.

If this is true, why follow God? Why be righteous? Much like ancient Egyptians, the righteous of all time have been "all about" the afterlife. God is a spirit, and the righteous long for spiritual blessings; physical blessings, to the righteous, are above and beyond what is expected or deserved (John 4.24; II Corinthians 3.17; 4.11-5.4). Jesus said, "None is good, save one, that is, God" (Luke 18.19). Romans says, "all have sinned, and come short of the glory of God" (Romans 3.23). No one deserves blessings, but God, ultimately, does not deal with the righteous according to what they deserve (Titus 3.5). This is the greatest blessing of all (Psalms 32.2).

Just because tragedy befell Akhet-Aten does not mean that the God that Akhenaten worshiped abandoned him. God allowed righteous Abel to be murdered, but, according to the Bible, God did not abandon Abel; God didn't even abandon Abel's blood, and thousands of years after the fact, God still remembered (Genesis 4.10; Matthew 23.35; Luke 11.51; Hebrews 11.4). Akhenaten did not see himself as abandoned either. Indeed, in the heartbreaking scene preserved outside Meketaten's death chamber, the rays of Aten continued to shine comfort and to lend strength. Aten was there to help Akhenaten's family bear tragedy. If Akhenaten was worshiping the God of the Bible in righteous obedience, God will remember and honor his service *forever*. In fact, God may have stated specific remembrance of the Amarna experiment in the curious wording of heavenly rewards expressed in Revelation 7.16, "neither shall the sun light [beat down] on them, nor any heat."

Tutankhamun and Ankhesenamun

It has been suggested that what really killed Akhenaten was his utter disappointment over the rejection of Atenism by Egyptians.[633] The long-term reward that Akhenaten sought was life after death, but in the short-term, he had hoped to convince others to seek and to follow the teachings of the God of Egypt. Though there's reason to believe that a tiny remnant of Akhenaten's religion persisted, sadly, in his efforts to convert Egypt, he largely failed.[634] Yet, in the most profitable way, perhaps Akhenaten didn't fail (Mark 8.16). Solomon said, "Let us hear the conclusion of the whole matter: Fear God, and keep his commandments: for this is the whole duty of man. For God shall bring every work into judgment, with every secret thing, whether it be good, or whether it be evil" (Ecclesiastes 12.13-14). Ultimately, no one, other than God, can judge Akhenaten. However, a consuming reverence and devotion to one God is obvious to any student of Amarna. If Aten was the God of the Bible, Akhenaten achieved his whole duty. Akhenaten identified and glorified *the* God of Egypt.

Citations

1. Dodson & Dyan 130; Silverberg 19; Reifstahl 61
2. Tyldesley, *Pharaohs* 124; Grosvenor 102; Reifstahl 80; Redford, *Akhenaten* 35; Bille-De Mot 27
3. Bille-De Mot 28
4. Moran 93
5. Ikram 79, 179; Aldred 259; Booth 106; Grosvenor 106; Reifstahl 79; Tyldesley, *Pharaohs* 122
6. Bille-DeMot 37; O'Connor 257; Tyldesley, *Pharaohs* 125
7. Newby 101; Silverberg 43; Shaw 267
8. O'Connor & Cline 32
9. *Ancient Egypt Unearthed*
10. Reeves & Wilkinson 174
11. Aldred 146
12. Newby 127; Reeves & Wilkinson 177; Shanks & Meinhardt 16; Silverberg 29
13. Newby 100
14. O'Connor & Cline 6; Redford, *Akhenaten* 35-36; Reifstahl 78
15. Booth 105
16. Dodson & Dyan 144
17. Newby 101; Bille-De Mot 16
18. Fletcher 68, 71; Grosvenor 102
19. Dodson & Dyan 144
20. Raymaekers 31
21. Assmann 31
22. Booth 105; Aldred 259
23. Shanks & Meinhardt 16; Gore; Silverberg 41, 159-160; Aldred 173-175, 181
24. Raymaekers 32; Gore; Aldred 85, 262; Redford, *Akhenaten* 60
25. Aldred 88
26. Aldred 88
27. Aldred 178, 260
28. Aldred 71
29. Booth 106; Shanks & Meinhardt 18; Redford, *Akhenaten* 175; Silverberg 19, 53; Breasted, *Development* 319
30. Silverberg 34
31. *Ancient Egypt Unearthed*; O'Connor & Cline 75; Tyldesley, *Pharaohs* 122, 125; Reifstahl 177; Aldred 239; Bille-De Mot 31, 39
32. Bille-De Mot 26; Reifstahl 61
33. Dodson & Dyan 142; O'Connor & Cline 134; R. Smith 64
34. Dodson & Dyan 142; Bryan 23; Gore; Tyldesley, *Pharaohs* 127
35. Booth 113; Dodson & Dyan 142; Davies 20; Assmann 169-170; Redford, *Akhenaten* 141; Gore; Aldred 85, 266-268; Silverberg 56-57
36. Redford, *Akhenaten* 51
37. Booth 110; Tyldesley, *Pharaohs* 127; Newby 119; Dodson & Dyan 142; Redford, *Akhenaten* 54; Aldred 180
38. Silverberg 216
39. Redford, *Akhenaten* 177
40. Newby 123
41. Gore
42. Bille-De Mot 31
43. Fletcher 16; Aldred 19; Redford email 23; Bille-De Mot 130; Silverberg 79; Shanks & Meinhardt 16
44. Silverberg 52; Bille-De Mot 54
45. Kemp 265
46. Bryan 150
47. Bryan 206
48. D. Stewart 50; Lange & Mirmer 533; Petrovich 14
49. Bryan 142
50. Bryan 350
51. Fletcher 16
52. O'Connor & Cline 51
53. O'Connor & Cline 28; Bryan 40; Lange & Mirmer 379; Breasted, *Development* 76
54. D. Stewart 51; Newby 93; Silverberg 49
55. Davis 72; Beegle 69; Greenberg 68
56. Silverberg *ix*
57. O'Connor & Cline 291; Silverberg 166; Redford email
58. Redford, *Akhenaten* 176; Aldred 279
59. Bryan 151
60. Bille-De Mot 54; Silverberg 70; Greenberg 66
61. Beegle 69, 73
62. Beegle 25
63. Beegle 24; Silverberg 202; Greenberg 65
64. Beegle 73; Bille-De Mot 170
65. Kitchen, *Reliability* 346; Winlock, *Excavations* 10
66. Davis 72
67. Hamlyn 90
68. Breasted, *Development* 337
69. Kitchen, *Reliability* 347; Lewy, *Origin* 2; Aling, *Egypt* 31-32
70. Beegle 25; Assmann 23, 46; Bille-De Mot 31
71. Docker
72. Bauval & Gilbert 100-101
73. Bauval&Gilbert 89; Breasted, *Development* 144, 149
74. Bauval & Gilbert 125
75. Aldred 261
76. Shanks & Meinhardt 34-35
77. Shanks & Meinhardt 50
78. Bryan 156
79. Bille-De Mot 30; Silverberg 7
80. Rawlinson 335
81. Bryan 144
82. Aldred 239
83. Breasted, *Development* 334
84. Aldred 71
85. Shanks & Meinhardt 23; Redford, *Akhenaten* 172; Aldred 244
86. David 47; Silverberg 4
87. Newby 123
88. Redford, *Akhenaten* 176; Bille-De Mot 54
89. Silverberg 71
90. Booth 122
91. Redford, *Akhenaten* 176; Aldred 279
92. Bille-De Mot 57; Silverberg 163; Breasted, *Records II* 390
93. Aldred 60; Silverberg 59
94. Tyldesley, *Pharaohs* 128; Aldred 273
95. Silverberg 49
96. Raymaekers 32
97. Silverberg *xii*; Booth 115
98. Aldred 269; Ray 62
99. Bille-De Mot 44
100. Assmann 168
101. Assmann 168
102. Redford, *Akhenaten* 170; Silverberg 33; Redford email
103. O'Connor & Cline 272; Booth 118; Tyldesley, *Pharaohs* 125; Dodson & Dyan 142; Hamlyn 90; Lange & Mirmer 379; Redford, *Akhenaten* 67; Aldred 71
104. Raymaekers 28
105. Silverberg 33
106. Redford, *Akhenaten* 176
107. Silverberg 62, 76
108. D. Stewart 71
109. Silverberg 138
110. Silverberg 78; 197
111. Winsey 12
112. Aldred 111,112;Booth112;Newby126; Fletcher 15

113. Bille-De Mot 42
114. Murnane 155; Bille-De Mot 58
115. Aldred 245
116. Path, "Is There a Creator?"

117. Dodson & Dyan 142
118. Aldred 44
119. Murnane 69; Silverberg 60; Davies 21
120. Tyldesley, *Pharaohs* 133
121. Booth 115; Butler 255
122. Silverberg 94
123. Booth 118; Redford, *Akhenaten* 143; Aldred 247
124. Silverberg 214; Booth 115; Redford, *Akhenaten* 142; Aldred 269
125. Aldred 268; Silverberg 48
126. Redford, *Akhenaten* 186
127. Booth 115; Shaw 254; R. Smith 46
128. Bille-De Mot 78
129. Aldred 268
130. Smithsonian clip
131. Tyldesley, Pharaohs 133-134; Dodson & Dyan 146; Silverberg 132
132. Silverberg 93
133. Silverberg *xiii*
134. Booth 118; Redford, *Akhenaten* 72
135. Aldred 112
136. Aldred 275
137. Rawlinson 361
138. Redford, *Akhenaten* 138
139. El-Sabban *xii*; Shaw 283
140. Tyldesley, *Pharaohs* 103; Rawlinson 335
141. Dodson & Dyan 142; Shanks & Meinhardt 19
142. Gore; Bille-De Mot 43
143. Booth 117; Gore; Bille-De Mot 43
144. Aldred 18
145. Raymaekers 29
146. Redford, *Akhenaten* 63; R. Smith *xiv*
147. Redford, *Akhenaten* 62; Raymaekers 29; Aldred 259; Silverberg 97, 214, 217; Ray 60
148. Bille-De Mot 76; Silverberg 95
149. Tyldesley, *Pharaohs* 132
150. Aldred 259; Bille-De Mot 81
151. D. Stewart 65
152. Shanks & Meinhardt 20
153. Bille-De Mot 93, 95
154. Ray 61
155. Silverberg 94
156. Booth 123; Shanks & Meinhardt 20; R. Smith *xiv*
157. Booth 124; Steele 20; Dodson & Dyan 150; Redford, *Akhenaten* 191; Silverberg 132, 185
158. Silverberg 62
159. Shanks & Meinhardt 20
160. Silverberg 94
161. Assmann 170; Redford, *Akhenaten* 204
162. Tyldesley, *Pharaohs* 130; Bille-De Mot 93
163. Redford, Akhenaten 78
164. Redford, *Akhenaten* 138; Raymaekers 27
165. Aldred 249
166. Glausiusz; Silverberg 95
167. Bille-De Mot 78
168. Breasted, *Records II* 410
169. Silverberg 94
170. Bille-De Mot 81
171. Redford, *Akhenaten* 59, 133; Raymaekers 31
172. Strouhal 228; El-Sabban *xii*
173. Aldred 240
174. Bille-De Mot 89
175. Silverberg89;Bryan145;IpuwerStz XII;Aldred 242

176. Shanks & Meinhardt 26
177. Redford, *Akhenaten* 176
178. Redford, *Akhenaten* 177
179. Aldred 112, 303
180. Booth 124; Redford, *Akhenaten* 147; Raymaekers 30; Aldred 18, 275; Shaw 282
181. Newby 126; Aldred 240; Bille-De Mot 130
182. Breasted, *Records II* 400
183. Redford, *Akhenaten* 178
184. Booth 113; Dodson & Dyan 142
185. Rawlinson 360
186. Aldred 279
187. Redford, *Akhenaten* 179
188. Aldred 241; Shaw 8
189. Booth 118
190. Aldred 66
191. Silverberg 82-83
192. Redford, *Akhenaten* 178
193. Redford, *Akhenaten* 180
194. Parkinson, *Sinuhe* 134
195. Aldred 241
196. Booth 118
197. Aldred 303
198. Bille-De Mot 83; Shaw 284
199. Bille-De Mot 84
200. Breasted, *Records II* 402
201. Aldred 111
202. Bille-De Mot 89
203. Booth 118
204. Murnane 179-180; Aldred 112; R. Smith 65, 98
205. Butler 249
206. Silverberg 82
207. Redford, *Akhenaten* 151
208. Aldred 300
209. Silverberg 139
210. Aldred 304
211. Gore
212. Tyldesley, *Pharaohs* 126; Redford, *Akhenaten* 148; Moran *xv*
213. Aldred 190; Moran *xxxiv*
214. Kemp 291; Moran *xvi, xix*
215. Newby 114; Van Seters 163
216. Bille-De Mot 54
217. Aldred 191
218. Moran 101
219. Moran *xvii*
220. Moran *xxxiv*
221. Moran 140
222. Davis 32
223. Silverberg 41; Aldred 260
224. Silverberg 123
225. Redford, *Akhenaten* 200; Hoerth, *Peoples* 275
226. Moran 214
227. Pfeiffer 49; Moran 143; Gray 135
228. Pfeiffer 47; Murray 39
229. Beegle 32
230. Hoerth, *Archaeology* 216; Wiseman 5-6; Lewy, *Origin* 7
231. Hoerth, *Archaeology* 217
232. Hoerth, *Archaeology* 218
233. Moran 393
234. Moran 138
235. Moran 153
236. Moran 196
237. Moran 230
238. Silverberg 123; Wiseman 42
239. Pfeiffer 50; Silverberg 124
240. Silverberg 128
241. Moran 265, 380-92; A. Myers 336, 718; May 93

242. Moran 280
243. Moran 283

244. Moran 297
245. Moran 317
246. Moran 317
247. Moran 318-319
248. Moran 349
249. Moran 343
250. Moran 340
251. Moran 328-334; May 59
252. Pfeiffer 51
253. Assmann 30
254. Assmann 31
255. Silverberg 162
256. Newby 116; Beegle 31; Lewy, *Origin* 8; Lewy, *Hābirū* 604; Gray 141, 156, 171-172
257. Pfeiffer 53; Wiseman 7; Lewy, *Origin* 5; Lewy, *Hābirū* 594-595
258. Newby 94
259. Beegle 32
260. Newby 116; Silverberg 116; Lewy, *Origin* 2, 7
261. Beegle 32; Lewy, *Origin* 1
262. Moran 331, 334; Lewy, *Origin* 3
263. Moran 273
264. Aldred 111
265. Aldred 178-280
266. Redford, *Akhenaten* 194; Butler 256; Hoerth, *Peoples* 275
267. Redford, *Akhenaten* 138
268. Aldred 130; R. Smith 65-66
269. Aldred 303-304
270. Aldred 180
271. Aldred 190; 272
272. Murnane 170; Redford, *Akhenaten* 144
273. Tyldesley, *Pharaohs* 134; Silverberg 126; Breasted, *Development* 319

274. Redford, *Akhenaten* 202; Butler 256
275. Newby 123; Redford, *Akhenaten* 199
276. Silverberg 105
277. Moran 115
278. Moran 238
279. Moran 248-250
280. Redford, *Akhenaten* 202; Bille-De Mot 132
281. Moran 249
282. Moran 256
283. Silverberg 117-118
284. Moran 244, 251
285. Moran 244
286. Redford, *Akhenaten* 202
287. Moran 197
288. Redford, *Akhenaten* 201; Moran 249
289. Moran 303
290. Moran 233
291. Petrovich 15
292. Silverberg 197; Breasted, *Records II* 393
293. Moran 235; Aldred 282
294. Moran 140
295. Pfeiffer48-49;Silverberg 116, 119-124, 128; Aldred 283; Newby 128, 130; Spalinger 161, Moran 243, 268
296. Moran 133
297. Moran 307
298. Pfeiffer 50; Moran 298
299. Aldred 283; Moran 306-307
300. Silverberg 123
301. Moran 328, 332
302. Silverberg 116; Moran 270

303. Moran 340
304. Moran 275, 328
305. Moran 273
306. Moran 155
307. Moran 326
308. Moran 140
309. Moran 162

310. 310. T. Stewart 14
311. 311. Moran 245, 252
312. 312. Moran 242
313. 313. Moran 193
314. 314. Moran 137, 218
315. 315. Moran 188
316. 316. Moran 132
317. 317. Moran 174
318. 318. Moran 249
319. 319. Moran 243
320. 320. Moran 206
321. 321. Moran 181
322. 322. Moran 267; Greenberg 44
323. 323. Moran 162, 269
324. 324. Silverberg 142
325. 325. kitchen, *Reliability* 183
326. 326. Davis 47
327. 327. Hawass 40
328. 328. Bille-De Mot 16
329. 329. Tyldesley, *Pharaohs* 127
330. 330. Tyldesley, *Pharaohs* 122; Dodson & Dyan 130
331. *Ancient Egypt Unearthed*; Moran 44

332. O'Connor & Cline 61; Hawass 43
333. Parkinson, *Sinuhe* 31
334. Butler 259; Silverberg 77
335. Freud 141; Raymaekers 30; Silverberg 191, 207
336. Silverberg 191
337. O'Connor & Cline 9; Dodson & Dyan 142; Silverberg 165

338. Redford, *Akhenaten* 79
339. Booth 106; Bryan 350; Silverberg 165
340. Bille-De Mot 80
341. Booth 105; Silverberg 42, 52, 54, 215; R. Smith *xiv*
342. Redford, *Akhenaten* 204
343. Silverberg 63
344. Booth 106; Assmann 153; Aldred 259
345. Shanks&Meinhardt 16;Aldred 259; Aling, *Egypt* 62
346. Aldred 260
347. Aldred 260; Bille-De Mot 130
348. Bille-De Mot 169; Silverberg *xiv*, 51; Ray 63
349. Aldred 239; Silverberg 50
350. Freud 22; Shanks & Meinhardt 15; Assmann 169, 171; Aldred 113; Kitchen, *Reliability* 331
351. Lange & Mirmer 374; Bille-De Mot 169; Silverberg 50, 191
352. Ray 63
353. Silverberg 75
354. Breasted, *Records II* 389
355. Ray 63
356. Silverberg 8
357. Silverberg 79
358. Redford email; Bille-De Mot 169, 171
359. Hamlyn 28
360. Silverberg 6
361. Hamlyn 30; Lange & Mirmer 379
362. Hamlyn 30; Rawlinson 359
363. Lange & Mirmer 379
364. Bille-De Mot 169

365. Hamlyn 90
366. Silverberg 6
367. Hamlyn 28
368. Shanks & Meinhardt 13; Aldred 240
369. Watterson 170
370. Rawlinson 358
371. Silverberg 6
372. Bille-De Mot 171
373. Butler 250
374. Silverberg 4
375. Newby 124
376. Ray 63
377. Shanks & Meinhardt 12; Ray 63
378. Shanks & Meinhardt 14
379. O'Connor & Cline 35
380. Newby 118; Bille-De Mot 44; Ray 63, 65
381. Dodson & Dyan 142; Assmann 153
382. Redford, *Akhenaten* 176
383. Shanks & Meinhardt 14; Docker
384. Butler 250; Silverberg 74
385. Aldred 111; Bille-De Mot 43
386. Tyldesley, *Pharaohs* 128
387. Murnane 167; Bille-De Mot 53; Bryan 162; Redford, *Akhenaten* 139; Gore; Ray 64
388. Breasted, *Records II* 410
389. Assmann 153; Aldred 259
390. Silverberg 80; Murray 38
391. Aldred 100; Shanks & Meinhardt 21
392. Redford, *Akhenaten* 186; Aldred 278
393. Shanks & Meinhardt 26; Assmann 168
394. Ray 64
395. Aldred 246
396. Aldred 247
397. Breasted, *Development* 339
398. Redford, *Akhenaten* 176
399. Redford, *Akhenaten* 177
400. Silverberg 98
401. Aldred 247
402. Aldred 247
403. Silverberg 203
404. Silverberg 208; Greenberg 59
405. Silverberg 198
406. Silverberg 199
407. Silverberg 204
408. Butler 255
409. Moran 39
410. Silverberg 79
411. Shanks & Meinhardt 11
412. Shanks & Meinhardt 34; Assmann 37
413. Silverberg 90
414. Booth 122; Shanks & Meinhardt 25; Ray 66; Aldred 273; R. Smith *xiv*
415. Silverberg *xiii*
416. Silverberg 202
417. Shanks & Meinhardt 12
418. Silverberg 77
419. Redford, *Akhenaten* 189
420. Redford, *Akhenaten* 190; Breasted, *Records II* 410
421. Newby 123; Silverberg 217 '
422. Booth 118
423. Tyldesley, *Pharaohs* 133
424. Raymaekers 26; Aldred 262
425. Assmann 153; Aldred 60; Ray 62
426. Seals
427. Silverberg 199
428. Breasted, *Records II* 391-392
429. Aldred 47-49; Breasted, *Records II* 395-397
430. Silverberg 199
431. Assmann 185
432. Bille-De Mot 43
433. Breasted, *Development* 9
434. Howard 484, 20, 564, 168
435. Breasted, *Records II* 389; Aldred 240; Shanks & Meinhardt 24
436. Breasted, *Records II* 417
437. Breasted, *Records II* 389
438. Breasted, *Records II* 408-409; Aldred 240
439. O'Connor & Cline 291; Aldred 240
440. Redford, *Akhenaten* 186; Aldred 278
441. Hamlyn 30
442. Aldred 100
443. Aldred 241; R. Smith 23, 57
444. Breasted, *Records II* 412
445. Murnane 55
446. Silverberg 76, Shanks & Meinhardt 19
447. Newby126; Shanks & Meinhardt 110; Bille-De Mot 169
448. Shanks & Meinhardt 28
449. Silverberg 193-194; Bille-De Mot 169
450. Bille-De Mot 83
451. Pfeiffer 43; Bille-De Mot 169
452. Bille-De Mot 171
453. Breasted,*History* 371-375; Silverberg 192; Assmann 180-191; Newby 126
454. Raymaekers 29
455. Silverberg 213
456. Bille-De Mot 25
457. Redford, *Akhenaten* 52; Booth 110; Moran 61
458. Silverberg 40
459. Tyldesley, *Pharaohs* 134; Assmann 25; Aldred 282; Silverberg 126
460. Vos 255
461. Butler 257
462. Booth 117; Bille-De Mot 59
463. Butler 249
464. Vos 309-310
465. Beegle 74
466. Ray 61
467. Dodson & Dyan 144
468. Butler 249
469. Murray 38; Silverberg *xiii*
470. Silverberg 70
471. Aling, *Ramses* 131; Hoerth, *Archaeology* 141; Hoffmeier 11
472. Booth 115; Redford, *Akhenaten* 142
473. Tyldesley, *Pharaohs* 134
474. Booth 118
475. Booth 113
476. Redford, *Akhenaten* 176
477. Butler 257
478. Raymaekers 31
479. Silverberg 81
480. Ray 65
481. Breasted, *Development* 330
482. Breasted, *Development* 324
483. Redford, *Akhenaten* 138-139, 175; Silverberg 58
484. Booth 122; Silverberg 57
485. Butler 256, 259; Aldred 245
486. Booth 116
487. Aldred 248; Silverberg 54
488. Newby 113
489. Silverberg 138; Ray 62
490. Butler 257
491. Booth 115
492. Silverberg 105
493. Butler 257
494. Bille-De Mot 60; Booth 115

495. Silverberg 58
496. Raymaekers 31; Butler 259
497. Redford, *Akhenaten* 72
498. Booth 122
499. Raymaekers 28; Breasted, *Development* 332
500. Bille-De Mot 89
501. Redford, *Akhenaten* 178
502. Redford, *Akhenaten* 178-179; R. Smith 95
503. O'Connor & Cline 272; Newby 125; Aldred 240; Silverberg 77; Breasted, *Records II* 389
504. Silverberg 40
505. Raymaekers 29
506. Silverberg 76
507. Bille-De Mot 58
508. Davies 9, 10
509. Davies 7
510. Tyldesley, *Pharaohs* 130; Dodson & Dyan 144, 147
511. Dodson & Dyan 146; Aldred 261; Silverberg 48; R. Smith 82
512. Dodson & Dyan 146, 153; Ray 70
513. Bille-De Mot 171; Shanks & Meinhardt 16; R. Smith 79
514. Booth 110; Aldred 261
515. Booth 115; Tyldesley, *Pharaohs* 133
516. Aldred 18; Shaw 284
517. Silverberg 103
518. Bille-De Mot 81
519. Silverberg 103
520. Aldred 304
521. Raymaekers 29
522. Bille-De Mot 81; R. Smith 124; Breasted, *History* 227
523. Silverberg 54; R. Smith 125
524. Bille-De Mot 38; Harris & Weeks 142; Booth 110
525. Silverberg 40; Redford, *Akhenaten* 52
526. Aldred 106; Newby 113; Booth 110
527. Tyldesley, *Pharaohs* 127
528. Aldred 66, 67, 80, 173, 175
529. Booth 110; Aldred 173
530. Silverberg 42
531. Bille-De Mot 38, 94-95, 118
532. Redford, *Akhenaten* 186
533. Aldred 180, 279
534. Bille-DeMot81;Aldred 279;Redford,*Akhenaten* 186
535. Bille-De Mot 12
536. Butler 255
537. Redford, *Akhenaten* 186
538. Butler 256; Redford, *Akhenaten* 205; Assmann 27
539. Assmann 25
540. Moran 107
541. Aldred 283

542. Assmann 39
543. Assmann 42
544. Silverberg 93
545. Redford, *Akhenaten* 186
546. Aldred 226
547. Gore; Aldred 227; Booth 125
548. Silverberg 93; *King Tut Unwrapped, Royal Blood*
549. Booth 125
550. Silverberg 93; *King Tut Unwrapped, Royal Blood*
551. Aldred 226
552. Booth 125; Gore
553. Aldred 289; Redford, *Akhenaten* 149; Silverberg 149; Booth 125
554. Oakes & Gahlin 447
555. Redford, *Akhenaten* 205; Aldred 287; Booth 125; Dodson & Dyan 156; R. Smith 94
556.
557. Booth 113-124; Silverberg 129, 130, 136
558. Silverberg 130
559. Aldred 230
560. Bille-De Mot 147; Ray 62
561. Aldred 227; Booth 125
562. Redford, *Akhenaten* 79
563. Redford, *Akhenaten* 186
564. Tyldesley, *Pharaohs* 127; Aldred 283; Booth 110; Reeves &Wilkinson 47,118; Dodson&Dyan 144
565. Booth 124
566. Silverberg 130
567. Dodson & Dyan 150; Aldred 110
568. Aldred 289; Booth 124
569. Aldred 227
570. Redford, Akhenaten 192-193

571. 570. Aldred 293
572. 571. Dodson & Dyan 150; Booth 113
573. 572. Aldred 227
574. 573. Redford, *Akhenaten* 150, 186; Gore
575. 574. Silverberg 126; Redford, *Akhenaten* 193; Booth 105; Gore
576. 575. Booth 125
577. 576. Silverberg 135
578. *King Tut Unwrapped: Royal Blood*

579. Booth 115; Bille-De Mot 153
580. Booth 118
581. Reeves & Wilkinson 119-121
582. Aldred 113
583. Silverberg 134; Booth 125
584. Silverberg 135
585. Booth 124
586. Redford, *Akhenaten* 205; Bille-

De Mot 81
587. Silverberg 131
588. Silverberg 133
589. Silverberg 131
590. Redford, *Akhenaten* 205
591. Redford, *Akhenaten* 207
592. Silverberg 134
593. Ray 71
594. Silverberg 127
595. Ray 71
596. Redford, *Akhenaten* 206
597. Redford, *Akhenaten* 207; Booth 106; Silverberg 30; Breasted, *Records II* 408
598. Ray 71
599. Silverberg 136
600. Bille-De Mot 82; Aldred 300
601. Redford, *Akhenaten* 206; Silverberg 99
602. Silverberg 147
603. Silverberg 101
604. Newby 123
605. Aldred 296; Redford, *Akhenaten* 205
606. Silverberg 137; Ray 68
607. Silverberg 135
608. Aldred 299
609. Silverberg 139
610. Booth 126
611. Dodson & Dyan 150; Redford, *Akhenaten* 207
612. Redford, *Akhenaten* 217
613. Redford, *Akhenaten* 218
614. Redford, *Akhenaten* 221
615. Ray 70; Dodson & Dyan 143
616. Redford, *Akhenaten* 221
617. Aldred 298
618. Aldred 300; Silverberg 148
619. Gore; Booth 125
620. Redford, *Akhenaten* 208; Assmann 27
621. Aldred 295; Ray 67
622. Aldred 295; Silverberg 139
623. Raymaekers 30
624. Silverberg 140; Ray 71
625. Aldred 181
626. Dodson & Dyan 153
627. Ray 68, 71
628. Redford, *Akhenaten* 67; Butler 258; Silverberg 150; R. Smith *xiv*
629. Silverberg 149; Redford, *Akhenaten* 91
630. Ray 77
631. Dodson & Dyan 143; Silverberg 139, 141
632. Shaw, eBook 283-290
633. Butler 259
634. Silverberg 135
635. Silverberg *xiv*; Shaw 285-286; Kitchen, *Reliability* 331

Conclusion

Evidence in Egyptian history supports the biblical account of the Hebrew sojourn in that great country.

The Bible tells the story of a pharaoh that, through the power of God, acquired unrivaled wealth and power with the discerning assistance of a vizier he named Zaphenat-Pa'aneah (Zatenaph-Ipi-ankh(u), or Ipi—for short), during a time of severe drought and famine. Egyptian history reports that Mentuhotep II was a wealthy pharaoh who, at the beginning of the Middle Kingdom, rose to unrivaled power. He had a vizier named Ipi, whose ka-priest, Heqanakhte, leaves vibrant record of a severe drought and famine.

Ipi, who is better known to Bible students as Joseph, brought his father, Jacob, his eleven brothers, and their wives and children to Egypt to live. They were given the best accommodations in Egypt and were allowed to settle in the rich farmland of the Delta where they exercised their livelihood as shepherds, sufficiently separated from Egyptians who found shepherds and Joseph's non-Egyptian family to be culturally offensive. According to prophecy, the Hebrews increased in numbers and became "great" in the land of Egypt, partly because they, with God's blessing, had enjoyed tremendous financial gain during a time when most others had suffered devastating financial loss.

Egyptian history speaks of—and the archaeological record confirms—mysterious foreigners who inhabited the Delta at the beginning of the Middle Kingdom. They lived in Avaris, a city that housed shepherds. The population of Avaris grew exponentially. Evidence of extensive, exotic trade indicates that the residents of Avaris had ample means. The thriving Syro-Palestinian community seems to have cohabited tranquilly beside Egyptians for decades, but eventually, perhaps following a catastrophe that made Avaris temporarily uninhabitable, the foreigners, known in Egyptian history as the Hyksos, invaded and conquered Memphis. They became "great" in the land of Egypt and ruled for over half a century to around a hundred years, during Egypt's Second Intermediate Period.[1]

The book of Exodus then introduces a pharaoh who was unaware of or was unimpressed with the story of Joseph. He subdued the Hebrews and pressed them into service as slaves, building treasure cities to support his army.

Egyptian history explains how the remarkable accomplishments of Joseph could have been forgotten. During the reign of the Hyksos, Egypt was divided. The Hyksos dominated Lower Egypt but held sway over much of the region, including parts of Upper Egypt and, certainly, into Canaan, where the Hyksos even maintained a second capital. However, a weak government in Thebes claimed dominion over Upper Egypt until the end of the Seventeenth Dynasty, when a young pharaoh named Ahmose was thrust into the arena. Since the rulers in Thebes were essentially cut off from northern Egypt for generations, Ahmose was uninformed and uninterested in the history of Lower Egypt except for the chapter of the Hyksos, the enemies that he utterly despised. Ahmose is remembered as the pharaoh who finally, successfully defeated the Hyksos, subdued them, and pressed them into service as slaves, quarrying stone for the pharaoh's building projects. Treasure cities, to house supplies that support operations of the military, would have been especially useful to Ahmose, who is the pharaoh credited with establishing a standing army in Egypt.

However, the Bible suggests that fear and mistrust of the Hebrews persisted in the administration of Egypt. A pharaoh, concerned about the potential might and the increasing number of Hebrew slaves, issued an edict ordering the slaughter of all newborn Hebrew males. When this law proved ineffective, the throne amended the decree, ordering Hebrew mothers to cast their own infant sons into the Nile. Yet one Hebrew mother, Jochabed, bravely resisted the pharaoh's egregious command. She fashioned a reed basket and set her precious baby adrift on the water. Pharaoh's daughter discovered the small ark, had mercy on the crying infant, defied her father's law, and adopted the Hebrew baby as her own son. She even hired Jochabed to act as the baby's wet-nurse. Moses is recorded in scripture with having one brother and one sister.

Likewise, the early New Kingdom saw the rise of an amazing young woman. Hatshepsut was the beloved daughter of pharaoh Thutmose I. Though her father was a hardened military general who had been appointed to the throne through the bloodline of her mother, Hatshepsut was not militaristic. She was, however, extremely bold and was willing to defy both convention and Egyptian law, proclaiming herself to be the first (known) woman to wear the title of pharaoh. Yet, a mysterious character played an integral role in Hatshepsut's life, family, and career; his name was Senenmut. By all accounts, Senenmut was precious to Hatshepsut and is usually associated with Neferure, Hatshepsut's daughter. Both Hatshepsut and Neferure seem to have been strangely close to Senenmut's lowly mother who, based on the interpretation of grave goods, had been hired to act as a wet-nurse for the royal family. Further tomb evidence indicates that Senenmut had one surviving brother and one surviving sister. A broad examination of Senenmut suggests that Hatshepsut loved him like a mother, that Senenmut was her adopted son.

Of course, the biblical account continues in the story of Moses. Though he had been raised in the royal household, at the beginning of middle age, Moses fled Egypt for fear of his life. He had killed an Egyptian taskmaster and feared retaliation from the sitting pharaoh who also may well have viewed Moses as a threat to his throne. The fugitive did not seek refuge in Canaan, the traditional home of his biological ancestors but fled to Midian where he lived for forty years.

When Hatshepsut was near fifty years old, around the time of her death, Senenmut disappeared. Hatshepsut's stepson, Thutmose III, became the undisputed pharaoh of Egypt. Then, for nearly twenty years, Thutmose III repeatedly campaigned into Palestine as he obsessively pursued the illusive "Prince of Kadesh," a fugitive accused of threatening pharaoh's authority. Eventually, Thutmose III captured the "prince of Kadesh," then unexplainably let him go. Afterward, Thutmose III returned to Egypt and turned his attention to attacking, vehemently, the memory of Senenmut and his relationship to Hatshepsut.

At eighty years old, Moses, following the instructions of God, returned to Egypt. The scriptures report that the pharaoh who had sought to kill Moses was dead, and a new pharaoh occupied the throne. Moses, with his brother Aaron, confronted the sitting pharaoh with this command of God: release the Hebrew slaves and allow them to serve a higher authority. The message did not sit well with the king. He was an excessively proud person and would not relinquish his authority easily. As a result, Egypt suffered a series of ruinous plagues, culminating in the *devastating* death of all first born in Egypt who were not protected by the blood of a sacrificial lamb marking the door of their house. The pharaoh, who obviously was not a first-born son, survived the tenth plague; but in his grief over the death of his own first-born son, agreed to allow the Hebrew slaves to leave Egypt, then changed his mind. He, along with his army, chased after the escaping Hebrews, followed them into the divided Red Sea but drowned when God closed the waters back over pharaoh, his army, his horsemen, and his chariots.

Forty years after the disappearance of Senenmut, the pharaoh who was occupying the throne of Egypt was Amenhotep II, the braggart son of Thutmose III. Of all the super egos that ever filled the double crown, Amenhotep II was arguably the most inflated. He certainly considered himself destined to be the undisputedly unequalled king of kings for all time, even though he was not the first-born son of either his mother or of Thutmose III. Amenhotep II is a person who would not have responded well to anyone challenging his authority or the authority of his god, Amun-Ra, who Amenhotep II was quite confident was the king of gods! Amenhotep II died suddenly, in middle age, and from all appearances in good health. Furthermore, there are indications in his tomb to suggest that Amenhotep II died of drowning.

Due to the death of pharaoh's first-born son in the tenth plague, the subsequent pharaoh to the king who drowned in the Red Sea could not have been the heir apparent. Furthermore, due to the destruction of Egypt's army, the new pharaoh's military strength would have been severely compromised. He would have inherited a nation in shambles. The tenth plague alone would have seriously undermined the productivity and skill level of the Egyptian workforce. Certainly, the effectiveness and power of Egyptian deities would have been suspect since they were specifically targeted in the plagues. Yet, the Bible is silent about events that transpired in Egypt immediately following the Hebrew exodus.

Egyptian history strongly indicates that Thutmose IV, the successor to Amenhotep II, was not the first-born prince. In fact, he may not have been the second or the third born! It is very likely that Thutmose IV, a mere teenager at the time of his father and brothers' untimely deaths, never expected to be king. The strength of Egypt's military at the beginning of Thutmose IV's reign is questionable at best because Egypt was attacked on her own soil! The young pharaoh successfully thwarted the Nubian invasion, but he probably did so with an army of raw recruits since there are multiple records of vigorous recruitment, training efforts, and outright conscription during his tenure. Simultaneously, Thutmose IV made unprecedented, concerted efforts to forge treaties with Egypt's enemies. Diplomacy vigorously replaced conquest in the new administration—and it was genuinely a new administration; Thutmose IV, unlike pharaohs before or after him, inherited almost no officials to serve in his court. Substandard workmanship in trades across Egyptian culture also indicate a sudden loss of experienced leaders and skilled workers during the reign of Thutmose IV. Marked increases in tombs at the rise of Thutmose IV suggest a record number of dead. But perhaps most intriguing is the shift in religious loyalty displayed by the Great House. Thutmose IV did not regard Amun-Ra with supremacy; instead a new, but old God came to the fore: Aten, the Lord of All. Therefore, in the exodus, God redeemed two peoples! He rescued his people, Hebrews, from slavery; and for a shining moment, beginning with Thutmose IV, the Lord of All rescued—from slavery to false gods—those Egyptians who chose to be his people and who followed his leading.

According to the Bible, when the Hebrews left Egypt, they plundered the land, and God caused Egyptians to be favorably disposed to relinquishing their riches. Of course, much of the goods that God directed the Hebrews to abscond from Egypt were later implemented to fashion religious artifacts intended for use in the intricate worship he would prescribe in the Law of Moses. Yet, God robs no man nor owes any debts.

Perhaps it should not be surprising then that Egypt soon experienced a golden age. Crops were plentiful, peace prevailed, and gold poured into the land during the reign Thutmose IV and his son, Amenhotep III.

For forty years, after leaving Egypt, the Hebrews wandered in the wilderness of Sinai. Then, under the leadership of Joshua, they entered Canaan and began the conquest that God allowed to fulfill the promise he had made to their ancestor, Abraham. Sometime within the first five years of the invasion, Joshua asked God for specific aid to procure a Hebrew victory during a particularly difficult and crucial battle. God answered Joshua, and the biblical account says that the sun stood still for an entire day.

Around forty years after the death of Amenhotep II, letters began to bombard Egypt from governors and vassals in Palestine. Canaan was under severe attack! Lands of the pharaoh were in grave jeopardy! A renegade group of assailants, identified in the Amarna letters in vague terms as the 'Apiru/Habiru, are generally believed, at some point, to be synonymous with the Hebrews. Deliverance and support of any kind was *begged* from Egypt in the Amarna tablets. Yet, no significant help was forthcoming, because sometime during the first five years of a new pharaoh, Amenhotep IV, a radical revolution was sparked in Egypt. Amenhotep IV changed the focus of the empire, changed the capitol city, changed the national religion, and changed his own name. Transfixed, the circle of the sun and the God symbolized by it had captured the attention and the imagination of Akhenaten, and his devotion to Aten was all consuming.

The Bible includes Psalm 104, which strongly indicates God's acceptance and involvement in the writing of words preserved in that particular hymn. Psalm 104 echoes (if not directly quotes) Akhenaten's *Hymn to the Aten,* which is preserved and duplicated in tombs of Akhet-Aten. Akhenaten's radical adoration, therefore, was recognized and approved by the God of the Bible. This was the God that Akhenaten worshiped.

Individually, any of the above concurrences could easily be dismissed as coincidence or as circumstantial. But when one considers that this string of evidence represents 500 years of sequential biblical and Egyptian history, reason dictates that the convergence cannot be coincidental. Evidence in Egyptian history supports the biblical account of the Hebrew sojourn in that great country.

Nevertheless, it's obvious to anyone familiar with the current understanding of Egyptian history that the theory expressed in this book does not agree with the accepted historical timeline. According to the Bible, the Hebrews sojourned in Egypt for 430 years, from the day Jacob entered the land to the day of the exodus

(Exodus 12.41). Yet the time allotted by the current chronology from the dawning of the Middle Kingdom to the death of Amenhotep II is 594 years! That's a difference of 194 years! The timelines don't agree; but then, Seti I disagrees with the modern timetable too.

At the end of the reign of Horemheb and at the rise of the Nineteenth Dynasty, Seti I celebrated his namesake, Seth, and established the Seth Cult of Ramses.[2] To commemorate the occasion, Seti I erected a stela to mark 400 years since Seth had last been acclaimed as the premier god in Egypt. Perhaps, as Dr. Bietak contends, it was little more than propaganda to legitimize the throne for the non-royal family of Ramses; still, according to the knowledge of Seti I, it seems that it had been 400 years since the rise of the Seth worshipers, the infamous Hyksos.[3]

According to the current time line, however, Seti I grossly miscalculated. The last year of Horemheb, according to current convention, is 1295 BC; 400 years before then would have been 1695 BC, one year into the reign of Neferhotep I, the first king of the Thirteenth Dynasty.[4] Could it possibly be that Neferhotep I was actually a Hebrew, that the first pharaoh of the Thirteenth Dynasty was really the first Hyksos king? Or, could it be that Neferhotep I was connected in some other significant way to the Hebrews? Perhaps that's why Hatshepsut desired to be preserved in statue, holding Neferhotep I's hand. Perhaps not all Hyksos kings were bad. Perhaps Neferhotep I was Hebrew, partly Hebrew, or perhaps his queen was Hebrew. But then, perhaps not. Perhaps Seti I should have just commissioned a 300 year stela instead, especially since no modern observer is really certain if the first Hyksos king came to power at the beginning of the Fifteenth Dynasty or not.

Yet, if it is assumed that Seti I was largely correct, it is fairly easy to calculate the approximate number of years between the death of Amenhotep II and the rise of Seti I. Thutmose IV reigned for 10 years, Amenhotep III reigned for 38 years, (allowing for a 12-year co regency) Akhenaten reigned an additional 5 years, Smenkhkare ruled perhaps about a year on his own, Tutankhamun reigned for about 10 years, Ay reigned for 2-4 years, and Horemheb was on the throne for 28 years. Therefore, a total of nearly 100 years transpired between the death of Amenhotep II and the rise of Seti I. If that 100 years is transposed to cover 100 years before Neferhotep I and then an additional 30 years is added to compensate for the difference between the biblical account of 430 years and the 400 years of Seti I's stela, then subtract 15 years for the time Joseph spent in Egypt before his family arrived, and the theory in this book only disagrees with the conventional timeline by about 45 years.

Still, when one considers that there seems to be more that we *don't* know about ancient times than what we do know, especially for arcane phases such as the Second Intermediate Period when reliable records are nearly non-existent and the unstable end of the Middle Kingdom when multiple pharaohs changed order in rapid succession, it is difficult to place great confidence in the accuracy of our modern timeline.[5] This uncertainty alone could account for the discrepancy between the conventional timeline and the time allowed in the theory of this book. It must also be considered that much of the information upon which the compilation of the modern timeline is made comes from documents that are known to be inaccurate and incomplete. The kings list provided by Manetho and by Diodorus Siculus, *The Royal Tablet of Karnak*, *The Royal Tablet of Sakkara*, and *The Royal List of Abydos* are all "incorrect."[6] They disagree with each other, except on one point: none of them lists Akhenaten!

Besides this, it is a known fact that ancient records were sometimes fabricated. After all, to ancient Egyptians, propaganda was more than powerful; it was prophetic. Thutmose III and Horemheb both fabricated the lengths of their reigns. Thutmose III was likely trying to eclipse the life of Senenmut, though most believe he was imposing his regency to encompass and supersede Hatshepsut. Nevertheless, he claimed to have ruled for 54 years, which is impossible, since he died in his mid-forties. Horemheb, too, attempted to cover the reigns of, at least, four pharaohs, presenting his reign as 59 years and directly succeeding Amenhotep III; however, Horemheb reigned less than thirty years.[7] In fact, Dr. Harris and Dr. Weeks contend, "[X-rays] have shown that the previous calculations of the ages at which various pharaohs died are incorrect, and therefore parts of the chronology of ancient Egypt will have to be altered, in some cases drastically."[8]

Allowances for discrepancies such as events that may have occurred concurrently, rather than sequentially, must also be taken into account. From the beginning of the Twelfth Dynasty, for instance, co-regency is an issue.[9] In the Amarna period alone, a time that spanned only around thirty years, there's a twelve-year discrepancy: did Akhenaten share the throne with Amenhotep III for a dozen years or not? Experts do not agree. Twelve years is a significant disparity within a thirty-year timeframe. The commonly accepted timeline for Egyptian history has many, many such discrepancies; therefore, the timeline is not reliable.

Nevertheless, no disrespect is intended toward the many experts who have labored intently to construct the currently accepted timeline. Certainly, they have taken the above observations into account and have tried very hard to compensate for the difficult variables. In fact, given the amount of time covered, it is amazing that the timeline seems to be as accurate as it is. Yet, most would concede that the timeline assigned for world history in general and for the history of ancient Egypt, to a degree, will always be a work in progress.

Perhaps Betsy Bryan expresses frustration with the timeline best:

There are those who recognize the pitfalls and rewards of examining chronological evidence, and there are those who consider issues with chronology to be little more than that which delays discussion.[10]

For that reason, the discussion in this book has given more credibility to the sequence of circumstances, people, and events rather than to where those particular subjects fall on a given chronological timeline. The similarity between the sequence of events in the biblical narrative from Genesis 37 through Joshua and the chronology of Egyptian history from the beginning of the Eleventh Dynasty through Akhenaten is uncanny.[11]

The God of the Bible, through the use of "men moved by the Holy Spirit," has written for us a book that is beyond compare. It is a spiritual book, but it's also history, poetry, science, geography, psychology, narrative, biography, and more. Infinite in its wisdom and perfect in its truth, transcending man's ability to duplicate; no earnest student of the Bible is disappointed. However, the Bible is not exhaustive; it tells about certain godly people across time, whose stories help to complete the overall purpose of the Bible, to present God's plan of salvation made available through Christ; but it does not tell the story of every faithful human being. That's why the study of Akhenaten is vital! Heroes of faith exist across time and space wherever there are those who diligently seek to know God and to obey his will. The God of the Bible *longs* to be the one God of every human being and the God of every nation, just as he was the God of Moses, the God of Akhenaten, and the God of Egypt!

Citations

1. Van Seters 154; Wiseman 87
2. Aling 130
3. Aling 131; Winlock, *Rise* 97
4. Rohl 20
5. Hoerth 141; D. Stewart 50
6. Silverberg 164; Van Seters 153
7. Silverberg 149
8. Harris and Weeks 176
9. Parkinson, *Sinuhe* 204; Petrovich 7, Shaw 149
10. Bryan 4
11. Hoffmeier 97

Bibliography

Aling, Charles F. "The Biblical City of Ramses." *Journal of the Evangelical Theological Society*. 25.2 (June 1, 1982): 129-133. Web. 1 September 2010.

Aling, Charles F. *Egypt and Bible History*. Grand Rapids, MI: Baker Book House Company. (1981). Print.

Aldred, Cyril. *Akhenaten King of Egypt*. London: Thames and Hudson Ltd. (1988). Print.

Allen, James P. "Heliopolis." *The Oxford Encyclopedia of Ancient Egypt*. Ed. Donald B. Redford, Oxford University Press, Inc., 2001. Middle Tennessee State University. 11 December 2011.
http://www.oxfordreference.com/views/ENTRY.html?subview=Main&entry=t176.e0302

Allen, James P. "Ramesses I." *The Oxford Encycloredia of Ancient Egypt*. Ed. Donald B. Redford, Oxford University Press, Inc., 2001 Middle Tennessee State University. 5 January 2012.
http://www.oxfordreference.com/views/ENTRY.html?subview=Main&entry=t176.e0601

Allen, James P. "Some Theban Officials of the Early Middle Kingdom." 15 April 2015.
http://gizapyramids.org/pdf_library/festschrift_simpson/01_allen.pdf

Allen, James P. The Heqanakht Papyri. New York: The Metropolitan Museum of Art. 2002. ebook.

Ancient Egypt Unearthed. Narr. Philip Madoc. Dir. Jill Morgan. Discovery Communications, LLV. 2009. DVD.

Assmann, Jan. *Moses the Egyptian*. Cambridge, MA: Harvard University Press. (1997). Print.

Axelrod, Alan. *Profiles in Leadership*. New York: Prentice Hall Press. (2003). Print.

Baron, Robert A. and Donn Byrne. *Social Psychology: Understanding Human Interaction*. Boston: Allyn and Bacon, Inc. (1978). Print.

Bauval, Robert and Adrian Gilbert. *The Orion Mystery*. New York: Crown Publishers, Inc. (1994). Print.

Beegle, Dewey M. *Moses, The Servant of Yahweh*. Grand Rapids, MI: William B. Eerdmans Publishing Company. (1972). Print.

Ben-Tor, Daphna. *Scarabs, Chronology, and Interconnections*. Fribourg, Switzerland: Academic Press Fribourg. (2007). Print.

Bible Reader Free. Hiddenfield Software. 2004. Web. 25 January 2011.

Bierling, Neal. *Giving Goliath His Due*. Grand Rapids, MI: Baker Book House. (1992). Print.

Bietak, Manfred. *Avaris; the Capitol of the Hyksos*. London, England: British Museum Press. (1996). Print.

Bille-De Mot, Eléonore. *The Age of Akhenaten*. London: Cory, Adams, & Mackay Ltd. (1966). Print.

Booth, Charlotte. *People of Ancient Egypt*. Brimscombe Port, Great Britain: Tempus Publishing Limited. (2006). Print.

Bolshakov, Andrey O. "Ka." *The Oxford Encyclopedia of Ancient Egypt*. Ed. Donald B. Redford, Oxford University Press, Inc., 2001. Middle Tennessee State University. 13 June 2012
<http://www.oxfordreference.com/views/ENTRY.html?subview=Main&entry=t176.e0369>

Breasted, James H. *A History of Egypt*. New York, NY: Charles Scribner's Sons. (1937). Print.

Breasted, James. H. *Ancient Records of Egypt, Volume 1*. Champaign, IL: University of Illinois Press. (2001). Print.

Breasted, James H. *Ancient Records of Egypt, Volume 2*. Champaign, IL: University of Illinois Press. (2001). Print.

Breasted, James H. *Development of Religion and Thought in Ancient Egypt.* Glouscester, MA.: Charles Scribner's Sons. (1970). Print.

Brier, Bob. *The Great Courses; Great Pharaohs of Ancient Egypt.* Dir. Jon Leven. The Learning Company Limited Partnership. 2004. DVD.

Brinkley, Joel. "Archeologists Unearth 'Golden Calf' in Israel." *The New York Times.* New York Times, 25 July 1990. Web. 28 September 2011.

Brock, Edwin. "Piecing it all Together; an Ongoing Study of the Later New Kingdom Royal Sarcophagi." *KMT* 2.1 (Spring 1991): 42-49. Web. 2 June 2011.

Brown, Chip. "The king herself: what motivated Hatshepsut to rule ancient Egypt as a man while her stepson stood in the shadows? Her mummy, and her true story, have come to light." *National Geographic* 215.4 (April 2009): 88. Web. 1 September 2010.

Bunson, Margaret. *The Encyclopedia of Ancient Egypt.* New York: Facts on File Limited. (1991). Print.

Bryan, Betsy M. *The Reign of Thutmose IV.* Baltimore: The John Hopkins University Press. (1991). Print.

Butler, Robert W. "Akhenaten, The Damned One: Monotheism as the Root of All Evil." *At the Interface: Probing the Boundaries* 63 (2011): 249-264. Web. 1 January 2011.

Cameron, Averil and Amélie Kuhrt. *Images of Women in Antiquity.* Detroit: Wayne State University Press. (1983). Print.

Casson, Lionel. *The Pharaohs.* Chicago: Stonehenge Press Inc. (1981). Print.

Champollion, Jacques. *The World of the Egyptians.* Genève, Swtizerland: Editions Minerva, S. A. (1971). Print.

Clayton, Peter A. *Chronicle of the Pharaohs.* New York: Thames and Hudson. (1994). Print.

Cloud, Rodney. Telephone conversation. 17 June 2014.

Collier, Mark and Bill Manley. *How to Read Egyptian Hieroglyphs.* Berkley, CA: University of California Press. (1998). Print.

Cottrell, Leonard. *Lady of the Two Lands.* Indianapolis, IN: The Bobbs-Merrill Company, Inc. (1967). Print.

Crans, Wayne J. "Culex pipiens: The Northern House Mosquito." *Rutgers Center for Vecotor Biology.* 7 July 1996. Web. 12 November 2011.

Curtis, Tim. "Read Through the Bible in a Year Lecture." Georgetown Church of Christ. 9 August 2017. Georgetown, TX.

David, Rosalie. *Egyptian Mummies and Modern Science.* Cambridge: Cambridge University Press. (2008). Print.

Davis, John J. *Moses and the Gods of Egypt.* Grand Rapids, MI: Baker Book House. (1971). Print.

Davies, N. de G. *The Rock Tombs of El-Amarna, Parts V & VI.* London: The Egypt Exploration Society. (2004). Print.

Der Manuelian, Peter. *Studies in the Reign of Amenophis II.* Hildesheim: Gerstenberg Verlag. (1987). Print.

Docker, John. "In Praise of Polytheism." *Semeia* (Winter 2001): 149. Web. 10 November 2011.

Dodson, Aidan and Dyan Hilton. *The Complete Royal Families of Ancient Egypt.* London, England: Thames & Hudson, Ltd. (2004). Print.

Dorman, Peter F. *The Monuments of Senenmut.* London, England: Kegan Paul International. (1988). Print.

Dothan, Trude and Moshe Dothan. *People of the Sea*. New York: Macmillan Publishing Company. (1992). Print.

Egypt Engineering an Empire. Narr. Michael Carroll & Peter Weller. Dir. Christopher Cassel. History Television Network Productions. 2006. Web. 19 April 2015. https://www.youtube.com/watch?v=sbPLXMeMm3

El-Sabban, Sherif. *Temple Festival Calendars of Ancient Egypt*. Wiltshire: Redwood Books. (2000). Print.

Engelbach, R. *Introduction to Egyptian Archaeology*. Cairo, Egypt: General Organization for Government Printing Office. (1961). Print.

ESV Study Bible. Wheaton, IL: Crossway Bibles. (2008).

Exodus Decoded, The. Narr. & Dir. Simcha Jacobovici. Associated Producers Production. Canada. 2005. DVD.

Expedition Unknown: Egypt's Lost Queens. Narr. Josh Gates. Dir. Douglas Segal. The Travel Channel. 2018. Television.

Expedition Unknown: Great Women of Ancient Egypt. Narr. Josh Gates. Dir. Douglas Segal. The Travel Channel. 2018. Television.

Feucht, Erika. "Family" *The Oxford Encyclopedia of Ancient Egypt*. Ed. Donald B. Redford, Oxford University Press, Inc., 2001 Middle Tennessee State University. 9 July 2011. http://www.oxfordreference.com/views/ENTRY.html?subview=Main&entry=t176.e0233

Fletcher, JoAnn. *Chronicle of a Pharaoh; the Intimate Life of Amenhotep III*. New York: Oxford University Press, Inc. (2000). Print.

Freud, Sigmund. *Moses and Monotheism*. New York: Vintage Books. (1939). Print.

Galford, Ellen. *Hatshepsut: The Princess Who Became King*. Washington D.C.: National Geographic Society. (2005). Print.

Gardiner, Alan. *Egypt of the Pharaohs*. London: Oxford University Press. (1961). Print.

Gill, David. "'Leaving Town' and 'Swedes': Edward Thomas and Amen-Hotep." *Notes and Queries* 248.3 (September 2003): 325-27. Web. 24 May 2010.

Glausiusz, Josie. "Body Image in Ancient Egypt." *Nature* 463.7277 (7 January 2010): 34. Web. 10 February 2012.

Gnirs, Andrea M. and James K. Hoffmeier "Military" *The Oxford Encyclopedia of Ancient Egypt*. Ed. Donald B. Redford, Oxford University Press, Inc., 2001 Middle Tennessee State University. 9 July 2011. http://www.oxfordreference.com/views/ENTRY.html?subview=Main&entry=t176.e0456.s0001

Gore, Rick. "Pharaohs of the Sun." *National Geographic* 199.4 (April 2001): n. pag.Web. 6 November 2011.

Gray, Mary P. "The Hābirū-Hebrew Problem in the Light of the Source Material Available at Present." *The Hebrew College Annual*. XXIX 1958. 135-202. Print.

Greenberg, Moshe. *Understanding Exodus*. Eugene, OR: Cascade Books. (2013). Print.

Grosvenor, Melville Bell. *Ancient Egypt*. Washington D.C.: The National Geographic Society. (1978). Print.

Hamlyn, Paul. *Egyptian Mythology*. New York: Tudor Publishing Co. (1965). Print.

Harris, James E. and Kent R. Weeks. *X-Raying the Pharaohs*. New York: Charles Scribner's Sons. (1973). Print.

Hattstein, Markus. *Lost Civilizations*. New York, NY: Parragon. (2009). Print.

Hawass, Zahi. *The Lost Tombs of Thebes; Life in Paradise*. New York: Thames & Hudson. (2009). Print.

Hawass, Zahi and Francis Janot. *The Royal Mummies: Immortality in Ancient Egypt*. Vercelli: White Star Publishers. (2008). Print.

Hayes, William C. *Royal Sarcophagi of the XVIII Dynasty*. Princeton: Princeton University Press. (1935). Print.

Hetherington, E. Mavis and Ross D. Parke. *Child Psychology, a Contemporary Viewpoint*. New York: McGraw-Hill Book Company. (1975). Print.

Hoerth, Alfred J. *Archaeology and the Old Testament*. Grand Rapids, MI: Baker Books. (1998). Print.

Hoerth, Alfred J., Gerald L. Mattingly, and Edwin M. Yamauchi. *Peoples of the Old Testament World*. Grand Rapids, MI: Baker Books. (1994). Print.

Hoffmeier, James K. *Israel in Egypt*. New York: Oxford University Press. (1996). Print.

Holness, Alfred. *Egypt as Seen in Scripture and on the Monuments*. Glasgow, Scotland: The Glasgow Bible and Book Depository. (1900). Print.

Hornung, Erik. *The Valley of the Kings*. New York: Timken Publishers, Inc. (1990). Print.

Howard, Alton H. *Songs of the Church*. West Monroe, LA: Howard Publishers. (1977). Print.

Hussein, Ahmed Elyas. "Similarities in the World of the Indian Ocean: Interaction of Cultures—Roots and Routes." *Canadian Association of Aftrican Studies Annual Conference/Canadian Council of Area Studes Learned Societies*. April 27-May 1, 2005. Web. 28 July 2011.

Ikram, Salima. *Death and Burial in Ancient Egypt*. London: Pearson Education Ltd. (2003). Print.

"Is There a Creator?" *Through the Wormhole*. Narr. Morgan Freeman. Dir. Lori McCreary. The Science Channel. 9 June 2010. Television.

James, T.G.H. *The Hekanakhte Papers and Other Early Middle Kingdom Documents*. New York: The Metropolitan Museum of Art. 1962. Print.

Janot, Francis and Zahi Hawass. *The Royal Mummies; Immortality in Ancient Egypt*. Vercelli, Italy: White Star S.p.A. (2008). Print.

Josephus, Flavius. *The Complete Works of Josephus*. Grand Rapids, MI: Kregel Publications. (1981). Print.

Kees, Hermann. *Ancient Egypt: A Cultural Topography*. Chicago, IL: University of Chicago Press. (1961). Print.

Kemp, Barry. *Ancient Egypt; Anatomy of a Civilization*. New York: Routledge. (2006). Print.

Key Word Study Bible. Chattanooga, TN: AMG Publishers. (1977). Print.

King Tut Unwrapped: Life and Death. Narr. Nick Schatzki. Dir. Brando Quilici. The Discovery Channel. 2009. Television.

King Tut Unwrapped: Royal Blood. Narr. Nick Schatzki. Dir. Brando Quilici. The Discovery Channel. 2009. Television.

Kitchen, K. A. *On the Reliability of the Old Testament*. Grand Rapids, MI: Wm. B. Eerdmans Publishing Co. (2003). Print.

Kitchen, Kenneth A. "Ramesses II" *The Oxford Encyclopedia of Ancient Egypt*. Ed. Donald B. Redford, Oxford University Press, Inc., 2001 Middle Tennessee State University. 25 July 2011. http://www.oxfordreference.com/views/ENTRY.html?subview=Main&entry=t176.e0602

Kitchen, Kenneth A. "The Patriarchal Age: Myth or History?" *Biblical Archaeology Review* March/April 1995. 48-57, 88-95. Print.

Landman, Neil H., Paula M. Mikkelsen, Rüdiger Bieler, and Bennet Bronson. *Pearls: A Natural History*. New York: American Museum of Natural History. (2001). Print.

Lange, Kurt and Max Hirmer. *Egypt; Architecture, Sculpture, Painting in Three Thousand Years*. London: Phaidon Publishers, Inc. (1968). Print.

Leach, Bridget and John Tait. "Papyrus." *The Oxford Encyclopedia of Ancient Egypt*. Ed. Donald B. Redford, Oxford University Press, Inc., 2001 Middle Tennessee State University.
31 December 2011. http://www.oxfordreference.com/views/ENTRY.html?subview=Main&entry=t176.e0547

Leahy, Anthony. "Sea Peoples." *The Oxford Encyclopedia of Ancient Egypt*. Ed. Donald B. Redford, Oxford University Press, Inc., 2001 Middle Tennessee State University.
21 September 2011. http://www.oxfordreference.com/views/ENTRY.html?subview=Main&entry=t176.e0643

Leca, Ange-Pierre. *The Egyptian Way of Death*. Garden City, NY: Doubleday & Company, Inc. (1981). Print.

Lesko, Leonard H. "Book of That Which is in the Underworld." *The Oxford Encyclopedia of Ancient Egypt*. Ed. Donald B. Redford, Oxford University Press, Inc., 2001.Middle Tennessee State University. 10 July 2011.
http:www.oxfordreference.com/views/ENTRY.html?subview=Main&entry=t176.e0100

Lewy, Julius. "A New Parallel Between Hābirū and Hebrews." *Hebrew Union College Annual*. XV 1940. 47-58. Print.

Lewy, Julius. "Hābirū and Hebrews." *Hebrew Union College Annual*. XIV 1939. 587-623. Print.

Lewy, Julius. "Origin and Significtion of the Biblical Term 'Hebrew.'" *Hebrew Union College Annual*. XXVIII 1957. 1-13. Print.

Luban, Marianne. "Queen Tiye and the Co-Regency." *Internet Archive WaybackMachine Beta*. 6:55:06. 25 October 2009. Web. 21 February 2012.

Ludwid, Emil. *Cleopatra The Story of a Queen*. New York: The Viking Press. (1937). Print.

Macalister, R. A. Stewart. *The Philistines Their History and Civilization*. Chicago: Argonaut, Inc., Publishers. (1965). Print.

Marowitz, Yvonne J. "Jewelry" *The Oxford Encyclopedia of Ancient Egypt*. Ed. Donald B. Redford, Oxford University Press, Inc., 2001 Middle Tennessee State University. 11 July 2011.
http://www.oxfordreference.com/views/ENTRY.html?subview=Main&entry=t176.e0362

Matthews, Victor H. and Don. *Old Testament Parallels*. New York, NY: Paulist Press. (1991). Print.

May, Herbert G. *Oxford Bible Atlas*. New York, NY: Oxford University Press. (1995). Print.

McWhirter, Norris. Guinness Book of World Records. Toronto: Bantam Books. (1986). Print.

Mertz, Barbara. *Temples, Tombs, and Hieroglyphs*. New York, NY: Coward-McCann, Inc. (1964). Print.

Meskell, Lynn. *Private Life in New Kingdom Egypt*. Princeton: Princeton Unviersity Press. (2002). Print.

Monet, Pierre. *Eternal Egypt*. New York, NY: The New American Library. (1964). Print.

Moran, William L. *The Amarna Letters*. Baltimore: The Johns Hopkins University Press. (1987). Print.

Morrison, Dan. "Ancient Egypt Cities Leveled by Massive Volcano, Lava Find Suggests." *National Geographic News*. National Geographic Society. 2 April 2007. Web.18 April 2012.

Murnane, William J. and Charles C. Van Siclen III. The Boundary Stelae of Akhenaten. London: Kegan Paul International. (1993). Print.

Murray, Margaret A. *The Splendour that was Egypt.* London: Sidgwick and Jackson Limited. (1963). Print.

Myers, Allen C. *The Eerdmans Bible Dictionary.* Grand Rapids, MI: William B. Eerdmans Publishing Co. (1987). Print.

Myers, Bernard S. *Art and Civilization.* New York, NY: McGraw-Hill, Inc. (1967). Print.

"Mystery of the Screaming Man." *Egypt Unwrapped.* Narr. J.V. Martin. Prod. Dir. Barny Revill. Atlantic Productions for National Geographic Channel. 2008. Television.

Newby, Percy Howard. *Warrior Pharaohs.* London, England: Faber and Faber, Ltd. (1980). Print.

Oakes, Lorna and Lucia Gahlin. *Ancient Egypt.* London, England: Anness Publishing, Ltd. (2002). Print.

O'Connor, David and Eric H. Cline. *Amenhotep III; Perspectives on His Reign.* Ann Arbor, MI: The University of Michigan Press. (2001). Print.

Oren, Eliezer D. *The Hyksos: New Historical and Archaeological Perspectives.* Philadelphia, PA: The University Museum. (1997). Print.

Papanek, John. *Egypt: Land of the Pharaohs.* Richmond, VA: Time-Life Books. (1992). Print.

Parkinson, R. B. "Sinuhe" *The Oxford Encyclopedia of Ancient Egypt.* Ed. Donald B. Redford, Oxford University Press, Inc., 2001 Middle Tennessee State University. 24 December 2011. http://www.oxfordreference.com/views/ENTRY.html?subview=Main&entry=t176.e0675

Parkinson, R. B. *The Tale of Sinuhe.* Oxford: Clarendon Press. (1997). Print.

Path, Winifred. 19 October 1995. Telephone.

Peloubet, F. N. Peloubet's Bible Dictionary. Philadelphia: The John C. Winston Company. (1925). Print.

Petrovich, Douglas. "Amenhotep II and the Historicity of the Exodus Pharaoh." *The Master's Seminary Journal* 17.1 (spring 2006): 1-30. Web. 17 January 2011.

Pfeiffer, Charles F. *Tell El Amarna And The Bible.* Grand Rapids, MI: Baker Book House. (1963). Print.

Pharaohs and Kings; a Biblical Quest. Narr. David Rohl. Dir.Timothy Copestake. Soul Purpose Productions. TLC. Silver Spring, MD. (1995). VHS.

Ramses: Wrath of God or Man? Narr. Morgan Freeman. Dir. Stephen Endelman. Discovery Communications, Inc. Cananda. 2004. DVD.

Rawlinson, George. *History of Ancient Egypt.* New York: Dodd, Mead & Company. (1882). Print.

Ray, John. *Reflections of Osiris.* New York, NY: Oxford University Press. (2002). Print.

Raymaekers, J. "Akhenaten-Ancient Egypt's Prodigal Son?" *History Today* 40.1(January 1990). Web. Academic Search Premier. 17 December 2011.

Redford, Donald B. *Akhenaten The Heretic King.* Princeton: Princeton University Press. (1984). Print.

Redford, Donald B. *A Study of the Biblical Story of Joseph.* Leiden, Netherlands: E. J. Brill. (1970). Print.

Redford, Donald B. "Exodus 1:11." *Vetus Testamentum* 13. 40 (1963): 401-418. Web.1 September 2010.

Redford, Donald B. "Mendes: City of the Ram and Fish; Microcosm of Ancient Egypt Lecture." Middle Tennessee State University. 20 October 2012. Murfreesboro, TN.

Redford, Donald B. *The Oxford Encyclopedia of Ancient Egypt*. New York: Oxford Universtiy Press, Inc. (2001). Print.

Redford, Donald B. "Questions About Aten." Message to Pamela O'Neal. 23 October 2011. email.

Redford, Donald B. "Trying to Understand." Message to Pamela O'Neal. 20 November 2011. email.

Redmount, Carol A. "Ethnicity, Pottery, and the Hyksos at Tell El-Makhuta in the Egyptian Delta." *Biblical Archeologist*. 58.4 (December 1995): 182-190. Web. 1 September 2010.

Reeves, Nicholas. *Ancient Egypt the Great Discoveries*. New York, NY: Thames & Hudson. (2000). Print.

Reeves, Nicholas and Ricahrd H. Wilkinson. *The Complete Valley of the Kings*. London: Thames & Hudson. (1996). Print.

Riefstahl, Elizabeth. *Thebes in the Time of Amenhotep III*. Norman, OK: University of Oklahoma Press. (1964). Print.

Roberts, Russell. *Rulers of Ancient Egypt*. San Diego, CA: Lucent Books. (1999). Print.

Robins, Gay "Women" *The Oxford Encyclopedia of Ancient Egypt*. Ed. Donald B. Redford, Oxford University Press, Inc., 2001 Middle Tennessee State University. 12 July 2011
http://www.oxfordreference.com/views/ENTRY.html?subview=Main&entry=t176.e0773

Roehrig, Catharine H. *Hatshepsut From Queen to Pharaoh*. New York, NY: The Metropolitan Museum of Art. (2005). Print.

Rohl, David M. *Pharaohs and Kings*. New York, NY: Crown Publishers, Inc. (1995). Print.

Romer, John. *Valley of the Kings*. New York: William Morrow and Company, Inc. (1981). Print.

ROM, Jim. "Biblical Treasure May be Forerunner of the Golden Calf." *The Guardian* (26 July 1990): 11. Web. 19 October 2011.

Ryholt, K. S. B. *The Political Situation in Egypt During the Second Intermediate Period*. Copenhagen, Denmark: Museum Tusculanum Press. (1997). Print.

Saleh, Mohamed and Hourig Sourouzian. *The Egyptian Museum Cairo*. Munich, Germany: Prestel-Verlag. (1987). Print.

Seals, Tom. "The Noachian Covenant and the Table of Nations: Genesis 9-10 Lecture." David Lipscomb University. 3 July 2012. Nashville, TN.

Secrets of Egypt's Lost Queen. Narr. Harry Prichett. Dir. Brando Quilici. The Discovery Channel. 4 December 2007. Television.

"Secrets of the Sphinx." *Egypt Unwrapped*. Narr. J.V. Martin. Prod. Dir. Barny Revill. Atlantic Productions for National Geographic Channel. 2008. Television.

Shanks, Hershel and Jack Meinhardt. *Aspects of Monotheism; How God is One*. Washington, DC: Biblical Archaeology Society. (1997). Print.

Shaw, Ian. The Oxford History of Ancient Egypt. Oxford: Oxford University Press. (2000). Print.

Shaw, Ian. The Oxford History of Ancient Egypt. Oxford: Oxford University Press. (2003). eBook. Web. 5 May 2015.
http://web.a.ebscohost.com.vwproxy.lipscomb.edu/ehost/detail?sid=0cf094d1-cc37-4090-889db526215514ef@sessionmgr4001&vid=0#db=nlebk&AN=380989

Silverberg, Robert. *Akhnaten The Rebel Pharaoh*. Philadelphia: Chilton Books. (1964). Print.

Silverman, David P. *Ancient Egypt*. London, England: Duncan Baird Publishers. (1997). Print.

Smith, F. LaGard. *The Daily Bible*. Eugene, OR: Harvest House Publishers. (1984). Print.

Smith, Ray Winfield and Donald B. Redford, *The Akhenaten Temple Project*. Warmisnster, England: Aris & Phillips Ltd. (1976). Print.

Soliman, Rasha. Old and Middle Kingdom Theban Tombs. London: Golden House Publications. (2009). Print.

Sourouzian, Hourig. "Merenptah" *The Oxford Encyclopedia of Ancient Egypt*. Ed. Donald B. Redford, Oxford university Press, Inc., 2001 Middle Tennessee State University. 26 July 2011
http://www.oxfordreference.com/views/ENTRY.html?subview=Main&entry=t176.e0448

Spalinger, Anthony. *War in Ancient Egypt*. Malden, MA: Blackwell Publishing. (2005). Print.

Stadelmann, Rainer. "Sety I" *The Oxford Encyclopedia of Ancient Egypt*. Ed. Donald B. Redford, Oxford University Press, Inc., 2001 Middle Tennessee State Universtiy. 26 July 2011
http://www.oxfordreference.com/views/ENTRY.html?subview=Main&entry=t176.e0657

Steele, Philip. *The Egyptians and the Valley of the Kings*. New York: Dillon Press. (1994). Print.

Stewart, Desmond. *The Pyramids and the Sphinx*. New York: Newsweek Book Division. (1971). Print.

Stewart, Ted. *Solving the Exodus Mystery*. Lubbock, TX: Biblemart.com. (1999). Print.

Strong, James. *Strong's Exhaustive Concordance*. Gordonsville, TN: Dugan Publishers, Inc. (1984). Print.

Strouhal, Eugen. *Life of the Ancient Egyptians*. Norman: University of Oklahoma Press. (1992). Print.

Szpakowska, Kasia. *Daily Life in Ancient Egypt*. Malden, MA: Blackwell Publishing. (2008). Print.

ten-Berge, R. L. and F. R. W. van de Goot. "Seqenenre Taa II, the Violent Death of a Pharaoh." *Journal of Clinical Pathology* 55.3 (March 2002): 232. Web. 1 September 2010.

Thomas, Robert L. *New American Standard Exhaustive Concordance of the Bible*. Nashville: The Lockman Foundation. (1981). Print.

Thompson, Frank Charles. *The Thompson Chain-Reference Bible, New American Standard.* La Habra, CA: The Lockman Foundation. (1983). Print.

Thompson, J. A. *Handbook of Life in Bible Times*. New York: Guideposts. (1986). Print.

Taburiaux, Jean. *Pearls: Their Origin, Treatment and Identification*. Radnor, PA: Chilton Book Company. (1986). Print.

Tyldesley, Joyce. *Egypt*. New York: Simon & Schuster Books for Young Readers. (2007). Print.

Tyldesley, Joyce. *Hatchepsut the Female Pharaoh.* London, England: Viking. (1996). Print.

Tyddesley, Joyce. *The Pharaohs.* London: Quercus Publishing Plc. (2009). Print.

Unger, Merrill F. *Unger's Bible Dictionary*. Chicago: Moody Press. (1977). Print.

Van Seters, John. *The Hyksos.* New Haven: Yale University Press. (1966). Print.

Velikovsky, Immanuel. *Ages in Chaos.* Cutchogue, NY: Buccaneer Books, Inc. (1952). Print.

Vos, Howard F. *Bible Manners and Customs.* Nashville, TN: Thomas Nelson Publishers. (1999). Print.

Watterson, Barbara. *The Gods of Ancient Egypt.* New York: Facts on File Publications. (1984). Print.

West, John Anthony. *The Traveler's Key to Ancient Egypt.* New York, NY: Alfred A. Knopf. (1985). Print.

Wilson, John A. *The Burden of Egypt.* Chicago, IL: University of Chicago Press. (1951). Print.

Winlock, H. E. *Excavations at Deir el Bahri 1911-1931.* New York: The Macmillan Company. 1942. Print.

Winlock, H. E. *In Search of the Woman Pharaoh Hatshepsut.* London, England: Kegan Paul. (2001). Print.

Winlock, H. E. *The Rise and Fall of the Middle Kingdom in Thebes.* New York: The Macmillan Company. 1947. Print.

Winsey, A. Reid. *Freehand Drawing Manual.* New York: Prentice Hall, Inc. (1950). Print.

Wiseman, D. J. *Peoples of Old Testament Times.* London: Oxford University Press. (1975). Print.

Woldering, Irmgard. *The Art of Egypt.* New York, NY: Greystone Press. (1962). Print.

y de la Torre, Walter Reinhold Warttig Mattfeld. "Site Proposals for Rephidim and Mount Horeb (Mount Sinai)." *Forbidden Knowledge: the Bible's Origins.* 17 December 2000. Web. 25 January 2012.

Zagorski, Nick. "Profile of Lonnie G. Thompson." Proceedings of the National Academy of Aciences of the United States of America. 25 July 2006. Web. 9 June 2012.

Zivie-Coche, Christine. *Sphinx: History of a Monument.* Ithaca: Cornell University Press. (1997). Print.

Zlotowitz, Meir. *The Family Chumash Bereishis.* Brooklyn, NY: Mesorah Publications, Ltd. (1989). Print.

Zodhiates, Spiros. *The Hebrew-Greek Key Word Study Bible.* La Habra, CA: The Lockman Foundation. (1977). Print.

Illustrations

Images in this edition are understood to be in the Public Domain or are classified as free to use. Every effort has been made to document images correctly and to find copyright holders. If there are errors or omissions they will gladly be rectified in subsequent editions.

Pg 2: Praefcke, Andreas. *Akhenaten, Nefertiti, and their Daughters.* Public Domain. Ägyptisches Museum Berlin, Inv. Web. 1 May 2012.
Pg 3: *Egypt Hieroglyphe4.* Public Domain. Wikimedia Commons. Web. 6 May 2012.
Pg 4: *Block from the Sanctuary in the Temple of Mentuhotep II.* Public Domain. Met. Museum of Art. Wikimedia Commons. Web. 1 May 2012.
Pg 10 : The Yorck Project. *Sennedjem Plowing.* Public Domain. DIRECTMEDIA Publishing GmbH. Wikimedia Commons. Web. 1 May 2012.
Pg 15: Captmondo. *The Narmer Palette.* Public Domain. Wikimedia Commons. 2 May 2012.
Pg 18: Markh. *Mentuhotep II's mortuary temple at Deir el-Bahri.* 2006. Wikimedia Commons. 3 May 2012.
Pg 20: Bodsworth, Jon. *Mentuhotep Seated.* 2007. Wikipedia. Web. 3 May 2012.
Pg 22: Biofeld of SPECTRE. *Hyksos.* 2007. Public Domain. Wikimedia Commons. Web. 2 May 2012.
Pg 24: Smith, G. Elliot. *Seqenenre Tao II.* 1912. Public Domain. Wikipedia. Web. 1 May 2012.
Pg 27: Udimu. *Ancient Egyptian Dagger.* Cairo Egyptian Museum. Wikimedia Commons. 10 May 2012.
Pg 30: O'Neal. *Jacob's Seal.*
Pg 32: Walters, Henry. *Scarab With Cartouche of King Sheshi.* 1911. Walters Art Museum. Wikimedia Commons. 10 May 2012.
Pg. 35: NebMaatRe. *Ibscha Relief Chnumhotep II.* 2008. Wikimedia Commons. Web. 3 May 2012.
Pg 37: Tupper, William Vaughn. *Statues of Shepherd Kings.* 1860-1890. Boston Public Library. Wikimedia Commons. 10 May 2012.
Pg 40: *Hyksos Woman Carrying a Child.* Free to Use and Modify. Google Images. Web. 2 September 2013.
Pg 46: *Ancient Egypt.* Public Domain. Internet Sacred Text Archive. Web. 11 May 2012.
Pg 48: Postdlf. *Hatshepsut.* 2005. Wikimedia Commons. Web. 4 May 2012.
Pg 51: Captmondo. *Block Statue of Senenmut and of Neferura.* 2008. Wikimedia Commons. Web. 5 May 2012.
Pg 55: Oilermann, Hans. *Chair from the Tomb of Ramose and Hatnofer.* 2008. Wikimedia Commons. Web. 5 May 2012.
Pg 56: Markh. *Thutmose III and Hatshepsut from the Red Chapel at Karnak.* Public Domain. Wikimedia Commons. Web. 11 May 2012.
Pg 59: Schengilli-Roberts, Keith. *Ostracon of Senenmut.* 2007. Wikimedia Commons. Web. 6 May 2012.
Pg 63: Monniaux, David. *Louxor Obelisk Paris dsc00780.* 2005. Wikimedia Commons. Web. 11 May 2012.
Pg 71: Schengili-Roberts, Keith. *Thutmose III.* 2007. Metropolitan Museum of Art. Wikimedia Commons. Web. 11 May 2012.
Pg 75: Meskens, Ad. *Mortuary Temple of Queen Hatshepsut.* Wikimedia Commons. Web. 11 May 2012.
Pg 78: Ignati. *Sarkophag Amenophis II in KV35.* 2009. Wikimedia Commons. Web. 12 May 2012.
Pg 81: Captmondo. *Elephantine Stele of Amenhotep II.* 2010. Kunsthistorisches Museum. Wikimedia Commons. Web. 11 May 2012.
Pg 86: Dalbera, Jean-Pierre. *Statue of Pharaoh Amenhotep II from the Museo Egizio.* 2008. Wikimedia Commons. Web. 12 May 2012.
Pg 108: Ignati. *Raum des Sarkophagus mit Szenen des Amduat.* 2009. Wikimedia. Web. 12 May 2012.
Pg 111: Siren. *Thoutmôsis IV Louvre.* 2005. Louvre Museum. Wikimedia Commons. Web. 12 May 2012.
Pg 114: *Brickmaking.* Public Domain. Greenhomedesign.co.uk. Web. 5 May 2012.

Pg 117: *Amenhotep II in Coffin*. ASAE III. 1902. Public Domain. Google Images. Web. 7 May 2012.

Pg 119: Sreejithk2000. *RAMmummy*. 2006. Wikimedia Commons. Web. 11 May 2012.

Pg 122: Faucher-Gudin and Insinger. *Procession of Philistine Captives*. 1903-1904. Wikimedia Commons. Web. 6 May 2012.

Pg 127: Xu Shane. *Dream Stele of Thutmose IV*. 2012. Used with permission. 30 June 2012.

Pg 132: Hajor. *Akhenaten, Pharaoh of Egypt*. Egyptian Museum, Cairo. Wikimedia Commons. Web. 6 May 2012.

Pg 133: Schengili-Roberts, Keith. *Queen Tiy*. 2006. Altes Museum, Berlin. Wikipedia. Web. 12 May 2012.

Pg 134: Parrot, A. *Colossal Statue of Amenhotep III*. 2011. Public Domain. British Museum. Wikimedia Commons. Web. 8 May 2012.

Pg 137: *Aten Disk*. Public Domain. Wikimedia Commons. 11 May 2012.

Pg 145: Schütze, Finsamer. *Small Temple of Aten at Tell el-Amarna*. Wikimedia Commons. Web. 11 May 2012.

Pg. 147: O'Neal. *Amarna Map*.

Pg 148: *Nefertiti*. Public Domain. Wikimedia Commons. Web. 7 May 2012.

Pg 151: AtonX. *Soldisken Aten*. Wikimedia Commons. Web. 6 May 2012.

Pg 153: Camocon. *Habiru or Apiru or 'pr.w*. 2008. Wikimedia Commons. Web. 12 May 2012.

Pg 155: *Amarna Akkadian Letter*. Public Domain. Wikimedia Commons. Web. 8 May 2012.

Pg 158: Kurihito. *Tombes d'El-Amarna-Représentation Dégradée Du Roi Sur Son Char*. 2008. Wikimedia Commons. Web. 12 May 2012.

Pg 177: *Boundary Stela "S" in Akhet-Aten*. Wikimedia Commons. Web. 12 May 2012.

Pg 185: Ollermann, Hans. *KV55 Sarcophagus (Cairo Museum)*. 2004. Egyptian Museum of Cairo. Wikimedia Commons. Web. 12 May 2012.

Pg 186: the Yorck Project. *Wandmalerel aus El-Amarana*. Public Domain. Wikimedia Commons. Web. 12 May 2012.

Pg 187: Bodsworth, Jon. *Amarna Princess*. 2007. Cairo Museum. Wikimedia Commons. Web. 6 May 2012.

Pg 187: Siren. *Princesse Amarna*. 2005. Louvre Museum. Wikimedia Commons. Web. 12 May 2012.

Pg 188: Schengili-Roberts, Keith. *Nefertiti with the Aten*. 2006. Altes Museum, Berlin. Wikimedia Commons. Web. 12 May 2012.

Pg 190: Schengili-Roberts, Keith. *Holding Hands-Fragment of Amarna Statue*. 2006. Altes Museum, Berlin. Wikimedia. Web. 12 May 2012.

Pg 191: Walters, Henry. *Daughter of Amenophis IV or Akhenaten*. 1930.Walters Art Museum.Wikimedia Commons. Web. 13 May 2012.

Pg 197: *Foreign Tributes Scene from an El-Amarna Tomb*. Public Domain. Wikimedia Commons. Web. 12 May 2012.

Pg 200: Schengili-Roberts, Keith. *Study of Akhenaten*. 2006. Ägyptisches Museum, Berlin. Wikimedia Commons. Web. 12 May 2012

Pg 206: Praefcke, Andreas. *Spaziergang im Garten Amarna Berlin*. 2006. Public Domain. Wikimedia Commons. 12 May 2012.

Pg 212: Xu Shane. *Great Sphinx of Giza and Khafre's Pyramid, Giza Plateau, Cairo*. 2012. Used with permission. 30 June 2012.

Index

Hathor 19, 63, 74, 95, 96, 97, 108, 205

Hatnofer 55-58, 60, 66

Hatshepsut 48-66, 68, 70-74, 80, 88, 89, 97, 99, 105, 108,133, 135, 213, 214, 216

Hebrew 3,8, 9, 11, 13, 14, 17, 18, 25-44, 47, 48, 50, 55, 58, 60, 62, 65-72, 74, 84-86, 90, 92-94, 97-99, 101, 103, 105-110, 115, 116, 118-125, 135, 137, 138, 140, 141, 144, 145, 153, 154, 156, 157, 159, 160, 162-165, 170, 172-174, 176, 177, 179, 180, 182, 185, 186,189, 198, 199, 205, 213-216

Hebron 26, 29, 32, 33, 36, 84, 86, 135, 156, 163, 205

Heqanakhte 10-12, 94, 213

Hecataeus 105

Hittite 26, 84, 119, 120, 122-124, 153, 159, 161, 164, 192, 198, 203, 205

Holy Spirit 20, 24, 167, 175, 182, 184, 189, 217

Horemheb 92,102,103, 119, 141, 164, 193, 196, 201, 203, 204, 216

Hormae 57, 58

Horus 17, 20, 24, 47, 53, 60, 107, 113, 126, 136, 151, 163, 169, 178, 183, 201

Hyksos 3, 13, 23-28, 30-44, 48, 50, 57, 58, 60, 65, 66, 69, 70, 72, 74, 79, 84-86, 99, 116, 118, 119, 121-123, 125, 153, 156, 166, 193, 198, 205, 213, 216

Hymn to the Aten 149, 189, 195, 202, 215

Iaret 111, 112

Imhotep 13, 140

Inet 51, 55, 56, 59

Intermediate Period, First 8-10

Intermediate Period, Second 13, 16, 23, 27, 41, 43, 213, 216

Ipi 10-12, 15, 16, 30, 138, 213

Ipuwer 12, 13, 23-26, 29, 33, 34, 36, 37, 39, 43, 44, 138, 150

Ishtar 47, 192, 193

Isis 47, 48, 60, 61, 64, 65, 95, 205

Israel 12, 26, 28, 29, 31, 35, 40-43, 60, 67, 69, 70, 86, 92, 93, 97, 106, 111, 116, 120, 122-125, 135, 137, 140, 142-144, 146, 152, 154, 157, 161, 164, 171-173, 176, 186, 189

Isaac 25, 28, 31, 34, 36, 67, 86, 121, 123, 160, 170, 173

Itj-Tway 16

Jacob 16, 25-36, 38, 39, 44, 67, 86, 157, 170, 172, 173, 213, 215

Jambres 90

Jannes 90

Jeroboam 69, 143

Jerusalem 30, 118, 135, 140, 142-144, 146, 154, 155, 160, 205

Jesus 43, 44, 58, 109, 138, 139, 167, 175, 176, 179-183, 198, 206

Jethro/Reuel 20, 65, 67

Job 26, 27, 43, 99, 161, 167, 179, 205

Jochabed 47, 55, 60, 63, 64, 66, 74, 213

Jonah 126, 167, 192

Jordan 30, 153, 155-157, 205

Joseph 3, 5-20, 25-38, 40, 42-44, 54, 58, 60, 65, 66, 74, 114, 140, 161, 162, 173,176, 198, 205, 213, 216

Josephus 30, 32, 34, 42, 43, 48, 54, 90, 94, 100, 114

Joshua 26, 28, 31, 84, 120, 123-125, 135, 136, 153, 154, 156, 159, 160-163, 180, 194, 204, 215, 217

Josiah 32, 140, 142-144, 175, 176, 193

Judah 26, 28, 30, 32, 35, 120, 135, 140, 142-144, 176

Kadesh 36, 72, 73, 80-82, 84, 85, 89, 119, 120, 159, 205, 214

Kamose 13, 24, 31, 35, 43, 49

Karnak 32, 42, 51, 64, 66, 72, 73, 80, 84, 90, 96, 97, 110, 116, 118, 141, 144, 160, 216

Khepri 24, 113, 115, 126, 134, 167, 183

Kiya 146, 170, 195, 196, 204

Law of Moses 26-28, 32, 44, 68, 74, 97, 165, 172, 174-177, 185, 189, 205, 215

Lebanon 36, 81, 154, 158, 163, 190

lepers 42, 95, 198

Levant 29-31, 36, 81, 101, 154, 159, 161, 204, 205

Libya 18, 42, 119, 120, 122, 123, 195, 198, 205

Luxor 42, 60, 96, 146, 165

Mamre 86

Manetho 28, 33, 34, 37, 39, 42, 95, 101, 116, 152, 161, 198, 216

Mediterranean 31, 33, 38, 47, 85, 116, 121-124

Megiddo 72, 73, 83, 85, 154, 161, 162, 176

Meketaten 146, 199, 200, 204, 206

Melchizedek 20, 26, 67, 138, 145, 152, 160

Memphis 9, 11, 16, 20, 23, 33-35, 38, 40-42, 60, 80, 81, 83, 96, 105, 113, 161, 190, 198, 203, 213

Mentuhotep II 5-19, 23, 29, 30, 37, 38, 54, 70, 138, 161, 213

Mentuhotep III 162

Mentuhotep IV 9, 16, 17

Merenptah 88, 108, 120, 123-125

Meritaten 146, 199-201, 204

Mesopotamia 6, 27, 47, 69, 156, 162

Middle Kingdom 5-15, 17-19, 23, 25, 29, 32, 33, 36, 52, 54, 59, 65-66, 90, 96, 103, 118, 138, 205, 213, 216

Midian 31, 36, 55, 62, 65, 67, 71, 72, 88, 89, 119, 157, 214

Milkilu 154, 155, 162

Miriam 54, 56, 58

Mitanni 82-84, 87, 133, 146, 159, 163, 192, 196, 196, 200

Moses 3, 12, 20, 26-28, 30, 32, 37, 39, 40, 43, 44, 47-58, 60, 62-74, 88-93, 95, 97, 99, 103, 104, 108, 111, 112, 114-122, 137-139, 144, 145, 152, 153, 157, 165, 170, 172-181, 185, 186, 198, 199, 204, 205, 213-215, 22

Mry 90, 102

Nebuchadnezzar 193

Biblical Index

232

About the Author:

Like the humble peasant woman who found some curious clay tablets while digging in the ruins of Amarna, this author doesn't claim to be special—but sincerely hopes she may have seen something that is.

www.ingramcontent.com/pod-product-compliance
Lightning Source LLC
Chambersburg PA
CBHW062016090426
42811CB00005B/870